THE EMERGENCE
OF AN INDUSTRIAL
LABOR FORCE
IN INDIA

THE EMERGENCE OF
AN INDUSTRIAL LABOR FORCE
IN INDIA

A Study of the Bombay Cotton Mills, 1854-1947

*

MORRIS DAVID MORRIS

University of California Press

Berkeley and Los Angeles

1965

FOR

Melvin Moses Knight

Acknowledgments

During the course of writing this book I became the debtor of a very great many people who provided aid, comfort, and criticism. To all of them I am deeply grateful. I must thank particularly Kantilal Hiralal Shah, Bobbsee Shah, and Kusum Thakore Chhatrapati who eased my work in Bombay in very special ways. Donald F. Gordon, my colleague for many years, tolerantly and generously gave time and thought to my intellectual problems. J. R. Huber and J. B. Gillingham lightened the burdens of authorship in ways available only to departmental chairmen. Douglass C. North, Director of the Institute for Economic Research at the University of Washington, always seemed able to find the little bits of help for me that made it easier to finish this work. And Mrs. Marijane Anderson, Secretary of the Institute, solved most of my practical problems in her usual intelligent and efficient fashion.

My research burden was made less arduous because of assistance from the following sources: R. G. Gokhale and his staff at the Bombay Millowners' Association, the University of Bombay School of Economics, Bombay Labor Office, the Bombay Archives and Secretariat, the India Office Library, and the University of Washington Library.

Parts of the research and writing were made possible by grants from the Rockefeller Foundation, the Ford Foundation Foreign Area Fellowship Program, the American Philosophical Society, and the Institute for Economic Research at the University of Washington.

M.D.M.

Contents

Abbreviations

BLO 1921   Labour Office, Government of Bombay. *Report on an Enquiry into the Wages and Hours of Labour in the Cotton Mill Industry [1921]* (1923)

BLO 1923   Labour Office, Government of Bombay. *Report on an Enquiry into the Wages and Hours of Labor in the Cotton Mill Industry [1923]* (1925)

BLO 1926   Labour Office, Government of Bombay. *Report on an Enquiry into Wages and Hours of Labour in the Cotton Mill Industry, 1926* (1930)

BLO 1934   Labour Office, Government of Bombay. *General Wage Census*. Part I: Perennial Factories. *Third Report. . . . May, 1934* (1937)

BLO, Deductions from Wages 1926   Labour Office, Government of Bombay. *Report of an Enquiry into Deductions from Wages or Payments in Respect of Fines* (1928)

BLO, Wages and Unemployment 1934   Labour Office, Government of Bombay. *Wages and Unemployment in the Bombay Cotton Textile Industry* (1934)

BMOA   Bombay Millowners' Association. *Report of the Bombay Millowners' Association*

BSEC 1928–29   Government of Bombay. *Report of the Bombay Strike Enquiry Committee, 1928–29*. Vol. I (1929)

Census   *Census* for year indicated

FA   Presidency of Bombay. *Annual Factory Report* for the year indicated

FC 1875   *Report of the Commissioners Appointed by the Governor of Bombay in Council to inquire into the condition of the operatives in the Bombay Factories. . . .* (1875)

FC 1885   *Report and Proceedings of the Commission Appointed to Consider the Working of the Factories in the Bombay Presidency* (1885)

FC 1890   *Report of the Indian Factory Commission, Appointed in September 1890* (1890)

FC 1906   India. Textile Factories Labour Committee. *Report of the . . . Committee Appointed . . . December 1906 . . . .* (1907)

ICEC 1948   *Interim Report by the Industrial Conditions Enquiry Committee* (1948)

ICEC 1950   *Final Report of the Industrial Conditions Enquiry Committee* (1950)

IDC 1921	Industrial Disputes Committee. *Minutes of Evidence* (1921)
IDC 1922	Industrial Disputes Committee. *Report of the Industrial Disputes Committee* (1922)
IFLC 1908	India. Factory Labour Commission, 1908. *Report . . . 1908.* 2 volumes (1908)
IIC 1916–18	India. Indian Industrial Commission. *Report of the Indian Industrial Commission, 1916–18. With Minutes of Evidence.* 5 volumes (1918)
ITB 1927	India. Tariff Board. *Report of the Indian Tariff Board (Cotton Textile Industry Enquiry), 1927.* 4 volumes (1927)
ITB 1932	Indian Tariff Board. *Report of the Indian Tariff Board Regarding the Grant of Protection to the Cotton Textile Industry* (1932)
ITB 1934	Indian Tariff Board. *Cotton Textile Industry, 1934.* 4 volumes (1934)
ITJ	*Indian Textile Journal*
ITJ Jubilee Souvenir	*The Indian Textile Journal: Jubilee Souvenir 1890–1940*
LG	*Labour Gazette*
LIC 1946	Labour Investigation Committee, Government of India. *Main Report* (1946)
LIC, Enquiry 1946	Labour Investigation Committee, Government of India. *Report on an Enquiry into Conditions of Labour in the Cotton Mill Industry in India* (1946)
Mehta, CMI	S. D. Mehta, *The Cotton Mills of India, 1854–1954*
Mehta, ICTI	S. D. Mehta, *The Indian Cotton Textile Industry: An Economic Analysis*
PW	Department of Statistics, India. *Prices and Wages in India*
RCL 1892	Great Britain. Royal Commission on Labour. *Foreign Reports.* Volume II. *The Colonies and the Indian Empire* (1893)
RCL 1929	Royal Commission on Labour in India (1929–1931)
SRBG	*Selections from the Records of the Bombay Government*
TLIC 1938	*Report of the Textile Labour Inquiry Committee, 1937–38.* Vol. I. *Interim Report* (1938)
TLIC 1940	*Report of the Textile Labour Inquiry Committee.* Vol. II. *Final Report* (1940)

sponse to proletarianization. Virtually no attention has been given to the problems of mobilizing a labor force and disciplining it to the requirements of Indian industry. Yet the availability of a work force untrammeled by traditional restrictions or social and sentimental barriers to mobility is one crucial element in the economic development of an industrial society. To what extent has the lack of such a mobile labor force inhibited the growth of Indian industry? How greatly have the sentiments of agricultural attachment, the religious tenets of caste and family, and the continued existence of rural occupations operated to limit the mobility of labor and the free flow of a work force into the factories of India? Has the problem of mobilizing such factory labor differed significantly from that which faced the nations of the West? In other words, is the problem of achieving this precondition of industrialization in India different in kind or merely in tempo from the pattern elaborated by countries of the North Atlantic nucleus?

Once having obtained a work force of adequate proportions, what have been the consequences of this achievement? What were the problems of taking a motley collection of rural folk of varying sociocultural traditions and assimilating it to factory work with its rationalized production processes, its simple repetitive tasks, its pace set by the machine, and its duration set by an employer?

Although there is complete agreement that in India today unemployment both overt and covert is widespread, there has been almost equally uniform agreement among industrialists, officials, and scholars that industrial development in India before 1947 was seriously handicapped by the difficulty of mobilizing a stable, disciplined labor force of adequate size. This was the considered judgment of the Indian Factory Labor Commission of 1908: "The position of the operative has been greatly strengthened by the fact that the supply of factory labor undoubtedly is, and has been, inadequate; and there is, and has been, the keenest competition among employers to secure a full labor supply." [2]

The classic statement on the subject appeared in 1931 in the report of the Royal Commission on Labor in India:

Throughout the greater part of its history, organized industry in India has experienced a shortage of labor. A generation ago, this shortage was apt at times to become critical. . . . [After 1905] the position became easier in the factory industries, but even in these, before the [first world] war, few employers were assured of adequate labor at all seasons of the year. . . . Perennial factories . . . have now reached a position in which most of them have sufficient labor at all seasons and there is a surplus of factory labor at several

---

[2] *IFLC 1908*, I, p. 19.

CHAPTER I

Nature of the Problem

The career of the industrial labor force during the expansion of modern industry has attracted considerable attention, but scholarly studies have been concerned primarily with the social response of the work force to the new industrial environment, specifically with the growth of trade unions and labor movements. However, the economic historian is preoccupied with more than this. He is concerned with all the changing patterns of economic institutions, recognizing these as techniques which evolve to deal with allocative relations which are themselves changing. Viewed thus, the early phase of an industrial revolution introduces a new technology that sets new problems and demands new solutions. Factors of production have to be mobilized in different ways, and institutions have to be changed to accomplish this. Seen in these terms, many more dimensions are added to the historical analysis of early industrialization as it involves the labor force. A new range of intellectual issues appears. We now must enquire into the creation of new labor markets and changing patterns of labor deployment, into the enhancement of skill and occupational mobility, the habituation of the work force to novel obligations and routines, and the development of new wage structures. In short, we must investigate how the early entrepreneurs solved the problems of recruiting, organizing, and administering the labor force. The focus of analysis shifts from social protest to social administration, from a stress on the horrors of industrialization to an analysis of the clumsy grapplings with new problems and the efforts made to handle them, first with traditional devices and then gradually with painfully formulated new techniques. When the phenomenon is viewed in these terms, even trade union development can be studied with fresh insight as the instrument of social discipline and administrative coördination.

These general comments about the limited intellectual range of past labor force studies apply with particular force to studies on the history of the industrial labor force in India.[1] Such detailed scholarship as there has been is almost entirely preoccupied with the emergence of Indian trade unions and labor movements, with the work force re-

---

[1] The term India throughout refers to the pre-1947 boundaries.

centers. . . . Speaking generally, it would be true to say that the turning point came during the last five years. Up to that stage, labor tended to have the upper hand in that there was competition for its services; since then the tendency has been for the workers to compete for jobs.[3]

The same point was recently made by an American scholar who referred to "the excess of jobs over job-seekers which typified Indian industries for the period between 1900 and 1935" and by the official historian of the Indian cotton textile industry.[4]

Not only is this purported shortage of labor supposed to have affected directly the rate of industrial growth in an adverse way; it is supposed to have shaped also the behavior and attitudes of workers coming into industry. Put briefly, the behavior pattern is described in one of two ways. One line of analysis suggests that, labor being short in industry, employers had to scramble for their work force and make all sorts of concessions which weakened their hold on the workers. The employees, because of the absence of effective employer-imposed discipline, were able to indulge in the luxury of all too frequent returns to the villages to which they were unyieldingly devoted.[5]

The alternate and essentially contradictory hypothesis recognizes the potential surplus of labor in the countryside that was available for urban employment. It argues that as a consequence of this surplus employers were able to abuse workers unmercifully. Since working conditions in the factories were intolerable, labor tended to remain in the villages or was very quickly forced back to the land by utter exhaustion.[6]

Whatever the specific line of causation accepted by scholars, the general conclusion is that workers retained their rural links to an extent which limited the supply of labor for industrial development. As a consequence, disciplined urban-industrial (i.e., proletarian) types of behavior did not develop. The failure of a proletarian outlook to appear was accompanied by the purported high rates of absenteeism and labor turnover and the slow growth of trade unions in Indian industry.

Interestingly enough, neither of these hypotheses nor the conclusions

---

[3] *RCL 1929*, "Report," p. 21.

[4] Oscar A. Ornati, *Jobs and Workers in India* (Ithaca: The Institute of International Industrial and Labor Relations, Cornell University, 1955), p. 35; and Mehta, *CMI, passim.* See also Max Weber, *The Religion of India* (Glencoe, Illinois: The Free Press, 1958), p. 114.

[5] *IFLC 1908*, I, pp. 18–19; *IDC 1922*, p. 1; *RCL 1929*, "Report," p. 22; and Mehta, *CMI*, p. 118.

[6] *IFLC 1908*, I, pp. 81–93; Mehta, *CMI*, p. 119; G. B. Jathar and S. G. Beri, *Indian Economics*, II (7th ed., London: Oxford University Press, 1945), pp. 76–77; and D. R. Gadgil, *The Industrial Evolution of India in Recent Times* (4th ed., London: Oxford University Press, 1942), pp. 127–130.

drawn from them have been tested by any substantial exploration of the historical material. Generally, what has been written is either tautological in character or deficient in analysis. Much of the literature tends to base interpretation on hypothetical psychological and sociological propositions which themselves are highly suspect. Moreover, the methodology is questionable. The historical argument typically rests on scattered fragments of evidence taken indiscriminately from all areas of the country and from all sorts of industry, seasonal and perennial, large-scale and small-scale; it relates to all kinds of labor, casual and permanent, unskilled and skilled. It is impossible to generate a satisfactory analysis from this sort of mélange, particularly during a period when modern industry was making only its first timid mark on the economy and there was no national market for labor.[7]

Another weakness of the studies of the economic history of the labor force is the tendency to ignore the possible contributions of formal economic theory to these investigations. Though it would be pretentious to attempt to apply truly sophisticated economic analysis to nineteenth- and early twentieth-century developments in the absence of better data, the use of even elementary theoretical notions from economics can be extremely useful. Not only will the introduction of these tools help to synthesize the evidence into a more satisfactory framework, but their employment will also point the way to the formulation of new problems.

I have suggested that satisfactory studies of the creation of an industrial labor force cannot be made on an all-India basis. To get at the meaning of this process, case studies are essential. This study is an attempt to contribute to the satisfaction of this need by a detailed study of the creation of a labor force in the cotton textile industry of Bombay City from its inception in the 1850's to 1947.[8]

Concerned as I am with the problem of how a labor force is mobilized and organized for factory employment during the early stages of industrialization, my study had to make use of an industry where the factory system had been fairly well developed. In India as in Britain nearly a century earlier the cotton textile industry was the pace setter of industrialization. It was India's first factory industry, and it remains even today

---

[7] Studies in the field of modern Indian economic history generally suffer from the tendency to work on an all-India basis. For some comments on this and other problems in the field, see M. D. Morris and B. Stein, "The Economic History of India: A Bibliographic Essay," *Journal of Economic History*, XXI, No. 2, June 1961, pp. 179–207.

[8] By 1947 the main lines of the process with which I am concerned had been almost entirely worked out.

the most important.[9] Moreover, the industry was Indian in origin, and Indian entrepreneurs were almost entirely responsible for its expansion. These features made it an obvious choice for a first study.

Given my view that all-India studies tend to be too diffuse for precise analysis, the cotton textile industry also offered the advantage of concentration of activity. The two obvious centers in terms of length of history were Bombay City and Ahmedabad. By all other tests of importance as well — number of mills, number of spindles and looms installed, output, capital invested, and employment — the two cities represented the most important concentrations of textile production in the country.[10] Having narrowed the choice, I had no difficulty in finally selecting Bombay as the focus of my study. First, it was the city in which the modern textile industry and genuine factory production began, and despite many vicissitudes, it has remained the country's foremost textile center. Second, unlike the situation in Ahmedabad, the Bombay work force is heterogeneous. It has been drawn from many areas whereas Ahmedabad's labor has come mainly from near-by districts. Certain aspects of the economic history of the labor force could be explored only in the more complex Bombay situation. Third, the Bombay industry has had a long and bitter tradition of industrial conflict. There have been more labor disputes in the Bombay cotton textile industry, and they have been of greater intensity than in any other place or industry in the country. The trade unions which have emerged have had a complicated, tumultuous, and unstable career. Ahmedabad, in this regard too, is less interesting because it represents a special case. Industrial relations have been more peaceful, and its trade unions have been relatively stable. These conditions were not typical of India generally but were due to the personal influence of one man, M. K. Gandhi. Fourth, and not least, the the records for Bombay are more extensive and more easily accessible than the Ahmedabad materials.

On the other hand, a great deal has been written about the Bombay textile work force. Virtually all reports and studies have emphasized the difficulty of recruitment and the failure to achieve a stable, disciplined, efficient work force. In the face of virtually unanimous agreement that Bombay textile mills suffered from a halting uncertain

---

[9] For some data on the relative importance of employment in various factory industries, see C. A. Myers, *Labor Problems in the Industrialization of India* (Cambridge: Harvard University Press, 1958), p. 17. For a comparison of value added in Indian manufacturing industries, see Department of Economic Affairs, Ministry of Finance, Government of India, *Final Report of the National Income Committee, February 1954* (Delhi: Manager of Publications, 1954), p. 66.

[10] S. D. Mehta, *CMI*, pp. 234 and 265.

supply of labor and that the labor that did come into the factories did not respond with that degree of stability, reliability, and efficiency on which productive operation depended, is there anything new and worthwhile that historical analysis can add?

I think there is a great deal that can be contributed by a historical study. Careful analysis will throw quite a novel light on the whole process of labor force creation. The evidence will show that contrary to the canonical view, the supply of labor for industrial requirements was not hard to get. The material will also indicate that the level of labor force performance was almost entirely set by the nature of industrial organization and operation. In other words, the basic quality of labor performance as it emerged in the cotton textile industry was the result of employer policy and responses to market forces and not the consequence of labor force psychology or social structure.

In considering these problems there are some important matters of definition. Most of these can be considered as they arise, but I must say a few words here about the concept of labor discipline as I use it. When I speak of a disciplined industrial labor force I am referring to a body of workers who are responsive to the technical requirements of industry, to the "web of rules" at the work place, and to the incentives (and disincentives) of the market mechanism. The determination of the degree of discipline must be based on the use of measurable behavioral indexes.

In some circles the term labor commitment has been substituted for labor discipline. I object to the use of the word commitment because that term tends to carry with it a psychological component. As Moore and Feldman tell us, "Commitment involves both performance and the acceptance of the behaviors appropriate to an industrial way of life." [11] In other words, the use of the term lays stress on the "phenomenon of internalization or moral conformity" as crucial to the functioning of an industrial system.[12]

I do not propose to examine the problem in detail, but let me briefly indicate two major difficulties raised by the introduction of this psychological element. First, it is very difficult to measure the degree of psychological "acceptance" at any moment in time, and it is impossible to measure the phenomenon as it existed historically. Second, it is not clear what psychological commitment to the industrial system means. Kerr and Segal have implied that commitment must be to a specific set of

---

[11] W. E. Moore and A. S. Feldman (eds.), *Labor Commitment and Social Change in Developing Areas* (New York: Social Science Research Council, 1960), p. 1.

[12] *Ibid.*, p. 9.

property relationships as well as to a specific set of technological requirements.[13] This suggests the questionable proposition that a labor force that collectively identifies itself with revolutionary political objectives is of necessity not committed to the requirements of industrial production.

The technical requirements of the industrial system can tolerate a very wide variety of "attitudes." For example, is the American worker who eagerly seeks as much free time as possible for fishing and hunting and who has a yen to retire to a farm truly "committed"? Is the Indian worker who strikes frequently and disruptively "committed"? The answer may be ambiguous in psychological terms. But the answer in both cases is affirmative so far as the effective functioning of modern enterprise is concerned.[14] This does not mean that other systems of organization and greater doses of "identification" would not extract superior levels of performance from the work force. However, such a notion implies the existence of some absolute standard by which to measure "acceptance." A major complicating factor is that the productivity of an industrial system is not solely a matter of technological potential as qualified by the degree of labor force "acceptance" of the system. There are market relationships and the entrepreneur's involvement in them which will fundamentally affect the level of performance in industry. Given these difficulties of meaning and measurement, I exclude the psychological component from my definition.

This study does not pretend to be a complete description of all aspects of the career of the Bombay cotton textile labor force. It is by design limited to those topics which bear directly on the specific problems of recruitment and the establishment of factory discipline. But even on the issues with which it deals, I am not completely satisfied. Weaknesses of the data, particularly on the quantitative side, have forced me to leave gaps although I am, of course, convinced that the main lines of the argument are correct. It is possible that others will uncover new materials which will clarify ambiguities and complete the record. I am not particularly hopeful that this will occur.[15] It is more likely that we will have to

---

[13] C. Kerr and A. Siegal, "The Structuring of the Labor Force in Industrial Society," *Industrial and Labor Relations Review*, VIII, No. 2, January 1955, p. 163.

[14] Although my analysis will suggest that high rates of strikes, absenteeism, and labor turnover are consistent with the existence of a disciplined labor force, there are many scholars who see these primarily as evidence of protest against the acceptance of the new imperatives of the industrial work community. See, for example, C. Kerr, F. H. Harbison, J. T. Dunlop, and C. A. Myers, "Industrialism and Industrial Man," *International Labor Review*, LXXXII, No. 3, September 1960, pp. 246–247.

[15] The main source of new materials, if they still exist, would be the records of individual mills, particularly for the period before World War I.

explore the same problems in other regions and in other sectors of the economy to resolve some of the issues left unsettled by this study.

There are other important reasons for studying these problems in other sectors of the Indian economy. The economic historian should be more concerned with the general pattern of economic change and adjustment than with the specific case. In this study I am not only interested in comprehending the dynamics of industrial labor force creation in Bombay; I am ultimately concerned with possible generalizations about labor force creation in India as a contribution to the nineteenth- and twentieth-century Indian economic history. This involves a comparative analysis of a number of cases. I would suggest that to explore the full array of problems and emerge with satisfactory conclusions on an all-India level requires the study of at least four other instances — the steel industry, railways, coal mines, and plantations.[16] An analysis of this kind, properly controlled, could also make some substantial contribution to our understanding of the world-wide process of labor force creation during the early stages of industrialization. It might lend greater precision and realism to one of the variables we must incorporate into a general theory of economic change and growth.[17]

Unfortunately, a great deal of monographic work is necessary before we can have a truly adequate picture of the early stages of labor force creation even in India. Recognizing this, I think it useful to suggest to readers with an interest in these matters some of the types of problems which need examination and some of the lines along which analysis might proceed. Therefore, throughout the study I have felt free to indicate specific questions the investigation of which might prove useful. In this sense, the study is as much a syllabus of further work to be done as it is an investigation in its own right.

Let me say a few words about the data that were available. Beginning with the first Bombay Factory Commission investigation in 1874, various committees and commissions have produced a spate of reports from which much can be drawn. From its inception in 1921 the Bombay Labor Office produced reports, surveys, and a monthly *Labour Gazette* which are valuable sources. The annual reports of the Bombay Mill-

---

[16] An analysis of these four industries should provide a sufficient range of variation to permit satisfactory generalizations. I hope at some future time to publish the results of a study of the creation of an industrial labor force at the Tata Iron and Steel Company plant at Jamshedpur, 1907–1957.

[17] For a brief attempt at some international comparisons, see M. D. Morris, "The Recruitment of an Industrial Labor Force in India, with British and American Comparisons," *Comparative Studies in Society and History*, II, No. 3, April 1960, pp. 305–328.

owners' Association provide a very useful series from 1875; and the files of the *Indian Textile Journal*, which began publication in 1890, are equally important. In addition there are numerous other sources which will be noted, but unfortunately the period from the industry's beginning to 1875 is *terra incognita*. No substantial information seems to have survived. The very earliest phase of labor force creation, in some ways the most interesting, has only been hinted at in later material.

The cotton textile industry of India, and especially the Bombay sector of it, is perhaps better served by an abundance of statistics than almost any other major part of the economy. Nevertheless, appearances are deceptive. At every point the statistics are subject to serious question, and this study must depend, as historical studies unfortunately so often must, on the qualitative rather than on the quantitative evidence. I shall invoke statistical data wherever possible, but the intention is that they should provide rough orders or magnitudes rather than precise relationships.

CHAPTER II

Economic Development of Bombay City

There is no adequate economic history of Bombay and its hinterland. I have tried to work out enough information, based on the scanty data that are available, to lay the foundation for subsequent discussion. Consequently, I have stressed the general pattern of economic activity before 1870 and the city's population growth.[1]

During the whole of the British period Bombay was, with Calcutta, one of the two largest and most important cities in India. Bounded within the confines of a long narrow island, Bombay is separated from the mainland by a small creek. In 1864 the island-city had an area of about 18.6 square miles. Between 1860 and 1947 reclamation along its shore line added another six square miles to its area. By the time of the 1951 census Bombay was a city of 2.3 million people crowded into an area of 25.3 square miles.[2]

Although Bombay has the finest natural harbor in India, the island had no significance before the appearance of the British. The great sweeps of traditional Indian history completely bypassed or barely encompassed it.[3] Small ships of the preindustrial era did not require deep or extensive harbors. The important factor was ease of communication with productive hinterlands and overseas markets. For the pre-eighteenth century trade of the Indian Ocean, Broach and Surat to the north of Bombay were better located. Both these entrepôts had easier land communication with the resources and markets of northern India, and both were closer to the main traditional overseas markets on the Persian Gulf and the Red Sea. By contrast, Bombay was not only cut off from effective contact with the Indo-Gangetic plain and farther away from the Persian Gulf and Red Sea ports; it was also isolated from easy

---

[1] Much of the information of the development of Bombay comes from S. M. Edwardes, *The Rise of Bombay: A Retrospect* (Bombay: The Times of India Press, 1902); S. M. Edwardes, *The Gazetteer of Bombay City and Island* (3 vols., Bombay: The Times Press, 1909); and *Materials Towards a Statistical Account of the Town and Island of Bombay* (being Vol. XXVI, Parts 1–3 of the *Gazetteer of the Bombay Presidency*, Bombay: 1893.)

[2] *Census 1864*, p. xi; and Government of Bombay, *Greater Bombay District Census Handbook (Based on the 1951 Census)* (Bombay: Government of Bombay, 1952), p. 2.

[3] Edwardes, *Gazetteer*, I, Ch. 3.

communication with central India by the steep Western Ghats. Moreover, the region behind these Ghats, the Deccan Plateau, traditionally
did not generate products for substantial interregional or international
trade.[4]

In 1661 Bombay Island with its estimated population of 10,000, was
ceded to the British by the Portugese.[5] It was not until the early
eighteenth century that the town began to grow steadily as an important
East India Company entrepôt. Surat and Broach, engulfed by political
difficulties, declined to insignificance whereas Bombay benefited from
the generally improved circumstances of the East India Company,
from the island's militarily defensible position and the security of its harbor.[6] The growing commercial importance of Bombay encouraged the
Company to import Parsi shipbuilders from Surat and establish a ship-
yard in 1735. The yard prospered as a center for the construction and
repair of ships in the international and country trades, and by 1781 it was
employing more than 500 native workers.[7]

There is no way to determine the rate at which population grew in the
eighteenth century, but we know that it expanded rapidly under the
Company's policy of "toleration and progress." The records show a
steady influx of weavers, goldsmiths, ironsmiths, construction workers,
and traders. The evidence suggests that by 1780 the population of the
island had risen to about 100,000.[8] We also know that even at the beginning of the eighteenth century, the island, incapable of providing for
itself, was dependent on the mainland "for Merchandise, Timber, or
Provisions, from whence only such things must come. . . ."[9] Thus, as
population grew, an increasingly elaborate trade network with the
mainland was created. This inability to sustain itself and the growing
dependence on an ever-widening hinterland have been continuing characteristics of the Bombay economy.[10]

---

[4] For a general description of the regional geography, see C. D. Deshpande,
Western India: A Regional Geography (Dharwar: Student's Own Book Depot,
1948).

[5] Edwardes, *Gazetteer*, I, p. 152.

[6] Anonymous, *A Description of the Port and Island of Bombay* (1724), p. 4.

[7] R. A. Wadia, *The Bombay Dockyard and the Wadia Master Builders* (Bombay:
privately published, 1955), gives the history of this enterprise which survived into
the second half of the nineteenth century.

[8] For pre-1800 estimates of population, see Edwardes, *Gazetteer*, I, pp. 142–
158. The economic developments associated with this expansion are described in
the sources already cited and in James Forbes, *Oriental Memoirs* (2d ed., London:
1834), I, pp. 96–97 and II, p. 380.

[9] Anonymous, *A Description of the Port and Island of Bombay*, pp. 4, 16, and 33.

[10] "Bombay" in *The General Gazetteer . . . Originally Written by R. Brookes*,
M. D. (8th ed., London: 1794); and Basil Hall, *Fragments of Voyages and Travels*.

We have four estimates of population in Bombay for the period 1806 to 1814, varying between 180,000 and 236,000. It is probable that the permanent population at the end of the Napoleonic Wars was somewhere in the neighborhood of 160,000 to 180,000 people.[11] Three features of the Bombay population which are matters of some significance for later discussion should be noted at this point. First was the cosmopolitan character of the population, even at this early period. By the time of Hall's visit in 1812, the diversity of caste, religious groups, and geographical origin constituted one of the island's striking characteristics.[12]

A second feature was "the migratory or floating portion of the natives who come and go according to the seasons and other circumstances." [13] Hall estimated this migratory element to constitute nearly one-third addition to the permanent population of the time, the numbers fluctuating according to the "periods of public excitement or high commercial enterprise."[14] Who these people were and where they came from is uncertain. Many seem to have come from long distances, and others were agriculturists from surrounding districts who sought employment on the island during their slack periods.[15]

A third characteristic was the role of famines which periodically drove people from the surrounding regions and more distant parts into the city. Mackintosh estimated that some 72,000 famine victims poured into Bombay during the great famine of 1803–04.[16] Captain Hall stated that the famine of 1812–13 drove 20,000 onto the island.[17]

This very brief discussion suggests that Bombay's population grew from a few thousand at the beginning of the eighteenth century to more than 160,000 in the early nineteenth century. The evidence indicates a fair degree of mobility in the surrounding areas, a mobility which cannot be attributed to British land policy or to the results of British indus-

---

Second Series, III (2d ed., Edinburgh: 1852), pp. 39–40.

There is need of a study of the impact of Bombay's growth on the economic development of its hinterland along lines suggested by F. J. Fisher, "The Development of the London Food Market, 1540–1640," *Economic History Review*, V, No. 2, April 1935, pp. 46–64.

[11] A good summary of these estimates and their sources can be found in Edwardes, *Gazetteer*, I, pp. 158–161.

[12] Hall, *op. cit.*, pp. 11–15; and other sources previously cited.

[13] *Ibid.*, p. 43.

[14] *Ibid.*, p. 49.

[15] *Materials Towards a Statistical Account of the Town and Island of Bombay*, II, p. 275.

[16] Edwardes, *The Rise of Bombay*, p. 235.

[17] Hall, *op.cit.*, Chaps. I–III. In these chapters Hall gives a very vivid description of the effect of famines in the Gujarat on Bombay's population.

trial competition, both of which were nineteenth-century phenomena.[18] Similarly, the evidence points to the existence of seasonal labor migrations and famine additions to the Bombay population even in the period preceding British rule.[19]

Bengal and Madras had come under East India Company control in the mid-eighteenth century, but on the western side of the continent British power remained restricted to Bombay Island and a few outposts until the Maratha empire was finally destroyed in 1818. The period between this event and 1870 is in many ways the most interesting part of the city's economic development. During this era the beginnings of modern transport facilities into the Western Ghat hinterland were established; international trade connections, culminating in the opening of the Suez Canal in 1869, were developed; modern commerce and banking institutions were built up; and the basis was laid for the industrialization which followed. Unfortunately, this is a period for which there is very little detailed information.

The evidence suggests a very rapid growth of population in the half century between 1814 and 1864.

TABLE I
Population of Bombay, 1814–1864 [20]

1814	180,000
1830	229,000
1846	566,000
1864	816,562

Although none of the pre-1864 estimates can be given great credence, there is little reason to doubt that in the early 1850's the population was in the neighborhood of a half-million.[21] On the basis of the expansion of economic activity which we know was taking place on the island in the first half of the nineteenth century, such growth does not seem un-

---

[18] I assume that in-migration was far more important than natural increases in accounting for Bombay's population growth. This is suggested by the records as well as by the very high death rate which characterized the island.

[19] For general confirming discussion, see *The Monthly Miscellany of Western India*, I, 1850, pp. 239–240. The importance of the floating population should not be taken to imply the absence of a permanent population in the city. Though there is no certain way to prove the point, the records leave the impression that population growth was accompanied by an increasing number of people staying on as permanent residents.

[20] Data for 1814, 1830, and 1846 comes from sources used by Edwardes, *Gazetteer*, I, pp. 160–163. The 1864 figure comes from *Census 1864*.

[21] Presidency of Bombay, *Annual Report, 1862–63*, p. 116, throws doubt on the validity of the pre-1864 census returns.

reasonable.[22] Our knowledge of the particularly vigorous growth of enterprise between 1846 and 1864 makes it equally plausible to accept the
idea of continuous population expansion during this period. Whatever
its specific weaknesses, the 1864 census was probably reasonably accurate in its over-all total. What, then, were the features of Bombay's
economic development which contributed to this rapid population
growth?

The dissolution of the Maratha empire made possible the establishment of uninhibited British hegemony and order over almost the whole
of western India. The elimination of political instability directly contributed to the expansion of commerce.[23] The opening of the Bhore
Ghat in 1830, the first major roadway through the Western Ghats,
further stimulated trade, making possible the substitution of bullock
carts for pack animals and the consequent sharp reduction in freight

TABLE II

Commodity Foreign Trade Moving Through Bombay,
1801–02 to 1870–71 [24]

(In millions of rupees)

Period	Imports	Exports	Total
1801–02	7.2	8.0	15.2
Annual average for decade ending			
1809–10	7.3	9.8	17.1
1819–20	9.3	10.7	20.0
1829–30	14.9	20.4	35.3
1839–40	19.5	35.1	54.6
1849–50	32.4	49.9	82.3
1859–60	53.9	91.7	145.6
1869–70	119.6	261.5	381.1
1870–71	115.2	248.2	363.4

[22] One contemporary source describes the tremendous influx of population into
Bombay, commenting that the city attracted all sorts of "vagrants." "The Native
Poor of Bombay," *The Bombay Quarterly Review,* IV, No. 8, October 1856, pp.
235–272, particularly pp. 253–254.

[23] Kenneth Ballhatchet, *Social Policy and Social Change in Western India, 1817–
1830* (London: Oxford University Press, 1957).

[24] Edwardes, *Gazetteer,* I, p. 418. Another measure of the increase in international
trade is the fact that between 1839–40 and 1843–44 the number of pieces of mail
going through Bombay to and from London nearly tripled. R. J. F. Sulivan, *One
Hundred Years of Bombay: History of the Bombay Chamber of Commerce, 1836–
1936* (Bombay: Times of India Press, n.d.), pp. 51–54.

charges.[25] At the same time, Bombay's international commerce was stimulated, in part at least, by the East India Company charter revisions of 1813 and 1833. During this period the main imports were sugar, metals and metal manufactures, and textile products; opium and raw cotton were the dominant exports.[26]

After 1800 Bombay became increasingly the nearest port of call for the traffic of the Indian Ocean as well as for the trade with Europe and Asia.[27] And although bulk freight continued to move around the Cape of Good Hope until the opening of the Suez Canal, important maritime improvements steadily reduced the average time of shipping between Bombay and London.

The expansion of trade during the first half of the nineteenth century resulted in a multiplication of the island's commercial facilities. The old system of agency houses was gradually replaced by joint-stock banks, the first of which was established in 1840. Insurance companies developed quickly; by 1851 there were twenty-five carrying on business in Bombay. And as early as 1836 the Bombay Chamber of Commerce was organized by a group of English and Indian merchants.[28]

---

[25] J. M. Maclean, *A Guide to Bombay* (3d ed., Bombay: 1877), p. 68; and C. W. Grant, *Bombay Cotton and Indian Railways* (London, 1850), p. 149.

[26] Edwardes, *Gazetteer*, I, pp. 514–521. Edward Thornton, *Statistical Papers Relating to India* (London, 1853), p. 67, pointed out that Bombay had become the entrepôt through which the bulk of India's cotton exports flowed.

[27] Cargoes from traditional west coast ports like Surat and Broach were shipped by country craft to Bombay, from where they were transshipped by ocean-going vessels to their ultimate destinations.

[28] D. E. Wacha, *Shells from the Sands of Bombay* (Bombay: K. T. Anklesaria, 1920), pp. 335–337; Edwardes, *Gazetteer*, I, pp. 288–312; and Sulivan, *op. cit.*, p. 10.

One interesting characteristic of nineteenth-century Bombay enterprise suggested by the formation of the Chamber of Commerce is the extent to which economic activity was not dominated by Europeans but was shared by local merchants. This is worth noting because the phenomenon runs counter to the usual view held by scholars that Indian entrepreneurs did not respond to the commercial and industrial opportunities of the nineteenth century. Moreover, the response in Bombay was quite different from that which characterized Calcutta at the same time. A Calcutta journal in 1864 commented that "Calcutta may take to herself the glory of being the Metropolis of British India, but she can hardly presume to place herself on a par with the sister Presidency of Bombay in matters of trade and general enterprise." Quoted in *Bombay Saturday Review of Politics, Literature, and Commerce*, VI, No. 15, 9 April 1864, p. 341. See also *ibid.*, VI, No. 36, 3 September 1864, p. 843, for a sophisticated discussion of the difference between the two cities.

The vigor and enterprise of Indians in Bombay can be seen in the role they played in the "share mania" of 1861–1865. Useful sources on this period, apart from those already given, are D. E. Wacha, *A Financial Chapter in the History of Bombay City* (2d ed., Bombay: A. J. Combridge & Co., 1910); Bombay Bank Commission

The two decades before the outbreak of the American Civil War seem to have been particularly prosperous. The Chamber of Commerce reported that between 1841–42 and 1851–52 the import of cotton cloth had doubled in quantity and of cotton yarn had trebled. During this period Bombay became the great entrepôt for the distribution of British manufactures in Asia.[29] And the 1850's apparently were a period of equally impressive commercial growth. The Collector of Customs reported that during the five years to 1857–58 imports more than doubled in value; exports showed a slower but similar expansion, rising by a third during the same period.[30]

Expansion of international trade stimulated complementary activities. There was continuous construction of port facilities, and to meet the need for more space there were land reclamation and the erection of new buildings.[31] The Bombay dockyard also responded to this burgeoning trade. In 1847 at least 2,000 workers were employed to build ships for the East India Company, the navy, and for private shippers. The first steamship was built in 1829, and a number were constructed subsequently. In the first decades the materials for iron ships had to be imported, but in 1851 an eighty-ton steamer was built entirely from locally manufactured components.[32] In addition to the dockyard, there was also

---

Minutes of Evidence (3 vols., London: HMSO, 1869); *The Late Government Bank of Bombay: Its History* (London, n.d.); and *Papers Regarding the Management of the Bank of Bombay during the Late Commercial Crisis* (2 vols., Calcutta: Superintendent of Government Printing, 1868).

The contrast between Bombay and Calcutta was not only commercial but extended into the industrial sphere as well. An official reported in 1908 that "an examination of joint stock companies will show that Bengal is far behind Bombay in the inauguration of purely indigenous concerns." J. G. Cumming, *Review of the Industrial Position and Prospects of Bengal in 1908* (Calcutta: Superintendent of Government Printing, 1908), p. 4. The distinction between Bombay and Calcutta should not be attributed solely to the role of the Parsis in the economic life of Bombay. Although Parsis were extremely important, Muslim, Jain, and Hindu entrepreneurs were also of enormous significance, even in the first half of the nineteenth century. For example, in the economic activities of the 1850's and 1860's it was a Hindu merchant, Premchund Roychund, who was the key figure. See Bombay Bank Commission, *op. cit., passim.*

All these propositions suggest the need for a comparative study of economic responses in Bombay and Calcutta during the nineteenth century. I am certain that such an investigation would lead us to a complete reinterpretation of the nature of Indian behavior in the presence of economic opportunity.

[29] *Bombay Chamber of Commerce, Report, 1852–53* (Bombay, 1853), pp. 23–25 and 268 ff; and Sulivan, *op. cit.,* pp. 21–23.

[30] *Ibid.,* p. 61.

[31] *A Guide to Bombay from the Bombay Times Calendar of 1855* (Bombay 1855), pp. 81 ff.

[32] Wadia, *op. cit.,* pp. 176, 269–289, and 322. After 1850, for a host of reasons, the Bombay dockyard declined in importance.

the East India Company ordinance factory which as early as 1823 employed nearly a thousand permanent and temporary workers in its gun-carriage section.[33]

The 1850's were a decade of great public works activity throughout India. Improvements in internal communications — post, telegraph, and railways — directly contributed to the growth of Bombay's commerce. The first railway in India was opened in 1853 between Bombay and Thana, a distance of twenty-one miles. By the middle 'sixties one line had been extended eastward over the Bhore Ghat toward the central India cotton-growing tracts, and another line had been pushed northward to Ahmedabad and the cotton areas of Gujarat.[34] The railway operations required the establishment of railway workshops and the expansion of foundry facilities for maintenance and repair work.[35]

Expansion of transport facilities was not limited to railroads. Apart from the international developments already mentioned, there was a substantial growth of the coastal trade. As early as 1847 nine steamers were operating out of Bombay, of which the Bombay Steam Navigation Company had five plying between Colombo, Surat, and Karachi. These, plus the hundreds of coastal sailing craft, hauled passengers as well as cargo.[36]

Much of the expansion of water and land transport facilities was associated with the developing trade in raw cotton of which so large a proportion was being channeled through Bombay into international markets. This activity required other facilities. For example, by the early 1850's there were a number of steam cotton presses in operation, baling cotton for export. Some of these enterprises were quite large, one employing about a thousand workers.[37]

The beginnings of cotton textile factory production accounts for some of Bombay's growing economic activity in the later 1850's. Construction of the first mill began in 1854, and production started in 1856.[38] By 1860 there were six more in operation, and in July 1860 one Bombay newspaper boasted:

---

[33] H. A. Young, *The East India Company's Arsenals and Manufactories* (Oxford: Clarendon Press, 1937), p. 202.

[34] The first railways were constructed on the assumption that Indians, for social and religious reasons, would not travel. Financial estimates were based entirely on freight movements. This was immediately proved wrong. Passenger traffic quickly became a major revenue source. "Railways in Western India," *Bombay Quarterly Review*, I, April 1855, pp. 304–307.

[35] Maclean, *op. cit.*, p. 138.

[36] Edwardes, *Gazetteer*, I, pp. 393 and 399; Edwardes, *The Rise of Bombay*, pp. 272–273; *The Monthly Miscellany of Western India*, I, 1850, p. 231.

[37] *A Guide to Bombay from the Bombay Times Calendar of 1855*, p. 99.

[38] Mehta, *CMI*, pp. 13–17.

Whatever may be the state of other parts of India, it is manifest that Bombay feels neither anxiety nor apprehension regarding the future of the empire. Capital was never more plentiful amongst us than at present, nor the spirit of enterprise more powerful. Money, to the amount of nearly a quarter of a million pounds sterling, has been invested during the last fortnight in the establishment of manufactories calculated to promote industry and assist in the development of the resources of the country. Bombay has long been the Liverpool of the East, and she is now become the Manchester also. Factory chimney-stacks already meet the eye on every side, and when the numerous companies recently formed are in full operation, Western India will have cause to be proud of her capital. In 1850 we question much if even the model of a cotton mill had found its way to Bombay; but now the tall chimneys of half-a-dozen factories tower solemn and somber above the surrounding buildings.[39]

This economic ebullience was given a speculative twist by the outbreak of the American Civil War and the cessation of cotton exports from the American South. Although Indian cottons had a poor reputation for quality, the crisis in the European textile industries forced increasing dependence on India as a source of the raw material. Cotton prices soared, and incomes from exports rose sharply during the Civil War period. Then, when the war ended, cotton prices and incomes from its export declined almost as precipitously. Since there has never been an adequate study of this important event, it is not easy to analyze the relationships involved. There is no question, however, that the rising prices of cotton exports, following two decades of nearly uninterrupted expansion in Bombay, triggered a mighty speculation that engulfed public officials as well as private citizens.[40]

---

[39] Quoted in Edwardes, *The Rise of Bombay*, pp. 264–265. The growth of steam-powered enterprises during the 1850's and early 1860's was great enough to require the passage of a smoke abatement law. Presidency of Bombay, *Annual Report, 1862–63*, p. 98.

[40] The main sources on the Civil War boom have been cited in footnote 28, above. See also A. Siegfried, "Cotonniers aux Indes," *Revue de Paris*, LVII, December, 1950, pp. 12–28. Romesh Dutt, *The Economic History of India in the Victorian Age* (7th ed., London: Routledge and Kegan Paul, 1950), p. 347, claims that the value of cotton exports from India rose from £5.6 millions in 1860 to £37.6 millions in 1865 and then declined sharply. D. R. Gadgil, *The Industrial Evolution of India in Recent Times* (4th ed., London: Oxford University Press, 1945), p. 16, reported that the average price of Indian cotton rose from As. 3-7 to As. 11-5 per pound between 1860 and 1864 and then dropped.

Though much has been made of the enormous flood of wealth that poured into the hands of the peasantry, it seems clear, first of all, that rising prices of cotton apparently affected only those districts of western India where cotton was grown. Second, statistics of cotton exports in physical rather than value terms do not confirm the tales of enormous increases in cotton production. In 1861 one million bales of cotton were exported from Bombay. There were sharp falls and rises in

With the stimulus of such economic activity — new reclamation works, building and road construction, expanded transport facilities, new industry, and growing commerce — people poured into the city, bringing the total population to 816,000 in 1864. If we accept the 1846 estimate of 566,000 people, this represents a 44 per cent increase in eighteen years. Certainly, all contemporary observers agreed that the expansion of population after 1845 was rapid and that it reached explosive proportions between 1856 and 1864.[41]

The end of the Civil War in the United States led to the collapse of the "share mania." The fall of cotton prices was accompanied by even wider consequences. There was a sharp contraction of credit, which was worsened by the London financial crisis of 1866 and the collapse of the Bank of Bombay in 1867.[42] The termination of many of the more ambitious and speculative construction projects certainly reduced employment opportunities. We do not know what the immediate effects were, but the census of 1872 reported that the island's population had fallen to 644,000. Contemporaries accepted the fact that the 21 per cent decline in population was "accounted for by the migration from Bombay of the swarms of adventurers and laborers from all parts of India and from abroad who were attracted to the city by the speculative enterprises and the high prices of labor which marked the season of unexampled prosperity enjoyed by Bombay during the American War." [43]

There has been a tendency for historians to assume that the Civil War speculation was entirely responsible for booming economic activity in Bombay. I have already shown that the evidence indicates that Bom-

---

exports, but the 1861 figure was not exceeded until 1865 when 1.1 million bales were exported. The source for these figures is "A.B.F.," *Statistical Tables Relating to Indian Cotton* (Bombay, 1889), Table 29, p. 59. If these figures are at all reliable, they suggest an amazingly inelastic supply curve for cotton output over the short run and suggest some of the problems inherent in Indian agriculture, problems which were and are as much technical as institutional. For a rather sophisticated analysis of the inelasticity of cotton supply during the American Civil War, see Samuel Smith, *The Cotton Trade of India* (London, 1863). For some of the technical problems of Indian agriculture, see Louise E. Howard, *Sir Albert Howard in India* (London: Faber and Faber Ltd., 1953.)

[41] Wacha, *Shells from the Sands of Bombay*, pp. 421–422; *Presidency of Bombay, Annual Report*, for the years 1862–63 through 1866–67; H. Conybeare, "Report on the Sanitary Requirements of Bombay," *SRBG*, New Series, No. XI, 1855.

[42] *Papers Regarding the Management of the Bank of Bombay during the Late Financial Crisis* (2 vols., Calcutta, 1868); and Bombay Bank Commission, *Minutes of Evidence.*

[43] Maclean, *op. cit.*, p. 87. See also *Census 1872*, p. 1. In 1864 one journal worried that "the slightest check to the labor market would fill Bombay with starving laborers . . . who could cause trouble." *The Bombay Saturday Review*, VI, No. 2, 9 January 1864, p. 25.

bay's expansion had a substantial foundation and had been going on for many years before the "share mania" exploded upon the city. During the Civil War further important public and private construction programs were undertaken and many of them continued after the boom collapsed. In fact, a significant part of modern Bombay's physical plant dates from the period 1864 to 1872.[44] The solid nature of the city's economic growth is reflected in the fact that the 1872 population figure was still 78,000 (13.8 per cent) more than it was in 1846.[45] Bombay remained more populous than either Calcutta or Madras.

This is not the place to undertake an analysis of the economic history of Bombay after 1870. Suffice to say that the great port was favored by the opening of the Suez Canal in 1869 and by the continued expansion of railway facilities into the hinterland. Moreover, it proceeded to become one of the two most important manufacturing centers in the country and the most important textile producer. But the economic career of Bombay after 1870 reflected to a considerable degree the unstable pattern of growth which characterized the entire Indian economy before 1947. Some indication of this can be seen from the record of population growth after 1864.

TABLE III

Population of Bombay City, 1864–1951 [46]

Year	Population	Per cent change over previous census year
1864	816,562	. . . .
1872	644,405	−21.08
1881	773,196	19.99
1891	821,764	6.28
1901	776,006	−5.57
1906	977,822	26.01
1911	979,445	0.71
1921	1,175,914	20.06
1931	1,161,383	−1.24
1941	1,489,883	28.29
1951	2,329,020	56.32

---

[44] Edwardes, *Gazetteer*, III, *passim*; Edwardes, *The Rise of Bombay*, pp. 279–300; letter of Governor Frere to Sir J. Lawrence, in Bombay Bank Commission, *Minutes of Evidence*, III, p. 76; and D. E. Wacha, *The Rise and Growth of Bombay Municipal Government* (Madras: G. A. Natesan and Co., 1913), pp. 88–89.

[45] It is, of course, possible that the decline in population between 1864 and 1869 was even greater and that the 1872 figure already reflects the effects of economic recovery.

[46] From census reports for the various years.

As I have already pointed out, the population decline recorded in 1872 apparently was a response to the collapse of the Civil War boom. Many workers, unable to find employment, evidently returned to the rural areas from whence they had come. The population increase recorded by the census of 1881 seems a consequence of the restoration of economic expansion in Bombay in the 1870's.[47]

The decline in 1901 seems to have been the aftermath of the great plague epidemic. Shortly after its outbreak, in late 1896, a great exodus began and by the end of January 1897 the official estimate was that "some 400,000 people — about one-half of the entire population of the City — had fled." [48] Although the worst of the plague was felt in 1897, there were periodic recurrences and one of the harshest outbreaks occurred at the time of the 1901 census when more than four hundred people were dying each day.[49] What is surprising is that the city's population did not show a more dramatic decline.[50]

The special census of 1906 attempted to recompute the population under more normal conditions. The 1911 census indicates relatively slow growth but is distorted by the fact that it is compared with the 1906 figure rather than with 1901. The enumeration occurred at a time of very bad business conditions.[51] The 1921 figure reflects the World War I expansion of economic activity. The slight decline in 1931 was associated with "severe epidemics, a heavy business slump and several years of bad trade, which . . . combined to depress the figures for the last years of the decade." [52] The increases in population since 1931 have been the result of World War II prosperity, the expansion of old industries, the growth of new ones and, after 1947, the tragic consequences of partition.

---

[47] It is possible that the famine of 1877–78, which affected large parts of the Presidency, may have accounted for the high rate of increase implied by the 1881 census. Speaking of the tide of famine migration into Bombay, the Municipal Commissioner commented that "we have no exact record of the actual population at that momentous period when an appalling flood of destitution had swept into this city; for a short period the approaches to the city were guarded and the wanderers counted: in 1877, from the 15th of August to the 30th of September, 36,258 destitute entered the city. . . ." *Census 1881*, p. 1.

[48] J. K. Condon, *The Bombay Plague* (Bombay: Education Society's Steam Press, 1900), p. 130.

[49] *Census 1906*, p. 20.

[50] Disastrous famines in the Gujarat and Deccan districts in 1899 and 1900 contributed to a flow of people into Bombay at the same time that the residents were fleeing from the city. Edwardes, *The Rise of Bombay*, pp. 328–331.

[51] *Census 1911*, XI, p. 3.

[52] *Census 1931*, p. 9.

CHAPTER III

History of the
Bombay Cotton Textile Industry

(1)

In 1832 Charles Babbage, the first great analyst of modern industry, boasted:

> The produce of our factories has preceded even our most enterprising travellers. The cotton of India is conveyed by British ships round half our planet, to be woven by British skill in the factories of Lancashire; it is again set in motion by British capital; and, transported to the very plains whereon it grew, is repurchased by the lord of the soil which gave it birth, at a cheaper price than that at which their coarser machinery enables them to manufacture it themselves. . . . At Calicut . . . the price of labor is *one-seventh* of that in England, yet the market is supplied from British looms.[1]

But with India providing both raw material and markets, it was not long before attempts were made to establish factory production of cotton products in the country.[2] In fact, as early as 1817–18, only a few years after English cloth began to flow to India in large amounts, Englishmen set up a cotton mill near Calcutta. There were other isolated attempts in the years before 1850, none of them particularly successful. The industry had its real beginnings in western India in the 1850's, when we get a cluster of attempts at Broach, Ahmedabad, and Bombay.[3] It was the ac-

---

[1] Charles Babbage, *On the Economy of Machinery and Manufactures* (Philadelphia, 1832), p. 17.

[2] Though much more has been written about the cotton textile industry than any other in India, there is still no satisfactory economic history of it or of the Bombay section, its greatest part. The two best studies by far are Mehta, *CMI* and Mehta, *ICTI*. Unfortunately, both suffer from very serious limitations of many sorts, not the least being the lack of satisfactory documentation. D. H. Buchanan, *The Development of Capitalistic Enterprise in India* (New York: The Macmillan Company, 1934) contains a useful, short description.

This chapter does not attempt a complete economic history of the Bombay mills. Within the limits of current knowledge, it gives only as much information as will be relevant to an understanding of the development of the industry's labor force.

[3] For a brief summary of what is known about these early efforts see Mehta, *CMI*, pp. 3–27. Mehta's discussion of the initial Calcutta enterprise needs modification. He states that the mill cost £200,000 to construct when, in fact, this seems to have been the original cost of the cotton mill and four other connected enterprises,

tivity in Bombay, particularly the efforts of C. N. Davar (1814–1873), which led directly to the development of the modern industry.[4]

C. N. Davar's father, a wealthy Parsi merchant, was a broker for English commercial firms engaged in the India and China trade. In 1830 the young Davar entered the family business, and after the death of the father in 1837 he and his elder brother opened a brokerage firm which also operated as agent for English firms in the Asian trade. Widening experience and the encouragement of success led Davar to extend the sweep of his activities. In 1846–47 he coöperated with some English partners in the formation of the Commercial Bank of Bombay. Success here led to a number of further banking ventures and into other types of enterprises. Davar was an active figure in the establishment of the Bombay Steam Navigation Company, and in 1853 to 1855 he helped organize the Bombay Hydraulic Press Company and a large cotton-cleaning enterprise.[5]

---

a distillery, foundry, oil pressing operation, and a paper mill. The entire complex went bankrupt, not because the cotton mill was unprofitable but apparently because the original managing agency house, Messrs. Fergusson and Company, failed during the Calcutta crisis of the early 1830's. When purchased from the bankrupts, the cotton mill and the other enterprises were started again and functioned at least until 1840. In 1840 the cotton mill was being run by an all-India labor force, except for the superintendent. The Indians, it was claimed, were "very expert." See *Parliamentary Papers, 1831–32*, H.C., X, Paper 735-II, evidence of T. Bracken, pp. 154–155; and *Parliamentary Papers, 1840*, H.C., VIII, Paper 527, evidence of H. Gouger, pp. 116–119.

[4] There is only very sketchy information on Davar and the establishment of the first cotton mills in Bombay. Mehta, *CMI*, pp. 13 ff., gives the most detail, but without documentation. His most striking addition to our knowledge is the reproduction of the deed of agreement between Davar and the shareholders of the first cotton mill. *Ibid.*, pp. 26–27. Another important source is the short biography in *ITJ*, I, No. 2, November 1890, p. 27, which was based on information furnished by Davar's family. There is also material on Davar in the records of the Parsi *Panchayat* (Council) of Bombay. The important bits there can be found mainly in the *Panchayat's* records labeled "Parsi Prakash," II, *passim*. One can find pieces of information on the earliest mills in various issues of *ITJ* and S. M. Rutnagur, *Bombay Industries: The Cotton Mills* (Bombay: *The Indian Textile Journal*, 1927). P. R. Cola, *How to Develop Productive Industry in India and the East* (London, 1867) is also useful.

I had hoped that investigation of the great nineteenth-century textile machine firms of Lancashire, particularly Platt Brothers of Oldham, would throw more light on the subject. However, Professor W. A. Chaloner of the University of Manchester has been through the firm's records and reports that there is almost nothing on the Bombay connection. What information there is on British equipping of early Bombay industry appears in Professor Chaloner's essay, "John Galloway (1804–1894), Engineer of Manchester and his 'Reminiscences,'" *Transactions, Lancashire and Cheshire Antiquarian Society*, LXIV, 1954, pp. 111–112.

[5] To give a notion of the scale of some of these enterprises, the Bombay Steam Navigation Company was floated with a capital of one million rupees (approximately £100,000). *The Monthly Miscellany of Western India*, I, 1850, p. 232.

I have stressed the extensive interests of the Cowasji Davar because his activities were not untypical of the bigger Indian businessmen of Bombay at the time. Involved in the export and financing of raw cotton and the import of cotton textiles, it was inevitable that the notion of importing machinery and starting a textile mill would strike Davar or one of his contemporaries. Nevertheless, the boldness of Davar's conception in the face of considerable difficulties is impressive. Plans and machinery had to be imported. Skilled mechanics to guide the erection of the mill and equipment also had to be brought from Britain, as did the managerial talent. Coal and wood for fuel had to be brought by sea to Bombay. The only certain advantages were the availability of raw cotton and the existence of markets for yarn and cloth.

Davar apparently conceived the idea of establishing a modern cotton mill in 1851, but "the absence of trained work people, and the great risk of failure deterred him from entering actively into the enterprise for some time afterwards." [6] However, he did contact Platt Brothers of Oldham. Correspondence apparently convinced the English machine builders of the possibilities of such an undertaking. They appointed Davar their Bombay agent and offered to furnish plans and equipment at very moderate prices. With financing provided by more than fifty of Bombay's leading merchants, a joint-stock company capitalized at Rs.500,-000 was floated in July 1854.[7] The mill went into production in February 1856 and was sufficiently promising to encourage Davar to project a second enterprise in 1857, which started operations in 1859.

The "logic" of cotton manufacturing by modern techniques impressed more than one group of entrepreneurs at the same time.[8] In August 1854, a month after Davar's first venture was floated, another group of Bombay businessmen met to plan the financing of a cotton mill. This Oriental Spinning and Weaving Company, formally floated in 1855, was designed

---

[6] *ITJ*, I, No. 2, November 1890, p. 27.

[7] The records suggest that only two Englishmen were stockholders, and although the majority of investors were Parsis, members of other Indian communities were important participants. Mehta, *CTI*, p. 15. For this and other reasons it is risky to overstress the role of Parsis in the nineteenth-century Indian response to modern economic opportunities. On this point, see D. P. Pandit, "Creative Response in Indian Economy: A Regional Analysis," *Economic Weekly*, IX, No. 8, and No. 9, February 23 and March 2, 1957, pp. 283–286 and 315–317; and H. Acharya, "Creative Response in Indian Economy: A Comment," *ibid.*, IX, No. 17, April 27, 1957, 547–549.

[8] For contemporary estimates of the advantages and disadvantages of factory production of cotton textiles in India, see J. A. Mann, *The Cotton Trade of Great Britain* (London, 1860), pp. 75–79; letter of S. Laing, *The Economist*, XX, No. 998, 11 October 1862, pp. 1126–28; and Cola, *op. cit.*

as a composite mill, unlike Davar's two mills which initially produced only yarn. Going into production in 1858, the Oriental Mill proved even more profitable than Davar's enterprises, and others were encouraged to move into the field. Five companies were floated in 1860 and two more in 1861.[9] By 1862 at least four mills with 94,000 spindles and 2,150 looms were at work, and six others were under construction.[10] Some English observers were quick to draw the obvious implication. Describing the disastrous effects of British factory competition on Indian handloom production, R. M. Martin, using words reminiscent of Babbage's analysis only thirty years before, warned his countrymen:

It is too late to resuscitate an almost extinct manufacture; but there is a Nemesis in trade as in other human transactions; several steam-spinning and power-loom weaving establishments have been formed in different parts of India; and the cotton is wrought near the place of its growth, instead of being sent to Europe and returned as cloth, after traversing a distance of twenty to twenty-five thousand miles. The demand for the produce of these Anglo-Indian mills is increasing; cheapness of labor (two-pence a day), warmth of climate, cotton from contiguous fields grown at a rate varying from five to six farthings per pound, abundance of coal, to which may now be added increasing means of irrigation, facilities of transit, and available capital, all tend to promote economical production, and to enhance profits; so that even the present generation may witness the Lancashire manufacturer beaten by his Hindu competitor.[11]

A momentary halt to the construction of mills was forced in Bombay by the effects of the American Civil War boom and its financial aftermath,

_____

[9] Mehta, *CMI*, pp. 20–25.

[10] W. R. Cassels, *Cotton: An Account of its Culture in the Bombay Presidency* (Bombay, 1862), pp. 344–345. There is considerable confusion in the sources about the precise number of spindles and looms installed in these early mills. For example, S. M. Edwardes, *The Rise of Bombay: A Retrospect* (Bombay: The Times of India Press, 1902), p. 306, stated that there were 195,673 spindles and 2,700 looms working in 1862. But whatever the precise situation, the loom figures should do away with the widespread notion that the industry in its early stages had no weaving capacity. Buchanan, *op. cit.*, p. 201, is the most influential of recent sources for this incorrect view. There is strong evidence that weaving was an important part of the industry's activities from the beginning. Cola, *op. cit.*, p. 64, quotes a report to the Manchester Chamber of Commerce, dated March 1867, that stated that from 50 to 75 per cent of mill cloth sold in the Bombay bazaars was of local manufacture. Mehta, *CMI*, p. 41, gives some undocumented figures which indicate that in 1875 about 45 per cent of all yarn spun in the Bombay mills was being consumed by them in the production of cloth. Presidency of Bombay, *Annual Report, 1872–73*, p. xxii, reported that "the returns from Sind and Aden show . . . that Bombay-made cloth can, on equal terms, compete successfully with the produce of English mills."

[11] R. M. Martin, *The Progress and Present State of British India* (London, 1862), pp. 280–282.

but by 1870 progress was resumed.[12] By 1874 seventeen mills had been erected and by 1900 eighty-six had been built.[13]

The capital required to establish one of the early mills was not exceptional by the standards of contemporary Bombay finance. Davar's first venture was capitalized at Rs.500,000. The evidence suggests that the cost of starting an efficiently designed enterprise in the late 1850's and 1860's required between Rs.500,000 and Rs.1,500,000 (£50,000–150,000) for land, buildings, equipment, and inventory.[14] The mills were typically joint-stock ventures. The early promoters seem generally to have distributed their shares among a relatively small number of business associates, friends, and caste brethren. These enterprises were apparently almost entirely financed on a fully paid-up capital basis, with machinery and plant paid for in cash.[15]

After 1872 the industry expanded very rapidly, and new sources of capital were tapped. Potential local and English suppliers of coal, cotton, stores, machinery, and even buildings began to provide share capital in return for contracts for their products, or they made their contributions in the form of long-term contracts and deferred payments. Once mills got started, middle-class investors could easily be induced to offer their savings to successful ventures.[16]

The Bombay textile industry was initially conceived and financed by Indians. Lacking details, it is impossible to establish the extent to which non-Indians participated in the early ventures, but it was not until 1874, after seventeen Indian-dominated mills had gone into operation, that the first English sponsored and financed company was established.[17] In

---

[12] Presidency of Bombay, *Annual Report, 1866–67*, pp. 334–335; Mehta, *CTI*, pp. 32–33.

[13] Statistics on the establishment of Bombay mills come from the annual reports of the Bombay Millowners Association and Rutnagur, *op. cit.*, pp. 9–37. These figures do not allow for mills dismantled during the period. For a year-by-year record of the number of mills in existence in Bombay, see Appendix I.

[14] Cola, *op. cit.*, pp. 52–63; *The Late Government Bank of Bombay: Its History*, Appendix A, pp. 87–91; Rutnagur, *op. cit.*, p. 245. Mehta, *CMI*, pp. 14–15, gives some figures on capital mobilized for other types of enterprises at the same time.

[15] *ITJ*, II, No. 17, February 1892, p. 95; *ITJ*, V, No. 51, December 1894, p. 54; Rutnagur, *op. cit.*, p. 46; P. S. Lokanathan, *Industrial Organization in India* (London: G. Allen & Unwin, Ltd., 1935), pp. 22–23; Mehta, *CMI*, p. 93; N. G. Hunt, "Banks and the Indian Cotton Industry," *ITJ Jubilee Souvenir*, p. 39.

[16] S. Saklatvala, "The Indian Cotton Textile Industry," *ITJ Jubilee Souvenir*, p. 307; Lokanathan, *op. cit.*, pp. 28–31. Many of these suppliers did not hold on to their shares but unloaded them after the company had gotten under way and its share prices had (hopefully) risen. *ITJ*, II, No. 17, February 1892, p. 95; *ITJ*, V, No. 51, December 1894, p. 54.

[17] Rutnagur, *op. cit.*, pp. 9–37, gives the names of many of the early entrepreneurs and their predominantly indigenous origin is clear. Mehta, *CMI*, p. 15, states that the two English participants in Davar's first mill took only 13 per cent of the shares.

1875 a report prepared for British textile interests pointed out that Indian mills "are almost exclusively owned by natives, and are under native supervision." [18] Although other British financed mills were started after 1874, foreign capital never amounted to more than a few per cent of total investment in the industry.[19]

The economic career of the industry in Bombay lends itself to division into three major phases: from its inception to about 1890, 1891 to 1922, and from 1923 to 1947. The initial period was marked by extensive growth, by the rapid entry of new firms and a concentration on yarn production. The second period was characterized by a slower rate of entry of new units, the expansion of old units, an increasing emphasis on weaving, and a shift to finer count production.[20] The third period is nota-

---

[18] "Report on Bombay Mills by Mr. John Robertson of Glasgow," *BMOA 1875 and 1875–76*, p. 74.

[19] Statistical Department, Government of India, *Financial and Commercial Statistics of British India*, 12th issue (Calcutta: Superintendent of Government Printing, 1906), p. 361.

The fragmentary evidence indicates that British capital invested in the Bombay mills came from merchants resident in Bombay. If we look at the problem of foreign investment in terms of the source where capital was generated rather than in terms of the nationality of its owners, it seems clear that virtually all the British capital came from local sources. See, for example, the career of James Greaves whose firm controlled six Bombay mills. *ITJ*, XXXII, No. 374, November 1921, p. 61.

In fact, it might be useful to reëxamine the entire question of nineteenth-century foreign investments along these lines, laying stress on the transfer of real resources from Britain to India rather than on the claims to property accumulated by Englishmen in India via reinvestment of earnings. There would be serious problems of conceptualization, but if we could do it I suspect that we would challenge the notion that large-scale transfers of real resources from Britain to India were important in the nineteenth century. The same technique applied to British investments elsewhere during the period might well suggest that the real resource burden of foreign investment on Britain was much less than Ragnar Nurkse suggested in "The Problem of International Investment Today in the Light of Nineteenth Century Experience," *Economic Journal*, LXIV, No. 256, December 1954, pp. 744–758. A discussion along this line can be found in H. J. Habakkuk, "Free Trade and Commercial Expansion, 1853–1870," *Cambridge History of the British Empire*, Vol. II (Cambridge: Cambridge University Press, 1940), Chapter XXI, pp. 792–798. See also J. Knapp, "Capital Growth and Export," *Economic Journal*, LXVII, No. 267, September 1957, pp. 432–444.

[20] In 1865 there were only ten mills working; by 1890 fifty-nine more had been opened. After that date the rate of entry slowed sharply. Between 1891 and 1921, the last occasion on which a new mill came into operation, only twenty-eight units were added. These figures do not allow for mills which went out of operation. See Rutnagur, *op. cit.*, pp. 10–24.

The greater stress on weaving in the second period is indicated by the rates at which spindles and looms were added. Between 1865 and 1890 the number of spindles installed increased by 658 per cent while looms increased by only 308 per cent; but between 1890 and 1922 spindlage rose a mere 64 per cent while loomage

ble for retrenchment, reduction in the number of mills, and increasing sophistication of product, technology, and organization.[21]

Although there are no statistical data to which I can usefully appeal, contemporary evidence seems to show conclusively that, barring minor crises, the industry was extremely prosperous before 1891. It is impossible to be precise about what "extremely prosperous" means. In the absence of profit figures, the prime evidence must be the very high rate of new entry into the industry which I have already mentioned.[22] However, John Robertson, discussing the situation in 1875, pointed out that "Notwithstanding all disadvantages . . . the success of the Bombay mills has been considerable judging from the dividends paid during the last few years." [23] Another contemporary observer also commented that in the early 1880's some mills "paid back all the subscribed capital in four years. . . ." [24]

The second period, 1891 to 1922, is somewhat more complex. In the decade after 1890 a number of developments threatened the prosperity of the Bombay mills. A series of short-run difficulties — the silver crisis

increased 375 per cent. (Calculated from the statistical appendix in *BMOA* for the relevant years). Not only was there greater stress on weaving; there was also a shift toward production of finer products. A simple measure of this is the fact that in the year 1901–02 only 11.8 per cent of Bombay's yarn production was in counts of "21s" or higher while in 1921–22 "21s" counts or above represented 29.2 per cent of the total output. Statistical Department, Government of India, *Statistics of Cotton Spinning and Weaving in the Indian Mills* for these years.

[21] For general descriptions, see Mehta, *CMI*, particularly Chapters XI and XII; and Ness Wadia, "The Industry in Retrospect," *ITJ Jubilee Souvenir*, p. 16.

[22] Some aspects of the difficulty of getting at profit data can be inferred from the series of articles by B. J. Padshah, "The Cotton Industry of India and the Cotton Duties," *ITJ*, XIII, No. 147, December 1902, *et seq.* Actually it is impossible to get satisfactory profit information of any sort before the 1930's at the earliest. For example, The Indian Tariff Commission, as late as 1926, found it virtually impossible to penetrate the problem with any degree of confidence. See *ITB 1927*, I-IV, passim. All profit figures used in this study must, therefore, be treated with extreme caution.

[23] *BMOA 1875 and 1875–76*, p. 76. Robertson visited Bombay as the representative of a group of potential British investors to determine whether the mill industry was a fruitful outlet for British capital. Despite his comments on the industry's profitability, he seems to have cautioned his principals against investment in Bombay. He feared that the rate at which new mills were being opened would very quickly lead to overproduction of low-count products. He also pointed out that the lack of an adequately trained work force — expansion forcing its steady dilution with new recruits — made it unlikely that the mills could evade the dangers of oversupply of coarse products by a shift to the production of finer-count yarns and cloth. *Ibid.*, pp. 75–78. See also *ITJ*, V, No. 57, June 1895, p. 203.

[24] "Report of the Chief Inspector of Factories and Workshops for the Year Ending 31 October 1887," *Parliamentary Papers, 1888*, XXVI, Command 5328, p. 116.

of 1893, bubonic plague, famines in the countryside — disturbed the industry and hampered profitable operations. Longer-run tendencies also began to manifest themselves. Internationally, the rapid growth of textile factories in Japan and China undermined the stability of Bombay yarn markets in East Asia. Domestically, Bombay producers were beginning to face more serious competition from the increasing number of up-country mills.

It is difficult to tell what happened to profits. Some comments referred to "properly administered" mills paying dividends of 10 to 20 per cent. And in the very bad year of 1894 the three Petit mills showed a profit of 26 per cent on capital.[25] But this latter case was certainly exceptional. The evidence generally seems to suggest that during this decade it was harder to make a profit. Entrepreneurs had to react more quickly and precisely to the changing character of the market, shifting the emphasis of their product-mix in the direction of finer count yarns and toward greater concentration on cloth production.[26]

In one way or another the industry did readjust. And after 1901 economic conditions once again improved.

Although by all impressions the pre-1891 boom was not recreated, Table IV indicates that between 1905 and 1914 gross profits on paid-up capital averaged 27.1 per cent.[27] Following the outbreak of World War I and the curtailments of cloth and yarn imports from Britain, profits rose to unprecedented levels. During the six years 1917 to 1922, while paid-up capital was being inflated, gross profits averaged 75.6 per cent and reached the incredible figure of 102.7 per cent in 1920.[28] Dividends paid

---

[25] *ITJ*, V, No. 57, June 1895, p. 204; *ITJ*, VII, No. 82, July 1897, p. 233; *ITJ*, VII, No. 84, September 1897, pp. 288–289; *ITJ*, IX, No. 99, December 1898, pp. 66–67; *ITJ*, IX, No. 100, January 1899, pp. 99–100; and *ITJ*, IX, No. 108, September 1899, p. 339.

[26] For discussion of this adjustment process, see Mehta, *CMI*, Ch. VI, and Ness Wadia, *op. cit.*, p. 16. The importance of the greater stress on weaving is indicated by the fact that after 1895, with the single exception of 1920, composite mills as a group earned higher average profits than mills concentrating on spinning only. And by the end of World War I only a few mills had not added looms. *ITJ*, XXXII, No. 373, October 1921, p. 12.

[27] Profits net of depreciation and managing agency commissions averaged 10.3 per cent during this same period. For a host of reasons, gross profits are a better measure of performance for the matters with which I am concerned. The fact that profit rates ran at these levels during a period believed less profitable than the pre-1890 era suggests something about the high rates of profits in the earlier period.

[28] Even net profits (after deducting depreciation and agency commissions) averaged 60.5 per cent during the 1917 to 1922 period, reaching a peak of 83.1 per cent in 1919. Computed from *ITB 1927*, IV, p. 73.

TABLE IV

Gross Profits in the Bombay Cotton-Mill Industry, 1905–1924 [29]

(Per cent of paid-up capital)

Year	Gross profits
1905	55.1
1906	51.5
1907	30.8
1908	21.3
1909	18.6
1910	8.8
1911	8.1
1912	38.2
1913	26.7
1914	14.1
1915	27.4
1916	39.0
1917	76.6
1918	53.4
1919	99.7
1920	102.7
1921	82.7
1922	38.5
1923	13.0
1924	1.9

out between 1917 and 1922 amounted to nearly 168 per cent of paid-up capital, reaching a peak of 40 per cent in 1919.[30]

The boom ended in 1922 and the industry entered its third stage, a period of fundamental difficulties. The steadily expanding competition from Japanese producers and mills elsewhere in India forced considera-

[29] Computed from *ITB 1927*, IV, p. 73. These figures were prepared for many years by J. A. Wadia, a leading figure in the industry. They can be found in a number of places, including the *ITJ*. There are occasionally slight variations in the figures between one source and another, but these are usually not significant. The prime difficulty is that we do not really know what these figures mean. Wadia never described his method of compilation. We do not know how many mills were included. There are many other questionable aspects to the data. Moreover, these over-all figures gloss over the wide range of profitability among mills in any year. For example, in 1912 profits on capital for fifty-nine mills ranged from 4.5 per cent to 65.2 per cent. *ITJ*, XXIII, No. 273, June 1913, pp. 296–297.

[30] *ITB 1927*, I, p. 20. Mehta, *CMI*, p. 156, reports that in 1920 twenty-six mills declared dividends of 40 per cent and more. Ten of these paid 100 per cent and two companies paid more than 200 per cent. He does not make clear whether this was on original capital or on some other base. For another discussion of the 1917–1922 situation, see Freda Utley, *Lancashire and the Far East* (London: George Allen & Unwin, 1931), pp. 310–318.

ble readjustment and adaptation during the next decade and a half. Basic technological and organizational changes were required. The industry was handicapped by the fact that it came out of the boom with the capital value of its virtually unmodified plant enormously inflated. In addition to the burden of its very high fixed costs, formidable labor unrest made the process of adaptation a particularly troublesome one. The domestic consequences of the international depression made progress even harder.[31]

It was not until the outbreak of World War II that the situation eased noticeably. Once again the curtailment of foreign competition gave a fillip to the Bombay mills. Moreover, military needs increased demand and countries that formerly had depended on other suppliers now turned to India for cotton textiles. Prosperity continued beyond the end of hostilities. Unlike the 1920's, however, no great collapse terminated this boom. Independence and the development of a planning economy introduced new elements into the situation.

(2)

The first mills seem to have been laid out with care, and effort was made to obtain the most modern equipment possible. However, in the period after 1870, when it became obvious that there was easy money to be made, eager speculators with little, if any, technical advice also rushed to take advantage of the opportunities and erected mills which were technically deficient. In Bombay these represented a minority of cases, but they contributed to the very general phenomenon, the increasingly wide diversity of types and efficiency of equipment and layout in the industry. Technological diversity also became typical within individual mills; additions to and modifications of plant resulted in new technology and patterns of operation being superimposed on the old. This characteristic within mills and in the industry generally provoked a number of serious problems, not least in the use of labor.[32]

---

[31] Ness Wadia, *op. cit.*, p. 16; Mehta, *CMI*, Chs. XI and XII. There is need for a thorough examination of the career of the Bombay industry during the interwar period. There has been a good deal of moralizing on the subject, stressing the speculative propensities and incompetence of managements. Very little attention has been paid to the impact of changing world and national demand or to the fact that the Bombay industry did, in fact, reorganize itself substantially during the period 1925 to 1939. That the readjustment took the form of bankruptcies and serious writedowns of capital was inevitable. How else could the market mechanism perform, particularly in an economy marked by generalized stagnation? Mehta, *loc. cit.*, has the most sophisticated discussion of the process but it is all too brief.

[32] For the speculative origins of many mills, see Lokanathan, *op. cit.*, pp. 28–31; and Buchanan, *op. cit.*, p. 204. For general discussions of the technological history

Compared with the situation in England where Bombay bought all of its equipment, wage rates of course were very low, and the industry tended to substitute labor for capital wherever possible.[33] Historically, this showed itself in the very slow introduction of many labor-saving innovations. For example, some departments — notably mixing and winding and reeling — were not mechanized until after World War I. In other departments, as in weaving, there was a tendency to employ labor-intensive rather than labor-saving equipment.[34] The low wage rates encouraged a series of other characteristics: the use of short-staple cotton, high machine speeds, and the production in each mill of a vast variety of products.[35] These features were all linked and had, as we shall see, an enormous effect on the organization and utilization of the labor force.[36]

It is impossible to say anything precise about labor costs as a proportion of total costs. As late as 1926 even the Indian Tariff Board with its

of the industry, see various articles in *ITJ Jubilee Souvenir*; and Mehta, *ICTI, passim.* The system of financing mills by selling shares to potential suppliers of equipment also contributed to the lack of technological standardization which characterized many firms. For an extreme case of technological chaos, see the history of the Dharumsey Mill in *ITJ*, I, No. 11, August 1891, pp. 176–177; and D. E. Wacha, *The Life and Life Work of J. N. Tata* (Madras: Ganesh and Co., 1915), p. 72.

[33] *ITJ*, IX, No. 102, March 1899, p. 153; Mehta, *ICTI*, p. 67, footnote 42.

[34] For example, as late as 1951 less than 3 per cent of all looms in Bombay were of the automatic type. *BMOA 1951*, statistical appendix. For an interesting example of mill calculations on this problem, see the discussion of the economic feasibility of introducing the Northrup loom into Bombay mills at the beginning of this century. *ITJ*, XIII, No. 149, February 1903, pp. 133–134. See also *ITB 1927*, I, pp. 143–144; and *ITB 1927*, II, pp. 139 and 353 ff.

[35] Mehta, *ICTI*, pp. 78–81; *ITJ*, I, No. 9, June 1891, p. 130; and *ITJ*, XXIV, No. 285, June 1914, pp. 319–320; and A. S. Pearse, *Indian Cotton* (Manchester: International Federation of Master Cotton Spinners and Manufacturers Association, 1915), pp. 221 and 225.

[36] There is a tendency among scholars to imply that the Bombay mills were technologically unimaginative, tending always to imitate the Lancashire industry. Buchanan, *op. cit.*, pp. 204–206; D. P. Joshi, "Developments in the Preliminary Processes of Weaving," *ITJ Jubilee Souvenir*, p. 125; P. S. Lokanathan, "The Managing Agency System: Can It Survive?" *ITJ Jubilee Souvenir*, p. 45. A careful study of technological usages and organizational structure indicates that the Bombay mills were perfectly willing to deviate from Lancashire experience in many ways. The very rapid shift from mule to ring spinning, the integrated spinning and weaving operations, the managing agency system of organization — all represent significant deviations from the British example. The particular choices made by the Bombay industry during its history would seem to be better explained by an analysis of cost-price relationships and factor proportions than by an appeal to a special millowner psychology. For some general insights on the slow development of an Indian machine-building industry, see Nathan Rosenberg, "Capital Goods, Technology and Economic Growth," *Oxford Economic Papers*, XV, No. 3, November 1963, pp. 217–227.

facilities had trouble making sense of the data.[37] The information it did get suggests that in the 1920's labor costs constituted a relatively small proportion of total costs. Possibly the most reliable judgment came from the economist, G. Findlay Shirras, who estimated the over-all cost of labor at between 12 and 17 per cent of total costs.[38] In 1932 the Indian Tariff Board estimated total labor costs for producing plain gray cloth in a group of eleven representative mills, of which four were in Bombay, at 24.85 per cent. This figure exaggerates labor costs because of the failure to include interest, depreciation, and managing agency commissions.[39] Including these costs would certainly have reduced total labor costs below 20 per cent. It is probably safe to assume that labor costs during the 1920's and early 1930's ranged between 15 and 20 per cent of total costs.[40] For a number of reasons, it is most unlikely that labor costs were higher during the earlier decades.[41] If anything, they should have been somewhat lower.[42]

(3)

For the greater part of its history, certainly into the 1920's, the Bombay mill industry was quite generally treated as a milch cow to be drained

---

[37] *ITB 1927*, I-IV, *passim.* particularly II, p. 231, and IV, p. 365. Not only were the mills secretive about their accounts, but their costing techniques left much to be desired. *Ibid.*, II, pp. 164 and 212; and *ITB 1932*, p. 95. For an explicit discussion of some of the problems of calculation of costs, see *ITB 1932*, pp. 95 ff. Even in the 1950's "not more than a score" of mills in all India could provide reliable cost information. Mehta, *ICTI*, p. 84.

[38] *ITB 1927*, IV, p. 334. One mill in Delhi reported that wages constituted 5.2 per cent of the cost of production of yarn and 8.86 per cent of the cost of production of cloth. *Ibid.*, IV, p. 375. The Bombay Textile Labor Union spoke of labor costs averaging 10 to 15 per cent. *Ibid.*, III, p. 470.

[39] Cost of cotton was estimated at 61.77 pies per pound and manufacturing and other costs at 62.50 pies. Labor cost in eleven Bombay mills was calculated at 49.40 per cent of total manufacturing costs. *ITB 1932*, pp. 98 and 222.

[40] S. A. Palekar, *Problems of Wage Policy for Economic Development* (New York: Asia Publishing House, 1962), pp. 160–161, shows wage costs in the Indian cotton textile industry in the years 1946 to 1955 ranging from a low of 19.94 per cent to a high of 28.64 per cent. These estimates also overstate labor costs by the exclusion of interest, depreciation, and managing agency commissions.

[41] Padshah, writing in 1903, estimated labor costs at 7 per cent of the total cost of producing yarn and 15 per cent of the cost of producing cloth. *ITJ*, XIII, No. 156, September 1903, pp. 378–379.

[42] Equipment, fuel, freight charges, and management costs all were very high during the early decades and tended to fall. At the same time, the slow shift into finer counts of product and the greater concentration in weaving as opposed to spinning should have raised relative labor costs. Mehta, *CMI*, p. 51. However, the issue is too complex to be resolved here. It requires a special study.

of profits at all costs. There is no doubt that the managing agency system was one factor contributing to this attitude, often inducing slackness, corruption, and a speculative fever where discipline, integrity, and a long-range view were needed. Even though the managing agency made possible the financing of early Indian enterprises under circumstances where capital might otherwise not have been forthcoming, it also introduced difficulties that cannot be minimized.[43] This is not the place to discuss the system's historical development, but a few points must be made because they ultimately bear quite heavily on the proper understanding of the labor problem.

The managing agents were usually venturers in many fields, and the cotton mills they promoted were viewed as enterprises from which profits could be drawn in various ways. Typically holding a controlling interest at the time a mill was established, the agents frequently divested themselves of all but a minor shareholding interest as time went on. But before reducing their proprietary stake they managed to fix their grip as managing agents, often in perpetuity and with rights to sell the agency to others without recourse to the shareholders.[44] As stockholders they were obviously concerned with the dividends that efficient mill operation would produce, but as managing agents they had other sources of income as well. For example, during the period before 1886 all managing agents were paid a commission on mill output regardless of the profitability of the enterprise's operations.[45] In addition, both by contractual

---

[43] There is a tendency in the literature to attribute much greater responsibility for evil to the managing agency system than the institution deserves. Many of the faults pointed to can be duplicated in the West where this institution did not develop. It is more likely that the behavior exhibited was a function of the stage of economic development. The so-called speculative behavior, the preoccupation with short-run profits, would seem to have been a rational response to the market situation in an underdeveloped economy. For some part of the general argument along these lines, see H. G. Aubrey, "Industrial Investment Decisions: A Comparative Analysis," *Journal of Economic History*, XV, No. 4, December 1955, pp. 335–351. However, the managing agency was the vehicle through which much manipulation occurred in India. We need a good reëxamination of the agency system. The best existing analysis is Lokanathan, *op. cit.* For brief descriptions, see Buchanan, *op. cit.*, pp. 165–172; V. Anstey, *The Economic Development of India* (3d ed., London: Longmans, Green and Co., 1949), pp. 113–115 and 501–505; *ITB 1932*, Chap. V; and Rutnagur, *op. cit.*, pp. 49–65.

[44] Lokanathan, *op.cit.*, Chap. I.

[45] In one reported case the agents from their commission alone in a period of ten years earned more than the value of the mill. The other shareholders did much less well. Rutnagur, *op.cit.*, p. 62. "The mischievous system of commission on production" encouraged agents to produce yarn and cloth regardless of the state of the market. It provided a built-in incentive to keep the mills functioning. *ITJ*, IX, No. 99, December 1898, p. 66, charged that during the bubonic plague epi-

right and by virtue of the authority they exercised, managing agents set themselves up as suppliers of raw materials and services to the mills they ran.[46]

The *Indian Textile Journal* almost from its inception in 1890 began to attack the system's abuses. In 1894 and 1895 it published a series of articles which criticized all aspects of the institution.[47] This was only the beginning of a continuing assault which has lasted virtually to the present. In 1898 the *Times of India* joined in the bitter criticism. For my purposes the "evilness" of the system is irrelevant. What is important is that to some considerable extent profit maximization for the decision-making group in the enterprise, the managing agents, did not relate specifically to the efficiency of the cotton mill itself but to the wider and more complex system of commercial relationships of which it was merely a part.[48]

Though in some firms the tautly efficient management of the cotton mill maximized profits for the managing agents, the system was so organized that this was not the most likely outcome. Profit maximization for the controlling group occurred most systematically if the mills were run in a way that did not necessarily maximize mill profits.[49] Such a system encouraged the establishment and perpetuation of certain types of

demic of 1896–1898, when the labor force was completely disorganized, European technicians urged that the mills should be closed. However, "the agents, whose interests lay in a commission on production per pound," kept the mills operating. For other sources making the same charge, see "Report of the Chief Inspector of Factories, 1887," *op.cit.*, p. 116; *FA 1897*, p. 7; and L. Fraser, *India Under Curzon and After* (London: W. Heinemann, 1911), pp. 331–332.

There is some evidence that the very rapid shift from mule to ring spinning, once it was proved practical, was stimulated by the very much higher output possible with ring spindles. Agents, paid a commission on output, found such an innovation most attractive. Mehta, *CMI*, p. 84. The principle of commission on output began to be replaced by a system of commission on profits in a few progressive mills in the 1890's. However, as late as 1913, of the fifty-nine mills registered under the Indian Companies Act, more than half had still not shifted to the system of payment on profits. *ITJ*, XXIII, No. 275, August 1913, p. 369.

[46] Lokanathan, *op.cit.*, pp. 46–47; *ITB 1932*, pp. 79 and 86–87. These features were not restricted to the Indian managing agency system. They also appeared in the United States, even in the early New England textile enterprises. R. K. Lamb, "The Entrepreneur and the Community," in *Men in Business* (W. Miller, ed.). (Cambridge: Harvard University Press, 1952), Chap. IV.

[47] "The Bombay Cotton Mills: Their Defects in Management and How to Remedy Them," *ITJ*, V, Nos. 50–57, November 1894 to June 1895.

[48] For example, the high profits made by the industry in 1912 seem to have been the result of cotton speculations in which the mills engaged. *ITJ*, XXIII, No. 272, May 1913, pp. 261 and 290. The speculative emphasis in mill operation was noted very early in the industry's history. See Cola, *op.cit.*, p. 64.

[49] Lokanathan, *op.cit.*, *passim* and particularly pp. 299–300; Rutnagur, *op.cit.*, pp. 49–65.

administrative organization and behavior inside the mills which were important in determining the kind of labor recruitment and disciplinary practices that developed and persisted.

Although the managing agents were responsible for over-all policy, day-to-day operations were in the hands of a manager, and the working of the various departments was typically under the direction of carding, spinning, and weaving masters and their assistants. Below this administrative and technical cadre were the jobbers immediately supervising the workers in each department. In the earliest years the administrative and technical staff had to be brought from England, but very quickly Indians began to take over as masters and managers. By 1895, the first date for which we have detailed information, more than half of all staff positions in the Bombay mills were held by Indians.[50]

The formal description of mill administration suggests the lines of authority familiar in the West. The manager directed the operation of the mill according to policy generally determined by the managing agents. Among his other responsibilities was the establishment and maintenance of work discipline. The department heads, though primarily responsible for the technical processes, were also formally responsible for the detailed discipline of the labor force in their sections. In this latter duty they were supposedly aided by their subordinates, the jobbers.

In fact, this pyramid of authority did not exist. Although it is difficult to describe precisely a pattern of authority which obviously varied from mill to mill, the system existing from the beginning did not give great power to the manager. For example, although the department heads and their assistants were nominally responsible to him, they were neither appointed nor discharged by the manager but by the managing agent.[51] This illustrates a common feature, the practice of managing agents intervening in details of mill management to a degree unknown in Lan-

[50] *Ibid.*, pp. 293–294; and G. N. Vaidya, "Cotton Mill Staff in Bombay," *ITJ Jubilee Souvenir*, p. 203. Though Lancashire practice encouraged the upward movement of aggressive and competent workers into managerial posts, this was certainly not the case in Bombay. So far as I can determine, there are virtually no examples of ordinary mill hands moving into the managerial and technical cadre. The highest post to which a mill hand could aspire was that of a departmental jobber. *RCL 1929*, "Report," p. 29. Mehta, *CMI*, p. 111, suggests some upward mobility but his point is not bolstered by any supporting evidence and it is largely contradicted by what biographical data there are. Rutnagur, *op.cit.*, pp. 697 ff, provides a collection of capsule biographies. The few relating to mill technicians suggest that these people started their mill careers as apprentices destined for managerial or technical posts. Apart from other restrictions, mill hand illiteracy must certainly have functioned as a major barrier to upward mobility.

[51] *ITJ*, VIII, No. 88, January 1898, p. 102; Mehta, *ICTI*, pp. 62–63.

cashire. Not only did this encourage extensive nepotism, but it led mill staff to identify their loyalties with the agents rather than with the managers.[52] As might be expected, such a system resulted in a high rate of turnover of mill managers and staff with obvious unfavorable consequences on mill administration and operations.[53]

Apart from these special features which weakened the power of the manager, we must also recognize that the jobber was far more influential than his position in the hierarchy would lead an outsider to conclude. Historically, the mills were unwilling to invest in a large and efficient staff of highly trained middle supervisors. In the absence of a solid middle management cadre, the jobber became, as we shall see, the key figure in labor recruitment and labor discipline. This was the case during the early decades; it was also true until very close to the end of the period with which I am concerned.

The jobber . . . is almost ubiquitous in the Indian factory system and usually combines in one person a formidable series of functions. He is primarily a chargeman. Promoted from the ranks after full experience of the factory, he is responsible for the supervision of labor while at work. In a large factory there may be a hierarchy of jobbers for this purpose, including women overseers in departments staffed by women. He has also, on many occasions, to act as assistant mechanic, and to help in keeping the machines in working order. So far as the worker is given technical training, the jobber is expected to provide it. He is not, however, merely responsible for the worker once he has obtained work; the worker has generally to approach him to secure a job.[54]

Although the mill manager and, above him, the managing agents were the ultimate authorities shaping the general terms of work in the factory, it was the jobber who, in effect, determined and maintained the specific quality of labor recruitment and discipline.[55] The role of the jobber was

---

[52] There are frequent references to extensive espionage in the mills sponsored by the agents and often designed to keep the manager under surveillance. *ITJ*, VIII, No. 88, January 1898, p. 102; and Mehta, *ICTI*, pp. 74–76.

[53] On the general weakness of the manager, see *ITJ*, III, No. 35, August 1893, pp. 224–225; *ITJ*, V, No. 54, March 1895, p. 134; *ITJ*, XIX, No. 228, September 1909, p. 405; and *ITJ*, XX, No. 229, October 1909, p. 2. Mehta, *ICTI*, pp. 73–76, suggests this for more recent times. The issues of *ITJ* can be studied to illustrate the very high turnover rate for mill staff. See also Mehta, *CMI*, 108–110; and "Report of the Chief Inspector of Factories, 1887," *op.cit.*, p. 115. Even allowing for the fact that many of the higher staff were foreigners who returned home after a tour of duty, the turnover rate seems to have been exceptionally high. *ITJ*, VI, No. 62, November 1895, p. 44. The rapid expansion of mills encouraged this phenomenon.

[54] *RCL 1929*, "Report," p. 23.

[55] On occasion the jobber was powerful enough to gain the support of the managing agents and defy the authority of the manager. For one such example, *ITJ*,

both cause and consequence of the systematic unwillingness of the managing agents to invest in expensive middle management supervisory staff.

(4)

The Bombay Millowners Association (BMOA) has been since its formation the representative organization of the Bombay mills and, although its membership has fluctuated, at all times the vast majority of Bombay mills were affiliated to it. The Association came into existence in 1875 as an instrument of self-protection against Lancashire pressure on Parliament. It was organized to oppose unfavorable tariff legislation and the passage of a factory act which Bombay millowners felt was a Lancastrian device to raise their costs.[56]

Since its formation the BMOA, representing the industry on all public issues, has been the acknowledged spokesman for the Bombay mills. For all the authority it achieved so early, the Association was not able to unify the mills for common action in matters of internal industry organization. Although on some issues the Association was able to obtain a degree of formal unity and collective action, its lack of punitive powers left it without as much authority as might appear from the formal record.[57]

The millowners, an unruly and opportunitic group, rarely missed the chance to break an agreement for convenience's sake. This was particularly true in matters affecting the technical organization of the industry and the administration of the labor force. In defense of the BMOA it must be pointed out that the organization was merely the executor of democratically determined policy. Its weakness lay in its frequent inability to enforce on its members those decisions which its executive committee may have made. As a result, in writing a history of the development of the labor force in the Bombay cotton textile industry it is wise to avoid reading too much into the Association's formal resolutions and its official records and programs. All of its policies must be tested in the light of the results which emerged.

III, No. 35, August 1893, pp. 224–225. Mehta, *ICTI*, p. 75, further comments that "Another implication of the instability of the . . . officer cadre lies in their inadequate command of the jobbers, who are apt to regard themselves as the permanent, and the former as the transient, unstable elements, with obvious undesirable reactions throughout the labor force."

[56] S. D. Saklatvala, *History of the Millowners' Association, Bombay* (Bombay: 1931), p. 1. For a history of the factory act agitation, see A. Mukhtar, *Factory Labour in India* (Madras: The Annamalai University, 1930), pp. 12–16; and *BMOA 1875 and 1875–76*, p. 52.

[57] *IFLC 1908*, I, p. 31; and Lokanathan, *op.cit.*, pp. 306–307.

CHAPTER IV

Supply of Labor

(1)

S. D. Mehta, the official historian of the cotton textile industry, has recently reiterated the commonly accepted proposition that the Bombay mills suffered chronic and severe shortages of labor which inhibited the expansion of the industry until 1921.[1] A careful study of the supply of labor available suggests that this view needs drastic revision.[2]

In order to discuss the supply of labor, it will be useful briefly to consider the rural sector from which the majority of the work force initially came. There have been no satisfactory studies of the economic relationship of the countryside with the growing urban centers of nineteenth- and twentieth-century India. This is not the place to undertake such an analysis, but there are important interpretive consequences which flow from certain traditional notions about the rural areas. Let me, therefore, point to three features which are almost always ignored.

First, we must recognize that the historic balance between men and resources in most areas of the subcontinent was always precarious, and equilibrium was sustained only by the systematic working of the checks of war, famine, and epidemic. Such vitality as has been claimed for the traditional order before the nineteenth century tended, on the whole, to be the vitality of no alternatives.[3]

Second, we must also recognize that even before the establishment of British rule a significant proportion of the population already was landless or cultivated plots which yielded submarginal incomes. These groups, apparently present in all areas of the country, had to eke out

---

[1] Mehta, *CMI*, Chap. IX and pp. 81–83, 97–99, and 225.

[2] It is important to stress that my concern here is with the supply of raw unskilled labor. Rapidly developing industries, particularly in underdeveloped areas, can be expected to be short of the skills for which there has been no previous need. The failure to distinguish between raw and skilled (or at least experienced) labor supply accounts, I believe, for much of the argument of shortage in the industry.

[3] For a brief analysis along these lines, see M. D. Morris, "Towards a Reinterpretation of Nineteenth-Century Indian Economic History," *Journal of Economic History* XXIII, No. 4, December 1963, particularly pp. 608–610.

their existence by working for others.[4] Finally, and as a partial consequence of the two features already mentioned, there were movements of
people from one district to another during the traditional period.[5]

The point of all this is to suggest that the European Industrial Revolution did not burst upon India in the first half of the nineteenth century
and smash a primitive utopia in which all owned land and where the
population was immobile because of high levels of well-being. This was
a society which historically had been making Malthusian adjustments
to its environment; the existence of a quasi-proletariat and population
migration were two socio-economic manifestations of this historic condition.

Western India was no exception to these generalizations. A careful
reading of the innumerable settlement reports for districts in the Bombay Presidency yields hints of the existence of a rural proletariat or
quasi-proletariat at mid-century.[6] An official report, attempting to grapple "with the allegations that are frequently made as to the poverty and
want of the lower classes," produced evidence which leads me to the
conclusion that in the 1880's at least 30 per cent of the rural population
of Bombay Presidency was in continual economic difficulty, being forced
to engage in at least some wage labor to eke out an existence. The greater

---

[4] The records are extremely vague on this point for at least one very obvious
reason. Most of the economic materials for the Mughal and early British periods
were the product of an official concern with land tenure and land revenue and
ignored the landless parts of the population. The only scholarly study of the early
landless labor groups that I know relates to Madras Presidency. See Dharma
Kumar, "The Growth of Agricultural Labour in Madras Presidency in the Nineteenth Century" (Unpublished Ph.D. dissertation, Cambridge, University, 1962),
where it is suggested that in 1800 agricultural laborers may have formed 10 to 15
per cent of the total population. For an abbreviated version, see D. Kumar,
"Caste and Landlessness in South India," *Contemporary Studies in Society and
History,* IV, No. 3, April 1962, pp. 337–363.

On the point of the existence of substantial underemployment, there is an interesting reference relating to 1823. In that year the Commander in Chief in India
reviewed the performance of the Bombay gun-carriage factory. Pointing out that
for efficiency's sake it would be desirable to introduce steam-power equipment
into the plant because of the difficulty of getting skilled workmen, he commented
that this was not a generally desirable policy "owing to the myriads of half-em-
ployed people in India." Quoted in H. A. Young, *The East India Company's
Arsenals and Manufactories* (Oxford: Clarendon Press, 1937), p. 201.

[5] See Irfan Habib, *The Agrarian System of Mughal India* (London: Asia Publishing House, 1963), pp. 116–117 and 120–122.

[6] For example, it was estimated that in the Kolhapur District more than 8 per
cent of the population were agricultural laborers, a figure which ignored artisans,
miscellaneous, and "inferior and predatory classes." D. C. Graham, "Statistical Report on the Principality of Kolhapur," *SRBG,* N. S., VIII (Bombay, 1854), pp.
140, 142, and 162. See also W. M. Hearn, "Statistical Report of the Colaba
Agency," SRBG, N. S., VII (Bombay, 1854), pp. 11–12.

bulk of these, perhaps 15 to 20 per cent of the rural population, had no significant claim to any land.[7]

Patel claims that the proportion of agricultural laborers to the total agricultural population of Bombay Presidency was increasing, that by 1901 this group totaled "more than thirty per cent," and it continued to increase during the twentieth century.[8] There are serious doubts about the accuracy of his estimates, but the evidence is clear that during the whole of the nineteenth century and the early twentieth century a substantial population in the rural areas was landless or nearly so and was dependent for survival on various forms of wage labor.[9] These groups of landless laborers and submarginal peasants constituted a large part of the potential labor force for the Bombay cotton mills.

The next question that has to be answered is whether or not there were geographical or social barriers inhibiting the flow of labor into Bombay. With regard to the geographical issue, it is true that western India did not possess adequate land-transport facilities until the spread of railways after 1854. In the absence of adequate feeder lines, even these affected only limited areas. But long before the building of railways there was a large and growing land trade between Bombay and the rest of western India. Where there was great commerce there had to be a great movement of people, if only by foot.[10]

---

[7] Director of Land Records and Agriculture, *Report on the Economic Condition of the Masses of the Bombay Presidency* (Bombay, 1888). The quotation is from *ibid.*, p. 51.

[8] S. J. Patel, *Agricultural Labourers in Modern India and Pakistan* (Bombay: Current Book House, 1952), pp. 21–25.

[9] Patel's analysis suffers from a twofold weakness. There is the implication that the proletarianization of the countryside was a nineteenth-century product, a proposition which I think the early settlement reports dispose of. There is also the assumption that a large part of this *apparently* increasing phenomenon was a function of the disruption of handicrafts. It is possible that the growth of population and the absence of any substantial increase of urban occupations did increase relative land pressure. I stress the uncertainty of the growth of landless labor because we know virtually nothing about the changing character of economic activity in the critical period 1850–1914. The decline of traditional activities was being offset by the rise of new occupations, even in the rural sector. For example, D. and A. Thorner, *Land and Labour in India* (London: Asia Publishing House, 1962), pp. 70–81, have shown how weak are the assumptions regarding the "de-industrialization" of India. See D. R. Gadgil, *The Industrial Evolution of India* (4th ed., London: Oxford University Press, 1945) who also suggests that the orthodox view cannot be uncritically accepted. It is even possible that the notion that traditional handicrafts were destroyed in the nineteenth century is not in accord with the real situation. For a tentative argument on this point, see Morris, *op.cit.*, pp. 612–613.

[10] For some estimates of land trade with Bombay in the 1840's, see C. W. Grant, *Bombay Cotton and Indian Railways* (London, 1850), pp. 95–97 and 149.

Sea transport was far easier, and passenger as well as freight traffic was extensive. Some regular coastal ferries were operating at the end of the eighteenth century, and in the early 1850's steam and sailing vessels were hauling passengers to and from Bombay by the thousands each year.[11] By the 1880's even the most isolated parts of the Ratnagiri District had been brought into contact with Bombay through the elaborate development of water transport.[12] All the evidence indicates that there were no significant physical barriers to movement to Bombay from the countryside during the nineteenth century.[13]

A great deal has been written about the stabilizing effects of Indian rural social structure — joint family, caste, and village organization — and how social relationships acted as barriers to population mobility. There is no evidence that bears out this proposition.[14] It is probably safe to say that the Indian population historically has been as mobile as, for example, the populations of western Europe at equivalent stages of economic development.[15]

---

[11] Hearn, *op.cit.*, pp. 96–98; *Monthly Miscellany of Western India*, I, 1850, v. p. 231; and "Prospects for Improved Shipping Accommodation in Bombay Harbour," *The Bombay Quarterly Review*, V, April 1857, pp. 385–397. In 1851 one writer referred to the "thousands of Natives, Mohamedans, Parsees, Hindoos, and Portugese [who] are conveyed, annually, in the steamboats that ply between Bombay and Surat. . . ." "The Bombay Railway," *The Bombay Quarterly Magazine and Review*, I, No. 2, January 1851, p. 142. In the mid-1860's the operation of the railway line between Bombay and Ahmedabad forced a reduction of sea fares to as low as 10 per cent of what they had previously been. Deck passenger fares in 1865 between Bombay and Surat were down to Rs. 1 and Rs. 1/8/0. *Bombay Saturday Review*, VII, No. 1, January 7, 1865, p. 7.

[12] "Papers Relating to the Introduction of the Original Survey Settlement into 144 Villages of the Sangameshvar Taluka of the Ratnagiri Collectorate," *SRBG*, N. S., CLXXI (Bombay, 1885), p. 21.

[13] A qualification to this statement is the fact that during the monsoon season, mid-June to mid-August, most sea travel stopped and land movements were sharply curtailed.

[14] For some discussion of how little we know of the link between caste and migration, see M. D. Morris, "Caste and the Evolution of the Industrial Workforce in India," *Proceedings of the American Philosophical Society*, CIV, No. 2, April 1960, particularly pp. 125–127.

[15] M. N. Srinivas and A. M. Shah, "The Myth of the Self-Sufficiency of the Indian Village," *The Economic Weekly*, XII, No. 27, September 10, 1960, pp. 1375–1377. It is true that mobility of population in India has been historically limited. My point is that it is entirely inappropriate to deduce from this the proposition that social structure was responsible for the phenomenon. Village studies cannot be used to prove a purported relationship between social structure and limited mobility because until very recently anthropologists were not interested in the kind of materials needed to furnish answers to this problem. However, certain characteristics of the Indian economy will suggest economic reasons for restricted mobility. During the nineteenth and early twentieth centuries new

If we look at the evidence from the Bombay end, where economic alternatives to rural existence were available, it seems clear that the Indian social structure cannot have been a decisive barrier to the flow of population needed for urban economic expansion. The growth of Bombay's population is, itself, the best evidence of rural mobility and, as has been indicated in Chapter II, all the evidence suggests that the rate of movement of people from the countryside was a more or less direct function of employment opportunities. For example, the population in Bombay City increased very rapidly between 1830 and 1864, from 229,000 to nearly 817,000. It seems clear that this enormous increase was directly linked with the city's economic expansion and the demand for labor it induced.[16] What is particularly noteworthy is that this same period is one during which there seems to have been a general improvement in the state of the agricultural sector of western India.[17]

It is true that some of this migration to Bombay was seasonal, reflecting a search for work during the slack periods in the countryside. But it is equally important to recognize that much of the temporary migration

economic opportunities were limited. There were no great tracts of virgin land capable of easy exploitation; nor was there any continuous and systematic expansion of the urban industrial economy. In these circumstances large population shifts could not be expected. But when opportunities occurred people moved. For example, the total emigration of Indians to British overseas colonies between 1834 and 1937 amounted to more than 30 million people. Commenting on this phenomenon, Kingsley Davis concluded: "We may assume . . . that the pressure to migrate, in an economic sense, has always been great enough to provide a stream of emigrants much larger than the actual stream, given the opportunity. In other words, the demand has been less than the supply." K. Davis, *The Population of India and Pakistan* (Princeton: Princeton University Press, 1951), p. 99.

[16] I am assuming that the bulk of this population growth came from immigration rather than from natural increases of the already present Bombay population. There are good reasons for this assumption. First, the rapidity of population growth makes it necessary for in-migration to have occurred, especially when Bombay sex ratio and age composition are considered. Second, descriptions of sanitary conditions and the high death rate during the period makes it virtually impossible for any conceivable birth rate to account for the rate of population growth recorded. On health and sanitation during the early 1860's, see A. H. Leith, "Report on the Sanitary State of the Island of Bombay," *SRBG*, N. S., LXXX (Bombay, 1864.) Third, all commentators of the period are agreed that there was a constant and rapid addition to population by immigration. Precisely what groups moved into Bombay is, of course, another issue. Variations in the ease and cost of physical movement and in rural economic conditions may have affected the composition of Bombay's immigrants.

[17] N. V. Sovani, "British Impact on India Before 1850–57," *Cahiers d'Histoire Mondaile*, I, No. 4, April 1954, p. 868. There is no necessary contradiction between prosperity in agriculture and migration of labor out of agriculture. See, for example, D. F. Humphrey, "Forces of Disequilibrium and World Disorder," *American Economic Review*, XLIV, No. 2, May 1954, pp. 552–564.

was certainly a function of the seasonality of Bombay's labor force requirements. A large proportion of employment opportunities on the
island during this period as in later years stemmed from construction
and shipping demands which were markedly affected by the monsoon.
In other words, the strong seasonal element of much of this migration
was caused not only by the nature of economic activity in the countryside but also by the seasonal fluctuations in demand for labor in the
city.[18]

The census data after 1864 also seem to point conclusively to the fact
that migration was responsive to the economic opportunities available
on the island. When these sources of employment and income dwindled,
the flow of labor into Bombay slowed up and could even be reversed,
as the 1872 census showed.[19] It was not the call of opportunity or "traditional ties to the land" that lured labor back to the countryside, for the
collapse of commercial activity in Bombay after 1865 was accompanied
by the disintegration of rural prosperity as well. The return to the rural
areas after 1865 was the only recourse, a counsel of despair.[20]

(2)

It is clear that the rural population was responsive to economic opportunities in Bombay. Now the critical questions are, was this labor
reluctant to offer itself for factory employment? And was the supply of
raw labor adequate to the expanding requirements of the cotton textile
industry?

A glance at the statistics will, of course, show that labor did move
into the mills. The data indicate that from the industry's beginning, the
trend of average daily employment was rising and reached a peak of
154,000 in 1927. Employment declined in 1928 and remained below the
1927 level until 1938. During World War II employment steadily rose
to 213,000 in 1945. In 1947, my terminal year, employment on all shifts
averaged 207,000.[21]

But the mere presentation of statistics does not prove anything. It is
not enough to describe the rate at which labor came into the mills. We

---

[18] See, for example, S. M. Edwardes, The *Gazetteer of Bombay City and Island*
(3 vols. Bombay: The Times Press, 1909), II, pp. 57–58.

[19] "But when the crash came, and Company after Company collapsed, the
laborers that had been engaged in reclamation and other works were discharged,
and finding no further employment in Bombay, returned to their villages in the in-
terior." *Census 1872*, p. 1.

[20] On the deteriorating state of the rural sector after 1864, see Gadgil, *op.cit.*,
pp. 24–32.

[21] See Appendix I.

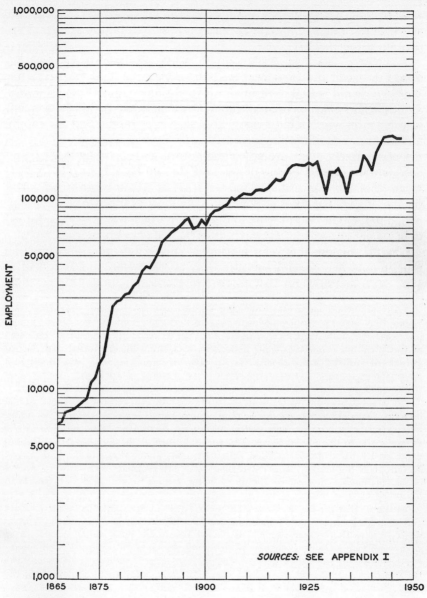

CHART I. Average daily employment on all shifts in Bombay cotton mills, 1865–1947 (semilogarithmic scale).

want to know whether, given market demand for yarn and cloth, the rate
at which labor moved into the factories served to limit the industry's expansion before 1922.[22]

The obvious first test of labor supply adequacy involves an examination of the trend of wages over time. Put very simply, a generalized labor
shortage should reveal itself in an upward-sloping wage trend. So long
as industrial expansion occurs without any significant upward movement
of wage rates we should be reasonably safe in assuming that the supply
of labor is not an inhibiting factor.

Unfortunately, there are no contemporary wage data until 1882, and
there are no specific figures of any sort that go back before 1875. This
means that it is impossible to tell the level at which wages were set in
the late 1850's, how rates responded to the Civil War boom or what happened to them in the subsequent decade. In other words, we are forced
to begin our analysis twenty years after the industry's inception.[23]

Chart II suggests that wage movements in the industry can be divided
roughly into five general periods: 1875 to 1906, 1907 to 1913, 1914 to
1923, 1923 to 1937, and 1937 to 1947.[24] The first period, 1875 to 1906,

[22] All authorities agree that raw labor supply was no problem after 1922. Between 1922 and 1941 unemployment was the critical problem. And even though
the expansion of demand created by World War II required substantial expansion
of the labor force, no one claims that there was any difficulty mobilizing the required labor. *RCL 1929*, "Report," p. 21; *BMOA* annual reports, 1921–1947; *LG*,
issues for 1921–1947; *TLIC 1938; TLIC 1940;* Mehta, *CMI*, Chs. XI-XIII; and
ICEC 1948, p. 24.

[23] It is probably safe to conjecture a bit about the movement of wages in the
first two decades. Whatever the level at which wages were set in the first mills,
it is likely that rates rose very swiftly during the Civil War boom because of the
dramatic rise in the cost of living. The weekly issues of the *Bombay Saturday Review* for 1864 and 1865 are filled with comments about rising prices and wages.
At one point the journal commented that "it is, indeed, marvelous how the poorer
classes in Bombay manage to live at all in these hard times." *Ibid.*, VI, No. 7, 13
February 1864, p. 183.

We know that the industry was badly disrupted by the post-Civil War collapse
and it is likely that wages fell. If we compare discussion in 1864 of the general
wage level with the statement of an ex-millowner in 1867, there is the strong
suggestion that wage rates had dropped drastically. *Ibid.*, VI, No. 37, 10 September 1864 and P. R. Cola, *How to Develop Productive Industry in India and the
East* (London, 1867), p. 61. Bombay business did not begin to recover until the
early 1870's and it was not until then that new mills began to open. Consequently, it is safe to assume that there could have been little if any stiffening of wage
rates until then.

[24] It should be made clear that the index in Chart II attempts, however im-
perfectly, to measure the movement of hiring-in rates, the cost of recruiting raw
labor for the industry. See Appendix III for a discussion of the data and problems involved.

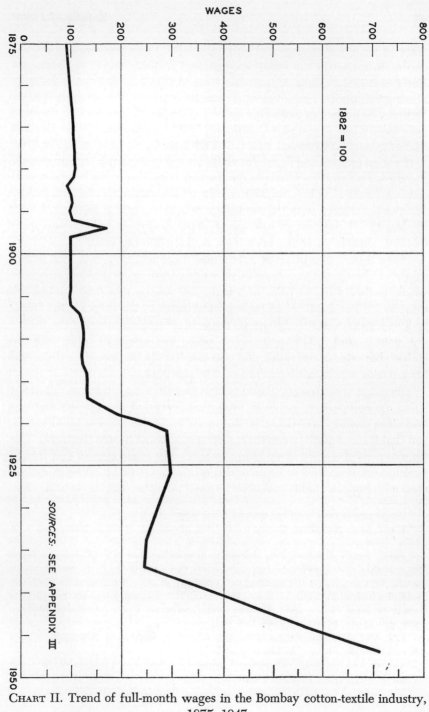

CHART II. Trend of full-month wages in the Bombay cotton-textile industry,
1875–1947.

shows a remarkable degree of wage stability. If for the moment we exclude 1875, we can say that the constancy is quite startling. There is a
slight rise of 7.5 per cent from the base year, 1882, to a peak in 1890.
During this period employment increased by nearly 86 per cent.[25] After
1890 the index began to decline and by 1898 had fallen back to the base
year level where it remained until 1907.[26] This occurred despite the fact
that employment between 1890 and 1906 rose by more than 70 per cent.

If we go back to the figure for 1875, which comes from a noncontem-
porary source and may have a downward bias, the index between that
date and 1882 rises by only 9.4 per cent while employment increased by
135 per cent. Even with the possible upward bias given to the index by
the low 1875 figure, wages rose only 17.6 per cent during the fifteen years
to 1890 while labor in the mills increased by 336 per cent.[27]

There is only one piece of independent quantitative evidence which
might challenge the conclusion that wages were quite stable during the
whole period, 1875 to 1905. This is a 1906 source which compared job
rates in 1875 and 1905.[28] An unweighted index of the rates for the twenty-five occupations listed suggests a rise of 27 per cent during the thirty-
one year period.[29] Although such a wage increase is at odds with the
stable character of my index, the rise can hardly be thought substantial
for a period when employment rose 586 per cent.

There is a very strong possibility that the 1875 rates were understated
since the comparison, made in 1906, was intended to show how wages
had risen during three decades. But apart from this there is another reason that the comparison produces a strong upward bias in the trend. The
figures used did not reflect hiring-in rates but some sort of full-month
average earnings and incorporated the upward drift of earnings associated with improvements in skill over time.[30] In other words, it seems clear

---

[25] Employment data used are derived from Appendix I.

[26] I will have something to say a bit later about the special circumstances of
1897.

[27] For a reason I will explain shortly, it is possible that the 1875 figure is on
the low side and therefore exaggerates even the modest wage increase that is
shown. This conclusion is supported by testimony of some Bombay mill managers
in 1888 which quite explicitly states that basic hiring-in rates had not risen in the
decade or more before 1888. *Bombay and Lancashire Cotton Spinning Inquiry,
1888,* pp. 34–35, 61–62, 176 and 188–191.

[28] *ITJ,* XVI, No. 191, August 1906, pp. 330–331. It is from this source that I
derived the data for my 1875 index number.

[29] Use of the fourteen occupational categories that are comparable to those
included in my index does not affect the result.

[30] See the commentary which accompanies the figures. *Ibid.,* p. 331.

that this source qualifies only very modestly, if at all, the stability conclusions to be drawn from my index.[31]

It is possible that some might argue that in India for one reason or other, wage rates might be unresponsive to the pressures of labor shortage. However, the facts do not bear out any such notion. In 1897, when plague caused thousands of workers to flee the city and when mills were desperately short of hands, wages rose more than 68 per cent in a few short months.[32] This exceptional increase to a peak of 171.6, a level not again touched until the inflation-ridden years at the end of World War I, supports a conclusion that there was no shortage of labor during the period of the industry's most rapid expansion. Given the experience of the plague year, one can only conclude that had there been a need for more labor than actually presented itself at going rates, we would expect to see the evidence reflected in a sharply rising wage trend.

The second period, 1907 to 1913, opened with an upward rise in the level of wages to a new but subsequently sagging plateau. It is not easy to explain why the rise in 1907–08 was so pronounced, but there seems little question that the sustaining of this generally higher level of wages must necessarily be attributed to the rising cost-of-living to which all observers referred.[33] The years from 1908 to World War 1 were not on the whole very prosperous ones.[34] As we will see, unemployment seems to have been serious in 1909 to 1911. The fact that wages tended to stick at the 1907–08 level seems to have been a function of the rising cost of living and did not reflect any adverse change in the supply of labor.

---

[31] That this rise did not reflect any difficulty in obtaining raw labor is suggested by a letter from a mill manager in the same issue of *ITJ. Ibid.*, p. 339. See Mehta, *ICTI*, p. 29, who also concludes that wage levels were "remarkably stable" during the entire period.

[32] For the best short statement, with wage data, of what happened to wage rates in 1897, see *FA 1897*, p. 8.

[33] K. L. Datta, *Report on the Enquiry into the Rise of Prices in India*, (Calcutta: Superintendent of Government Printing, 1914), I, pp. xiii, 176, 181–182 and 186; *BMOA 1908*, xiv; and *ITJ*, XVIII, No. 209, February 1908, p. 136; *ITJ*, XIX, No. 224, May 1909, p. 267; *ITJ*, XX, No. 237, June 1910, p. 290; *ITJ*, XXI, No. 250, July 1911, p. 351.

There is no satisfactory study of price movements in Bombay. The Datta study has serious defects and has been sharply criticized by D. H. Buchanan, *The Development of Capitalistic Enterprise in India* (New York: The Macmillan Company, 1934), pp. 350–352; and V. Anstey, *The Economic Development of India* (3d ed., London: Longmans, Green and Co., 1949), p. 447. For a recent attempt to measure the real value of monthly money wages, K. Mukerji, "Trend in Real Wages in Cotton Textile Mills in Bombay City and Island, from 1900 to 1951," *Artha Vijnana*, I, No. 1, March 1959, pp. 82–95.

[34] *BLO 1921*, Appendix F, pp. 108–109.

There is one alternate source of evidence which can be used to test wage movements between 1905 and 1914. J. A. Wadia for many years compiled a record of industry performance.[35] One figure he provided was the industry's annual wage bill, which, when divided by employment for the same year, yields an annual income figure per worker. Though this estimate does not measure wage rate movements, a strong upward trend might at least cast doubt on the validity of my wage index.

Though there are some rather sharp movements, the general pattern of the per capita annual income data in Table V suggest no significant contradiction to the proposition that labor was not in short supply during the prewar decade, in spite of the fact that between 1905 and 1914 average daily employment rose by 18 per cent.

TABLE V

*Index of Average Annual Income
per Worker Employed, 1905–1914*[36]

	1905=100	
1905 ....100.0	1910 ....108.4
1906 .... 95.7	1911 ....108.4
1907 .... 97.9	1912 ....108.1
1908 .... 95.4	1913 .... 99.3
1909 .... 95.8	1914 .... 95.5

During the third period, 1914 to 1923, the wage rate level rose sharply. The cost of living during World War I seems to have outstripped rises in wages, suggesting that as before, it was the inflation of prices and not a shortage of labor that accounted for the upward wage trend.[37]

The interwar years required a contraction of the labor force as the industry struggled to resolve its economic difficulties. And between 1926 and 1937 there was a steady fall in the level of wages.[38] After 1937 the

---

[35] For a compilation of these figures for 1905-1924, see *ITB 1927*, IV, pp. 73–75.

[36] For wage bill data, *loc.cit.* Employment data used were taken from Appendix I below. There are a number of obvious problems which make the Wadia figures treacherous to use. Not only do we not know how they were compiled, but they include salaries of clerks, supervisors, and management as well as wages of production workers.

[37] Mukerji, *op.cit.*, pp. 89 and 92–93. Between 1914 and 1921 average daily employment rose by more than 34 per cent. As has been shown in Chapter III, profits during this period soared to astonishing heights. Had labor been in short supply, the industry could well have tolerated more rapid wage increases than were granted.

[38] Employers found it difficult to reduce wages as the cost of living fell. Much of the labor unrest from 1923 on stemmed from mill-hand efforts to protect their money wage rates as prices declined.

trend reversed, and wages rose swiftly during World War II to the 1947 peak. But as in World War I, it seems clear that wages lagged behind wartime price rises and were pulled upward only by the cost-of-living.[39] This seems to support the conclusion that no real shortage of labor developed even during the period when employment increased by 53 per cent.[40]

On the whole, allowing for all the weaknesses inherent in my index, the behavior of wages seems to support a conclusion that at no time between 1875 and 1947 was there any systematic shortage of labor. This is, of course, a conclusion sharply at variance with traditional notions. To avoid dependence solely on the statistical evidence, let me examine the qualitative material that is available. What light does it throw on raw labor supply?

(3)

Unfortunately, there is almost no material on labor recruitment problems of the first mills. We know that in 1865 the ten mills employed fewer than 6,600 people. The Bombay population at the time was more than 800,000. It is reasonable to suppose that the insignificant labor requirements of the first mills were easily satisfied.[41] The only contemporary record I have found relates to the Kurla Spinning and Weaving Mill, established in 1860.[42] In 1864 a Bombay journal described it as having 28,000 spindles and 475 looms in operation.

The native element consists of upwards of a thousand hands, all told, although there are seldom more than 750 at work at one time. . . . But little difficulty is experienced in procuring labor. "We take," said the manager, "the first person who offers himself, and the younger he is the better. If he is good for anything it very soon peeps out. If he is worthless he goes about his business." The mill is very popular with the natives.[43]

---

[39] Mukerji, *loc.cit.* In fact, so far as I can tell all World War II increases came from the rising Dear Food Allowance which was adjusted to the cost-of-living index. There seem to have been no increases in basic rates. During World War I, the situation was somewhat different. In addition to provision of a Dear Food Allowance, basic rates in some occupations also rose. See *PW* for 1914–1921. However, at that time the Dear Food Allowance was not automatically geared to the cost of living.

[40] Employment measured from 1937 to 1945, the peak year.

[41] The profitability of these mills supports this judgment.

[42] Kurla, where this and one other mill were located, is on the mainland, just beyond Bombay Island. The careers of these two enterprises were so closely linked to the history of the industry in Bombay proper that they must be included in any discussion of the Bombay cotton textile industry.

[43] *Bombay Saturday Review*, VI, No. 17, April 23, 1864, p. 391. A later description of this mill's career, *ITJ*, I, No. 11, August 1891, pp. 176–177, stated

If this mill, located away from the main centers of Bombay's population, was able to recruit a satisfactory supply of labor, it would seem that none of the other mills can have had trouble. Certainly after the Civil War boom had collapsed there could have been no difficulties. Labor moved out of Bombay because of lack of employment opportunities.

In 1874, the next date for which we have information, the Bombay Factory Commission investigated the need for factory legislation. By this time the industry was expanding very rapidly, with a large number of new mills coming into operation.[44] The commission was not concerned with the supply of labor but it did elicit a few bits of information which indicated that raw labor supply was no problem. One mill manager, Mr. Bowler, testified:

Q. Is there any difficulty here in supplying mills with labor?
A. No, none.
Q. Supposing mills in Bombay were doubled, do you think there would be any difficulty then?
A. No.[45]

An official in another mill stated that there was no problem getting raw labor for new mills but that skilled labor was a problem, "for it takes years to train up persons to it." [46]

It is worth noting that the millowners opposed legal limitations on the hours of work not because they would create or intensify a labor shortage but for the opposite reason that restrictions might handicap the growth of an industry that was providing employment to a large group of people.[47] Between 1875 and 1885 the number of mills working rose to forty-nine, but still there were no complaints of labor shortage.[48]

The second factory commission, which took testimony in 1884, provided the first official occasion on which questions regarding the supply of labor were explicitly asked. The testimony makes it clear that even during this period of rapid increase in the number of enterprises there

that "At first there was a great difficulty in getting workpeople. . . ." This is a case where a contemporary account seems clearly better than one written three decades later.

[44] See Appendix I and S. M. Rutnagur, *Bombay Industries: The Cotton Mills*, (Bombay: *The Indian Textile Journal*, 1927), p. 14.

[45] *FC 1875*, p. 75.

[46] Mr. Alcock, *ibid.*, p. 82.

[47] M. N. Banajee, *ibid.*, p. 68. See also the conclusion of the millowner representatives on the commission, *ibid.*, pp. 3–5.

[48] During the legislative career of the bill that ultimately became the Factories Act of 1881, the millowners continued their opposition in the same terms, that the law would inhibit employment possibilities for needy people. See *BMOA 1875 and 1875–76*, pp. 53 and 57; *BMOA 1878*, p. 13; and *BMOA 1879*, p. 12.

was no shortage of potential mill hands. Of the large number of mill representatives testifying, only five reported that their labor supply was inadequate and four of these were complaining of the shortage of trained operatives. Only one mill claimed that some of its machinery was idle. The Inspector of Factories best summarized the situation:

The supply of skilled labor is less than the demand. There is undoubtedly a rush for employment by unskilled hands when a new mill is opened, but inducements have to be offered to trained hands . . . to leave their former employment. By unskilled hands I mean men, women, and children who have not previously been employed in mills. I do not think it strange that outsiders should seek employment in new mills, because it is simply a question of increased wages.[49]

Between 1885 and 1892 average daily employment rose by nearly 57 per cent. But testimony to the Royal Commission on Labor in 1892 indicated that there continued to be no labor supply problem. In fact, there is some evidence that a surplus pool of experienced labor had already emerged. As one government official described the situation: "Very nearly a lakh [100,000] of workers are engaged in the textile trades in Bombay, of which number about 20,000 are women. Of the total number of a lakh, about 25,000 have only irregular employment, taking the place of absenteeism and so forth.[50]

---

[49] *FC 1885*, p. 27. This conclusion was bolstered by the testimony of a mill-owner whose factory was just being completed. "My experience has been that there is a great rush for employment in new mills." Mr. Jugmohundas, *ibid.*, p. 132.

Most of the explicit testimony on labor supply will be found in the answer to the Commission's question 16. In four of the five cases where there is some implication of shortages, it is clear that the representatives were talking of experienced labor. For example, Mr. Barrett spoke of being short of labor but at the same time was cutting down on employment of women. *Ibid.*, p. 58. In the one case where the spokesman testified that some of his looms were idle, this was a temporary phenomenon caused by widespread malaria. This employer preferred to keep his machinery idle rather than recruit inexperienced hands. Mr. Mody, *ibid.*, pp. 94 and 97. As I have already suggested, a shortage of trained labor was to be expected in circumstances where new mills were springing up as rapidly as was the case in Bombay at this time. The evidence is quite convincing that new mills were pirating experienced hands from older enterprises. As one manager pointed out: "There is a larger demand for trained hands, and these being scarce are leaving us as new mills spring up. I think the situation of the mill has something to do with this owing to the distance from the mill to the operatives' houses. New mills offer inducements [to experienced workers] in the way of higher pay." Mr. Sorabji, *ibid.*, p. 18.

[50] Mr. Drewett, *RCL 1892*, p. 132. For supporting testimony, see Factory Inspector Moos, District Collector Campbell, and M. N. Lokhunday, *ibid.*, pp. 128, 134, 136, and 172. See also *FC 1890*, p. 3.

There is one piece of evidence that is typically cited to support the contrary point of view. In 1888 J. N. Tata, owner of a mill in Kurla, wrote to the government and to the Millowners' Association, urging that the Bombay mills institute a formal system of labor recruitment in northern India. Failing to get support at that time, he resurrected the scheme in 1892 and again in 1897. His proposal has been interpreted as evidence of labor shortage. A careful reading of the correspondence and Wacha's discussion of it, as well as the lack of interest shown by other millowners, suggest that this is an incorrect interpretation.[51] Tata was primarily concerned with the shortages of labor that might develop in the future if the industry continued to expand at the rate it had between 1882 and 1888 and the consequences of this on work-force militancy. As Mr. Tata wrote in 1888:

No doubt, Bombay being the center of all trade and the port of transit nearest to Europe, a larger number of the unemployed will find their way here. But it should be borne in mind that the older operatives are now getting educated and beginning to have a faint glimmer of their true position in the industrial development. They pretty freely know when to strike and when to demand higher wages. And as they grow in strength and in the perception of their rights it is not unlikely they may prove as much a source of trouble and anxiety as the operatives in Lancashire and elsewhere. We fear there are many chances of larger number of strikes by and by and it would be prudent to provide against their occurrence as far as it may be possible for the millowners to do. Combination and dear wages are the rocks ahead of which the millowners sought to steer clear.[52]

Tata wanted to draw workers from many regions to make the threat of "combination and dear wages" less likely in the future. He argued that such a program would "provide against the contingency of scarcity which, though not keenly felt now, will be so . . . in the future years and at the same time prevent large strikes. A judicious admixture of Bombay men with men from the Upper Provinces would have a most wholesome effect." [53]

---

[51] S. D. Mehta, "Professor Morris on Textile Labour Supply," *Indian Economic Journal,* I, No. 3, January 1954, p. 336. For the record of the Tata proposal, see D. E. Wacha, *The Life and Life Work of J. N. Tata* (Madras: Ganesh and Co., 1915), pp. 72–97; *BMOA 1892,* pp. 11–12 and 43–45; *BMOA 1896,* pp. 149–160; and *BMOA 1897,* pp. 4–6.

[52] Wacha, *op. cit.,* pp. 83–84.

[53] *Ibid.,* pp. 85–86. Wacha, whose comments are particularly useful since he helped draft the proposal, is explicit that Tata was concerned with the "future as more mills multiplied." *Ibid.,* pp. 77–78. Tata's initial proposal had its origins in personal experience. Having bought a bankrupt mill at Kurla in 1887, he had some labor problems during the early part of 1888. There seems to have been an adequate supply of adult mill hands but they struck, charging that he paid less than had been

Tata's renewal of his proposal in 1892 was again directed to the threat of combination, for this was a time of depression and strikes as millowners attempted to cut wages.

Tata's scheme got no support from his fellow millowners either in 1888 or in 1892. However, in 1897, at the height of the bubonic plague epidemic, when labor was truly in very short supply, the Tata plan to recruit labor in northern India was taken up by the millowners. It failed largely because the mills refused to pay going rates in Bombay to the new recruits.[54]

From examination of all available evidence, it seems completely clear that there were no problems of recruiting raw labor at any point between the industry's inception and 1892. In that year the *Indian Textile Journal*, looking back to the beginnings of the industry and its subsequent rapid growth, spoke of the prejudices against factory work which early observers had predicted would be encountered.

These prejudices were acknowledged to be great, and years of uphill work were anticipated before they could be successfully destroyed. It caused general surprise, therefore, when it was found that workpeople were induced to enter the mills without any great difficulty and to take to the work of tending to the various machines.[55]

The easy labor supply situation continued until the end of 1896 when the situation changed dramatically. The outbreak of bubonic plague drove people out of the city by the thousands. At some periods during the first half of 1897 fewer than one fifth of the mill hands were at work, and jobbers went out onto the streets to recruit whatever labor they could find to man the idle machines. But even before the epidemic ended, workers started returning to the mills. In July 1897 the BMOA

agreed, was paying on piece rather than time-rates, and was withholding wages. There may have been a slight shortage of child labor at one point, partly owing to the isolated location of the mill and perhaps in part owing to the trouble with the adults. However, it was not a labor shortage which affected production in 1888. Tata was completely reëquipping his new acquisition and the machine manufacturers found "it difficult to execute orders within a reasonable time." High costs of fuel and raw materials were other factors. At any rate, by 1890, this labor supply problem, to the extent that it may have existed, was solved. *Ibid.*, pp. 80, 82, and 92–93; *RCL 1892*, p. 137; and East India (Factories Act), *Return to an Address of the Hon. House of Commons, 15 April 1889*, p. 76.

[54] *BMOA 1896*, pp. 149–150 and 156–160; *BMOA 1897*, pp. 4–6; *ITJ*, VII, No. 81, June 1897, pp. 207–208; and *ITJ*, IX, No. 99, December 1898, p. 65.

[55] *ITJ*, II, No. 16, January 1892, p. 62. See also the statement of the Factory Commission of 1890: "Our enquiry has further shown that there will be no difficulty whatever in getting as many men as may be required." *FC 1890*, p. 3. The evidence given to the *Bombay and Lancashire Cotton Spinning Inquiry, 1888*, also confirms this point.

chairman reported that "there is today a sufficient number of trained men to keep all our machinery going." [56] However, in August there occurred another even more virulent outbreak of plague and another great flight of workers. But the shortage of labor never became as serious as during the first epidemic, and by mid-1898 the situation had eased sufficiently to permit the mills to terminate the daily payment of wages to operatives, a device introduced during the worst period. [57] Although there were recurrences of plague in subsequent years, its disruptive effects on the labor market declined sharply. [58]

In August 1898 the Association chairman expressed some concern over a possible labor shortage to be caused by the demands from new mills then under construction. [59] But his fears were unfounded. In fact, by the end of 1899 mills were shutting down or working short time because of the sharp decline in market demand. Wages were being cut in many mills and unemployment rose sharply as the industry worked at one quarter its usual rate. [60] Even when business improved after 1901 output expanded without any visible evidence of labor shortage.

During the boom of 1904 to 1906 an increasing number of mills began to extend the traditional hours of work, but this lengthening of the workday to fourteen and fifteen hours was not prompted by any recruiting difficulties. Labor, except for skilled workers, remained adequate through April 1905, even for the few mills working double shifts. [61] There may have been a slight shortage in August 1905 when "one or two mills" had trouble getting labor for a second shift. [62] But by the end of 1906

---

[56] *BMOA 1896*, pp. 147–148.

[57] For the impact of the plague epidemics on industry operations, see *BMOA* annual reports for 1896–1898 and *FA 1897*, pp. 7–9.

[58] It is hard to say why workers ceased fleeing from Bombay at the onset of each new plague outbreak. Experience may have induced contempt for its dangers. The spread of the disease to all parts of the Presidency may have removed the special terror of Bombay. The very serious famines in western India during the years 1896 to 1902 may have served as the stick of necessity, forcing labor to come to or remain in the city. *ITJ*, XV, No. 175, April 1905, p. 197; Presidency of Bombay, *Report on the Famine in the Bombay Presidency, 1899–1902*, I (Bombay: Government Central Press, 1903), p. 10.

[59] *BMOA 1897*, p. 81.

[60] *ITJ*, X, No. 115, April 1900, pp. 188 and 190; *FA 1900*, pp. 1 and 3.

[61] *BMOA 1904*, pp. 155, 160, and 162.

[62] *BMOA 1905*, p. viii; *ITJ*, XVII, No. 196, January 1907, p. 106. Few mills seem to have attempted double-shift working until the reorganizations of the late 1920's. This should not be interpreted as evidence of labor shortage. Lengthening the workday seems to have been the preferable and economically more rational device. A longer workday had virtually no effect on labor costs. Mill hands were mainly paid on output. Time-rated workers and clerical and supervisory staff could be required to work longer hours without premia. *ITJ*, XV, No. 178, July 1905, p. 317. On the

the flush of the boom had faded and many mills began working short time, a situation which continued into 1907.[63]

The period 1908 to 1911 was one of great general economic activity in Bombay, but it was a time of considerable economic instability for the cotton mills and gross profits steadily declined.[64] Mills individually responded to the unsatisfactory demand situation by periodic closures, short-time working, and the operation of only part of their equipment.[65] Nevertheless, in 1908 there appeared widespread reports of shortages of labor, complaints which continued through 1911. Testimony to the Indian Factory Labor Commission led it to conclude that "the supply of factory labor is, and has been inadequate, and there is, and has been, the keenest competition among employers to secure a full labor supply." [66] We have already seen that this conclusion was incorrect as it related to the period before 1908. Secular expansion of the Bombay textile industry had not previously been inhibited by any difficulties in the recruitment of labor. How meaningful were the claims of shortage in the years 1908 to 1911, especially in the face of the depressed condition of the industry? Let me examine the evidence that is available.

The evidence presented to the factory commission of 1908 was very crude. No attempt was made to define precisely the concept of labor shortage, and the commission gathered no statistical evidence worthy of the name that can be used to throw light on this point. All we have are the qualitative statements of witnesses, and these are often very ambiguous. However, a careful study of testimony given by the representatives

---

other hand, double-shift working required the addition of expensive permanent managerial staff which was not considered desirable in an industry where gluts of production were so frequent. Expansion of managerial staff often meant recruitment of foreign masters. Not only were their salaries enormous by Indian standards, but foreigners typically had to be given a three-year contract.

[63] *ITJ*, XVII, No. 199, April 1907, p. 193. The BMOA annual reports for 1905 to 1907 and *FC 1906* indicate no lack of labor to expand output. The only complaints were about the low level of skill and the bad state of labor discipline. See, for example, *BMOA 1907*, pp. ix and xiii.

[64] During this period there was a great amount of public works construction as well as private construction activity. Edwardes, *op. cit.*, I, p. 322; *ITJ*, XXI, No. 250, July 1911, p. 351. For declining gross profit figures in the textile industry, see Table IV, p. 30, above.

[65] It is difficult to determine the precise pattern of operations for the years 1908 to 1911. However, for evidence of closures, short-time working, and partial operation of equipment see *ITJ*, issues for 1908 to 1912; and BMOA annual reports for 1909 to 1912, particularly the "remarks" column in the statistical appendix attached to each of these reports.

[66] *IFLC 1908*, I, p. 19. Although the Commission's conclusion related to the whole of India, it was in large part based on testimony from representatives of forty-four of Bombay's eighty-six mills.

of forty-four mills makes it quite clear that only one or two mills, at most, suffered from any difficulties. There seems no doubt that every witness who reported shortages of labor also at the same time indicated an ability to recruit substitutes. As one mill representative said in a typical comment, "we have to cope with an insufficiency of labor, and have to engage substitutes. . . ." [67] What emerges from the evidence are widespread complaints of absenteeism, labor turnover, and frequency of strikes, but no difficulty in finding labor to keep the machines manned.[68]

I must conclude, therefore, that in 1908 the labor supply was quantitatively adequate for all mill needs. This judgment is bolstered by two facts. 1908 was a year of declining prosperity with profits falling and millowners contemplating short-time working and wage reductions.[69] Moreover, not one mill representative who opposed the proposal for a statutory limitation on hours of work which the 1908 commission was considering suggested that such legislation might make the labor supply situation more difficult. Yet one would suppose that in the face of a

---

[67] S. David, *IFLC 1908*, II, p. 76. Only the representative of the Western India Mill explicitly claimed that he "could not get sufficient hands for substitutes, and the mill was always short-handed." *Ibid.*, II, p. 91. But it is difficult to determine the meaning of even such an apparently explicit statement. For example, the witness from the Kurla Spinning and Weaving Company reported that he "was always short of hands. . . ." and then went on to say that he paid less than the going rate. *Ibid.*, II, p. 78. One would hardly call this a genuine labor shortage.

[68] These conclusions are drawn from a careful study of testimony by mill representatives in *IFLC 1908*, II. For a more detailed examination of this testimony, see M. D. Morris, "Some Comments on the Supply of Labour to the Bombay Cotton Textile Industry, 1854–1951," *Indian Economic Journal*, I, No. 2, October 1953, pp. 147–148. A member of the Indian Civil Service who independently investigated the situation concluded that no shortage of labor existed in Bombay in 1908. S. H. Fremantle, "The Problem of Indian Labour Supply," *Journal, Royal Society of Arts*, LVII, May 14, 1909, pp. 511 and 513. The chairman of the BMOA made it quite clear that the issues were the instability of the work force, its growing awareness of its own power, and the frequency of strikes. *BMOA 1908*, p. iv.

[69] In testimony to the Factory Commission, witnesses made reference to the fact that there was not enough labor to make two-shift working possible. See evidence of witnesses numbered 39, 40, 42, 45, 56, 62, 65, 74, and 76, *IFLC 1908*, II. Not only is it unclear whether these witnesses were referring to the possibility of shortages or merely the lack of experienced workers, but given the deteriorating economic situation, two-shift working was not, in fact, being contemplated. These statements came in response to questions by the factory commission on the general issue of further legislation to regulate hours of work.

On the weakened circumstances of the mills and the move towards short-time working and attempts to lower wages, see *ITJ* for 1908 and 1909, particularly XVIII, No. 211, April 1908, p. 232; XIX, No. 217, October 1908, p. 36; and XIX, No. 222, March 1909, p. 191.

shortage of labor the idea of legally restricting the hours of work would have provoked precisely that argument.[70]

The complaints of labor shortage in subsequent years, if they are taken to refer to generalized scarcities, are equally meaningless. For example, in the spring of 1910, when a leading millowner was telling his colleagues that "we are suffering not only from a paucity of skilled but also that of unskilled labor," many of the mills were working short time and the industry had just gone through a long period in the previous year when as many as 22 per cent of the looms had been shut down at one time.[71] Or again, in July 1911, the *Times of India* was saying that "Bombay is experiencing for the present what is veritably a labor famine. The mills especially have been hard hit. As one millowner put it: 'The demand for hands is simply enormous.'" [72] But virtually at the same time, in March and April 1911, twenty to twenty-five mills were entirely closed because of the lack of demand for cotton products.[73]

It is difficult to ferret out the precise situation when one is confronted with comments as chaotic as these. Nevertheless, a detailed reading of the BMOA annual reports and the *Indian Textile Journal* for the years 1909 to 1911 suggests that as before, the millowners were really complaining about mill-hand instability and truculence and not about shortages.[74] Faced by weak and unstable market demand, the owners

---

[70] In fact, a substantial number of witnesses favored a restriction of hours.

[71] *BMOA 1909*, p. vii; *ITJ*, XIX, No. 228, September 1909, pp. 416, 433, 436; *ITJ*, XX, No. 233, February 1910, pp. 160–161; and *ITJ*, XX, No. 238, July 1910, p. 345.

[72] Quoted in *ITJ*, XXI, No. 250, July 1911, p. 351.

[73] *ITJ*, XXI, 246, March 1911, p. 191.

[74] An important industrialist with a penchant for statistics attempted to estimate the extent of labor shortages that had developed between 1908 and 1912. See D. E. Wacha, "Bombay Mill Labour: A Statistical Analysis," *ITJ*, XXIV, No. 285, June 1914. Unfortunately the article is quite hopeless. Wacha merely took the increase in numbers of spindles and looms and multiplied these by a questionable labor-use factor to come up with an estimate of labor required. Apart from the fact that he assumed no productivity gains, he totally ignored the state of the market which kept a substantial part of the industry's equipment idle in 1909, 1910, and 1911. Even by his own estimates, there was no shortage of weavers during the period. He suggests a shortage of children (which the mills preferred to use) but no shortage of adult spinners. In fact, the total claimed shortage of child spinners according to Wacha's calculations amounted to less than 2 per cent of the total spinning employment in 1912. Even by his own estimates, this was a shortage that could have been easily overcome by the use of adult spinners, i.e., by raising wages. Actually, my wage index does show a slight rise between 1912 and 1913, all of which is accounted for by wage increases in certain spinning occupations. See *PW* for 1912 and 1913. The essay is interesting because it explicitly indicates the lack of quantitative data on which an analysis could be based.

attempted to cut wages, shut down their mills and equipment, and work short time whenever the immediate circumstances warranted. The rising cost of living during 1907 to 1912 made it difficult for mills to force wage rates down, and mill hands resisted efforts to impose short-time operations. There were a number of strikes over these issues. Moreover, the combination of unstable employment expectations in the mills and greater employment opportunities elsewhere in the city because of the construction boom seems to have made the workers more prone to drift into and out of the industry.[75] It was this instability and proneness to strike that was bothering the employers. This conclusion is supported by the fact that there was no shortage of substitute labor and no machines standing idle for want of hands to man them. The evidence of wage movements seems to be further corroboration of the view that the problems the industry faced were not caused by any failure of the supply of labor but were the result of the conditions within the industry. This seems to be confirmed by the industry's experience in 1912 when business conditions improved markedly. Output rose and so did employment requirements. Yet the supply problem was admitted easier.[76] It is clear that when the industry could offer promise of reasonably stable employment, supply of labor was no issue.[77]

Between 1912 and 1922 average daily employment rose by nearly forty thousand, about 36 per cent. Despite the great expansion induced by wartime demand, there were no generalized shortages of labor to limit output.[78] The labor force certainly grew more refractory as the cost of living skyrocketed. There were occasional shortages of skilled labor of various sorts, but the lack of an adequate influx of labor into the mills was not an employer complaint, although seasonal instability was.[79] In

---

[75] See *ITJ*, issues XX, No. 237, June 1910, p. 321; XXI, No. 250, July 1911, pp. 350–351; and XXIII, No. 274, July 1913, p. 330.

[76] Wacha, "Bombay Mill Labour: A Statistical Analysis," *op. cit.*, p. 318. Between 1910–11 and 1912–13 yarn output rose 13.5 per cent and cloth output rose 12.2 per cent. Statistical Department, Government of India, *Statistics of the Production of Yarn and Woven Goods in the Indian Cotton Mills* for these years. In the same period employment rose by more than 5 per cent.

[77] Interestingly enough, between 1910 and 1912 annual per capita wages fell from Rs.249.1 to Rs.241.5. These figures were obtained by using employment data in Wacha, "Bombay Mill Labour: A Statistical Analysis," *op. cit.*, Table A p. 317; and Wadia's industry wage bill data *ITB 1927*, IV, pp. 73–75. Both sets of figures must be treated with great caution. The per capita wage movement differs from that shown in Table V above because different employment figures were applied to Wadia's wage bill. However, even Table V shows stability of per capita wages between 1910 and 1912.

[78] Expansion of production was inhibited by the inability to import additional equipment during this period. *BMOA 1921*, p. viii.

[79] In mid-1916 the BMOA chairman reported that labor supply was easier than

fact, during 1919 the BMOA decided against a proposal for general double-shift working not because of any lack of raw labor but because "Bombay . . . suffers from the disability of having no housing accommodation within it for the extra 100,000 to 150,000 men required for the second shift, nor would the sanitary conditions of Bombay permit of such an influx of men for some time to come." [80]

At the very height of the double-shift controversy, in February 1921, one of the Association's most distinguished figures commented:

Even in Bombay today, with all these recruiting grounds at Ratnagiri and other places, what we find is that there is no scarcity of labor to speak of. We are always looking out in Bombay here and there and everywhere for an adequate supply of labor and we do not find any difficulty in obtaining it, with increased wages and other privileges. [81]

In 1922 the prosperity in Bombay came to an end; the long interwar crisis was upon the industry. Henceforth, the concern was not one of adding to total labor supply but of achieving more efficient use of existing labor. Even between 1940 and 1945, when average daily employment on all shifts rose 52 per cent, the industry reported that the supply of labor was, in general, entirely adequate for its needs. [82]

The qualitative evidence suggests quite clearly that at no point did the Bombay mills suffer from a lack of a supply of raw labor to meet the growth needs of the industry. Nor, as I have shown, does the behavior of wages square at all with any theory of labor shortage. I have already

---

it had been before the war. *ITJ*, XXVI, No. 307, April 1916, p. 213. One commentator remarked that labor was being drawn in from the countryside by the availability of jobs. *ITJ*, XXVII, No. 319, April 1917, p. 195. The exhaustive investigation by the Indian Industrial Commission made no reference to any labor shortages in Bombay, but there was a specific reference to seasonal instability. See A. E. Mirams, "Memorandum of Evidence," p. 17, filed as separate statement at end of *IIC 1916–18* "Report."

[80] *BMOA 1919*, p. 52. See also questions 22067 and 22074-77, Indian Fiscal Commission, *Minutes of Evidence*, III (Calcutta 1923), pp. 977–978; and BMOA annual reports for 1919 to 1921 for discussions of the housing problem. It is possible that millowners were unenthusiastic about double-shift working because there was widespread public feeling that they should provide mill-hand housing out of their own resources. *ITJ*, XXVII, No. 319, April 1917, p. 195; *ITJ*, XXVII, No. 320, May 1917, p. 242; and *ITJ*, XXVIII, No. 325, November 1917, p. 53.

[81] Wacha, quoted in Mukhtar, *Factory Labour in India* (Madras: Annamalai University, 1930), p. 194 n. The BMOA annual reports for 1919–1921 continually assumed that double-shift working would produce "the influx of extra labor it would involve." *BMOA 1921*, p. 45.

[82] *RCL 1929*, I, Part 1, p. 399. From January 1926, *LG* reported monthly on the state of the labor supply. The sole exception to the general adequacy of labor occurred in early 1942 when Japanese military successes caused a brief, panicky exodus of people from Bombay. *BMOA 1941*, p. iii; and *BMOA 1942*, p. ii.

indicated that labor costs were historically a relatively small proportion of total costs and the industry was one in which profit expectations until 1922 were generally quite high. Had a labor shortage been endemic, one would expect wage rates to have risen rapidly and steadily. Certainly, this is what happened between 1896 and 1897, the one period when all are agreed that labor was in very short supply. But otherwise, wages tended to be "remarkably stable." [83] During the periods when money wages did rise, the cause was most certainly a rise in the cost of living.

My conclusion is also supported by the technical history of the industry. Given difficulty in recruiting mill hands, one would have expected a shift from more labor-intensive to more capital-intensive methods of production. Instead, in the 1890's we find the industry shifting rapidly from mule spinning to ring spinning which, given the particular production patterns in Bombay, would seem to indicate a movement toward greater labor intensity. Moreover, refusal to introduce the Northrup loom or other forms of automatic weaving equipment after 1900 and reluctance to mechanize the mixing and winding and reeling departments until after World War I are also pieces of evidence pointing to persistent adequacy of the general labor supply. [84]

(4)

Where did the Bombay mill work force come from? We have no explicit information for the first half century but the census reports of 1911, 1921, and 1931 give us some fairly detailed information.

At least three interesting features are exhibited by these two tables. [85]

---

[83] Dr. Mehta, who has argued most vigorously for the thesis of labor shortages, has written: "There is general agreement that the wage levels [in Bombay before 1914] were remarkably stable. . . . In view of the general complaint of labor shortage made by Indian industry and noted as late as 1930 by the Royal Commission on Labor, it is remarkable that this position should have been maintained." Mehta, *ICTI*, p. 29. Elsewhere, Mehta has gone on to recognize that when shortages did occur "the industry did not view with any particular concern the prospect of paying higher wages" when, at least until 1910, "the profits of a normal year equalled or exceeded the wage bill." Mehta, "Professor Morris on Textile Labour Supply," *op. cit.*, p. 336. Dr. Mehta would not have found the combination of relatively stable wage rates and very high profits at all paradoxical had he recognized the obvious economic implication for the supply of labor.

[84] The only alternative explanation that comes to mind is the possibility that Bombay millowners were not responsive to profit-maximizing notions but were bound by certain nonmaterial, spiritual considerations. However, such a charge has never been leveled at them by anyone at anytime.

[85] A very large number of interesting issues could be discussed, drawing information from the data on which Tables VI and VII are based. However, most of these would take me into an examination of the districts and regions from which population moved and away from my specific concerns.

TABLE VI

Place of Origin of Cotton-Mill Work Force, 1911–1931 [86]

Place of origin (miles from Bombay)	Per cent of total mill hands		
	1911	1921	1931
1–100	7.48	5.13	3.62
101–200	63.44	50.07	38.26
201–300	2.68	4.98	4.71
301–400	3.37	2.67	1.30
401–500	0.62	3.46	1.98
501–750	0.28	1.50	0.99
751 and more	3.05	10.65	14.62
Unidentified migrants	8.16	2.67	8.19
Born in Bombay	10.92	18.87	26.33
Total	100.00	100.00	100.00

TABLE VII

Districts Providing Main Supply of Cotton-Mill Work Force, 1911–1931 [87]

District	Distance from Bombay (miles)	Percent of total mill hands		
		1911	1921	1931
Ratnagiri (Konkan)	(101–200)	49.16	35.53	25.37
Satara (Deccan)	(101–200)	7.27	6.63	5.15
Kolaba (Konkan)	(1 –100)	6.22	4.47	3.04
Poona (Deccan)	(101–200)	5.65	6.18	5.72
Kolhapur (Deccan)	(301–400)	3.07	1.85	0.51
Ahmednagar (Deccan)	(201–300)	1.46	2.99	2.01
United Provinces	(Over 750)	3.05	9.42	11.82
Total of above districts		75.88	67.07	53.62

First, the largest proportion of mill hands came from the 101 to 200 mile circle. The vast majority of these came from the Ratnagiri district and, generally speaking, the bulk of the immigrant work force came from the Konkan districts south of Bombay and the Deccan plateau east of Bombay. The Gujarat districts north of Bombay seem to have contributed only a very small proportion of the textile workers. Nonstatistical evidence suggests that this general pattern existed from the beginning of the industry's history.

The second feature is that with the passage of time there was a ten-

---

[86] See Appendix IV for sources and discussion of methods of construction.

[87] See Appendix IV for sources. All the Konkan and Deccan districts fell within the boundaries of Bombay Presidency. The United Provinces figure for 1911 is probably an understatement, reporting migrants from only two districts of the region.

dency for mill hands to be drawn from a greater number of districts and from increasingly distant areas. If one looks at Table VII, it appears that in 1911 the six most important Bombay Presidency districts contributed 72.83 per cent of all mill hands in Bombay. By 1921 the proportion from those districts had fallen to 57.65 per cent and by 1931 to 41.80 per cent. Other regions were contributing a rising proportion to the work force.[88] As part of this phenomenon, mill hands were coming from districts farther away, notably from areas 751 miles and beyond which included virtually all districts of the United Provinces (now Uttar Pradesh.) It was in the United Provinces that the BMOA attempted to recruit labor in 1897 and failed. Yet without any formal effort this particular region began to contribute an increasingly large supply of labor to the mills. In 1911 the United Provinces districts furnished at least 3.05 per cent; in 1921 the proportion rose to 9.42, and in 1931 to 11.82 per cent of total mill hands.[89] Put more generally, the census data indicate that between 1911 and 1931 the proportion of mill hands coming from distances 501 miles and more rose from 3.33 per cent to 15.61 per cent. And the BMOA surveys suggest that the trend continued, with 19.29 per cent in 1940 and 22.4 per cent in 1954 coming from distances of more than 500 miles.[90]

These figures should put an end to the frequently argued view that Indian workers would not move long distances, that the ideology of the society and its social institutions tended to keep the population restricted to the neighborhood of its traditional residence.[91]

---

[88] On the other hand, a 1940 BMOA survey, if it can be trusted, suggests that the trend was reversed. In that year, according to this survey, the six Bombay districts listed in Table VII accounted for 72.28 per cent of all mill hands. See R. G. Gokhale, *The Bombay Cotton Mill Worker* (Bombay: Millowners' Association, 1957), pp. 117–118. I find this a dubious conclusion. There are serious methodological flaws in this 1940 survey by the Association. See Appendix IV below.

[89] From sources cited in Appendix IV. The BMOA 1940 survey suggests that this trend continued. In that year, United Provinces districts contributed 13.55 per cent. Gokhale, *op.cit.*, pp. 117–118.

[90] Gokhale, *op.cit.*, pp. 87–89. It is inappropriate to argue that World War I was the incentive for the appearance of workers from such long distances. The 1911 figure for more than 500 miles includes a very small number of districts and possibly understates the true situation at the time. As early as 1892 the District Collector referred to the "rail-borne shoals of Lucknow, Cawnpore and Delhi Inlaka or Musalman hand-loom weavers [who] have found occupation in Bombay Mills. . . ." *RCL 1892*, p. 128. Thus the increase from 3.33 per cent in 1911 to 12.15 in 1921 may be exaggerated.

[91] The particular sources of mill labor and the changing importance of the streams of migrants are matters that need detailed analysis. It is easy to say that labor flowed from poor districts, but this is hardly an adequate explanation. Why did labor from some districts, such as Kathiawar, which provided large additions to the

The third important feature, suggested in Table VI, is the increasing proportion of the mill work force born in Bombay. This occurred despite the fact that the mill labor force was expanding rapidly until 1922. And in the interval 1911 to 1921 it occurred in contrast to the declining proportion of Bombay-born in the city's total population.

TABLE VIII

Proportion of Total Bombay Population
and Mill Hands Born in Bombay
1911–1931 [92]

Year	Total population (Per cent)	Total mill hands (Per cent)
1911	19.6	10.92
1921	16.0	18.87
1931	24.6	26.33

(5)

There is no consistent series that shows the changing sex and age composition of the mill work force. I, therefore, have attempted to construct one from the data that are available.

The most striking feature, especially when compared with the sex and age distributions of textile work forces in other countries during the nineteenth and early twentieth centuries, is the relatively limited use of women and children.[93] Even in the earliest years for which we have evidence adult males never constituted less than 69 per cent and women never more than a quarter of the total work force. Children, legally defined, never exceeded 5.6 per cent.

The proportion of female mill hands seems to have remained remarkably constant at between 20 and 25 per cent of the work force until 1931 when the figure began to decline. The reduction can be attributed to the widespread adoption of night-shift working after that date. Prohibited by law from working nights, women could not be added to the second

city's population, not become important in the mills? Why did the traditional sources of mill labor — Ratnagiri, Satara, Poona, Kolaba, etc. — apparently become of declining importance? To answer these questions we need a great deal of research that goes far beyond the scope of this study into the economic and social structure of the districts which supplied Bombay's migrants. We also need an examination of the growth of other employment opportunities in Bombay.

[92] *Census 1931*, IX, Part I, p. 14, gives figures on the Bombay-born part of the total Bombay population. Information on the Bombay-born part of total mill-hand population is taken from Table VI above.

[93] For a comparison of the situation in various countries in the 1930's, see *BLO 1934*, p. 10.

TABLE IX
Average Daily Employment of Men, Women, and Children in
Bombay Cotton Mills (All Shifts), 1884–1947 [94]
(Per cent)

	Adults				Adults		
Year	Men	Women	Children	Year	Men	Women	Children
1884	76.50	22.20	1.30	1919	77.47	20.33	2.20
1892	69.80	24.63	5.57	1920	77.72	20.38	1.90
1893	69.22	25.87	4.91	1921	77.96	20.49	1.55
1894	70.47	24.74	4.79	1922	79.50	19.68	0.82
1895	71.01	24.74	4.25	1923	79.09	20.46	0.45
1896	71.11	25.38	3.51	1924	78.10	21.49	0.41
1897	72.91	23.30	3.79	1925	77.66	22.15	0.19
1898	73.81	22.37	3.82	1926	77.34	22.62	0.04
1899	73.54	23.54	2.92	1927	77.88	22.10	0.02
1908	74.02	22.23	3.75	1928	78.23	21.77	. . .
1909	75.12	21.36	3.52	1929	78.56	21.42	0.02
1910	75.35	21.00	3.65	1930	77.11	22.86	0.03
1911	76.09	20.34	3.57	1931	78.01	21.96	0.03
1912	75.62	20.69	3.69	1934	81.06	18.94	. . .
1913	75.46	20.61	3.93	1937	84.08	15.92	. . .
1914	75.45	20.37	4.18	1939	85.07	14.93	. . .
1915	75.86	19.65	4.49	1944	87.86	12.14	. . .
1916	76.03	20.59	3.38	1947	88.83	11.17	. . .
1918	78.04	19.89	2.07				

[94] See Appendix II for absolute figures and for sources.

and third shifts.[95] Another factor contributing to the diminishing significance of women in the work force may have been the increasing use by
Bombay mills of their yarn in the production of cloth, thus reducing the
need for reelers, a predominantly female occupation.[96]

Right from the inception of the industry women seem to have been
employed predominantly in the cotton cleaning, winding, and reeling
departments — sections in which power equipment was not generally
used until well after the end of World War I [97] Some were employed as
sweepers and on spinning frames.[98] They never seem to have been employed as weavers.[99]

It has been suggested that factory legislation played some role in
restricting the use of women to departments in which power was not
used. The Factories Act of 1891 was the first to limit their hours of work.
It has been said that because the hours of adult males remained unregulated there was a strong tendency to use women only in those departments where "processes are for the most part carried on with hand
machines, which are not connected with the engine, and therefore do
not require attention from the time of starting to that of closing the
mill." [100]

There are at least three obvious reasons why this explanation is inadequate. First, there seems to have been no change in the proportion of
women employed after 1891 as compared with the period before. The
data in Table IX suggest, if anything, a rise in the percentage of women
employed in the 1890's as compared with 1884. This would, of course,
not preclude a simultaneous shift of women into a more limited range of
jobs in the cleaning, winding, and reeling departments. However, two
other features seem to take care of this possibility.

The argument that attributes the restricted use of women to the influence of factory legislation ignores the fact that women were employed

---

[95] The Factories Act of 1911 prohibited the employment of women or children
between 7:00 *p.m.* and 5:30 *a.m.*

[96] Mehta, *CMI*, p. 168.

[97] Women largely dominated the winding and reeling departments.

[98] For the early situation, see *FC 1885*, particularly the answers to question 60.
For quantitative evidence on female job patterns during the interwar years, see the
various wage surveys conducted by the Bombay Labor Office between 1921 and
1934.

[99] This seems clear in *FC 1885*, answers to question 60; B. H. Saklatvala, *IFLC
1908*, II, p. 82; and the Bombay Labor Office wage surveys. In fact, in 1934 a survey of the 214 cotton mills in the Bombay Presidency showed that "with the exception of seven women in one mill in Dharwar, no women are employed as
weavers." *BLO 1934*, p. 11.

[100] *FA 1892*, p. 15.

in spinning departments not only before 1891 but afterward as well. We have no statistical data for the period before 1921, but the evidence already cited suggests that the proportion of women employed as spinners before 1890 cannot have been very large.[101] On the other hand, data for the interwar years indicate that women employed as ring piecers, doffers, gaiters, and tarwallas, though a small proportion of total employment in these occupations, constituted a not insignificant proportion of all women employed in the industry.[102] If anything, the proportion of women in these occupations may have risen rather than fallen after 1891.

Finally, the argument ignores the qualitative evidence that the concentration of women in a few departments, primarily in those where the tasks were unmechanized, predates the Factories Act of 1891 and seems to go back to the very earliest years. It is this fact, the restricted use of women right from the industry's beginnings, that has to be explained, is difficult to explain, and is not explained by reference to the influence of factory legislation. Why did not the Bombay mills initially reproduce the Lancashire pattern of utilizing women on a very wide scale in a broad spectrum of jobs on both the spinning and the weaving sides?

There is certainly no clear evidence, but it may be possible to suggest a reason stemming from the fact that this was and is a society in which virtually all women married, married very young, and bore children at a very early age. The responsibilities of family life, especially in an immigrant situation which left the supporting elements of the joint family in the countryside, probably made women an unreliable sort of labor. For example, the manager of one of Bombay's largest mills commented that before 1890 he had tried to use women in many departments. He had given up the experiment not because of the legal restrictions on their hours of work but because "the women always had their household duties to perform. . . ."[103] John Robertson suggested the same point in 1875 when he reported that "females are found to be irregular

---

[101] The pre-World War I evidence suggests that only some mills employed women in their spinning departments. *FC 1875, passim; FC 1885, passim.*

[102] Women in these occupations as a proportion of total women employed amounted to 14.6 per cent in 1921, 12.5 per cent in 1923, 26.0 per cent in 1926, and 12.7 per cent in 1934. See *BLO 1921; BLO 1923; BLO 1926;* and *BLO 1934.* The 1926 figure, based on a survey of nineteen mills, seems grossly out of line with the other investigations which were based on tabulations from virtually all mills. I have no explanation for this discrepancy apart from the very strong possibility that the *BLO 1926* sample was unrepresentative.

[103] B. H. Saklatvala, *IFLC 1908,* II, p. 82. See also Factory Inspector Moos. *RCL 1892,* p. 136.

and troublesome, and are only employed as reelers and winders," employments that did not affect the main operations.[104]

This explanation of the restricted use of women in Bombay is not completely satisfying. For example, right from the beginning mills in Ahmedabad and other up-country centers used women much more extensively in spinning departments than was the case in Bombay. Moreover, though in Bombay the winding and reeling departments were overwhelmingly staffed by women, this was not the case elsewhere.[105] My explanation, to be conclusive, should apply equally to all textile centers.

There are some hints that variations in the employment of women derives in part from differences in social custom. Apparently only lower caste women would work alongside of men, and Bombay mills seem to have employed a smaller proportion of these than did mills in other centers.[106] But if this was in fact the case, we must still explain why the Bombay industry did not make greater use of lower caste women in order to achieve a higher proportion of women in the workforce.[107] The fact that no serious attempts were ever made to use them more extensively would seem to add some additional support to my proposition that there were no shortages of potential male millhands.[108]

---

[104] *BMOA 1875 and 1875–76*, p. 75. The winding and reeling departments worked with hand-powered equipment. They were organized to permit the employment of large numbers of women on what amounted to part-time work.

Even before the passage of the Factories Act of 1891 women in these departments typically came to work later and, except during very busy periods, would leave earlier than the men. They were also customarily allowed to leave the mills during the day to feed their children. However, where women worked in departments and on jobs linked to the main power source they worked the same hours as men. See *FC 1875; FC 1885; FA 1892*, pp. 12–16; evidence of BMOA and Bombay Textile Labor Union, *RCL 1929*, I, Part 1, pp. 397 and 342; and *BLO 1934*, p. 56.

[105] Some notion of the differences in patterns of employment of women by department in Bombay as compared with up-country centers can be obtained by a study of the tables in the various wage surveys conducted by the Bombay Labor Office between 1921 and 1934. For impressions of the nineteenth-century situation, see Mr. Jones, *FC 1885*, p. 34; Mr. Moos, *RCL 1892*, p. 13; *ITJ*, II, No. 23, August 1892, p. 218; and *ITJ*, X, No. 120, September 1900, p. 356.

[106] This is a difficult point to prove because it is not always clear whether sources were referring to low caste or to untouchable workers.

[107] The impression I have is that some employers, at least, feared that if they employed untouchable-caste women they would then be forced to employ untouchable-caste men. There is a hint of this in the testimony of B. H. Saklatvala, *IFLC 1908*, II, p. 82. There are occasional references to a reluctance on the part of mills to employ untouchables. However, this bias seems to have diminished in later years. On the general problem of caste, see section (6) of this chapter.

[108] In fact, the Factory Commission of 1890 made this point explicitly. "The difference in the wages between male and female operatives is, in most places, so

Children always seem to have been employed on a very small scale in the Bombay mills, and there are few tales of horror of the sort which we associate with the early cotton mills of Britain. The problem of estimating the proportion of children in the labor force is complicated by changing legal definitions of a child. One source estimated that in the late 1870's children made up 10 per cent of the work force, but it is impossible to tell what was intended by the notion of "children." [109] The 1881 census reported that 23.76 per cent of the mill workers were persons less than fifteen years of age. Apart from the fact that this figure is much larger than any others I have been able to find, the category included persons far older than those defined as children by factory legislation until 1922.[110]

There are no reasonably precise data until 1892 at which point my series shows that children (persons aged nine through thirteen) made up 5.6 per cent of the labor force.[111] From then until 1899 their share in the labor force declined. In 1908 the percentage of children employed stood at a slightly higher level than in 1899, and rose to 4.5 per cent of the labor force in 1915 — the highest point in the twentieth century. From then on the proportion of children declined steadily to insignificance.

Violations of the law probably resulted in some understatement of the proportion of children employed. Violations were probably substantial just after the passage of the first factories act in 1881 and most likely reached a peak during the boom of 1904 to 1906.[112] However, I am convinced that adjustment for illegal use (if we could estimate this figure) would not raise very much the proportion of children actually employed. Not only was enforcement reasonably efficient, but the over-all demand for children was really quite small. D. E. Wacha, calculating the number of children needed in the industry for the jobs on which they were

small that the millowners will not hesitate to substitute male adult labor, on which no restrictions are laid, for female labor which could, under the proposed amendment of the law, be worked only for 11 hours. Our enquiry has further shown that there will be no difficulty whatever in getting as many men as may be required." *FC 1890*, p. 3. See also the statement of G. Cotton, *BMOA 1891*, pp. 211–212.

[109] J. M. Maclean, *A Guide to Bombay* (5th ed., Bombay: 1880), p. 126.

[110] *Census 1881*, Table 124, pp. 174–178. The Factories Act of 1881 defined an employable child as one between the ages of seven through eleven. In 1891 this was raised to nine through thirteen; in 1922 it was raised to fourteen through seventeen.

[111] For these and other figures on employment of children, see Appendix II.

[112] W. O. Meade King, "The Indian Factories Act, 1881, with the Alterations Therein Proposed," Memorandum to the Secretary to Government, 24 June 1882, pp. 6–8; and L. Frazer, *India Under Curzon and After* (London: W. Heinemann, 1911), pp. 330–336.

typically employed, estimated that the maximum required in 1912 would have been not more than 5.2 per cent of the total work force.[113]

(6)

One who writes about the creation of an industrial labor force must obviously examine the relationship of caste to the process. Yet anyone who examines the literature must be struck with the paucity of material on the subject. Though there has been a good deal of general comment, we know virtually nothing specific about the relationship of caste to the entire phenomenon of industrialization. The basic data are extremely sparse, and scholars have tended to neglect the subject. The distinguished anthropologist, M. N. Srinivas, not long ago complained that "next to nothing is known about the social background of industrial workers. . . ." He went on to point out that information on the functioning of caste in the city "is conspicuous by its absence." [114]

In general terms there has been a widespread tendency to argue that rural migrants to the cities have been not only economically but also socially the most depressed groups. The implication is that there has been a disproportionately large outflow from rural areas to the cities of low caste people, most specifically of untouchable groups.[115] It is certainly true that low caste groups of all kinds did constitute an overwhelming proportion of migrants to Bombay from an early date.[116] But this is not a very startling proposition since these groups made up a very substantial proportion of the total rural population. Before anything more precise can be said, we must examine the evidence more carefully.

For example, it is sometimes suggested that untouchables tended to move to the cities first, and higher caste groups began to move in sub-

---

[113] Wacha estimated that in the years 1909 to 1912 actual employment of children never rose above 3.65 per cent. He was writing of the need the industry had for more children, and his very liberal estimate of the number of children the industry could use came to 5.1 or 5.2 per cent of the total labor force, depending on how one calculates from his figures. These were derived from his article, *ITJ* XXIV, No. 285, June 1914, p. 318.

[114] M. N. Srinivas, "Social Anthropology and the Study of Rural and Urban Societies," *The Economic Weekly*, XI, Special Number, January 1959, p. 137. For an examination of the state of our knowledge on the subject, see Morris, "Caste and the Evolution of the Industrial Workforce," pp. 124–133. The analysis in this section follows that of the article.

[115] *Ibid.*, pp. 125–126. I use "low caste" to include not only untouchable but also what are sometimes called "intermediate" castes.

[116] For example, in the years 1864, 1872, and 1881, low castes made up between 59 and 64 per cent of the total Bombay City population. See the census reports for these years.

sequently.[117] This is not borne out by the Bombay census data summarized in Table X. Neither is it possible, on the evidence, to sustain the proposition that the flow of untouchables was disproportionately high.

TABLE X

Untouchables as a Proportion of Total Bombay
City Population, 1864–1941 [118]

Year	Per cent	Year	Per cent
1864 .... 3.97		1911 .... 9.09	
1872 .... 4.86		1921 .... 11.53	
1881 .... 6.36		1931 .... 8.88	
1891 .... n.a.		1941 .... 8.15	
1901 .... 9.38			

Table X shows that in 1864, after a period of extremely rapid population growth, less than 4 per cent of the population was classified as untouchable.[119] Although their proportion seems to have risen rather steadily, even at the 1921 peak untouchables represented less than 12 per cent of the total population of Bombay. And between 1921 and 1941, the last date for which there are any figures, the proportion dropped rather sharply. Moreover, it was only in the period beginning in 1901 that the proportion of untouchables in the city's population rose above the 7 to 8 per cent ratio that untouchables seem to have represented in the total population of Bombay Presidency.[120]

Ignoring the unreliability of census caste data, which is a serious matter, Table X does suggest that the rate of increase of untouchables in the Bombay City population was greater than the average, at least between 1864 to 1901 and 1911 to 1921.[121] But it is not possible to leap

[117] C. A. Myers, *Labor Problems in the Industrialization of India* (Cambridge: Harvard University Press, 1958), pp. 39–40.

[118] Calculated from census data for various years. In 1864 and 1872 I used figures for "Hindu outcastes" which *Census 1881*, p. 14, indicated were untouchables. Beginning in 1881, I included the following castes in the untouchable category: Bhangi, Halalkore, Chambhar, Mochi, Dhed, Mahar, Holiya, Wankar, Mang, and Madig. For 1941, I used the group labeled "Scheduled Castes." The figures for 1881 to 1931 probably slightly understate the proportion of untouchables in the total population. This is suggested by the fact that in *Census 1941*, pp. 89–91 and 103–105, the castes I have named represented 85.1 per cent of the total of all "Scheduled Castes."

[119] None of the pre-1864 evidence suggests that untouchables were moving into the city at a high rate.

[120] Based on comparisons with the Presidency census data for the period.

[121] On the weakness of caste data, see the relevant sections in the censuses for 1911–1931.

immediately to the conclusion that untouchables showed a greater tendency than other groups to migrate to the city. Two specific issues must first be dealt with. First, we would have to come to some conclusion about differential caste group fertility rates before we could determine that the different rates of increase of various caste groups in Bombay City were a function of migration rather than of birth rates in the city itself. This is not an insignificant issue since Davis reports that fertility tends to be inversely related with social (i.e., caste) status.[122]

Second, even if we could be certain that differential caste group increases in Bombay were due entirely to immigration, we still could not conclude that the increased proportion of any specific group was the result of distinctive pressures in the countryside on this group. The changing proportions in Bombay might merely have reflected shifts in the districts from which migration was occurring and different caste proportions within these districts. Until we get detailed studies which relate caste composition of migrants to the caste composition of the cohort populations from which they derived, it is not at all appropriate to advance any easy generalizations on the propensities of untouchables or of any other groups to migrate to the city.[123]

Having made these general observations, let me now examine the caste data available for mill workers.

Table XI certainly shows that untouchables represented a very small proportion of total mill labor. However, when we note that untouch-

---

[122] Davis, *op.cit.*, pp. 73–74. The census data I have examined but not explored in detail at least leaves open this possibility for untouchables in Bombay City. The censuses for 1872 and 1881 report that about 20 per cent of the untouchables in the city had been born there. Unfortunately, the caste data in the 1911 and 1921 censuses do not yield this information. However, if we assume that the reported number of immigrant untouchables represented virtually all of this immigrant group, the remaining untouchables (i.e., those for whom no birthplace is given and who might possibly be Bombay-born) represented in 1911 and 1921 a higher proportion of total Bombay population than in either 1872 or 1881. For the sources on this, see Appendix V.

[123] The census commissioners certainly treated the increase of untouchables in Bombay as an immigration phenomenon. See *Census 1881*, p. 41; *Census 1921*, IX, pp. 20–21.

One would probably be safe to suggest as a first approximation from the census data that before 1864 untouchables were much less likely to move to Bombay than other groups and that afterwards they tended to move in at a slightly more rapid rate than all other groups combined, at least until 1921. However, it would take detailed investigation to see whether this was exceptional or whether there were other specific caste groups which also moved in at rates higher than the average. The declining proportion of untouchables 1921 to 1941 suggests that when economic opportunities were not great, as they were not in Bombay during the period, untouchable castes tended to lose out.

TABLE XI

Untouchables as a Proportion of Bombay City
Population and of the Bombay Mill Labor Force,
1872–1941 [124]

Year (1)	Untouchables as a proportion of total Bombay population (2)	Untouchable mill hands as a proportion of total mill labor force (3)
1872	4.86	0.99
1881	6.36	2.11
1891	n.a.	n.a.
1901	9.38	n.a.
1911	9.09	9.05
1921	11.53	11.91
1931	8.88	11.28
1941	8.15	13.81

ables constituted a relatively small proportion of the total Bombay population, this fact is not particularly startling. However, the table does suggest that the industry began by using untouchables in very insignificant numbers, even when compared with their proportion of the all-city population. Gradually their share of mill employment rose to a level somewhat above their proportion in the city's population.[125] In other words, Table XI runs against the notions that untouchables were the earliest recruits to the industry or that they ever provided the bulk or even a substantial proportion of the total labor force. These figures set some outer limits to the role of untouchables in the industry, but they tell us very little more.

The next issue we must examine is the degree to which caste influenced specific occupational patterns. There is a tendency to argue that industry is caste-blind for a number of reasons. It may be because no single caste can provide an adequate supply of labor, because it is impossible to determine specific caste affiliation in an industrial situation, because employers are uninterested in caste affiliation, or because all castes are willing to do all work in industry. It is not infrequently suggested that some or all of these features result in the

[124] Figures in column 2 come from Table X. The figures in column 3 are based on calculations discussed in Appendix V.

[125] The rise between 1931 and 1941 is probably a statistical fiction. It is safer to assume that the proportion of untouchables to total mill labor remained approximately constant between 1921 and 1941. See Appendix V for a discussion of this point. But even if their share of mill employment did not rise between 1921 and 1941, it remained stable while the untouchable proportion of total city population fell.

mixing of workers in such a fashion as to lead to the ultimate under-mining of the caste system. Kingsley Davis advanced an extreme version of this view, saying: "If industrialization proceeds rapidly [in India], . . . the caste system will have essentially disappeared by the end of this century." [126]

Although such propositions suggest something, right or wrong, about the ultimate impact of factory employment, they tell us noth-ing about caste groups as they have existed in industry. They contribute nothing to our understanding of why, in the early decades of the Bombay mill industry's career, the proportion of untouchables was insignificant and why that proportion gradually increased. It is possible that this trend was the result of purely accidental factors, but I think that what little evidence there is suggests that it was not. If accident is ruled out as an explanation, we must try to determine the degree to which caste affilia-tion tended to determine the general chances of being hired and the specific jobs for which hiring was done. If caste had any effect, we must explore the extent to which access to occupational opportunities was determined by the social attitudes of employers and their agents or stemmed from the labor force itself.

But first, we need statistical evidence of the extent to which the phe-nomenon of caste clustering was, in fact, found in the cotton mills. There is only one study available, the BMOA 1940 survey of 37,639 workers in nineteen Bombay mills.[127] The survey shows that Marathas constituted more than half (51.8 per cent) of all male workers. They were found in large proportions in all departments. Of the other important groups, Bhayyas contributed 13.8 per cent to the total male labor force. Unlike the Marathas, they tended to cluster in certain departments. 53.8 per cent were in the "mixing to speed frame" departments and 17.2 per cent in the weaving sheds. But only in the former did they represent a large part (46.8 per cent) of departmental employment.[128] Harijans (un-touchables) contributed 11.9 per cent of all male employees. 72.5 per cent were employed in the ring-spinning departments where they made up 39.5 per cent of all male workers. Muslims, the only other large group distinguished, made up 5.2 per cent of total male workers. The 52.2 per cent employed in the weaving sheds constituted 6.9 per cent of the weaving operatives.[129]

---

[126] Davis, *op.cit.*, p. 176.

[127] Gokhale, *op.cit.*, p. 116. The survey covered nearly 27 per cent of 1940 em-ployment.

[128] In the weaving sheds they represented only 6 per cent of the male workforce.

[129] Women mill hands were much more restricted occupationally. Of all women, 85.9 per cent were employed in winding and reeling, and Marathas and Harijans were the dominant groups by far. Of all Maratha women, 92.4 per cent worked in this department, and 73.5 per cent of all Harijan women were employed there.

Looking at the survey data somewhat differently, were there any departments in which any of these groups was not found? As I have already suggested, Marathas were extremely important in all sections.[130] Bhayyas, though concentrated in certain sections, could be found in all departments as could the Muslims. Only the Harijans showed a restricted pattern of participation. Clearly, the most distinctive feature is that of a total of 1,240 workers in the weaving sheds only eighty (0.6 per cent) were Harijans, and they represented only 2.2 per cent of all Harijans in the work force.

In spite of this fact, we have to recognize that this survey really tells us very little about caste-clustering in the mills. I do not think it necessary to set down a precise definition of caste, but it is essential to recognize that I am using the term to refer to what are more precisely called subcastes (*jati*), endogamous and interdining groups which exist in territorially confined areas of the countryside. For any analysis of labor recruitment and the study of the behavior of rural recruits in an industrial environment, we must begin our study with those social groups which exhibit homogeneity and cohesive behavior in the countryside. It is entirely inappropriate to lump into larger groups because of similarity of name, function, social status, or region-of-origin subcastes that are not endogamous.[131]

I am not necessarily arguing that village subcaste (*jati*) relationships will ultimately prove to be the most relevant categories of social behavior inside the factory. In fact, it may well be that *jati* relations were irrelevant there. But when one is concerned with the historical process of creating an industrial labor force, analysis must begin with the existing social relationships in the villages from which the work force comes. This is crucial when the specific problem is the influence of caste on the process of recruitment and disciplining of rural migrants to urban-industrial employment. If these social groupings, so decisive in the villages, ceased to have relevance or were transformed in the factory environment, this does not diminish the original significance of *jati* as a category for the problem with which I am here concerned. It is precisely the transformation from *jati* to something else that becomes important to describe and evaluate. Unfortunately, research has not yet gotten this far. My difficulty is that investigators have tended to use the concept

---

[130] In five of the six departmental classifications of the survey, Marathas were a plurality or a majority of the workers. In the "mixing to speed frame" section, Bhayyas supplied more labor (46.8 per cent) but Marathas provided 31.5 per cent of the total in that section.

[131] I. Karve, "What is Caste?" *The Economic Weekly*, X, Annual Number, January, 1958, pp. 125–138.

caste to mean one thing (*jati*) in the description of village social structure and function and something quite different when describing industrial socio-economic behavior. In fact, the sources on the Bombay situation have systematically confused *jati* with district, region, language, occupation, or religion.

The 1940 BMOA survey poses grave difficulties precisely in these terms. Apart from serious questions about the representativeness of the sample, the so-called "caste" categories are really not that at all. The Hindu group, representing 92.4 per cent of all workers, was divided into six "caste" categories — Maratha, Kunbi, Bhandari, Bhayya, Kamathi, and Harijan.[132] Of these, only one — Bhandari — seems fairly clearly to represent a *jati*, and the employees so identified constituted only 2.7 per cent of the entire work force.

Neither Marathas nor Kunbis are single interdining, intermarrying entities. Both are clusters of endogamous groups. Moreover, Kunbis of various sorts have gradually incorporated themselves within the Maratha designation.[133] Bhayya is not a caste designation at all but a regional term referring to all groups from what is now Uttar Pradesh.[134] Kamathi also seems to be a regional rather than a *jati* classification.[135] And Harijan, of course, is an euphemism comprehending all depressed castes. In Bombay there were at least six major untouchable caste groups — Bhangi, Chambhar, Dhed, Mahar, Mang and Mochi — and a number of minor ones. Since these groups are mutually exclusive in the countryside, it is inappropriate to lump them together.[136] These conglomerate categories

---

[132] There was also a "miscellaneous" Hindu category that included 5.7 per cent of the total labor force.

[133] Karve, *op. cit.* For a brief discussion of the problem, see *Census 1921*, VIII, Part 1, pp. 183–184. *Census 1931*, pp. 41–42, listed eighteen different Maratha-Kunbi groups, including one catch-all category. Not infrequently the "term 'Maratha' in its wider aspect is used to indicate a number of castes from Brahmins downward." J. H. Hutton, *Caste in India* (3d ed., London: Oxford University Press, 1961), p. 20. On this point, see also *Census 1901*, p. 183, and *Census 1911*, VII, p. 278.

[134] Rutnagur, *op. cit.*, p. 319. *Census 1931*, pp. 184–193, listed nine different "caste" groups from the U. P. working in the Bombay mills and these nine represented fewer than 40 per cent of the total U. P. migrants working in the industry.

[135] M. M. Shah, "Labour Recruitment and Turnover in the Textile Industry of Bombay Presidency" (Unpublished Ph.D. dissertation, University of Bombay, 1941), p. 180.

[136] The situation in the countryside is even more complicated than this. The Maratha Chambhars, alone, are divided into at least six endogamous groups; Dhed is a term which covers at least fourteen endogamous divisions; and the name Mahar blurs the distinction among fifty-three endogamous groups. *Census 1911*, VII, pp. 249, 254 and 287.

are impossible to justify analytically if the basic issue is not only the functioning distinctiveness of the groups which ultimately become part of the industrial labor force but also the possible consequences of such exclusiveness inside the mills.[137] On the other hand, the fact that the BMOA used the general categories it did, raises the possibility that these broader distinctions were of greater operational significance than *jati*. If so, then it was not "caste" in the technically precise sense that was crucial in the industry.

The BMOA survey does suggest some regional-, linguistic-, and religious-, as well as caste-clustering in the mills of Bombay. [138] But the data also seem to indicate that the enclaves of workers were not preclusive. With the exception of untouchables in the weaving sheds, we find all major regional and religious groups and Hindus of all castes in every department.[139] This 1940 evidence seems to be supported by nineteenth-century reports. For example, in 1864 the Census Commissioner of Bombay wrote:

It is supposed that at one time caste determined the occupation that a Hindu was to follow. Now it is but a limited influence, and there are few castes of which the members will not engage in any occupation, and but few occupations in which the persons of any caste will not seek a livelihood.[140]

Seventeen years later another census commissioner, making the same point, added the comment: "Hindus have a very great capacity for adapting themselves to circumstances and necessities." [141] And in 1892 a factory inspector stated that the "refusal of men of one caste to work with those of the other has been singularly rare in the textile trade." [142] These judgments seem to be borne out by the absence of any substantive contradictory evidence.

----

[137] The BMOA survey also listed Muslims as a unitary category although here, too, rural endogamy actually fragments the superficial coherence of the group. *Census 1901*, XI, p. 201.

[138] In addition to Gokhale, *op. cit.*, p. 116, see R. C. James, "Labor and Technical Change" (Unpublished Ph.D. dissertation, Cornell University, 1957), pp. 103–117; Shah, *op. cit.*, pp. 179–180; J. H. Kelman, *Labour in India* (London: George Allen and Unwin Ltd., 1923), pp. 75, 86–87, and 134–135; Mehta, *CMI*, pp. 120–121; and *FC 1885*, p. 5.

[139] We actually cannot be certain of the almost complete exclusion of untouchables from the weaving sheds. Lumping all migrants from the Uttar Pradesh region under the "Bhayya" designation ignores the possibility that some, at least, of these people employed in the weaving sheds may have been untouchables. Moreover, 4.6 per cent of weaving shed employees were lumped into a Hindu "miscellaneous" category which also may have included untouchables.

[140] *Census 1864*, p. xviii.

[141] *Census 1872*, p. 42.

[142] *RCL 1892*, p. 136. See also *FC 1875*, p. 24.

The weaving sheds apparently were the only historically significant exception to the generalization that whatever the situation in the countryside, nothing prevented the employer from selecting freely from the Bombay labor market and assigning his recruits in any way he saw fit.[143] The explanation widely given for the situation in the weaving sheds is that whenever a weft bobbin was replaced, yarn had to be sucked onto the shuttle. If untouchables were employed, other groups working with the same shuttle would have been ritually defiled.[144]

Reasonable though the explanation may be, it is not possible to tell whether this is a complete explanation of the fact. After all, the mills apparently had little trouble getting Hindu and Muslim weavers to work together.[145] But even if the phenomenon has been correctly explained, it stands as a clear exception to the situation in every other department where "caste people and Harijans are found working promiscuously . . . side by side without religious stigma. . . ." [146] We would still have to answer the question: why here and nowhere else?

There is one aspect of the situation which has been largely ignored, the fact that historically the weaving department tended to be the highest paid section in the industry, with its relative advantage increasing over time.[147] In effect, the situation in the weaving sheds pitted all "clean" groups (including Muslims) against all untouchable groups. We must at least raise the possibility that the exclusion of untouchables was not entirely a caste phenomenon but was also a device to preserve the monopoly of particularly advantageous but very limited economic opportunities against newcomers.[148]

The weaving shed represents the one possible case where workers

---

[143] The bar to untouchables in the weaving sheds seems to go back to the earlier decades of the industry. *FC 1875*, p. 23; and *IFLC 1908*, II, p. 82.

[144] Shah, *op. cit.*, p. 216.

[145] I cannot tell whether this fear of ritual pollution affected only Hindus or Muslims as well.

[146] Shah, *op. cit.*, pp. 216–217.

[147] *PW* for 1882 to 1922. It will be recalled that the weaving section of the industry expanded much more swiftly than the spinning side, particularly after 1890.

[148] This possibility would be strengthened if we could find data which showed a tendency for exclusion of untouchables from the highest paid occupations in the mills, regardless of department. Unfortunately, there is no way to get at this information in the 1940 BMOA survey. However, there were more than weaver jobs in the weaving sheds and many of them were very highly paid. The fact that untouchables were apparently excluded from these jobs, despite the absence of any specific possibilities of pollution, supports my contention. See, also, G. R. Pradhan, "Untouchable Workers of Bombay City" (Unpublished Ph.D. thesis, University of Bombay, 1936), p. 43; Kelman, *op. cit.*, p. 86; and Shah, *op. cit.*, p. 216, for some examples which seem to support this notion.

would not permit the employers to use certain groups. To continue looking at the labor supply problem in terms of worker attitudes, there is one additional question to be raised. Were there any occupations in the mills which would not be accepted by all groups? There were none in the operating departments, but it is widely believed that there were certain ritually degrading tasks — sweeper jobs — which were accepted only by untouchable castes.[149] There is, however, no statistical evidence bearing on this point. The 1940 BMOA survey throws no light on the subject. But apart from this, certain problems are involved. To the extent that over time the flush toilet replaced the honey bucket in the mills, it is possible that the issue of ritual contamination became irrelevant.[150] However, even if we accept the fact that these tasks continued to exist, we are in no position to say that it was, in fact, only untouchable castes which were taking them.[151] And even if we could document the fact, we still could not be certain that this caste-clustering was a result of selection by workers rather than the selection of members of these castes for these jobs by the employers.

I have already implied that not only those who seek employment but also those who employ are intimately involved in the caste system and are as largely affected by its demands. The employer as a caste-affected person may seek to give employment to his caste brethren. If true, this would have made for the tendency for specific castes to have found employment in specific companies, if not in the industry itself. Although the evidence is not clear, such a pattern is not suggested.[152]

But even if the employer did not recruit labor from his own particular subcaste, he may still have had views and prejudices as to the appropriate distribution of jobs among available castes in terms of purported caste skills, appropriate mixing of groups and the like. On this point

---

[149] *FC 1885*, Appendix III, p. 197; *RCL 1929*, I, Part 1, p. 385.

[150] E. M. Forster once wrote: "Introduce water-closets and main-drainage throughout India, and all this wicked rubbish about untouchability will disappear." Preface to Mulk Raj Anand, *Untouchable* (Bombay: Jaico Publishing House, 1956), p. 6.

[151] In the absence of firm statistical evidence, the mere statement that the groups that did this work were untouchables proves nothing. It is not uncommon in India to identify as an untouchable any person engaged in a task traditionally viewed as the work of untouchable castes. See the comment on "Chamars," *Census 1911*, VII, p. 249; and E. W. Hopkins, *India Old and New* (New York: C. Scribner's Sons, 1901), p. 308 n.

[152] In fact, to the extent that employers and their agents were predominantly Gujarati whereas the work force was almost entirely non-Gujarati, it seems clear that the phenomenon did not affect recruitment of the labor force. On the other hand, there were obvious regional, linguistic, and other communal clusterings at the managerial level. But in the absence of detailed studies, it is impossible to determine their precise nature.

there are some scattered facts. There is no question that many employers at various times had specific notions about the adaptability of special groups — not necessarily caste groups — to specific types of work.[153] For example, many early mills seem to have sought out Julahas, a traditional group of Muslim handloom weavers, to employ in their weaving sheds. It has been said that these people were brought from long distances in the early years — from Upper India, Madras, and Calcutta — as well as recruited from among the group permanently resident in Bombay.[154]

There is also evidence that some of the early mills refused to employ untouchables. In 1874 the manager of the United Spinning and Weaving Mill reported: "No low-caste operatives are allowed to be employed in the mill." [155] In 1908 the manager of the D. Petit Mill not only stated that "There were no low caste men in the weaving shed," but he also made the point that "When a man applied for work, his caste was enquired in-to. Caste, in fact, was a great consideration." [156] And one of the reasons the Tata scheme of 1897 to recruit labor in the Uttar Pradesh region seems to have foundered is that the untouchable caste weavers — Kosto Mahars — who were available at the wages offered under the scheme were unacceptable to the millowners who sponsored the enterprise.[157]

But whatever the specific examples, they are exceedingly few in number. For the industry as a whole there seems to have been no generally formulated and explicitly maintained policy of caste selection.[158] It seems fairly safe to conclude that most of the changing pattern of group concentrations by department and mill had nothing to do with any clearly defined employer policy but were linked with the general methods of hiring labor and the preponderant power of the jobber in the process. The general influence of the jobber is analyzed in Chapter VIII. It is sufficient at this point to indicate that he played a decisive role in the

---

[153] For some suggestions on this point, Edwardes, *op. cit.*, pp. 207–208; A. R. Burnett-Hurst, *Labour and Housing in Bombay* (London: P. S. King and Son, 1925), p. 49; Shah, *op. cit.*, pp. 179–80. James, *op. cit.*, pp. 110–111, in fact, explicit-ly argued that "Mill management thinks and feels in geographical origin terms. . . . Management consciously considers and plans the 'community' composition of its mill. Prejudice concerning a community's efficiency and political proclivities are reflected in hiring practices."

[154] *ITJ*, XVII, No. 196, January 1907, p. 106.

[155] *FC 1875*, p. 23. This mill also employed very few Muslims. *Loc. cit.*

[156] *IFLC 1908*, II, p. 82.

[157] *BMOA 1897*, p. 5.

[158] Mehta, *CMI*, pp. 120–121. Kelman, *op. cit.*, pp. 86–87. Certainly, a number of early mills employed untouchables. *FC 1885*, pp. 5 and 144; *FC 1890*, p. 47. On the other hand, as late as the beginning of World War II, when untouchables were widely employed, it was said that there were some mills which employed very few or none at all. Shah, *op. cit.*, p. 179.

selection and retention of labor and thus very clearly must have been responsible for much of the specific caste or other group concentrations that existed in individual mills.[159]

This does not in itself explain the tendency particularly of untouchables to increase their share in mill employment before 1921. It is possible that the rapid growth of employment opportunities at various times contributed to this in one special way. As the industry increased its emphasis on cloth production, weaver wages rose relatively, and there seems to have been a shift of "clean" castes from spinning into the weaving sheds.[160] Though there is no evidence on this point, it is possible that the lower paid employments, particularly ring spinning, then became more easily accessible to untouchables.[161] Strikes and the opportunity for strikebreaking apparently also offered untouchables a channel for employment.[162] Once having established a foothold in the industry, they seem to have consolidated their position.

On examining the historical evidence as a whole, there seems little basis for arguing that any of the traditional features of the caste system as it may have functioned in the countryside affected the employer's ability to recruit labor as he saw fit. Whatever caste distinctions did persist in industry seem not to have imposed any obstacles to efficient utilization of workers or to profitable operation of the enterprises.[163] Moreover, many of these institutional carryovers from the rural sector seem to have broken down over time. It was, after all, a fact that the "refusal of men of one caste to work with those of the other has been singularly rare in the textile trade." [164]

There were, it is true, a few examples of employers providing separate welfare facilities based upon "caste" distinctions. For example, in the 1920's one mill had set aside a separate playing field for its untouchable

---

[159] See, for example, *ITJ*, III, No. 35, August 1893, p. 224.

[160] *ITJ*, XVII, No. 196, January 1907, p. 106; *IDC 1921*, p. 18.

[161] This also seems to be the device by which the early importance of Muslim weavers was diluted by Hindus. *ITJ*, XVII, No. 196, January 1907, p. 106; Mehta, *CMI*, p. 117.

[162] For example, during the 1929 general strike, it is claimed that B. R. Ambedkar, leader of the untouchables, undertook to supply strikebreakers for a number of mills. Mehta, *CMI*, p. 121. Shah, *op. cit.*, p. 179, suggests that strikebreaking was the way in which many new groups, other than untouchable, established themselves in the industry. On the other hand, it is possible that the strikebreaking role of untouchables has been exaggerated. See Appendix V and Chapter IX on this point.

[163] I have found not a single statement by an employer that caste distinctions had imposed any handicap in the recruitment or use of labor.

[164] *RCL 1892*, p. 136. On the gradual disruption of these features, *IFLC 1908*, II, p. 134; B. Shiva Rao, *The Industrial Worker in India* (London: George Allen and Unwin, 1939), p. 80; Shah, *op. cit.*, pp. 216–217; and Mehta, *CMI*, 120–121.

workers.[165] In some of the few cases where employers established can-
teen or dining facilities, separate arrangements were made for untouchables.[166] There is one report that "clean" caste women refused to use a
crèche because an untouchable *ayah* was employed to operate it. But
the same source indicates how quickly and easily the company was able
to eliminate the opposition.[167] In fact, the inescapable conclusion from
the evidence is that whatever distinctions did persist in the mills survived only because employers found it unnecessary to eliminate them.
Whenever and wherever industry operations required the disruption of
these traditional distinctions, they crumbled.

Let me make one final point. To the limited extent that group distinctions of a caste type did persist, they were clearly not based on *jati*
prescriptions of the traditional sort but, as in the weaving sheds, on much
wider elements — on a division between all untouchables and all other
workers. The persistence of this phenomenon seems to be more easily
explicable in terms of limited job opportunities rather than on the basis
of ritualized hostility of one *jati* toward another. In a society of enormous
poverty and very restricted employment opportunities there was an
overwhelming tendency for groups to preëmpt for themselves the mo-
noply of whatever jobs were available. Intruding groups, whatever their
character, were a threat to the tenuously held advantages which did
exist.[168]

---

[165] *LG*, VI, No. 5, January 1927, p. 442. On the other hand, the survey of recrea-
tional facilities from which this example is drawn implies that this was exceptional.
Ibid., pp. 442–443.

[166] Kelman, *op. cit.*, pp. 87 and 134–136; K. Dwarkadas, *Forty-Five Years with
Labour* (Bombay: Asia Publishing House, 1962), 146.

[167] *Loc. cit.*

[168] For example, it was easier, apparently, to integrate dining facilities than to
introduce untouchables into the weaving sheds.

CHAPTER V

Stability and Instability
in the Labor Force

(1)

Virtually all studies of the Bombay cotton textile industry accept the fact of high rates of labor turnover and absenteeism and stress the fact of the workers' connections with the countryside as being responsible for this historic lack of permanent attachment to mill employment. Some writers have emphasized the importance of the mill hand as landholder. Mehta, for example, referred to

the large number of workers . . . who came from classes which have a vested interest in agricultural land and other rural property and who, as a consequence, have only an unstable nexus with the towns of their migration. Only too often in the early decades a worker came to the mills, or for that matter to the city, to collect the cash required for adding an extra bit of land to his plot or for purchasing a new pair of bullocks. These wants satisfied, the man went back, probably never to return. . . . It was this state of affairs which led to the average working life of a worker in cotton factories being only 5 or 6 years as late as 1896.[1]

Others, claiming that the bulk of the operatives was recruited from land-less or virtually landless rural groups, have argued that the attachment to the countryside derived from the vitality and tenacious influence of joint family and village institutions.[2] Given these persistent links with the countryside, whether derived from landholding or social and religious relationships, the mill hand, it has been argued, came to the factory with the intention of remaining at work for only a short period. And his term of service in the mills, whether for a few years or many, was interrupted by frequent returns to the countryside, either to satisfy peak labor requirements on the land or for social, psychological, and religious reasons.

Our operatives are agriculturists first and agriculturists last. The period of their employment in the mills fills only a small portion of their lives. . . .

---

[1] S. D. Mehta, "Professor Morris on Textile Labour Supply," *Indian Economic Journal*, I. No. 3, January 1954, p. 334.

[2] The classic statement is found in *RCL 1929*, "Report," pp. 11–14. The horror of urban-industrial existence is sometimes stressed as a factor pushing the millhand back to the countryside. Mehta, *CMI*, p. 119; C. A. Myers, *Labor Problems in the Industrialization of India* (Cambridge: Harvard University Press, 1958), pp. 43–44.

They work a certain length of time until they have laid by sufficient funds to return to their native country. The attractions of their village hold them until all their resources are completely exhausted and necessity once more drives them back [to the Bombay mills]. . . . The outcome of this unsettled, vagrant life is loss of skill, no incentive to work their best, a lowering of their physical stamina, and a total lack of sympathy between themselves and their employers.[3]

Before examining the problems of labor turnover and absenteeism in detail, let me say a few things about the mill hand as a rural landholder. The most important point — and it cannot be stressed enough — is that we can say virtually nothing on this subject. There is no statistical material that throws light on the issue, and the casual observations of employers and officials are of little use on this point. We do not know what proportion of the early or later mill hands were landholders nor do we know whether there was any change in the proportion of landless to landholding operatives over time.[4]

I have been able to find only two bits of information which bear on the landholding status of mill workers. Of the thirty-six cotton mill operatives examined by the factory commission of 1890, thirty-one were born outside of Bombay. Of the sixteen of these who gave information on the subject, eleven (68.8 per cent) said that either they or their families held some property in their native village and five (31.2 per cent) had no landed connection.[5] The only other estimate was made by Dr. Nair in 1908. He estimated that no more than 20 per cent of mill labor in India could lay any claim to landholding status.[6]

---

[3] *BMOA 1918*, p. xii. See also *IFLC 1908*, I, pp. 18–19; and *RCL 1929*, "Report" pp. 13–14 and 17–19. Myers, *op. cit.*, pp. 36 ff. gives the best recent summary of current opinion on the subject.

[4] In the period before World War I it was generally assumed that landholding was an ubiquitous phenomenon in the countryside and, therefore, virtually all mill hands who came from the rural areas were landholders. In the years following World War I the problem of landlessness became a public issue and observers began increasingly to stress the fact that mill hands were likely to be drawn from the landless elements in the countryside. What is at stake, however, is the phenomenon I mentioned in Chapter IV, that landlessness was an important feature throughout the whole of the nineteenth century. We do not know to what extent mill hands were drawn from this particular segment of rural society. Employers and government officials were in no position to make judgments about the rural status of the employees, and evidence from these sources must be treated with considerable skepticism.

[5] *FC 1890*, pp. 22–50. Based on oral evidence given by Bombay mill hands to the Commission during its first twelve meetings.

[6] Dr. Nair's dissent to the main report, *IFLC 1908*, I, pp. 88–89. A survey at the end of my period reported that of 679 working-class (not necessarily mill hand)

There is no way to determine how accurately either of these widely disparate estimates represented the then current situation. Though we can get no valid estimate of the proportion of landless mill hands at any moment, there is some logical basis for assuming that the proportion increased over time. First, there is the evidence I have produced showing that a rising proportion of the labor force was born in Bombay. It is safe to assume that most of this group had no land in the countryside.[7] Second, there is some evidence that a growing proportion of very low caste groups, including untouchables, gained entry into the industry.[8] These tended to be landless elements in the countryside. Third, there was a growing pressure of population in the countryside from which mill hands were recruited.[9]

Unfortunately, these arguments for a rising proportion of landless mill hands in the labor force are based on an unproven first assumption. If the mill work force was made up of largely landholding persons in the early decades, then it is likely that the proportion of this group in the work force declined for reasons I have given. However, if mill hands were initially and persistently drawn from landless groups, the changes I have indicated would not have affected the proportion of landless mill hands at all.

Most scholars today would argue that whether or not mill hands were landowners was irrelevant to the problem of instability. They would accept the view of the 1929 royal commission that for social, psychological, and religious reasons the mill hands preserved their village connections and that historically they returned to their native places after relatively short working periods in the mills. Mehta, for example, describing the extent of this kind of labor turnover before 1900, has written that "rarely could one come across a man above forty-five among mill workers in Bombay . . . until 1900. As late as 1898, it was estimated that the average working life of a cotton mill worker was between five and six years." [10]

---

families, 45.1 per cent claimed to own some land in their villages. However, the significance of this is vitiated by the fact that of that group, only 5.9 per cent had a direct connection with the property. In the remaining cases, the land was worked by relatives or others. In other words, 54.9 per cent of the total group surveyed were landless and as much as an additional 42.4 per cent may well have been effectively landless. *LIC 1946*, p. 70.

[7] This need not necessarily be true but is the likely situation.

[8] See Chap. IV, Section (6) above.

[9] I am here assuming a growth in numbers of submarginal landholders as well as of landless laborers.

[10] Mehta, *CMI*, p. 119. See also *FA 1892*, p. 5; *ITJ*, IV, No. 37, October 1893, p. 6. D. and A. Thorner, *Land and Labour in India* (London: Asia Publishing House,

These widely accepted views on labor turnover are unacceptable on purely methodological grounds. First, there are no substantial statistics that give either mill-hand age or length of service until after World War I. Second, even if there had been a high labor turnover in the industry, it is possible that it was generated by a very small segment of the work force.[11] Third, high labor turnover in individual mills, which is all that observers could identify, must not be correlated automatically with a return to the countryside. High labor turnover in individual mills is clearly compatible with low rates of departure from the industry.[12] Finally, the fact that one rarely saw a mill hand older than forty-five before 1900, apart from the untrustworthiness of visual estimates of age, is perfectly compatible with long service in the industry. In 1900 the industry was to all intents barely thirty years old. If we assume, quite reasonably, that the average age of recruits into the work force tended to be very young, the rapid rate of growth in size of the labor force would obviously have kept the average age of mill hands below forty-five.[13] In other words, the evidence that is typically used to indicate high labor turnover rates does not in fact show this. The evidence is consistent

----

1962), p. 60, describing the all-India situation before 1939, said that "The rate of turnover in the mills was very high, running to 50 per cent or even 75 per cent per year."

[11] For example, the so-called strong evidence reporting 38 per cent labor turnover in a mill between January and June 1906 is worthless because it fails to consider this point. *IFLC 1908*, II, p. 60.

[12] To the extent that observers were accurately reporting labor turnover, they were only reporting what went on in individual mills with which they had experience. It was impossible for them to identify the destination of a worker who departed. M. M. Shah, "Labour Recruitment and Turnover in the Textile Industry of Bombay Presidency" (Unpublished Ph.D. dissertation, University of Bombay, 1941), p. 120, makes the point that the "high rate of labor turnover is largely due to the shifting of employees from plant to plant and then the question of fresh blood coming from the villages does not arise." Though he gives no documentation, his point is supported more or less by a Bombay Labor Office survey in 1927–1928 where it was reported that only "about 26 per cent" of terminations at a mill occurred for "going to native place." *LG*, IX, No. 5, January 1930, p. 458. See also *LIC 1946*, p. 107.

[13] What evidence there is suggests that the average age of first employment before 1900, and probably after, was less than twenty. A crude estimate based on testimony of workers to the 1890 Factory Commission indicates that average age of first employment was less than seventeen. *FC 1890*, pp. 22–50. Calculated from evidence given by thirty-six workers during the first twelve meetings. A survey of one hundred mill hands in 1913 produced exactly the same average age of first employment. G. K. Devadhar, "A Note on Cooperation among the Mill Hands," *Report of the Ninth Indian Industrial Conference* (Amraoti, 1914), p. 159. See also, *LG*, IX, No. 5. January 1930, p. 457, where a survey of 1,348 workers suggested that 59 per cent had started work in the mills before the age of twenty.

with low turnover rates, particularly if we are concerned with rates indicating departure from the industry rather than from individual mills.[14]

Unfortunately, there are no labor turnover data as such until after 1947, beyond the end of the period with which I am concerned.[15] However, there are some fragmentary length-of-service data relating mainly to the latter part of my period.

TABLE XII

Length of Service in the Bombay Cotton-Mill Industry, 1890–1955[16]
(In per cent)

Years of Service	1890	1927-28	1940	1955
Less than 5	72.2	37.5	29.5	9.7
5–9	11.1	23.4	28.5	34.0
10–14	5.6	15.9	18.8	25.6
15 and more	11.1	23.2	23.2	30.7
Total	100.0	100.0	100.0	100.0

[14] Length of service in the industry is the crucial measure for two reasons. First, in a growing industry there was bound to be movement of workers between one enterprise and another. Second, for reasons to be suggested in subsequent chapters, industry policy tended to militate against stability of employment in a single mill. One example should suffice here. Even workers who went on authorized leave had no claim to a job when they returned. They might be rehired, or they might be forced to find a new job. If they were taken back they were frequently recorded as new hands, thus inflating the labor turnover figures. *RCL 1929*, "Report," p. 26. On the absence of formal leave procedures, see *RCL 1929*, I, Part 2, pp. 298–299, 323–325.

[15] As late as 1940 there was not even an adequate statistical basis in mill records for determining labor turnover. *TLIC 1940*, p. 362. See also *LIC 1946*, pp. 105–107.

[16] 1890 data were tabulated from evidence of mill-hand witnesses, *FC 1890*, pp. 22–50. Twenty-six cases are involved. 1927–28 data come from *LG*, IX, No. 5, January 1930, pp. 457–461, and relate to 1,348 workers in the industry. This material can also be found in *RCL 1929*, I, Part 1, p. 14. Statistics for 1940 and 1955 come from the BMOA surveys reported in R. G. Gokhale, *The Bombay Cotton Mill Worker* (Bombay: Millowners' Association, 1957), pp. 101 and 124.

All these figures should be treated with great caution. *LG, op. cit.*, p. 460, suggests that the 1927–28 figures overstate real service time in the industry by incorporating periods of nonemployment. But even when the figures were adjusted to exclude the breaks in employment, the relationship with earlier and later years was not fundamentally changed. The readjusted data showed that 46.5 per cent of the sample had been in the industry for less than five years; 24.3 per cent had been in the industry for five through nine years; 13.9 per cent for ten through fourteen years; and 15.3 per cent for fifteen years or more. The ambiguity in the industry length-of-service data cannot be eliminated in the data for other years.

There is at least one fundamental element of bias toward understatement of length of service in the industry. The surveys report on workers at all stages of their careers rather than at the end of their working lives. This can be a substantial in-

Table XII indicates that even as early as 1890 mill hands were not completely birds of passage. More than 25 per cent of the very small sample had been employed for five years or more. And there is a very clear trend of increasing length of service. Two points ought to be made. First, although the average length of service in the industry rose between 1927–28 and 1940, there was no increase in the proportion of workers with fifteen years service or more. This is not particularly significant except as an expression of employer policy. Mehta has pointed out that after 1927 the industry went through a major reorganization which brought about "a reduction of 30 to 40 per cent in the labor force in less than fifteen years." [17] A substantial percentage of this reduction seems to have been accomplished by a discharge of older workers who could not or would not adjust to the needs of reorganized working.[18] Second, there is no evidence that the sharp decline in the percentage of workers with less than five years service between 1940 and 1955 resulted from any significant change in the psychology of the mill hands. As we shall see, the sharp increase in average length of service after 1940 was the result of changes in employment, tenure, and discharge policies in the industry.

The only explicit data available on length of service in the current mill come from the end of my period. Table XIII suggests a longer length of service in the industry than in a single mill, as one would expect. The 1927–28 survey data show that of the 1,348 workers interviewed, 643, 47.7 per cent, had been employed in only one mill. More than half had worked in two or more.[19] The 1890 and 1913 data suggest the same thing, as does another survey conducted in the early 1950's.[20]

---

fluence on surveys taken during or just at the end of periods of rapid labor force expansion as was the case in 1890, 1927–1928, and 1955. This bias would also affect the mill length-of-service data in Table XIII.

[17] Mehta, *CMI*, p. 170.

[18] The great strikes of 1928, 1929, and 1934 resulted in the discharge of many workers and their displacement by new mill hands.

[19] *LG*, IX, No. 5, January 1930, p. 459.

[20] In 1890, of the twenty-six cases employed more than one year, 48 per cent had worked in more than one mill. See *FC 1890*, pp. 22–50. In 1913, one hundred operatives had worked in an average of 2.37 mills during a Bombay career averaging seventeen years. Devadhar, *op. cit.*, p. 159. For the post-World War II survey, see P. N. Prabhu, "Bombay: A Study on the Social Effects of Urbanization on Industrial Workers Migrating from Rural Areas to the City of Bombay," in *The Social Implications of Industrialization and Urbanization: Five Studies in Asia* (Calcutta: UNESCO Research Centre on the Social Implications of Industrialization in Southern Asia, 1956), p. 63. This study is most unreliable. For some methodological and substantive criticisms, see M. D. Morris, "The Myth of 'Paradise Lost': Unesco's Study of Bombay Labour," *The Economic Weekly*, Vol. IX, Nos. 26–28, July 6, 1957, pp. 857–862.

TABLE XIII

Total Years of Service in Current Mill and in Industry,
1927–28, 1940, and 1955 (In per cent) [21]

	1927-28			1940		1955	
Years of service (1)	Service in industry (2)	Service in current mill (3)	Current service in Sassoon Mill (4)	Service in industry (5)	Service in current mill (6)	Service in industry (7)	Service in current mill (8)
Less than 5	37.5	53.0	60.1	29.5	36.1	9.7	17.1
5–9	23.4	20.5	22.4	28.5	32.3	34.0	35.3
10–14	15.9	9.1	9.2	18.8	15.6	25.6	22.1
15 and more	23.2	17.4	8.3	23.2	16.0	30.7	25.5
Total	100.0	100.0	100.0	100.0	100.0	100.0	100.0

Seen in this light, the evidence makes it proper to suggest that even quite early in the industry's history there was a significant proportion of the work force which had developed a long-term attachment to employment in the cotton textile industry, if not to employment in a single mill.[22] Over time this proportion rose substantially.[23]

---

[21] Columns (2), (3), and (4) come from *RCL 1929*, I, Part I, pp. 14 and 484. Columns (2) and (3) are based on a sample of 1,348 cases drawn from the entire industry. Column (4) is based on 1,725 cases from a special survey conducted by the Meyer Sasson Mill. The 1940 and 1955 data come from Gokhale, *op. cit.*, pp. 98, 101, 123, and 124.

The "service in industry data," columns (2), (5) and (7), are the same as appear in Table XII.

[22] Table XIII also shows a rising length of service in individual mills after 1927–28. As in the case of length of service in the industry, later evidence will suggest that the changing pattern was not the consequence of changed work-force psychology but a function of different employer policies. R. C. James, "Labor and Technical Change" (Unpublished Ph.D. dissertation, Cornell University, 1957), p. 242, points out that at least the 1940 and 1955 Bombay data compare very favorably with experience in the United States.

[23] The distinction between length of service in individual mills and in the industry should clarify the apparent contradiction between my interpretation and the widespread view that labor turnover was very high. Employers were reporting on the basis of experience in their own mills and were drawing the conclusion that workers who quit a mill were necessarily quitting the industry. This was, of course, an unwarranted assumption, but in the absence of industry-wide service records there was no way for employers to discover the error of this assumption. The phenomenon of increasing attachment to the industry was also hidden by the rapid expansion of employment before 1922. R. C. James, "Labor Mobility, Unemployment, and Economic Change: An Indian Case," *Journal of Political Economy*, LXVII, No. 6, December 1959, p. 546, has unfortunately perpetuated the notion that "the worker

This generalization can be supported in another way. It will be re-called that I have suggested that a growing proportion of mill hands seem to have claimed Bombay as their birthplace from 1911 on. The evidence given by mill hands to the 1890 factory commission shows that apart from those born in Bombay, another 25 per cent never returned to their native places.[24] If this feature of permanent migration is added to the rising percentage of Bombay-born mill hands shown in the 1911 to 1931 censuses, it indicates an even higher proportion of workers attached to the industry than I have dared suggest.[25]

---

went to a specific job based on a specific contact; when he lost it, he went home." On the whole, this seems not to have been the case.

[24] *FC 1890*, pp. 22–50.

[25] There has been a tendency among many observers to imply that only the Bombay-born part of the city's population contributed to the permanent labor force. All others were viewed as purely temporary residents in the urban setting. See, for example, *IDC 1922*, p. 1. Such a notion ignored the almost inevitable necessity of a city like Bombay to grow by immigration. The mere fact that a large proportion of the population had been born outside the city cannot be used as automatic proof of labor force instability. See M. D. Morris, "The Labor Market in India," in *Labor Commitment and Social Change in Developing areas*, edited by Moore and A. S. Feldman, pp. 178–179. One can find a slight modification of the traditional interpretation in *RCL 1929*, "Report," pp. 11–20. A more explicit revision is *LIC 1946*, pp. 69–71. However, even in these two sources the implication is that the development of an effectively permanent immigration of labor into Bombay was a post-World War I phenomenon. There is certainly no satisfactory basis for such an idea. Moreover, it runs counter to some evidence as, for example, the apparently permanent migration of certain Muslim weaving groups into the city. See *FA 1897*, p. 9; and A. R. Burnett-Hurst, *Labour and Housing in Bombay* (London: P. S. King and Son, 1925), pp. 10–13.

Moreover, even within the group that did not establish a permanent connection with the city there seem to have been many who indicated a fairly persistent attachment to the mills. There is some very sketchy evidence that a large proportion of the mill hands who returned permanently to their villages were replaced in the mills by other members of their own families. In other words, apart from the increasing proportion of urban-based mill proletarians there was also, possibly, an increasing proportion of village-based mill families. The system of jobber-hiring used by the mills tended to encourage this. *ITJ*, VI, No. 72, September 1896, p. 285; *RCL 1929*, "Report," pp. 12–13, and *LG*, IX, No. 7, March 1930, p. 720.

In my discussion I have assumed, perhaps illegitimately, that workers did not normally drift into other sectors of the Bombay economy. In the absence of other major year-round industries, the cotton mills probably offered the best opportunities for reasonably stable employment and income. There were complaints of inter-industry migration, although they seem to have been minor except during 1909 to 1911. See, for example, *ITJ*, XX, No. 237, June 1910, p. 321, and *ITJ*, XXI, No. 250, July 1911, pp. 350–351. This was a period when many mills were closed, and workers sought alternative employments. However, it is quite possible that the growth of general economic activity in the city during the century with which I am concerned may have encouraged much more interindustry labor mobility than I

(2)

Together with a short industrial work career, the most widely described and persistently criticized characteristic of the mill workers was
the apparently uncontrollable propensity to work irregularly.[26] From
1875, when records begin to be plentiful, absenteeism is the issue about
which employers complained most bitterly. Statistical detail is not available until quite late, but in 1889 an official estimated that the typical
mill hand worked an average of about three hundred days of the three
hundred forty-one on which the mills were open, an average absenteeism
rate of about 12 per cent.[27] The general run of comment in the decades
before World War I suggested an average daily absenteeism of 8 to 15
per cent.[28] Beginning in 1922 the Bombay Labor Office collected absenteeism data. These yield averages of about the same magnitudes as described by employers for the pre-World War I period.

have been able to identify. Moreover, it is clear that the mills used a great deal of
temporary labor to meet more than ordinary requirements. See *IFLC 1908*, I, p. 37.
Such a pattern of labor utilization certainly accounted for much of the work force
that was described as migratory. This situation was reinforced by the lack of any
effective distinction in the mills between purely temporary workers and those with
permanent status until the end of my period. Aspects of this problem will be considered, in later chapters. What is important, however, is the fact that once the
mills did establish a category of permanent workers who could not be discharged
arbitrarily, mill-hand stability became quite apparent. See James, "Labor and Technical Change," pp. 228 ff. In fact, James went so far as to refer to the "immobility
of the permanent worker," *op. cit.*, p. 235. This post-World War II change might
be attributable to some inexplicable transformation in the psychology or social
structure of the work force, but it is much more likely that the altered situation resulted from revised employment policies.
    [26] Writing of the post-World War II decade, Myers recognized that labor turnover
in the Bombay mills was particularly low, when compared to the separation rate in
American cotton textile mills. But he argued that absenteeism was very much higher
and in this sense the Indian worker is only "partially committed" to industrial employment. Myers, *op. cit.*, pp. 43–48.
    [27] East India (Factories Act), *Return to an address of the House of Commons, 15
April 1889*, p. 67.
    [28] The annual reports of the BMOA and the issues of *ITJ* have frequent references.
See also *IFLC 1908*, II, *passim*. A. S. Pearse, *Indian Cotton* (Manchester: International Federation of Master Cotton Spinners and Manufacturers Association, 1915),
pp. 223–225, describes one mill with an absenteeism rate of 23.8 per cent in October
1909 and 27.0 per cent in November 1909. This seems to have been exceptional. (In
fact, this was a period of very bad economic conditions and many mills were working
only part-time. I suspect that some of the methods of computation, to be discussed
below, explain this high figure.) Mehta, *CMI*, p. 118, claims that pre-World War I
daily absenteeism may have averaged as much as 50 per cent. He offers no evidence
of this. I have never encountered any such figure elsewhere and it must be dismissed
as wholly unlikely.

TABLE XIV
Annual Average Daily Absenteeism, 1922–1947 [29]

Year	Rate	Year	Rate	Year	Rate
1922	14.8	1931	9.3	1940	9.1
1923	15.1	1932	9.1	1941	9.6
1924	13.4	1933	9.2	1942	14.0
1925	12.2	1934	8.4	1943	10.8
1926	11.9	1935	7.9	1944	11.4
1927	8.5	1936	7.2	1945	11.4
1928	8.7	1937	7.6	1946	14.2
1929	9.8	1938	8.3	1947	14.4
1930	9.3	1939	10.5		

But the figures, which suggest a high (but not outrageous) rate of absenteeism, need much more critical examination than scholars have tended to give them. Some rather startling possibilities emerge after the methods of collection and calculation have been subjected to even a cursory scrutiny.

When the Bombay Labor Office started collecting absenteeism data it stated that "the number of mills reporting . . . varied from month to month, but, in general, [the average] represents reports from an overwhelming majority of the mills.[30] However, it is not likely that the weakness of coverage could be at the root of major difficulties. The serious problems stem from the methods of computation of the absenteeism rate in the individual mills.

The important question to ask is what were the mills reporting. The answer is that we don't know. During the entire period between 1922 and 1947 no one, least of all the Bombay Labor Office, could tell what the individual mills used as a base employment figure or what they included in absenteeism to measure against that base.[31]

---

[29] From *LG* for various years.

[30] See any of the early issues of *LG*.

[31] The Labor Office form was ambiguous and mills interpreted its demands as they saw fit. On the chaotic state of absenteeism data, see *ITB 1927*, II, pp. 223–224 and 242–243; *ibid.*, III, pp. 61–63. In 1929 the Government of Bombay commented that the Labor Office absenteeism data "cannot be considered to have reached a high degree of accuracy. . . ." *RCL 1929*, I, Part 1, p. 153. Even in the late 1930's, after the BMOA had started making serious efforts to improve the situation, differences in record keeping and reporting, not only among mills but in departments of the same mill, were enormous. Shah, *op. cit.*, pp. 10–12 and *passim*. After 1946 the combined efforts of the Labor Office and the BMOA resulted in improved reporting but the absenteeism data still did not distinguish between authorized and unauthorized absences or eliminate other critical ambiguities. Myers, *op. cit.*, p. 46; and Government of India, Ministry of Commerce and Industry, *Report of the Working Party*

How was the average daily labor requirement determined? Though not all mills used the same method, a typical one based the rate on the standard muster roll (SMR). A mill would estimate the maximum complement of workers needed to keep each machine and each department at full operation. This SMR provided the base against which abseentism was measured. But the actual number of workers needed daily was almost always a figure substantially below that given in the SMR. Thus the calculation of absenteeism which used the SMR as a base was inevitably destined to inflate the absenteeism rate.[32] Some mills seem to have added an allowance for substitute labor in the establishment of their SMR figures, which further inflated the base from which calculations were made. This sometimes added as much as 10 per cent to the SMR total.[33]

Not all mills calculated their absenteeism rate by relating SMR to average daily employment, but whatever the method it is generally clear that some serious problems emerge from what all the mills classified as absentees. Myers has said that the absenteeism rate is a manifestation by the Bombay worker of his "partially committed view of industrial employment. . . ."[34] But the critical issue here is that if we are to use absenteeism as a measure of indiscipline or noncommitment we must be certain that what is called absenteeism should in fact be identified with the worker's willful nonattendance at work. Many of the categories

---

for the Cotton Textile Industry (Delhi: Manager of Publications, 1953), pp. 222–223. One important point to keep in mind is that if the absenteeism data were so hopeless after World War I, they certainly can have been no better before then.

[32] *ITB 1927*, II, p. 282; *ITB 1927*, III, p. 61. Daily employment needs would typically be lower than the SMR figure for a number of reasons. There was typically some imbalance of equipment between one department and another. Even if by SMR standards full employment existed in some departments there could well be underutilized capacity in others. In addition, some equipment was always under repair. Moreover, changing market demand could operate to keep some equipment out of production. Historically, the main departments in which the SMR tended to be significantly in excess of normal daily employment requirements were winding and reeling, dyeing, bleaching, calendering, and finishing. Shah, *op. cit.*, p. 133. One example of the possible degree of distortion can be given. In 1907 A. K. Leslie reported that the nominal number of hands (the SMR) in his eight mills was 9,734, but he spoke of giving employment during a recent six-month period to an average of 5,639, or only 58 per cent of the SMR he made reference to. And this was a period of strong economic activity. *IFLC 1908*, II, pp. 58 and 60.

[33] *ITJ*, XIV, No. 159, December 1903, p. 81; *ITJ* XIV, No. 164, May 1904, pp. 235–236; *ITB 1927*, I, p. 135; *ITB 1927*, II, pp. 223–224, 282 and pp. 342; and *ITB 1927*, III, p. 61. See also Government of India, Ministry of Commerce, *op. cit.*, pp. 222–223.

[34] Myers, *op. cit.*, p. 45.

of nonattendance included by the mills violated this rule and thus tended to inflate the rate of absenteeism as a measure of lack of commitment.

First, the mills made no distinction between authorized and unauthorized leaves, nor did they identify absence by cause. This means that the absenteeism rate cannot be used as a satisfactory measure of willful absenteeism.[35] Second, mills often included as absentees workers they had laid off because of the state of the market.[36] It is probable, but not certain, that strikers were often reported as absentees. A final factor affecting the absenteeism rate stemmed from the fact that mills tended to carry on their rosters as absentees workers who had quit and had long since been replaced by others.[37]

All these factors tended to inflate the absenteeism figures, but another feature tended to work in the opposite direction. Weavers when absent were required to provide their own substitutes. Only when they did not were they listed as absentees.[38] Although it is as impossible to measure the effect of this as it is to estimate the influence of the other factors I have mentioned, it is my impression that the tendency toward overstatement of absenteeism definitely predominated. There is only one test of this judgment, but it seems conclusive. In July 1926 the Bombay Labor Office did a special study of nineteen mills and the survey attempted to classify absenteeism more carefully than was normal practice in the industry. This study produced an absenteeism rate of 8.26 per cent for the month. At the same time, the regular monthly survey yielded an absenteeism rate of 10.38 per cent, some 25 per cent higher.[39]

---

[35] *RCL 1929*, "Report," p. 26; Shah, *op. cit.*, p. 151; Myers, *op. cit.*, p. 46. A substantial part of the problem of definition arose out of the fact that until the late 1930's there was no provision in the industry for distinguishing permanent from temporary workers. Shah, working with the basic mill records at the end of the 1930's, couldn't sort this problem out. Shah, *op. cit.*, pp. 11–12 *passim*.

[36] There are numerous suggestions of this. See *RCL 1929*, I, Part 2, p. 311; *ITB 1927*, III, p. 62; and *LIC 1946*, p. 101.

[37] Shah, *op. cit.*, p. 11, says that as late as the 1930's there were mills where the names of departed workers were not dropped from the roster until an "auspicious" day, at which time all were canceled at once. Myers, *op. cit.*, pp. 47–48, pointed out that carrying long-absent workers on rosters may have inflated absenteeism rates but reduced labor turnover rates by an equivalent amount. Though correct, this point does not affect my discussion of labor turnover which is based on estimates of length of service.

[38] *ITB 1927*, III, p. 67.

[39] *BLO 1926*. Though the survey did not distinguish between authorized and unauthorized absences nor classify absence by cause, it did exclude certain of the more inflationary elements. See also *ITB 1927*, I, p. 134; *ITB 1927*, II, p. 61; *ITB 1927*, III, pp. 63–85; and *RCL 1929*, I, Part 1, 305–306. See, also, the remarks in *LIC 1946*, p. 101.

It is likely, therefore, that "true" absenteeism — i.e., correcting for these exaggerations — was well below the figures shown in Table XIV. This conclusion finds some support in the evidence for the decade after 1947. Between 1947 and 1957 average daily absenteeism among permanent mill hands dropped by more than 50 per cent, from 14.4 to 7.1 per cent.[40]

Myers, commenting on this post-1947 decline, has written: "Possibly more effective managerial policies and greater attachment to the job account for this decline; or changes in the method of data collection may explain it." [41] There is no question that part of the decline is attributable to improved reporting, and this part of the reduction must, of course, also be applicable to the earlier years with which I am concerned.[42] In other words, that part of the reduction in absenteeism rates attributable to improved reporting must be carried back to 1922 when the official series began. Moreover, we can assume that all estimates of absenteeism before this date can also be reduced because they too were inflated by the same factors that affected the official series.[43]

It is impossible to estimate the amount by which the published absenteeism rates should be reduced to arrive at a somewhat more accurate figure. However, my feeling is that on the average the corrected rate was probably always below 10 per cent, and I would suggest that this was not a very high figure, especially when we consider that illness alone probably contributed substantially to the total.[44]

To the extent that the remarkable decline in absenteeism after 1947 was not a result of improved reporting but was attributable to "more effective managerial policies," as Myers has said, it suggests a point very relevant for my period. A large part of absenteeism (and labor turnover as well) was more likely a consequence of employer policy than of worker psychology and social attachments. The following chapters are concerned with that possibility.

---

[40] *LG* for the period.

[41] Myers, *op.cit.*, pp. 45–46.

[42] The establishment of a defined class of permanent workers, combined after 1946 with a more precise definition by the Labor Office of what was to be reported, were two contributing factors.

[43] The fact that pre-World War I estimates were roughly of the same order of magnitude as the rates shown in the official series published from 1922 suggests to me that the same errors of inflation were present and must be allowed for.

[44] Apart from the statutory weekly day off, the mills after 1892 recognized a maximum of only eight other authorized holidays each year. *ITB 1927*, II, p. 356; *RCL 1929*, I, Part 2, p. 328. There were no provisions for sick leave or annual holidays.

(3)

Before I turn to these matters, I want to consider one other feature of absenteeism — the purported seasonal pattern. The seasonal cycle has always been attributed to the rural connections maintained by the mill hands. The best description of this seasonal return to the countryside was given to the 1929 royal commission.

The workers in Bombay City are in close contact with the villages from which they come. Those hailing from the neighboring districts of the city, who either own landed property or whose families have rented land, go to their villages every year before the setting in of the monsoon [early June] and return soon after the rains are over [early October]. In the months of April and May, therefore, there is a regular exodus, mostly to the Konkan. Workers who do not own lands or have not rented fields for cultivation usually go once a year either for the Shimga holidays [March] or during the Divali holidays [October or early November]. Workers who come from the Ghats generally go to their native places during the Navratri holidays [September to October]. Those coming from distant parts of the country, such as northern India and the United Provinces, go once in two or three years and stay at their native places for three to four months at a time.[45]

The statement suggests that absenteeism due to return to the villages was particularly great during the period March through October. In the absence of solid data, very little can be said, but it is useful to introduce a cautionary note which may prevent too easy acceptance of this widely held but only very weakly supported notion.[46] Actually, the monthly absenteeism statistics reported by the Bombay Labor Office from 1922 through 1947 show very little of the cyclical tendency one would antici- pate from the verbal descriptions.[47] Nor do the output data for the

---

[45] *RCL 1929*, I, Part 1, p. 7. Descriptions of similar sorts can be found in many places. See *Monthly Miscellany of Western India*, pp. 239–240; S. M. Edwardes, *The Gazetteer of Bombay City and Island* (3 vols., Bombay: The Times Press, 1909), I, pp. 214 and 322–323; and *IFLC 1908*, I, pp. 18–19.

[46] There was, for example, considerable disagreement on the exact period of peak absenteeism due to this cause. This can be seen from the testimony of two official BMOA witnesses to the Indian Tariff Board. Mr. Wadia said that absenteetism was at its highest in mid-May, June, and July. Mr. Mody claimed that July was one of the best (i.e., lowest) months for absenteeism and that February and March were very bad. *ITB 1927*, II, pp. 232 and 343. Actually, there is a serious question whether the phenomenon can be treated as absenteeism. To the extent that workers went away for such long periods, they had no assurance that their jobs would be waiting on their return. *ITB 1927*, II, p. 233.

[47] I have experimented with various statistical tests, none of which suggested any significant degree of seasonality in the absenteeism data. Not only are the data un-

period 1902 to 1928 show fluctuations compatible with the reports of widespread seasonal migration.[48]

It is possible, of course, that the pattern was historically more definite than the monthly absenteeism or output data show. Even here the evidence is not convincing. The traditional interpertation assumes that all workers except the small percentage from northern India made an annual trek to the countryside. But we have some suggestions that this was not the case. The mill-hand testimony to the factory commission of 1890 suggested that a very substantial proportion of the witnesses did not make the annual trek.[49] The 1913 survey of one hundred mill hands, all purporting to hail from the Konkan and Deccan districts of the Presidency, showed that only 35 per cent returned to the villages each year.[50] In 1929 the Manchester Mill reported that 22 per cent of its work force claimed not to have gone on this annual hegira.[51] And in the early 1940's we have a statement that of 679 working-class families surveyed, 38.7 per cent had not visited their village homes the previous year.[52]

Apart from these scattered bits of evidence which suggest that the annual migration was not the ubiquitous phenomenon that has been implied, there is another striking feature of the migration to and from Bombay that has been neglected. In response to a question raised by one of

---

satisfactory in general, but many years were affected by serious strikes. These features have to be considered before drawing any definite conclusions. However, the point is supported by B. Madhava and K. V. Krishna Sastry, "A Further Study of Statistics of 'Absenteeism' in Indian Labour," *Sankhya*, V, Part 2, 1941, pp. 215–222.

[48] The Statistical Department, Government of India, *Statistics of Cotton Spinning and Weaving in the Indian Mills*, published monthly data on "production" of yarn and cloth in the Bombay mills. If seasonal shortages of labor of the type described did in fact occur, I would expect that this would have shown up in a distinctive pattern in the output data. Analysis of variance applied both to cloth and yarn output do not suggest this at all. Once again, the data are defective. Although referred to as production data, they were really sales figures. See *ITB 1927*, II, p. 301. This means that actual production behavior may possibly have been hidden by changes in the inventory position. Apart from this ambiguity, there is another complication. Depending on the state of the market for the two products, composite mills (the typical type in Bombay) could consume the bulk of their yarn in the production of cloth or, if the market for cloth was weak, they could concentrate their sales on the yarn side. As a result, fluctuations in output of one or the other product would not be decisive.

[49] *FC 1890*, pp. 22–50. This testimony is difficult to quantify. Of thirty-six witnesses, thirty-one had been born outside of Bombay. Of these, fifteen either had never returned to their native village or returned only at long and irregular intervals.

[50] Devadhar, *op.cit.*, p. 159.

[51] *RCL 1929*, I, Part 1, p. 485.

[52] *LIC 1946*, p. 170.

the members of the Royal Commission on Indian Labor, the Bombay Labor Office undertook to collect data on the "yearly ebb and flow of population into Bombay [by sea] from the Kolaba and Ratnagiri districts and Janjira State. . . ." [53] The results, derived for 1926 to 1929, did show that May was the month during which the exodus reached its peak, as we might expect. But what is surprising is that there was also a very great influx of workers into Bombay during the pre-monsoon period. Even the Labor Office was puzzled enough to ask: ". . . if the industrial population . . . is drawn from the agricultural population which is required to be at home during the monsoon months, [why should there] be so large a flow of workers into Bombay in the two months preceding the monsoon?" [54] Its only explanation was that possibly

this may be due to the interchange of members of the same family whereby one who has had to leave his home in order to relieve the pressure on the family is replaced after a certain period of time by another member of the same family who works in Bombay for some time and then comes back. If this were not the case, there would be an acute shortage of labor in Bombay City during the monsoon months, but there are no signs of any such shortage and the mills and other industrial concerns have no difficulty in getting all the labor they require.[55]

Although there are serious deficiencies in this study, what it suggests about the very high rate of influx into Bombay at the same time that there was a very high rate of outflow seems borne out by a few casual references in earlier decades.[56]

---

[53] *LG*, IX, No. 7, March 1930, p. 718. The report of findings can be found *ibid.*, pp. 718–726.

[54] *Ibid.*, p. 720

[55] *Loc.cit.* The traditional explanation cannot be salvaged by arguing that the simultaneity of influx and outgo reflected movements to different regions with different peaks of agricultural labor requirements. The passenger movements related to a single agricultural region.

[56] The data cover a four-year period only, and during two of these there were great general strikes which certainly affected both inflow and outflow of people. A more important weakness is that middle-class traffic was not distinguished from working-class movements. Normally, middle-class travelers represented about a quarter of the traffic, but "on occasions of festivals, etc., this percentage is even greater." *Ibid.*, p. 719. It is quite possible, therefore, that the seasonal exodus from Bombay could well have been largely a middle-class phenomenon. This is significant in that the description of seasonal absenteeism and the movement to the countryside seems, in fact, to have been derived from the behavior of the population at large rather than of the working-class part alone. It is incorrect to take this all-city pattern and apply it to the cotton textile industry work force.

But to the extent that there was clearly some seasonal pattern of working-class migration, it must be recognized that the city attracted a great deal of casual labor

Apart from the fact that a substantial part of the labor force was probably not involved in the seasonal absenteeism cycle, at least in the terms traditionally described, it is important to note that the season of high absenteeism was also the period of greatest incidence of epidemic illness in the city — smallpox, cholera, malaria, and (after 1896) plague. Although there are no statistics, Maloney, who spent a good deal of time working on related topics, pointed out in the early 1920's that "the sickness rate among mill hands in Bombay is at its lowest in February, and then gradually rises until October, except for a small temporary fall in June corresponding with the advent of the monsoon. From October there is a rapid fall." [57]

In other words, seasonal fluctuations in absenteeism were certainly associated, at least in part, with seasonal variations in the incidence of disease. Not all seasonal variations in absenteeism can be associated with the persistence of the rural link.[58]

One added cause of fluctuations in absenteeism which had nothing to do with the rural connection may be identified. It rests on the fact that millowners seem to have included laid-off workers in their calculations of the absenteeism rate and that there were apparently seasonal fluctuations in demand for textile products. Mehta claims that there are seasonal peaks in market demand, with March to May and October to December being high demand periods and July and August the months of lowest demand.[59] If this was the historical pattern, it is quite possible that higher absenteeism rates in July and August were, in fact, merely a reflection of lay-offs in the industry.

---

which sought temporary employment during the slack season in the countryside. The cotton mills employed a great deal of temporary labor to meet peak period demand. *IFLC 1908*, I, p. 37. Apparently, one of these peak periods occurred in the spring. Mehta, *ICTI*, p. 165. This was also a period of great activity in construction and shipping. Edwardes, *op.cit.*, pp. 322–323. The return to the countryside has to be linked to the onset of the monsoon, when a great deal of activity in Bombay, notably in construction and shipping but also possibly in cotton textiles, declined sharply or ceased altogether. In other words, the migration pattern seems to have reflected to a very large degree the demand for labor.

There clearly is need for a careful study of seasonal population migration, linked to the cycles of general economic activity in Bombay.

[57] Quoted in Burnett-Hurst, *op.cit.*, p. 60.

[58] Employers had no statistics or other basis for concluding that all seasonal absenteeism was attributable to migration to the countryside. Occasionally mill officials did recognize that sickness was a factor. See, for example, *ITJ*, XV, No. 179, August 1905, p. 342.

[59] Mehta, *ICTI*, p. 165.

CHAPTER VI

Hours of Work

There was no artificial illumination in the Bombay mills until the end of the nineteenth century, and in its absence work was limited to the daylight hours. Dawn-to-dusk working began in the earliest mills and was universally imitated.[1] Although each mill worked its own schedule of hours, the typical mill worked thirteen to fourteen hours during the summer months and between ten and a quarter and twelve hours in the winter.[2] One witness explained the variation in hours worked by the different mills: "There are no standard hours of labor; each mill works as many hours as daylight allows them to; the number of hours varies with variations in lighting and processes in different mills; the new mills, long, high, and narrow, with nearly half of their walls fitted with windows, make much better time than the old mills do." [3]

The opening and closing of individual mills also tended to vary even during the same season. For example, the working hours of the Anglo-Indian Mill were timed by the factory inspector. He reported that in January 1884 the workday varied from eleven hours and fifteen minutes to eleven hours and fifty minutes; in June 1884 it fluctuated between thirteen hours and eighteen minutes and thirteen hours and fifty minutes.[4] The indefiniteness of the time at which a mill started to work caused difficulties.

The use of the steam whistle being prohibited by the municipality, and there being no public clock in the quarter of the town occupied by operatives, they are unable to tell the time, or to guess how long it is from daylight. In this uncertainty, and to avoid being late, they often find themselves arriving at the mill long before it begins work. These operatives who are too early may . . . be found lying about the approaches to the mill sleeping.[5]

---

[1] One source suggested that the first mills worked only eight or ten hours a day, but it seems that the Oriental Mill, which went into operation in 1858, initiated the principle of dawn-to-dusk working and it was quickly imitated. *ITJ*, X, No. 113, February 1900, p. 135; *ITJ*, XVII, No. 196, January 1907, pp. 106–107.

[2] Evidence for this and other aspects of hours of work can be found in *FC 1875*, *FC 1885* and *FC 1890*.

[3] Mr. Drewet, *RCL 1892*, p. 132.

[4] Mr. Jones, *FC 1885*, p. 32. These working times excluded the midday interval.

[5] *FC 1890*, p. 13. There is a similar description by W. O. Meade King, "The Indian Factories Act, 1881, with the Alterations therein Proposed," Memorandum

The time schedule during the day was also not fixed. Most mills claimed to stop work for half an hour during the middle of the day. Actually, if the typical mill stopped work at all during the day, it did so for no more than fifteen or twenty minutes. And there was no fixed time for the break to occur.[6] The time of closing was equally uncertain. Workers had no time pieces and there were no clocks in the mills. The worker knew that his day had ended only when the machinery began to slow down. As one worker plaintively commented, "Some mills whistle to close at one time and some mills whistle at another time." [7]

The hours for the majority of women, those working in the winding and reeling departments, were shorter than those worked by men. Women seem to have come in about an hour later and left an hour earlier, but each mill had different arrangements. The main feature, again, was the irregularity of hours.[8]

Market conditions and equipment permitting, the mills worked steadily through the year, averaging about eighty hours per week in the winter and as many as ninety-eight during the summer. Though one or two closed on alternate Sundays, the great majority had no regular days of closing. Most seem to have stopped for a few of the more important Hindu holidays but rarely did a mill stop work for more than thirty days during the year.[9] These were not full holidays for the operatives. On days when mills were not working, the mill hands still had to turn up and clean their machines, a task that could take as much as half a day and for which they were not paid.[10] Some mill managers favored a fixed

to the Secretary to Government, 24 June 1882, p. 2. In 1884, 5,500 workers signed a petition which complained about "the uncertainty at present prevailing in regard to the hour for starting work, . . . the source of great inconvenience to the workmen." *FC 1885*, p. 231. See also *IFLC 1908*, II, pp. 52 and 85.

[6] *FC 1885, passim.* Many workers claimed that the machines were not stopped at all during the day. *FC 1890, passim.*

[7] Genoo Babajee, *FC 1885*, p. 100. For a vivid description of the uncertainty of the work schedule during the day at the typical mill, see *ITJ*, I, No. 4, January 1891, pp. 59–60.

[8] These departments used hand equipment and the women were paid on a piecework basis. There was no special incentive to keep the women working especially long hours. The typical system seems to have been to keep large numbers of women on the roster, give each woman a fixed amount of work to do, leaving her free to depart when her stint was completed.

[9] John Robertson's report, *BMOA 1875 and 1875–76*, p. 75; *BMOA 1876*, pp. 106 ff, particularly pp. 116–117; *FC 1875 and FC 1885, passim;* and East India (Factories Act), *Return to an Address of the House of Commons, 15 April 1889*, pp. 64 and 66.

[10] John Robertson's report, *loc. cit.*; and *FC 1890, passim.* Employees were also required to turn up and clean their machines, always without pay, when equipment

day of rest each week, but the owners generally opposed this although they recognized that workers were taking some time off in the form of unauthorized absences.[11]

These were the conditions until the passage of the Factories Act of 1891. Apart from placing some added restrictions on child labor and limiting the workday of women to eleven hours, the new law imposed two statutory requirements which affected the work week. Although the daily hours of work of adult males remained unregulated, the act did require that there be a full half-hour shutdown of work at midday and that all employees be given a Sunday holiday unless some other holiday occurred during the week. Regulations issued in Bombay under the Act's authority made one additional modification. Workers were not to be required to come to the mills to clean their machines on holidays. Instead, once a fortnight, on the day preceding the statutory day off, the mills were to stop their operations at 4:00 P.M. and the workers would clean the machines until dusk without pay.[12]

Depressed conditions after 1890 produced for the first time some serious concern about the industry's long-term profitability. When the mills began working fewer days a week the chairman and some of the members of the Millowners' Association proposed that the mills work shorter hours rather than fewer days each week as a way of reducing the number of workers required and getting greater production at lower cost.[13] But none of the mills, not even those controlled by the persons making the proposal, limited its hours or attempted to standardize them.

At the same time a new development was laying the ground for an even greater diversity of hours in the industry. A few mills had installed electric lights in the 1880's, and in the early 1890's the movement began to gather momentum.[14] In 1896 the Collector of Bombay complained that

---

breakdowns kept the factories closed. *FC 1885, passim.* N. M. Lokhunday and Mr. Campbell, *RCL 1892*, pp. 169 and 174. See also, Mr. Cocker's testimony, *Bombay and Lancashire Cotton Spinning Inquiry, 1888*, pp. 87–88, that in 1887 his mill stopped only eighteen days and that on at least eight of those days the workers came in to clean their machines without pay.

[11] *FC 1885, passim.*

[12] BMOA statement, *RCL 1892*, p. 132. The weekly holiday provision was easily enforced. But the provisions for the midday break and the hours of work for women and children seem to have been frequently ignored. See *FA Reports* for 1892 and after; and various evidence in *FC 1906* and *IFLC 1908*, I and II.

[13] The argument was that the long workday required extra workers to spell the mill hands during informal breaks. A shorter and more regular schedule would permit the establishment of more systematic discipline. See the chairman's statement and the supporting comment by Mr. Wadia, *BMOA 1893*, pp. 133 and 136.

[14] Technical problems with electric generators seem to have been mainly responsible for the delayed acceptance of electric lighting.

seven or eight mills were engaging in night work. The Millowners' Association responded that one mill was using electric light merely to achieve a standard year-round twelve-hour workday. The others were working overtime only in the carding departments "because their carding machinery is not sufficient to keep the rest of their mills in full work. . . ." The Association concluded that "night labor, properly so-called, will meet with no sympathy at the hands of this Association." [15]

The Collector was unimpressed, fearing that "once a commencement is made by a few mills, others are likely to rapidly follow the lead and in self-defense resort to night labor." [16] Widespread night work did not become an immediate reality because of plague-induced disruption of the industry in 1897 and 1898 and the unfavorable economic conditions which lasted to the beginning of the century.[17] But by 1904 a large number of mills were working longer hours with the assistance of electric lighting. A few worked double shifts but the great majority extended the workday.[18] By August 1905 thirty-two of the seventy-nine mills were working from 5:00 A.M. to 8:00 P.M., with only the half-hour statutory midday break. Others were following this pattern as quickly as electric generators could be installed. A few employers, dismayed by the development, attempted in 1904 and again in 1905 to get the Association membership to agree to establish a fixed twelve-hour workday. A resolution was passed but it had no effect. Then Lovat Frazer, editor of the *Times of India*, started a campaign against the long hours and the general violations of the factory act. Despite Frazer's exposures, taken up by other papers, the millowners remained unmoved. The fifteen-hour day continued.

It is difficult to establish precisely what did happen, but there is no question that the labor market was badly disrupted. About half or more of the mills were working the fifteen-hour day; the others, unable to get electrical equipment, were forced to work the traditional dawn-to-dusk schedule. Some of the short-hour mills, losing hands to mills working longer hours where earnings were greater, were forced to shift to a system of daily payment to attract enough labor. At the same time, mills

---

[15] *BMOA 1896*, pp. 113–114. The issue of night work seems first to have been raised by the Collector in 1892. *BMOA 1908*, p. viii.

[16] *BMOA 1896*, p. 114. For detailed evidence on the extension of hours, see BMOA annual reports for 1903 to 1908; *ITJ* issues for 1905 and 1906; *IFLC 1908*, I and II; L. Frazer, *India Under Curzon and After* (London: W. Heinemann, 1911), pp. 131–136; and *FC 1906*.

[17] At the beginning of 1899 at least a dozen mills were working from daybreak to 8:00 P.M., *ITJ*, IX, No. 101, February 1899, p. 121.

[18] Mill reluctance to work double shifts seems to have been associated with the high cost of added supervision.

working long hours seem to have lost some workers who disliked the fifteen-hour day. The disorderly situation finally culminated in October 1905 in riots. Mobs of operatives roamed from one late-working mill to another, calling out workers, throwing rocks, breaking windows and, in one case, destroying the attendance sheets and other records kept by the timekeeper.[19]

These outbreaks occurred at an embarrassing time. The future King-Emperor and his consort were on their way to India, and it was feared that the continuation of long-hour working might produce working class riots while the Prince of Wales was visiting Bombay. The millowners found it politic to curtail night working temporarily. But as soon as the royal pair retired from the scene the same pattern of long *versus* short working hours was resurrected and continued throughout 1906. Early in 1907 the boom came to an end. Mills contemplated short-time working which meant fewer days but the same long hours. Faced with growing public hostility and the threat of government intervention, the governing committee of the BMOA made frantic but futile efforts to get millowners to coöperate in the restriction of hours.

The individualistic behavior of the employers clearly emerges during this period. Although the mere extension of the hours of work seems to have caused some of the trouble with the labor force, the truly disruptive element was the absence of any standardized working pattern among the mills. It not only resulted in a steady flow of mill hands from mill to mill, in search of the longer or shorter hours and equivalent income that suited each individual, but it also produced riots in the streets.[20]

The situation remained disorderly until the passage of the revised factory act in 1911 when the working hours of men were statutorily regulated. No man could be employed for more than twelve hours in any one day; neither could he start work before 5:30 A.M. nor finish after 7:00 P.M. unless the mill used a system of shifts approved by the factory inspector. There also had to be a half-hour work break after six hours of work. The weekly holiday provision was tightened to prevent continuation of the practice of requiring hands to clean machine on holidays. Regulations affecting women and children were stiffened. Not only did

[19] See *ITJ* issues for July–October 1905; Frazer, *op.cit.*, pp. 131–136; *BMOA 1905*, pp. vii–xv.

[20] Of twenty mills whose working hours were ascertained in 1908, one worked round the clock with two shifts; eight had fixed hours of work the year round but they varied among themselves from thirteen to fourteen hours, exclusive of the midday break; the remaining eleven, some with electric lights, had seasonally varying workdays. *IFLC 1908*, I, p. 82.

the law establish a fairly rigid framework within which the mills were forced to work, but it also created a system of enforcement which finally wiped out the wholesale evasions characteristic of the previous statute. From this time in the history of the Bombay mills variations in the length of the working day ceased to be a significant cause of unrest and instability. The state had intervened to bring order where the employers had been unwilling or unable to do so.[21]

The Factory Commission of 1908 had been established specifically to investigate the long hours of work exacted by the mills. The Commission recognized that differences in hours of work among mills accounted for some of the instability of the work force. It also recognized the need for improved supervision within the mills, but its fundamental conclusion was that shortening the hours would independently improve discipline and productivity.[22] However, reduction of the workday to twelve hours in 1911 did not seem to yield significant improvements in mill-hand work performance. Employers continued to complain about the undisciplined behavior of the labor force, its propensities to loiter, to be absent and unstable.[23] But as we shall see, this was not the consequence of any "natural" tendency of the Indian operative. The failure to achieve improved patterns of labor utilization and discipline stemmed from the character of the working rules and the quality of their application.

---

[21] There is no need to give a description of subsequent statutory curtailments of the length of the working day. Suffice to say that by the end of my period the mills were down to an eight-hour day and a forty-eight-hour week.

[22] *IFLC 1908*, I, 21–22.

[23] It is impossible to measure productivity changes with the evidence available. The employer's typical measure of mill-hand productivity was the number of machines an operative tended. However, this is not a useful device in the Bombay situation. Variations in the quality of raw material, count of yarn, speed of machines, balance of equipment between one department and another, and variety and quality of final products all have to be taken into consideration. The most sophisticated analysis of these factors can be found in Mehta, *ICTI, passim.*

CHAPTER VII

Work Regulations in the Mills

(1)

The cotton textile industry needed a growing supply of labor. The new workers it recruited rarely if ever possessed any previous experience in an industrial establishment, although it is probable that a large proportion had had some familiarity with rural wage employment.[1] These raw novices had to be converted into an army of disciplined mill hands, responsive to the general requirements of industrial work and to the special needs of the mills. One way of examining this development is to study the structure of rules and penalties which the mills imposed upon their employees. Analysis of the formal system of discipline followed by an analysis of the manner in which the system was actually enforced should throw considerable light on the kind of work force the industry was able to create. The discussion in this and the next chapter will make it clear that to a very large extent the industry got the kind of labor force it wanted.[2]

We know nothing about the kind of work rules laid down by the very early mills. Each mill as it came into operation seems to have prepared its own regulations. We do not know whether they were copied from Manchester or were based on earlier experience in other Indian enterprises. The rules were written or printed and a copy was posted somewhere on the premises.[3] Following the enactment of the Indian Factories Act of 1891, the Millowners Association held a general meeting to consider "the adoption of a uniform code of rules for the observance and guidance of workpeople," and a draft was prepared consisting of six-

---

[1] In later decades at least some part of the recruits may already have possessed factory experience in cotton mills up-country or in other industries. There is no satisfactory evidence on this point.

[2] Contrary to what one would expect, there seem to have been very few complaints about labor discipline in the early stages of the industry's career. Employer grievances begin to show up only after 1890.

[3] We know that in 1874 one mill had posted a list which consisted of fifteen regulations. Mr. Bhagubhoy, *FC 1875*, pp. 25 and 30. A copy of work rules had to be posted somewhere on the premises in order to establish employer authority under the general law of master and servant.

teen regulations.[4] A contemporary remarked that this proposal was "a fair representation" of the regulations under which mill labor typically worked.[5] The draft was never formally approved by the member mills, and each enterprise continued to operate with its own work code.[6]

Occasionally in subsequent years there were comments at annual Association meetings that it would be desirable to standardize work regulations, but no new attempt was made to formulate a code which would apply in all mills until the late 1920's. A uniform set of "Standing Orders" was introduced in 1931, but the provisions were not enforced. Finally, in the late 1930's, as a product of external pressure, standardization of work regulations among mills did become a reality.

(2)

What were the formal demands made by the employer upon mill hands in the early period? The draft regulations prepared by the BMOA in 1891, which seem to embody the main principles in force in all mills until at least 1931, were extremely general.[7] Operatives were required to turn up regularly at the time set by the mill, remain in the mill during the entire workday, perform their work as directed, and leave the establishment at the time designated. They were obligated to turn up even when the factory was not working, unless the employer gave formal notice that the mill would be closed for more than thirty consecutive days.[8] Mill hands were not to smoke except in designated places; they

---

[4] *BMOA 1891*, pp. 15 and 172–175.

[5] Mr. Drewet, *RCL 1892*, p. 132.

[6] I have found no explanation for the failure of the mills to agree to this standardized draft. In the absence of copies of work rules from individual mills, it is impossible to tell precisely how widely the BMOA draft was used as compared with individual mill versions.

[7] The BMOA draft of 1891 is the first example of working rules that is available. However, evidence suggests that it is not untypical of what existed from the beginning. See the early volumes of *ITJ* and *FC 1875* and *FC 1885*, *passim*. The evidence also suggests that although the industry underwent steady changes in technology and organization, the formal rules on work organization and labor discipline remained largely unchanged from the earliest days until the 1930's. *BLO, Deductions from Wages 1926*, pp. 15–20.

Appendix VI contains a copy of the BMOA draft code of 1891. The discussion which follows is based on this source. For a contemporary discussion of the proposal, see *BMOA 1891*, pp. 15 and 171–173.

[8] At least one witness claimed that this rule was "done merely with the object of preventing them [experienced hands] from seeking employment elsewhere." Mr. Lokhunday, *RCL 1892*, p. 169.

were not to steal company property, give bribes, strike, or conspire with others to leave the firm's service. And they could not quit without giving a month's notice.

How were these formal obligations enforced? It appears that regulations for enforcement were as general as the rules themselves. Apart from provision for outright discharge and forfeiture of accrued earnings for any offense, fines were the principal device used to guarantee work performance.[9] But the rules were not explicit on this and mentioned fines as an alternative only in cases of theft and smoking in undesignated places. In fact, fines were levied for tardiness, bad work, and a host of unspecified misdemeanors. Fines were also imposed for absence without leave, the so-called "double-khada system." For each day's unauthorized absence, two day's pay was forfeited.[10]

Control over work performance was bolstered by the method of wage payment. Piecework was the rule wherever it could be applied. The system has always been a powerful incentive and it is clear that it served as such among the mill hands.[11] Control over performance also was maintained by withholding wages. All regular workers were paid once a month. Theoretically this occurred fifteen to twenty days after the end of the month during which work was performed, but typically wages were not paid until close to the end of next month.[12] This meant that at all times the employer was holding no less than two weeks of a worker's earnings. Usually he was holding a minimum of a month's pay, but he could be holding as much as two months accumulated earnings against

---

[9] Confirmation can be found in various testimony, *FC 1875*, *FC 1885*, and *RCL 1892*.

[10] Mr. Helm, Mr. Edwards, and Mr. Dhunjeebhoy, *FC 1875*, pp. 21, 25, and 45. See also various evidence, *FC 1885*, and *ITJ*, I, No. 2, November 1892, p. 28. The working of the "double-khada" system is somewhat ambiguous. For those workers paid on a time basis the situation is clear. The uncertainty occurs in the case of the large proportion of workers who were paid on piece rates. What constituted a day's pay? Apparently, a worker not only received no pay for the day he was absent but he was not paid for his output on the first day back at work. See R. Bhicajee, *RC 1885*, pp. 98–99; and W. O. Meade King, "The Indian Factories Act, 1881, with the Alterations Therein Proposed," Memorandum to the Secretary to Government, 24 June 1882, p. 2. The implication in the bits of evidence that can be found is that there was an expectation of standardized output per day and the employer actually deducted the amount he expected a worker to earn in a day. This prevented the worker from soldiering on the job his first day back. *LG*, VI, No. 12, August 1927, p. 1109.

[11] Meade King, *op. cit.*, p. 3; and *Minutes by His Excellency Sir Richard Temple . . . 1878* (Bombay, 1878), p. 172.

[12] *FC 1875, passim*. See also Appendix VI, BMOA draft rule No. 4.

which fines could be levied.[13] Here, obviously, was a considerable disciplinary weapon.

Withholding wages served three objectives. First, by giving the employer a fund which guaranteed recovery of fines levied for bad work, damage to equipment, and other misdemeanors, it ostensibly forced the mill hand to maintain performance. Second, it was intended to inhibit labor turnover among trained hands.[14] Depending on the mill, workers were required to give two weeks or one month notice of intention to quit. Notice could be given only on the one or two designated days in a month. Failure to give notice at the prescribed time and on a prescribed form could result in forfeiture of all accrued earnings.[15] Some mills also decreed that if, after giving notice, an employee was absent or irregular in his work the notice to quit was voided and he was required to submit a new notice.[16] Third, the withholding of earnings was intended to protect the employer against strikes. Combinations or attempted combinations were cause for immediate dismissal and forfeiture of all accumulated wages.[17]

The formal system of discipline ran entirely against the workers. The rules permitted the employer to act against the employee almost without inhibition. For example, although the provision that workers had to give notice of intention to quit was ostensibly balanced by an equivalent

---

[13] There is a vast amount of evidence to the effect that mills often actually paid workers at the end of the second month or even later. See various evidence *FC 1875*; *FC 1885*; *FC 1890*; *RCL 1892*; *FA 1892*, pp. 6 and 15; *FA 1897*, pp. 10–11; and *IFLC 1908*, II, particularly pp. 51 and 106.

[14] Mr. Dadabhoy, *FC 1885*, p. 42; *BMOA 1896*, p. 135.

[15] BMOA draft rule No. 6, Appendix VI below; *IFLC 1908*, II, pp. 51, 106, 118, 157; and A. R. Burnett-Hurst, *Labour and Housing in Bombay* (London: P. S. King and Son, 1925), p. 57.

[16] *ITJ*, XXII, No. 257, February 1912, p. 170; and Mr. Talcherkar in 1917, quoted by Mukhtar, *Factory Labour in India* (Madras: Annamalai University, 1930), p. 157. To make quitting even less easy, workers could collect their accrued pay only on specified days. However, a special system developed as an informal device, making it easier for mill hands to move. Unable to collect his accumulated earnings when he departed, the employee would sell his wage claim at a discount for immediate cash to a jobber, moneylender or merchant. The purchaser would then take the purchased authorization (the "havala") and collect the millhand's wages at the designated time. For descriptions of the "havala" system, see *BLO, Deductions from Wages 1926*, p. 23; *LG*, VII, No. 1, September 1927, pp. 57–59; and *BMOA 1937*, p. 36. I have been unable to find references to this system before World War I. However, the methods of wage payment and the widespread informal financial transactions in the mills from the earliest years suggest that the "havala" phenomenon did exist in earlier decades.

[17] Mr. Dadabhoy, *FC 1875*, p. 42; and BMOA draft rules Nos. 12 and 13, Appendix VI below.

employer obligation, the regulations were general enough to permit the worker to be discharged at will. As one mill official said: "You will find that if the manager or agent is not willing to retain a man, he will be dismissed without notice." [18]

The rules provided that when a worker was discharged for "misconduct" the employer was free to deduct in the form of fines from accrued wages whatever he thought appropriate.[19] Certainly there was no channel of appeal for the worker inside the mill, and recourse to the courts was a feeble defense.[20] Fines were not light. The typical fine in the 1870's and early 1880's of two to four annas for being late to work amounted to the loss of as much as half to a full day's pay.[21] There are no statistics to indicate how heavy total fines were before World War I. However, one of the best run mills reported in 1892 that its fines constituted about "one per cent of the total amount of wages paid in a month." [22]

Although the formal system of rules was severe, regulation of the specific behavior of operatives at work was surprisingly lax.[23] The most obvious feature, the one that caught the eye of all observers, was the large number of idle workers visible in the mills. In 1884 mill officials estimated that at any one time in individual mills from 7 to 47 per cent

---

[18] Mr. Bhagubhoy, *FC 1875*, p. 29. On the ostensible responsibility of the employer, see mill evidence to *RCL 1892*, pp. 123, 137, and 138. BMOA draft rule No. 7, Appendix VI below, made a formal statement of the employer's obligation but also contained a qualification broad enough to permit discharge at will.

[19] BMOA draft rule No. 7, Appendix VI below. See also testimony of Mr. Moos and Mr. Campbell, *RCL 1892*, pp. 135–136 and 173–174.

[20] Mr. Lokhunday, *RCL 1892*, p. 171. There was some question as to the legality of forfeiture of wages in the manner described. See the letter of the BMOA attorney to the Association, *BMOA 1891*, p. 171. See also *BMOA 1896*, pp. 134–135. On the other hand, there is some evidence that when the mills posted their regulations they could impose the financial penalties. See the interesting court case described in *ITJ*, III, No. 27, December 1892, p. 64. Apparently one of the important functions of the small welfare organizations which cropped up after 1870 was to assist mill hands in the recovery of their back wages. After 1890 there seems to have been an increasing recourse to the courts for this purpose. In later years there were employer complaints that the small claims courts were favoring mill hands in suits for recovery of withheld earnings. One manager complained that this was "detrimental to ordinary discipline at the mill." *ITJ*, XX, No. 240, September 1910, p. 340.

[21] Genoo Babajee and Raghoo Bhicajee, *FC 1885*, pp. 98 and 100. Though it is impossible to be precise about the level of wages in the mills at this time, it seems likely that the bulk of workers received Rs.7 or less per month, which meant no more than As.4 per day. This seems to be supported by Mehta, *CMI*, p. 143.

[22] Evidence of Swadeshi Mills, *RCL 1892*, p. 171. This probably constituted a minimum figure. As will be shown subsequently, accounting procedures and techniques of levying fines tended to understate the money value of penalties.

[23] The behavior described in subsequent paragraphs is based on a very great deal of evidence in *FC 1875*, *FC 1885*, and *FC 1890*.

of the work force was not at its machines.[24] The 1890 factory commission
reported: "We have ourselves seen them [the mill hands] engaged in
drinking water, washing, smoking, and looking about." [25] In later years
this loitering became a major focus of employer complaints and was used
as proof of the undisciplined character of the mill labor force. But the
evidence makes it clear that in the years before 1920 the phenomenon
was part of the pattern of labor utilization deliberately chosen by the
mills.[26]

I have already pointed out that the morning starting time of the mills
varied not only from one season to another but also within the same
season. Perhaps because of this operatives were typically given some
rather vague grace period, up to half an hour after the mill opened, before they were considered late. Workers were not required to be at their
machines when the power was turned on but gradually drifted in to work.
Stopping time at the end of the day was also uncertain, occurring whenever the manager or an assistant, deciding that it was too dark to continue, shut off the power. Lacking clocks or a precise schedule of
stopping work, employees began to drift away from their machines when
shadows began to darken their work places.[27]

Even before the statutory work break was imposed in 1891, most mills
did stop their machines for at least a few minutes at some point during
the middle of the day. The interval, typically brief and of irregular duration, did not occur always at the same time. Neither before 1891 nor
after did employers intend this as the meal period. In the absence of
designated eating areas, workers snatched their meals where and at any
time they wished, either beside their machines or in the mill compound.[28] Nor did the mills attempt to establish regular breaks during
which operatives could smoke or relieve themselves. They went off as
the occasion demanded. The employer was only concerned that when a
mill hand took a break his machines were tended by others and did not
have to be stopped. In fact, something like an informal shift system was

---

[24] *FC 1885, passim.*

[25] *FC 1890,* p. 12.

[26] We shall, in fact, see that at least until the 1920's the employers made no attempt to change the system of work organization which made loitering an inevitable
and necessary feature of labor utilization.

[27] For a vivid description of the loosely scheduled working of the mills, see *ITJ,*
I, No. 4, January 1891, pp. 59–60; and *ITJ,* V, No. 53, February 1895, p. 115.

[28] *Bombay and Lancashire Cotton Spinning Inquiry, 1888,* p. 87. *ITJ,* XIII, No.
146, November 1902, p. 49; C. D. Panday, *IFLC 1908,* II, p. 96; and Bombay Textile Labor Union, *ITB 1927,* III, p. 453. As late as 1934, forty-five of the fifty-seven
working mills had no regular eating areas for the mill hands. *BLO 1934,* p. 65.

created to provide for meal, rest, and toilet breaks without interrupting work. As one important millowner described the situation:

Ninety percent of the work-people take their meals during working hours, some take from three to five meals per day during working hours; no restriction is put upon them as to the time they take. When they are away from work, at their meals, there is somebody else doing it, and this is the reason why so many people are employed. . . . During this period the operatives are allowed full liberty to go out, to take their meals, to smoke, or do anything they please.[29]

One factory commission attributed this behavior to the "nature and ingrained habits of Indian workers." [30] But this ignored the fact that the nature of mill organization and operation made it necessary for employees, if they wished to take a break, to be away from their machines for rather long intervals. Operatives, prohibited from smoking inside the mill, had to go into the compound. Moreover, most early mills did not provide toilet facilities either in the mill or in the compound. As late as 1875 employees in many firms had to leave the mill premises and relieve themselves in the fields outside the plant walls.[31] By 1885 most of the mills seem to have provided some toilets, but as they were invariably located in the compound employees still had to leave the mill building.[32] In fact, as late as 1929 the Factory Inspector still opposed, for sanitary reasons, the locating of toilets inside the mills.[33] Not only were the toilets situated at considerable distances from the work places, but until very

---

[29] N. N. Wadia, *FC 1885*, p. 77. See also *BMOA 1879*, pp. 92, 94 and 108; and *IFTC 1908*, II, *passim*. Only two or three mills attempted by a system of passes to regulate the number of workers away from the department at any time. *FC 1885*, pp. 100, 105, and Appendix B, p. 8.

[30] *FC 1906*, p. 12.

[31] *FC 1875*, pp. 9 and 80.

[32] As late as 1909 at least one mill still had its privies located near a cemetery some distance outside the mill premises. *BMOA 1909*, pp. 17–18. See also Lt. Col. Corkery, *IFLC 1908*, II, p. 44.

[33] T. W. Johnstone, *RCL 1929*, I, Part 2, p. 240. There was good reason for him to take this position. The condition of the toilets left much to be desired. Employers frequently complained that workers, having come from the countryside, wouldn't adjust to urban-style toilet facilities. For example, Mr. Leslie, *IFLC 1908*, II, p. 60. However, the Royal Commission of 1929, commenting on such complaints, reported: "Our observations have convinced us that he [the mill worker] can be brought to use them without serious difficulty, provided they are kept in decent order. He rightly refuses to use a latrine whose condition, by the very nature of its construction and supervision, is always filthy." *RCL 1929*, "Report," p. 56. See also Captain Houston, *IFLC 1908*, II, p. 56. This problem continued beyond the end of my period. See *TLIC 1940*, p. 307; and *ICEC 1950*, pp. 51–53.

late in the period there were insufficient numbers of toilets and workers had to queue to use them.[34]

The very high temperatures and humidity, the dust, and the lack of ventilation also made it necessary for the mill hands to take frequent breaks. Mills reported in 1884 that they deliberately kept the work temperature between ninety and one hundred degrees, using live steam to keep up the temperature and humidity to what was considered by them a technically necessary level.[35] The situation remained roughly unchanged until the 1920's, and despite subsequent improvements excessive temperature and humidity remained a subject of constant complaint by both government officials and trade unions.[36]

Apart from the nature of mill facilities and methods of production which made it necessary for workers to take informal breaks from their work, there were other features which contributed to the presence of large numbers of apparently idle people on factory premises.[37] For example, not until very late in our period did any mills provide lunchrooms where workers could buy food. As a consequence, workers had to provide their own food. A tradition developed under which many did not bring it with them when they reported to work. Instead, food was delivered to them in the mill by relations, boardinghouse keepers, or the *khanawala*. These people seem to have been pouring in and out of the mills at all hours of the day.[38]

Although mills did not provide formal eating facilities until very late, most mills apparently granted concessions to tea shops which were established in the compounds and workers could be served all through the

[34] *IFLC 1908*, I, pp. 6–13; *IFLC 1908*, II, pp. 44, 50, and 52; and Bombay Textile Labor Union, *ITB 1927*, III, p. 453. Henceforth, I shall use the abbreviation BTLU for the Bombay Textile Labor Union.

[35] *FC 1885, passim.* One English engineer serving in a local mill claimed in 1875 that ninety-five degrees was not too high because the air "is always kept in motion by the revolving of the machines." Mr. Alcock, *FC 1875*, p. 81. *ITJ*, VIII, p. 95, August 1898, p. 289, reported mills working at temperatures as high as 110 degrees.

[36] *RCL 1929*, "Report," pp. 57–59; *ICEC 1950*, p. 59.

[37] In 1884 one mill manager reported that in his mill as many as 47 per cent of the work people "are taking their meals, resting, or smoking at all hours." Mr. Hammett, *FC 1885*, p. 65. Although this was an extreme statement, most employers spoke of 10 to 20 per cent of the work force loitering about at any one time. See various testimony, *FC 1885* and *IFLC 1908*, II.

[38] *ITJ*, I, No. 3, December 1890, p. 37; *BMOA 1891*, p. 48; and *BMOA 1921*, p. 62. The *khanawala* in Bombay is a professional distributor who picks up lunch boxes at workers' homes and delivers them to the workers at their places of work. The activity seems to have appeared quite early and at the present time has developed into an incredibly elaborate and efficient system which brings food containers from far out in the suburbs into the center of Bombay. It is a phenomenon that deserves study.

workday. Each mill seems early to have granted also a concession to a barber who, having set up shop somewhere in the compound, did a roaring business during working hours.[39] In many mills, mothers were permitted to bring their infants with them and nurse them in the departments or in the compounds. If they were not allowed to bring their children with them, they were permitted to leave the mills periodically to feed them.[40] Another major source of people floating about in the compounds and departments existed because of the way in which workers were hired. Each morning large numbers of job seekers were permitted into the mill compounds and departments. Those needed were hired, and the others only gradually trickled off the premises.[41] The accounts and tabulations of loitering probably included these people and consequently probably overstated the actual number of employees involved.

A reading of all the early evidence makes it very clear that this loose pattern of work organization had been initially created by the employers, and for a very long period they were very well satisfied by it. For example, in 1891 an official spokesman described the situation in the following terms:

There are no very strict regulations. The Indian operative, who is paid by piece-work, is allowed to come in half-an-hour after time of starting work, . . . the popular notion of sunrise varying within limits of half-an-hour. He keeps a lien on his place by putting in substitutes. He can leave early in the afternoon, if necessary, and get his half-day's wages. . . . There is no rule or way of seeing him constantly at his post during the working hours of the mill. He is a perfectly free agent in that regard. He feels himself at liberty to take his meals between the hours of seven and twelve, to stretch his legs occasionally, to loiter in the compound, or perhaps have his shave and shampoo under little sheds in the mill compound whenever he pleases. The youngsters may be seen having snatches at leapfrog even on the mill premises. . . . The women have more grace allowed them as to their times of starting work. . . . When they have to look after sucklings they have perfect freedom to go to their place and be back at intervals during the day. In fact, the Indian operatives do not work against their customs or their natural inclinations, or their traditional habits. . . . Walk through a mill at any time of the day and two out of six operatives told off for sets of machines will not be seen; they are taking it in turns to be out in the compound . . . hardly 1 per cent of the

---

[39] As one observer remarked: "A barber is a recognized part of the establishment. . . ." *ITJ*, VIII, No. 88, January 1898, p. 95. *ITJ*, I, No. 4, January 1891, pp. 59–60; *Bombay and Lanchashire Cotton Spinning Inquiry, 1888*, p. 28; *BMOA 1935*, p. 19.

[40] *BMOA 1891*, p. 144; *IFLC 1908*, I, p. 60; *IFLC 1908*, II, pp. 47, 49, 59 and 102; J. H. Kelman, *Labour in India* (London: George Allen & Unwin Ltd., 1923), pp. 189–190.

[41] *BMOA 1930*, p. 280.

Indian operatives take their meals during their recess hours. Each has his own time, and takes it during the working hours. . . .[42]

This description is certainly excessively idyllic but it did receive the accolade of approval from the BMOA.[43] What is important is that the speaker quite explicitly indicated that the employers were free to modify the pattern if they so desired.[44]

The formal work rules which did exist, as I have said, were most general, and the employers made no attempt to see that the mill hands learned them. They were not brought to the attention of the employees in any formal fashion when they were hired or at any other time. Mills rarely posted more than one copy, the one necessary to comply with the provisions of the statute of master and servant. But the bulk of the mill hands could not have read the rules even had they been widely exhibited. The employers assumed that the rules would be "read by those who can read, and afterwards explained by them to others who cannot read." [45]

More important is the fact that the formal rules were casually and erratically enforced. Causes of discharge were not precise, and there seem to have been no clear circumstances which would evoke any explicit penalty. As one mill officer said, "It would depend on the nature of the fault. Some deserve instant dismissal, others may require a week's or a fortnight's notice." [46] Fines were invoked in equally casual fashion. Not only did standards vary among mills, but penalties were applied quite cavalierly in each mill and department. For example, the "double-khada" penalty for absence without leave was enforced in some mills but not in others. In some mills it was invoked against time-rate workers only. In one mill it was not used "except in glaring instances." [47] As one critic commented, "In no two factories are the departmental working or routine rules the same, and the majority of illiterate operatives, tacitly accepting them are wholly ignorant of the conditions under which they enter service." [48]

---

[42] Dr. K. N. Bahadhurji, *BMOA 1891*, pp. 44–45.

[43] For a full description of the circumstances under which this statement was made, *ibid.*, pp. 8–9 and 34–57. See also *FC 1890*, pp. 8–12.

[44] *BMOA 1891*, p. 45.

[45] Mr. Dhunjeebhoy, *FC 1875*, p. 36.

[46] *RCL 1892*, p. 123.

[47] Mr. Dunkerly and Mr. Wadia, *FC 1885*, pp. 55, 77, and 90; *ITJ*, I, No. 1, October 1890, p. 15; Mr. Wadia, *IFLC 1908*, II, p. 94; and H. A. Talcherkar as quoted in Mukhtar, *op. cit.*, p. 157.

[48] Statement of the Kamgar Hitwardhak Sabha to the Bombay Government, *ITJ*, XXII, No. 257, February 1912, p. 170. The wide diversity of rules and disciplinary practices was admitted by the BMOA in 1927. *BSEC 1928–29*, p. 178.

The evidence makes it clear that in the Bombay mills hours were long, and labor was subject to the arbitrary and largely uncontrolled authority of the employers. It is equally certain, however, that discipline at the work place was fundamentally lax and ramshackle. Why did the mill-owners insist on the factories operating for long hours but at the same time not worry overly much about how these hours were spent? [49] Was this an irrational entrepreneurial pattern? The answer is not an easy one, especially in the absence of direct evidence on the subject. However, there were certain characteristics of cotton mill operation in Bombay which seem to point to an answer.

Labor costs were a very small proportion of total costs of production and, with the vast proportion of operatives being paid piecework rates, wage costs were not significantly affected by slack discipline. Moreover, the mills produced coarse yarn and cloth which did not require great skill or sophisticated supervision. At the same time equipment costs were relatively very high, and the critical object was to guarantee the continued operation of the machines. This pressure was increased, during the first half-century particularly, by the fact that the managing agents, the decision makers in each mill, were paid a commission per pound of output. Thus the relative price of factors and the specific incentives for the entrepreneur were both strongly on the side of having the mills operate long hours, producing as much product as possible, without particular regard to labor efficiency.[50] In other words, this thoroughly rational economic judgment encouraged what seemed to so many outsiders to be a thoroughly wasteful use of labor.

(3)

We do not have information that makes it possible to develop any quantitative notions about the impact of discipline in the pre-World War I period. However, in 1926 the Bombay Labor Office investigated "the extent of the practice by which employers . . . are empowered to inflict fines upon their workmen." [51] The survey, covering seventy-six of the eighty-three mills in Bombay, essentially confirms the description

---

[49] *FC 1875, FC 1885, FC 1890, IFLC 1908,* II, all contain evidence which confirm this.

[50] Dr. S. D. Mehta seems to have been making the same point. See Mehta, *ICTI,* particularly p. 67, note 42, but also the implications of pp. 32–33, and 41–49.

[51] *BLO, Deductions from Wages 1926,* p. 1. After the survey was completed, the Labor Office solicited comments from various interested groups. These were published in *LG,* VI, No. 6 and 12 and *LG,* VII, No. 1, February, August, and September 1927. Among the groups responding were two trade unions and two social service organizations.

of formal mill discipline that emerges from the earlier qualitative evidence.[52] It not only highlighted the enormous diversity of mill practice but it also made clear that apart from outright discharge, fines were the major instrument for achieving employer objectives.

By this time all mills posted copies of the work rules, usually printed in three languages (Marathi, Gujarati, and English), in at least two prominent locations.[53] But only half the mills even claimed that they instructed a new worker as to their meaning; the others still expected him to find out about them in his own way. The published regulations continued to be most general, but in their answers to the Labor Office questionaire the mills produced a long list of offenses for which they might impose fines.[54] However, no mill posted lists of these offenses nor were specific fines attached to particular offenses.[55] Eleven mills set limits to fines that could be imposed on a worker in any month, but the overwhelming majority still claimed the right to appropriate a worker's full accumulated earnings for any offense.[56] All except one mill claimed that the worker was notified both of his offense at the time it occurred and the amount of the fine that was to be imposed.[57]

The survey collected some evidence on the amount of fines collected during the period January to October 1926. Although the figures suffer from many weaknesses, they do give some idea of the financial impact of mill discipline on the work force.[58] During the ten months sixty-six

---

[52] Though obviously there must have been some changes in practice over time, the general principles of formal discipline remained intact. *BLO, Deductions from Wages 1926*, pp. 15–20.

[53] *Ibid.*, p. 18. Apparently government factory regulations had insisted upon this.

[54] For offenses for which fines could be levied, see *ibid.*, pp. 15–20.

[55] A few mills did post in weaving departments lists of fines for certain common weaving errors. *Ibid.*, pp. 17–18.

[56] The eleven mills set limits either to the proportion fines could be of total monthly earnings (2 to 5 per cent) or to the absolute amount. *Ibid.*, pp. 18–19. It is impossible to determine the extent to which forfeiture of accrued earnings actually did occur. *Ibid.*, pp. 15–16; *LG*, VI, No. 12, August 1927, p. 1110.

[57] This was vigorously denied by the trade unions and social welfare agencies. *LG*, VI, No. 12, August 1927, pp. 1124–1125.

[58] Not all the mills gave detailed information. Moreover, the fines were understated by certain features of the system of discipline. For example, some mills penalized late or absent workers by excluding them from the factory for a fixed period. The loss of earnings involved in the suspension was a fine but the penalty showed up only as a reduction of the wage bill. Similarly with "double-khada" penalties for absence without leave. Weavers were typically fined by being forced to buy the cloth they were charged with spoiling. This showed up in mill books as a sale. Wages forfeited were not reported. *LG*, VI, No. 12, August 1927, p. 1110.

mills reported fines totaling Rs.118,707, or 0.25 per cent of the total wage bill.[59] Only thirty-one of these mills gave enough information to permit a breakdown of fines by type of offense.

TABLE XV

Number and Amount of Fines in Thirty-one Mills
January to October 1926 [60]

Nature of fine	Number of fines	Per cent of total fines	Total fines (rupees)	Per cent of total fines	Average size of fines (annas)
Breach of discipline or mill rules	15,089	10.2	3,101–12	7.8	3.29
Bad work	116,625	78.6	32,667–5	81.8	4.48
Loss or damage to property	8,746	5.9	2,833–11	7.1	5.18
All others[61]	7,890	5.3	1,329–1	3.3	2.70
Total	148,350	100.0	39,931–13	100.0	4.31

The total fines reported by the thirty-one mills amounted to 0.2 per cent of the total wage bill. Each worker was penalized an average of 2.3 times during the ten-month period and forfeited almost half a day's pay as a result.[62]

Special attention should be drawn to one type of fine not included in Table XV. Although all mills fined weavers for bad work, in forty-two the fine took a special form. The weaver was required to take the spoiled material, and the value of the cloth was deducted from his monthly earnings.[63] Sixteen mills employing 9,226 weavers gave information on the amount of these penalties which were much heavier on the average than those cited in Table XV. As compared with the average fine of Rs.0-4-4 shown there, the average deduction for spoiled cloth was Rs.5-12-6, more than twenty-one times as great. These weaving fines cost

---

The figures which follow must be recognized therefore, as representing a conservative statement of the situation.

[59] *BLO, Deductions from Wages 1926*, p. 26.

[60] *Ibid.*, pp. 24–25.

[61] Mainly for loss of identification tickets used to indicate presence at work. *Ibid.*, p. 25.

[62] Based on average mill hand's daily earnings of Rs.1–5–3 in July 1926. *BLO 1926*, p. 43.

[63] The majority of the forty-two mills deducted the retail value of the cloth; the others charged the wholesale price.

the average weaver the loss of more than three days' pay during the ten-month period.[64]

In spite of the formal rigor of the published regulations, the 1926 investigation suggests that these were tempered in practice. But it was precisely this, not the severity but the degree to which discipline was cavalier in its application, which caused difficulties. Moreover, there remained the wide areas of mill operation in which no attempts had been made to establish orderly routines of work. This is suggested by the absence of any attempt to establish regularly scheduled meal and rest breaks. In 1927 the Indian Tariff Board recommended that a definite half-hour recess be established so that workers might have a fixed meal time.[65] The BMOA opposed this on the ground that the mills had attempted such a scheme in 1920 but had dropped it after a short trial because of worker opposition.[66] In rebuttal, one manager pointed to the fact that at least one mill had introduced a system of fixed breaks for meals and rest "many years ago," and he claimed that "neither the management nor the operatives would care to go back to the undisciplined system which previously obtained there and still obtains, I believe, in every other Bombay mill." [67] All evidence points to the fact that as late as 1927 the mills had no serious interest in eliminating irregular work behavior and made little effort to do so.[68]

---

[64] Based on the average two-loom weaver's daily earnings of Rs.1–13–4 per day in July 1926. *BLO 1926*, p. 46. In individual cases the deductions for spoiled cloth could be quite heavy. Three specific examples report deductions amounting to 32.3, 46.6, and 55.2 per cent of actual earnings for one month. Statement of Social Service League, *LG*, VI, No. 12, August 1927, p. 1119. Of course, if the weaver was able to sell the cloth the penalty did not necessarily constitute a total loss. But the Labor Office pointed out that he "may not be able to sell it except at a considerable loss . . . and the incidence of the fine may therefore be very heavy." *BLO, Deductions from Wages 1926*, p. 20. This would be particularly true where mills charged the errant weaver the retail value of the spoiled product. The BTLU complained that bad weaving was frequently caused, not by negligence of the weaver, but by poor materials, defective equipment, or poor supervision. *LG*, VI, No. 12, August 1927, p. 1118.

[65] *ITB 1927*, I, p. 138.

[66] *BMOA 1928*, p. 14. I have found no evidence in the Association records to support this contention. However, in 1908 one manager did say that he had offered his men fixed meal periods but "the men would not agree to the proposal, as they said their dinners could not be brought all at one time." Mr. Shepherd, *IFLC 1908*, II, p. 72.

[67] Mr. Addyman, *ITB 1927*, IV, p. 294. The firm referred to may well be the one which had introduced this scheme as long ago as 1884. *FC 1885*, p. 77.

[68] For example, it was not until 1926 that the BMOA took up the suggestion of one of the leading millowners that barbers should be excluded from mill compounds. Its recommendation to the member mills was a peculiarly timid one and seems to

(4)

The 1927 report of the Indian Tariff Board set in motion pressures which ultimately forced the Millowners' Association to move in the direction of more effective discipline. The Tariff Board, examining the industry's appeal for protection, pointed out that because of the weakened competitive position of the Bombay mills the "only alternative to a reduction in wages is increased labor efficiency. . . ." [69] It recommended greater standardization of work and more rational labor deployment.[70] However, the efforts of a few mills to introduce rationalized working engendered fears of unemployment in a labor force which was already beginning to feel the pinch of declining employment opportunities.[71] The tense situation culminated in a great general strike which broke out in April 1928 and lasted until October.

Early in May 1928 the spokesmen for the mill hands, the Joint Strike Committee, published a series of terms — "The Seventeen Demands" — defining the conditions under which the strikers would return to work. These constituted a fundamental criticism of existing work discipline. Among other demands, the strikers insisted on the standardization of work rules and work practices in the industry.[72] A few days later the Association responded, conceding the need for "standardized rules and regulations for enforcing discipline." [73]

Another matter requiring immediate attention is a uniform set of rules for all mills in connection with disciplinary measures to be enforced on the operatives. . . . Such rules exist at all mills at present, but are not uniform nor in many instances properly enforced. A new set of Rules has been framed, and will be put up in all mills in due course. . . . The chief alterations . . . will be the abolition of the present practice of allowing operatives to take meals during the working hours. A special half hour recess will be provided . . . for this purpose. . . . Similarly, we deem it essential that certain matters which have been the subject of misunderstanding in the past between em-

---

have had no effect. *BMOA 1926*, pp. 137–138 and 550. Moreover, it was not until 1934 that the BMOA got around to recommending that mills should "tighten up discipline so as to prevent the taking of meals in mill compounds while the machinery was working and that mill compound tea shops where they existed should only be opened for business before and after working hours and during recess intervals. . . ." *BMOA 1934*, p. 19. Again, the recommendation was half-hearted.

[69] *ITB 1927*, I, p. 133.

[70] *Ibid.*, 209–210.

[71] Actually the introduction of the so-called "Efficiency System" began in early 1926, before the Tariff Board issued its report. For a comprehensive description of the new system, see *BSEC 1928–29*, pp. 154 ff.

[72] *Ibid.*, pp. 175–177.

[73] *Ibid.*, p. 7.

ployers and employees should be clearly defined so that there may be no ground for any grievances in the future. . . . Fines should be imposed in accordance with Rules devised for that purpose. . . . All fines recovered will be credited to a welfare fund, or utilized in some way for the benefit of the workers.[74]

But the two parties could not agree on the nature of the regulations and ultimately the matter was put into the hands of an official committee of inquiry headed by Sir Charles Fawcett.

The Joint Strike Committee objected to the standardized work rules which had been offered by the Millowners' Association. It complained that though the rules imposed restrictions on the conduct of operatives they did not establish any limitations on employer conduct.

The Standing Orders provide penalty for the workers going late; but not for the employers starting some machinery late or for not providing work in time or in sufficient quantity where the workers are paid by results. . . . Again there is provision for penalty for the absence on the part of the workers, but there is no provision for granting leave to workers. It is a misconduct on the part of the workers to be insubordinate but it is not a misconduct on the part of the Manager to treat the workers with discourtesy.[75]

The Fawcett Committee replied that

these remarks overlook the limitations which obviously apply to enunciating general conditions of employment, intended to enable an operative to know what are the main conditions affecting him . . . and his liabilities for disobedience, etc. We are not considering the drafting of a general Labor Code, in which conditions regarding the duties of employers towards their employees might properly be inserted.[76]

Having dismissed this union argument, the Fawcett Committee worked with the parties to develop a set of working rules which could be considered "fair and reasonable." [77]

The standing orders which emerged from the negotiations involved a rather significant break from the industry's traditions. The formal demands on the mill hands were made more precise as were also the penalties for violations of discipline. Certain protections for employees were laid down. Historically, all breaches of rules could result in summary dismissal and forfeiture of accrued earnings. The new regulations

---

[74] *Ibid.*, pp. 178–179.

[75] *Ibid.*, p. 13.

[76] *Ibid.*, pp. 13–14.

[77] *Ibid.*, p. 1. The standing orders first proposed by the BMOA and those accepted as "fair and reasonable" by the Fawcett Committee appear in parallel columns *ibid.*, pp. 180–187.

not only clearly distinguished those offenses for which fines would be exacted from the very few which could result in summary dismissal, but they authorized forfeiture of accrued earnings only if a worker quit without notice. Moreover, workers had to be notified of an offense in writing, and the penalty could be levied only by mill officers of specified rank. The Fawcett Committee guarded against abuse of the fining power by providing that fines were not to exceed a maximum of 2 per cent of an employee's total monthly earnings.[78] The worker representatives objected to the continuation of any system of fines, but the Committee concluded that

having regard to the low level of intelligence of most of the Indian workers in the mills of Bombay, it would be inadvisable to abolish fining, and that the time has not yet come when the management of a mill can safely rely entirely on mere supervision and cautioning as a substitute.[79]

The new standing orders were also designed to tighten up work procedures in a number of ways. One regulation not only formalized the long-standing tradition that workers were required to drop tickets bearing their work numbers at the timekeeper's office but included weavers in its provision. Historically, weavers had always been exempt from this requirement because they furnished and paid their own substitutes. The change was intended to encourage mills to be concerned with weaver absenteeism and thus more directly with weaver efficiency.[80]

The BMOA draft proposed to end the tradition of allowing mill hands to eat at any time by accepting the 1927 Tariff Board recommendation of a half-hour morning meal recess. To avoid a reduction in work time, the Association proposed to curtail the noon break by fifteen minutes and lengthen the workday by an equal amount. The longer workday was opposed by the unions, and on this point they were supported by the Committee. The proposal constituted a step toward the curtailment of one source of loose labor usage but under terms unacceptable to the employees. As a result the Fawcett Committee recommendation merely provided for the introduction of a recess at such future time when agreement could be reached between employers and mill hands.[81]

The Fawcett Committee work rules also introduced another restric-

---

[78] *Ibid.*, p. 52. The Committee favored discontinuance of the system of selling spoiled cloth to weavers. Feeling that the penalty generated great discontent, it proposed a compromise which, however, was not accepted by the employers. *Ibid.*, pp. 53–56.

[79] *Ibid.*, p. 51.

[80] *Ibid.*, pp. 25–27.

[81] *Ibid.*, pp. 21–23.

tion into the industry's free-and-easy utilization of the labor force. In the past, when machinery breakdowns occurred, workers were required to remain at the mill without pay. In fact, they could be required to attend such a shutdown mill for as long as thirty days or suffer forfeiture of their accumulated earnings. Moreover, mills had been free to "play-off" (layoff) workers at will and for unlimited periods when business conditions were bad while insisting that operatives give a month's notice before quitting. The new rules provided that when breakdowns occurred, hands kept in the mill for more than an hour would be paid for the entire period of stoppage. Workers who were played-off for seven days were free to quit without notice.[82] Moreover, the traditional requirement that employees had to give a month's notice of intention to quit was cut to fourteen days.[83]

The Fawcett Committe proposals contained two additional novelties which were intended to contribute to work-force stability. The Committee introduced the notion of a permanent employee into the industry for the first time. Newly employed workers could be discharged or could quit at will during an initial two-month period, but after that time a worker would become permanent and could be discharged only for cause.[84] The Committee also established provision for formal leaves. Up to this time there had been no regular arrangement for a worker who wanted to take time off. Even if he went on authorized leave, the mill hand never knew whether or not he had a job to return to. A new regulation provided that a worker on authorized leave was entitled to return to his position if he did not overstay his time.[85]

Finally, and perhaps most important, the new rules were to be standardized in all mills, and the Millowners' Association undertook responsibility for enforcing uniform application. Mills could no longer modify rules unilaterally or without notice but had to give workers and the BMOA two-months' notice in writing of its intention. Objections of workers and unions were to be received and considered, and a change could not go into effect until the BMOA had given written approval. In other words, rule changes were not to be arbitrarily introduced nor could they be made without consideration of their effects on the disciplinary pattern of the entire industry.[86]

The Fawcett Committee issued its report in March 1929. The general

---

[82] *Ibid.*, pp. 33–39. This regulation proved ambiguous and was modified in 1933. *BMOA 1933*, pp. 12–13.

[83] *Ibid.*, pp. 39–41.

[84] *Ibid.*, p. 29.

[85] *Ibid.*, pp. 28–29.

[86] *Ibid.*, pp. 17–20.

strike of 1929 and subsequent labor difficulties slowed the preparation of the new regulations. The Association completed its draft in 1931 and announced that all mills had introduced them by the beginning of 1932.[87] But the individualistic proclivities of the millowners made the announcement premature. In May 1934 only forty-four of the fifty-seven working mills had actually posted the new standing orders, and even in these mills the rules were being ignored or were not uniformly applied. For example, only forty-six mills had limits on the amounts of fines they levied, and only thirty-eight claimed to limit fines to 2 per cent of a worker's total monthly earnings. There were similar variations on many other matters. In other words, the tradition of individual mill discipline continued to operate virtually without change.[88]

The Association seems to have taken its responsibilities seriously. Although this first substantial effort to standardize disciplinary regulations and work organization came through outside pressures — the Indian Tariff Board recommendations (1927), the general strike demands (1928), and the Fawcett Committee deliberations (1928 to 1929) — the Association, once moved, made vigorous attempts to impose upon the mills a more orderly pattern of work and discipline. But its achievements were almost entirely frustrated by the anarchic propensities of the individual employers.

Faced with continuing labor unrest and the failure of the industry to solve its own problems, the Bombay Government enacted the Trade Disputes Conciliation Act in 1934. An official labor officer appointed under this law began to play an important role. With Association coöperation he attempted to get the recalcitrant mills to observe the rules they had ostensibly adopted.[89] It was not an easy task. His monthly reports show that only with difficulty could the mills be brought to apply the discipline of the standing orders with equity and objectivity.[90] Subsequent chapters will show that his efforts did not successfully ease the tensions which were wracking the industry. Finally the State was forced to intervene more drastically and directly, enacting a Payment of Wages Act which went into operation at the end of March 1937. The statute im-

[87] *BMOA 1931*, pp. v and 82–88. The Association adopted the standing orders recommended by the Fawcett Committee almost without modification, but the numbering of the clauses differed.

[88] *BLO 1934*, pp. 45–51 for a survey of some of the variations in mill practices.

[89] The BMOA appointed its own labor officer to coöperate with the Government Labor Officer. *BMOA 1934*, pp. iv and viii; *LG*, XIV, No. 4, December 1934, p. 274.

[90] The Government Labor Officer had only very limited powers. His dealings with the mills can be partly followed through his reports, printed monthly in *ITJ*, issues for 1935–1938.

posed for the first time a series of direct legal restrictions on employer disciplinary measures. It primarily affected the size and scope of the employer's authority to fine workers.[91]

The new law established nine basic offenses or omissions for which fines could be levied and specifically designated the mill officers with authority to impose fines. Total fines against a worker could not exceed 3.12 per cent of his earnings in a pay period. In order to guarantee effective standarization of discipline, mills were required to obtain official approval of their standing orders; and they had to maintain a record of gross wages earned by each worker, the nature, amount, and authority of each deduction, and the net wages paid. Fines collected could be expended only for welfare purposes approved by the government officer. Finally, withholding wages was eliminated as a disciplinary weapon. Not only were workers to be paid their wages within ten days of the end of the month or within two days after they terminated employment, but the law prohibited employers from forfeiting accrued earnings when a worker quit without notice.

In some ways the Payment of Wages Act merely gave statutory recognition to the standards of work discipline laid down by the Fawcett Committee in 1929 and accepted by the BMOA in 1931. The law strengthened the regulations by making the government responsible for greater standardization among mills and more systematic application within mills. But there were also certain fundamental modifications which were bitterly opposed by the Association's spokesman when the bill was being considered by the legislature in 1935. The Association claimed that the limitation on fines in any pay period would make it impossible to impose effective discipline on weavers.

. . . the value of cloth at present passing through the hands of the operative is much more than it was a few years ago [because of the shift to the weaving of finer cloth], and the small amount of fine contemplated in the Bill would neither bear any proportion to the monetary value of the damage inflicted nor act as a deterrent to bad or careless workmanship.[92]

The Association also opposed State control over the fines collected by the employer.

---

[91] Although the act was defined to include virtually all modern industrial enterprises, its basic concern was with the situation in the Bombay mills. For the text of the act, see S. N. Bose, *Indian Labour Code (Central)* (2d ed., Calcutta: Eastern Law House, Ltd., 1950), pp. 577–594. Historically, the Bombay cotton textile industry served as the laboratory within which most major experiments in all-India labor legislation were first attempted.

[92] *LG*, XV, No. 1, September 1935, pp. 49–50.

After all, when a fine is imposed, it necessarily follows that the employer has suffered at least a corresponding financial loss, and it is, therefore, really his money which is being credited to the fund, and provided it is spent for the benefit of the work people, there should be no outside interference at all.[93]

The third change against which the employers protested was the provision abolishing the right to retain accrued earnings when a worker quit without notice. It was argued that elimination of this penalty deprived the employer of effective protection against the defaulting mill hand.[94]

In spite of these arguments the statute became law in 1937, and the standing orders introduced by the BMOA in 1931 had to be revamped. The new regulations drafted in 1937 by the Association necessarily contained a more precise statement of mill-hand obligations and penalties. Because of the limitations on employer fining power imposed by the new law, the standing orders added a penalty not before widely used in the industry and never before explicitly mentioned. A worker guilty of serious misconduct could, in lieu of discharge, be suspended without pay for no more than four days.[95] Otherwise, the regulations as they affected discipline within mills remained much as those which had been formally introduced in 1931.[96]

Although the line of descent from the Fawcett Committee recommendations to the 1937 work rules — the so-called standing orders — is quite clear, it was the Payment of Wages Act of 1936 that actually shattered the traditional discipline which had been in force since the industry's beginnings. It is true that the proposals of the Fawcett Committee had been accepted virtually without modification by the BMOA in 1931, but the Association was unable to get effective voluntary compliance from its members. Even the government's labor officer was able to achieve only modest gains between 1934 and 1937. The 1936 statute removed large parts of the formal structure of labor discipline from the unilateral control of the mills. It transferred much of the punitive power against the mill hand from the collective (and only vaguely successful) authority of the Millowners' Association and placed it in the hands of public officers. The employers had begun to lose their powers of self-government and their right to shape their own labor discipline, powers they had exercised without inhibition for more than three quarters of a cen-

---

[93] *Loc. cit.*

[94] *Loc. cit.* The Fawcett Committee had merely qualified the traditional practice by allowing forfeiture of the last fourteen days' pay. *BSEC 1928–29*, pp. 41–44.

[95] There is no evidence on how widespread the penalty of suspension had been in the past, but it certainly had existed. *BLO, Deductions from Wages 1926*, pp. 6 and 21.

[96] A copy of the 1937 standing orders can be found in Appendix VII, below.

tury. Henceforth, the exercise of these powers was to become increasingly the responsibility of the State. In the subsequent reshaping of the industry's labor discipline, the Bombay Millowners' Association was to serve primarily as the handmaiden of public authority.

But even after passage of the Payment of Wages Act, much of the actual administration of the work force remained within the control of individual millowners and the BMOA. Only the regulation of the fining power had really been transferred to the State. The standing orders of 1937 provided that the employers were free, with the written consent of the Association, to modify and revise their working rules. Given the lack of authority of the Association, the mills in effect were still able to regulate their own disciplinary patterns to a very large extent. As a result, tension between work force and employers remained at a high pitch and in 1938 the State again intervened to further extend its control over work discipline by enacting the Bombay Industrial Disputes Act.[97] Apart from other issues with which it dealt, the law defined the matters to be covered in the standing orders. It required that every employer had to submit his standing orders to the Commissioner of Labor for approval. Once approved by the commissioner, they could not be unilaterally changed. The act stated that employers and employees were to give written notice of proposed modifications to each other and to designated public officers. Notice of change was required not only for matters affecting the standing orders themselves but also for variations in a host of other work relationships not explicitly described in the standing orders. These included proposed changes in labor deployment, systems of production, wages and hours, and withdrawal of any customary concessions, privileges, or usages. In event of failure to achieve direct agreement between employer and employees on a proposed modification, the issue had to be carried to government conciliators and arbitrators. Only after this procedure had been completed could unilateral changes be attempted.

Once again the powers of the employer were restricted by State intervention. With the passage of the Bombay Industrial Disputes Act the locus of control over working relationships in the Bombay mills had been almost completely shifted. Work discipline and organization, in the broadest sense, had become a matter of public regulation.[98]

---

[97] For an analysis of the act, which went into effect in 1939, see *LG*, XVIII, No. 3, November 1938, pp. 183–191.

[98] For a very explicit description of this shift in control, M. P. LaBouchardiere, "Some Aspects of the Bombay Industrial Disputes Act, and the Present Work of the Labour Officer, Bombay," *Indian Journal of Social Work*, II, No. 1, June 1941, p. 62.

CHAPTER VIII

Administration of the Work Force

(1)

We now have a reasonably detailed description of the regulations under which the work force was administered. The formal harshness of the work rules during most of the industry's history does not seem crucial in explaining the kind of work force that the industry got. That these rules varied among mills was probably only slightly more significant. To understand the character of the labor force which the industry created for itself, two additional features have to be taken into account. First, we must recall that the formal working regulations were so general as to permit the widest range of interpretation and application of discipline within each mill. Second, and fundamental to the entire situation, enforcement of work discipline was not a responsibility taken by upper management but came into the possession of the jobbers who, in effect, became the actual managers of the work force. In hiring and in the general powers of supervision, punishment, and discharge the jobber was largely able to exercise the power of the employer. Coming from the same social and economic strata as the workers over whom he tyrannized, typically illiterate, with no specialized training, and with no hope of promotion into managerial ranks, the jobber had no interest in the long-run efficiency of his mill. In fact, his own interests, as we shall see, were frequently at odds with the achievement of such an objective. As the 1929 Royal Commission wrote: "The effect of the absence of prospects [for promotion] is especially marked on jobbers. . . . The fact that the jobber has ordinarily no prospect of going further strengthens the temptation to take the fullest advantage of the position he has attained." [1]

It was his power and the way in which it was exercised that contributed so largely to the ramshackle discipline within individual mills and within the industry as a whole. And when reforms in work-force organization became urgent in the late 1920's and early 1930's, the power of the jobber had become so institutionalized, so imbedded in the scheme

---

[1] *RCL 1929*, "Report," p. 29. Mehta, *ICTI*, p. 71, has gone as far as to say that the "jobber . . . is the weakest link in the organizational setup of India's cotton mills."

of things, that the millowners could not themselves transform it.[2] Only through the powerful intervention of the State was the jobber slowly pried from his strategic position.

I have already pointed out that the earliest mill technicians were Englishmen who did not speak the local languages and therefore could not select labor directly or train it without assistance. They had to be provided with interpreters and others who assisted in the hiring and training of the initial mill workers. Apparently, some of the most aggressive of these initial mill hands were designated as jobbers and made responsible for producing gangs of new recruits, passing on their own newly learned skills, and overseeing the performance of the hands they had mobilized.[3] As additional mills were opened, the technicians either

---

[2] Technical and economic reorganization of the Bombay mills was necessary to meet the growing competition of newer upcountry and Japanese enterprises. And this required rather drastic changes in methods of labor utilization. *ITB 1927*, I. Though a few employers began to be interested in eliminating the jobber's power for reasons of efficiency, another aspect of the jobber's role — his function as a strikebreaker — became increasingly important at the same time.

[3] There is no contemporary evidence that tells us about the creation of the position of the jobber. All statements about its origin tend to have a highly conjectural, ex-post flavor. In the absence of anything more substantial, I have relied heavily on S. M. Rutnagur, *Bombay Industries: The Cotton Mills* (Bombay: *The Indian Textile Journal*, 1927), pp. 289 ff. So far as I can tell, there were two different groups in the early mills which are sometimes confused. Mehta, *ICTI*, pp. 67–68. The early interpreters who served as assistants to the Lancashire technicians were not jobbers. These people probably came from reasonably well-educated groups and tended to move up in the mill hierarchy, many of them replacing foreign technicians and higher officers. The jobbers, those responsible for actual recruiting, training, and overseeing small groups of workers, seem clearly to have been drawn from the beginning from the same broad groups from which the mill hands themselves came. This is suggested in the earliest contemporary evidence we have. See testimony of Bhana Naiak and Syed Tyab Ally, *FC 1875*, pp. 88–90; testimony of Sakoo, *FC 1885*, p. 141; and the oral evidence of Mr. Warden, *IFLC 1908*, II, p. 80. We should also not neglect the possibility that the Bombay mills were able to draw on workmen already trained to mechanical processes. Jobbers could well have come from the railway workshops and other kinds of enterprises where such experience was generated. See W. Walker, *Facts for Factories* (Bombay, 1857), p. 15; *Bombay Saturday Review*, VI, No. 17, 23 April 1864, p. 391; J. M. Maclean, *A Guide to Bombay* (3d ed., Bombay, 1877), pp. 138 ff; and D. E. Wacha, *The Life and Life Work of J. N. Tata* (Madras: Ganesh and Co., 1915), p. 7.

I have not touched at all on the development of a skilled class of artisans and mechanics in the cotton mills. Mehta, *CMI*, Chap. VIII, and Mehta, *ICTI*, Chap. III, deals slightly with this. The *ITJ* had general articles and notes on this subject before World War I. What is particularly noteworthy is that I have found no complaints in the literature of shortages, instability, inefficiency, or truculence relating to these skilled workers. There is need for a thorough investigation of the methods

trained their jobbers in the same way or raided them from existing mills. One advantage new mills had over older ones was that they often were able to lure not only the already experienced jobber but also many of the trained mill hands who worked under his direction.[4]

It is not infrequently suggested that although the jobber post was initially created to provide intermediaries between the Lancashire technicians and the work force, the position survived because of social and linguistic factors which continued to divide management from workers even after Indians began to take over positions in mill administration.[5] Indian administrators came almost entirely from literate middle-class ✓ groups. It is argued that this difference in social origins served as a barrier to effective contact with the mill hands. Moreover, management cadre tended to be drawn from one linguistic group (Gujarati) and workers came from another (Marathi).[6] This widely accepted explanation is not at all satisfactory. There seems no overriding reason for jobbers to have been given, even in the earliest decades, the effective responsibilities of hiring workers and administering the labor discipline. The same social and linguistic distinctions existed at the Tata Iron and Steel Company at Jamshedpur and in the railroad systems, yet in neither of these enterprises did we find the jobber (subforeman or overseer) developing the special power he developed in Bombay.

In the absence of satisfactory historical evidence, I can only presume to indicate an alternative possibility. I would suggest that jobbers did not by some socio-linguistic accident usurp their powers. It seems to me, rather, that they were intended to play the role of a middle management cadre from the beginning. Had they not been used to select and manage the work force, albeit in a subordinate capacity, it would have been necessary to employ other more expensive and perhaps no more efficient supervisory staff to perform the same functions. Given the fact that for a long while the technology of the industry was relatively simple, the

---

by which workers were trained for highly skilled tasks. I suspect that the role of the railway workshops will prove very important.

[4] W. T. Pomfret, *IIC 1916–18*, IV, p. 342; H.B.C., "Preliminary Thoughts on the Efficiency of the Bombay Textile Labour," *Journal of the Indian Economic Society*, II, No. 4, December 1919, pp. 212–213; *RCL 1929*, I, Part 1, pp. 432 and 502; and *RCL 1929*, I, Part 2, pp. 332 and 337.

[5] Indians appeared as mill officers very early. By 1895 nearly 60 per cent of all technicians were Indian. Rutnagur, *op. cit.*, pp. 293–294.

[6] As late as 1943 the BMOA thought it worth-while to publish a twenty-seven page English-Gujarati-Marathi glossary of mill terminology to help "Officers and Supervisory Staff of Mills who do not understand Marathi." The Millowners' Association, Bombay, *Glossary of Textile Terms (Used by Bombay Cotton Mill Workers)* (Bombay: Millowners' Association, 1943).

products quite coarse and work-force skills quite elementary, no one more sophisticated than the jobber was required. Jobbers needed no great skill to select labor and pass on what little training was necessary.[7] And by paying jobbers on the basis of the output of their subordinates wherever possible, strong incentives were applied to make certain that they kept the machines adequately supplied with labor and producing at top output.[8]

It was the jobber's task to see to the staffing of machines in his department or section. The industry very quickly became known as a source of expanding employment opportunities, and job seekers developed the custom of waiting at the mill gates each morning. When mill expansion required taking on more staff, or market demand warranted taking on more mill hands for a short period, or if there was more absenteeism on any day than could be taken care of by the use of operatives already in the mill, the jobber typically went to the gate in the morning and selected from among the expectant crowd those he wanted to employ.[9]

---

[7] The Bombay mills made absolutely no effort to establish any formal training program for new recruits. In fact, this was true even at the end of my period. Hands picked up whatever experience they needed by serving as unskilled workers or acting as unpaid assistants for friends or relations who were already employed. See evidence of the Bombay European Textile Association, *RCL 1929*, I, Part 2, p. 335; R. C. James, "Labor and Technical Change" (Unpublished Ph.D. dissertation, Cornell University, 1957), pp. 167 ff; and B. Shiva Rao, *The Industrial Worker in India* (London: George Allen and Unwin, 1939), pp. 90–91.

[8] The implication of most discussions of the 1920's and 1930's was that jobber power was and always had been an essentially irrational aspect of mill organization. But what, in fact, had occurred after World War I was that the Bombay industry's requirements had changed. In order to survive increased competition, the industry had to introduce a more sophisticated technology and much finer count products. In the absence of a broadly based system of public education, the traditional jobbers were not capable of performing the necessary new functions. This, I think, is the essential burden of Dr. Mehta's analysis. Mehta, *ICTI*, Chapter IV, particularly pp. 66–72.

[9] Mill-gate hiring seems to have existed as early as 1864. This is implied in the description in *Bombay Saturday Review*, VI, No. 17, April 23, 1864, p. 391. It is clearly suggested in various testimony, *FC 1885*, particularly the answers to question 16.

A few mills were initially established in quite isolated parts of the island, away from the main centers of population. Jobbers at these mills occasionally had to go out and recruit labor in the more populous parts of the city. But labor very quickly settled where mills were built and the development of public transportation at the turn of the century made labor more mobile within the city. When market demand encouraged all mills to increase output very quickly at the same time, jobbers might occasionally have to go to working class residences to recruit enough labor to meet

Making the jobber responsible for the recruiting of labor tended toward a certain fragmentation of the labor market. The jobber's position and income depended on his having an easily accessible supply of labor to meet fluctuating mill needs, and each jobber tended to create a small pool of labor around himself on which he could draw as needed.

Each jobber . . . is expected to find workers for his department. He realizes that failure to do so may result in his dismissal. Accordingly he endeavors to acquire an influence over his friends and acquaintances who live in the same or in neighboring chawls. He lends them money, advises them in family affairs and arbitrates in disputes. When labor is required, he uses the influence so gained and is generally successful in procuring hands. On occasions when he visits his village, he paints the life of a mill-worker in the brightest colors and endeavors to induce his relatives to leave their homes and fields for the more remunerative calling.[10]

This explains the evidence one finds of a tendency for workers to be concentrated in mill sections on the basis of relationship and place of origin. An English mill manager in the 1890's described the phenomenon:

. . . in the morning one of the overlookers or jobbers brought about a dozen hands in my presence, saying he had selected them for the purpose of replacing absentees and others who had left. I enquired through the interpreter as to the steps he had taken to find out the qualifications of the applicants, and he [the jobber] replied that they were *known* to him, being his caste fellows, and in some cases his neighbors.[11]

Not only did workers have a hard time finding employment except through a jobber connection, but the system tended to build loyalty to the jobber rather than to the employer.

The jobber's selection of new hands was theoretically subject to approval by the departmental master or mill manager, but inevitably the jobber's choice was decisive. His superior could only choose from those the jobber decided to present to him. At best, the manager would reject

---

short-term needs. The evidence suggests that the only important period when jobbers had to go into the streets and residential areas to find labor on a large scale was during the worst of the plague in 1897 and 1898. *FA 1897*, p. 8.

[10] A. R. Burnett-Hurst, *Labour and Housing in Bombay* (London: P. S. King and Son, 1925), pp. 46–47. See also Rutnagur, *op. cit.*, p. 326; and *BLO, Deductions from Wages 1926*, p. 17. However, it must be stressed that the evidence is quite clear that the jobber's basic responsibility was the overseeing of the labor in his section. He was not a labor contractor; he did not pay the workers who were his subordinates. His recruitment function was only an incidental aspect of his foreman's role.

[11] *ITJ*, III, 35, August 1893, 224.

obviously unsuitable recruits and order the jobber to submit another batch.[12]

In a society where employment opportunities were desperately needed and eagerly sought, the jobber became an important figure. With the power to grant or withhold employment, he was in a position to demand and obtain *baksheesh* or *dasturi* (fee, commission, bribe) from any worker seeking a job. The evidence suggests that this form of job purchase began very early. It was apparently sufficiently widespread to attract the attention of the Factory Commission of 1875.[13] Certainly in 1890 the system of paying for a job seems to have been ubiquitous. The *Indian Textile Journal* described successful applicants, male and female, paying anywhere from Rs.2 to Rs.5 for a job.[14] The Millowners' Association certainly was officially aware of the phenomenon because in 1891 its draft working rules contained a provision against the giving or taking of bribes.[15] The Indian Factory Labor Commission of 1908 got a great deal of evidence on *dasturi*, one witness testifying that there was a flat Rs.5 fee paid to get a job in either the spinning or weaving departments.[16] Employers entered only feeble denials, one manager agreeing that he "had heard of small sums being paid in the way of *dasturi*" but that he had "no knowledge of any sum as large as Rs.5 being paid." [17] The system continued into the 1920's. In 1926 the Bombay Textile Labor Union told the Indian Tariff Board that the system prevailed in virtually all mills, even those with exceptionally good managements.[18]

---

[12] *Ibid.*, 224–225. A factor contributing to the jobber's decisive role in hiring was the fact that in many mills the departmental heads arrived after work had started in the morning and after new hands had been taken on. Mr. Welsh, *IIC 1916–18*, IV, p. 75; M. S. Bhumgara, *RCL 1929*, I, Part 2, p. 501; BMOA evidence, *ibid.*, I, Part 2, p. 318; and Bombay European Textile Association evidence, *ibid.*, I, Part 2, pp. 331–332.

[13] On this occasion the mill officer and jobber questioned both denied the existence of *dasturi*. *FC 1875*, 30 and 89. However, at least one contemporary observer reported its presence. Wacha, *op. cit.*, p. 74.

[14] *ITJ*, I, 2, November 1890, p. 28. In 1893 it was said that jobbers took up to one month's earnings from successful job applicants. *ITJ*, III, No. 36, September 1893, p. 245. There are occasional references to payments for jobs in subsequent issues of *ITJ*. Workers testifying before the 1890 factory commission denied having paid for their jobs, but it is to be expected that employers, jobbers, and mill hands would all have reason to deny the existence of *dasturi* to an official body.

[15] Rule 14, Appendix VI. See also *BMOA 1893*, p. 17; *BMOA 1896*, p. 141.

[16] Mr. Nare, *IFLC 1908*, II, pp. 115–116. Another witness, *ibid.*, p. 111, said that the rate was 20 per cent of the first month's pay. This, at then current wages, would have involved much less than Rs.5.

[17] Mr. Cooper, *ibid.*, II, p. 149.

[18] *ITB 1927*, III, p. 547. On the basis of all the evidence the Tariff Board collected, it agreed with the union on the widespread extent of *dasturi*. *Ibid.*, I, p. 138.

The widespread existence of hiring *dasturi* had obvious consequences. It gave the jobber a powerful incentive to keep labor turning over as quickly as possible. As late as 1933 one mill official, describing his own experience, indicated the scope available to the jobber.

If the jobber is left to engage *badlis* [substitutes] from day to day, it is to his advantage to have each day as many fresh men as possible. By doing so, he is able to distribute his patronage as widely as possible, and thereby reap a very large harvest of graft. When the jobbers are in charge of *badli* engagement it is found that in addition to the total complement of permanent hands nearly thirty to fifty per cent of the full strength of the mill are working as mere badlis; of these, hardly ten per cent are persons who secure work for more than a fortnight in the aggregate while the rest get work for one or two days only in the month.[19]

It is clear that much of the labor was hired not on the basis of experience and efficiency but on the size of the payment the worker was willing to give. An equally consequential effect was, of course, the willingness of

---

Even the BMOA admitted its existence but claimed that it was dying out. *Ibid.*, II, pp. 351–352.

The ubiquity of *dasturi* would, of course, suggest the continued existence of a vast supply of labor desperately seeking employment and willing to pay for it. However, it has been suggested that *baksheesh*, to use a more general term, was a characteristic institution in all Indian life. Having paid it for services rendered in the countryside, the worker expected to pay it in Bombay. The implication here is that the existence of the phenomenon before World War I was more likely the expression of an unyielding social custom than a reflection of market forces, defying even the purported persistent shortage of labor. See J. H. Kelman, *Labour in India* (London: George Allen and Unwin Ltd., 1923), pp. 106–107; and M. C. Matheson *Indian Industry, Yesterday, Today and Tomorrow* (London: Oxford University Press, 1930), pp. 132–133. Though there may be some truth to this view generally, on the one occasion when labor shortages clearly did exist, during the plague epidemics of 1897 and 1898, *dasturi* vanished and workers were paid premia to take jobs.

The phenomenon of *dasturi* may be seen not only as evidence that labor was easily available at going rates; it suggests something more. By paying *dasturi*, workers were indicating that they were willing to work at a wage less than the employer was paying. In this sense, the employer was nominally paying a rate above the equilibrium price, the difference being taken by the jobber. The employer, in effect, was paying somewhat less to the mill hands and somewhat more to the jobbers than the pay roll suggested. One could argue that the jobber was being paid to organize the labor market and that in his absence the employer would have had to employ a middleman of some sort to do the job. It is possible that the jobber bore the risk and that this was reflected in short-run fluctuations in the *dasturi* part of his income. However, there is no evidence sufficiently detailed to permit a test of this proposition.

[19] *LG*, XIII, October 1933, p. 112. See also the evidence of the Bombay Textile Labor Union, *ITB 1927*, III, p. 439 *et seq.* The *ITJ* constantly made this point in its attacks on the principle of jobber hiring.

the jobber to keep hands who were not competent but who were willing to pay to hold their jobs.[20]

There were complaints about the evils stemming from the power of the jobber to hire labor, but they came mainly from outside observers and from an occasional manager.[21] The managing agents, the industry's policy makers, made no effort to change the system for seventy years. Even when the Tariff Board held its hearings in 1926 and the system came under violent attack, and proposals were made that hiring by jobber should be ended, the Millowners' Association opposed the suggestion.

To a large extent the jobbers bring the labor. . . . We think the jobbers are the men most competent to do that under the present circumstances. . . . I do not think otherwise we can fill up the places of our absentees or keep all the machinery going. Then jobbers are in touch with the men. The [department] assistants are not in touch with the men as much as the jobbers. . . . The labor of course is scattered over a big area; some in one district and some in another district, and it will make it very difficult for a person like a weaving master to try and control it.[22]

It was quickly pointed out that labor did not have to be recruited from all over the city since workers congregated at the mill gates. The employer representative then responded that departmental heads could not know the qualities of individual workers.

My point is that the jobber is one of them. Under Bombay conditions the jobber practically comes from the same class of men as the workman himself and therefore he is naturally in touch. Now the men who are above the jobbers do not belong to the same strata of life . . . and naturally are not in touch with the men. . . . You cannot easily get at them [the workers] unless you have some point of contact with them, which these superior officers do not enjoy at the moment.[23]

He went on to argue that the crowds at the mill gate were inadequate to supply either permanent or substitute workers at any time. "At the gates

---

[20] P. V. Deolalkar, "Textile Industries in India" (Unpublished Ph.D. dissertation, University of Bombay, 1927), pp. 212–213. One mill manager, Mr. Panday, pointed out in 1908 that as a consequence of allowing the jobber to do the hiring, it was possible to have a labor shortage inside the mill at the same time that a surplus existed outside, *IFLC 1908*, II, p. 97. The Bombay Textile Labor Union made the same point twenty years later. *ITB 1927*, III, p. 447.

[21] For an example of one manager who protested jobber exactions, see the case of Alfred Barratt, in Rutnagur, *op. cit.*, p. 668.

[22] *ITB 1927*, II, p. 347.

[23] *Ibid.*, p. 348.

we do not get a thousand people. Fifty or sixty come. Of course that makes a large crowd at the gate. But it does not mean that the spinning master can fill his requirements merely from that." [24]

The Tariff Board suggested the establishment of an employment center where unemployed workers could register and from which mills could recruit the labor they needed. The Association representative declared that this was "absolutely impossible." Not only was the proposal administratively unthinkable, but workers were so ignorant that they wouldn't use such a center. They could only be recruited by jobbers to whom they were bound "by all sorts of dealings. . . ." The employers obdurately maintained that the jobber system had to continue. It would end only when the level of work-force education had been raised.[25]

The Tariff Board, obviously disturbed by the chaotic state to which the jobber system reduced the process of selecting labor, was unimpressed by the Association's defense of its necessity. The board recommended that "all labor should be engaged directly by the officer of the mill in charge of the department which requires it or by a responsible assistant and not by the jobber." A system of direct employment was used in other cotton textile centers and "we see no reason why it should not be followed in Bombay." [26]

Shortly afterward the Association reported to the government that the industry was implementing this recommendation.[27] But in 1929 the Royal Commission discovered that nothing had, in fact, been done. The BMOA admitted that it had taken no official stand on the issue, the matter being left to individual mills.[28] Like the Tariff Board which preceded it, the Royal Commission issued a scathing denunciation of the system and recommended that each mill should appoint a special labor officer who would be responsible for all hiring.[29]

Faced by the obvious likelihood that the Royal Commission's conclusions would be adverse to the continuation of jobber hiring, at the end of 1929 the BMOA recommended to its members that "the policy of direct recruitment of labor should be encouraged" and that "a notice should be put up in all mills stating . . . that any heads of departments, assistants or jobbers accepting bribes from the work people would be in-

---

[24] *Loc. cit.*

[25] *Ibid.*, II, 348–352.

[26] *ITB 1927*, I, p. 139.

[27] *BMOA 1928*, p. 14.

[28] *RCL 1929*, I, Part 2, pp. 320–321. The evidence on the jobber system can be found scattered throughout *ibid.*, I, parts 1 and 2.

[29] *Ibid.*, "Report," pp. 23–25.

stantly dismissed." It requested that these policies be introduced before 1 February 1930.[30]

The Association might recommend but it was the millowners who had to dispose. In June 1930 the *Labour Gazette* reported that only forty-six of the sixty-eight working mills even claimed to have taken steps to encourage the direct recruitment of labor although all had posted notices against the taking of bribes.[31] In 1934 the BMOA told the Indian Tariff Board that the system of jobber hiring was on the wane and the jobber's recruiting power had been sharply reduced because the "final selection and appointments are made by the heads of the departments concerned."[32] But in fact jobber recruiting remained intact. As one mill officer stated, "in concerns where it was stated that the heads of departments are making the engagements directly, in practice it only meant that the heads of the departments merely approve of the engagements primarily made by the jobbers."[33]

The turning point in the transformation of the old system of jobber hiring occurred in 1934 with the passage of the Bombay Trade Disputes Act.[34] While the Government Labor Officer created by the law was moving directly against cases of bribery, the Association labor officer appointed to coöperate with him turned his attention to the root of the matter.[35] He submitted a proposal to control the employment of substitutes, one of the main sources of jobber power and corruption. The idea of this "*badli* [substitute worker] control scheme" was to establish a pool of substitutes with first claims to temporary and permanent jobs.

[30] *BMOA 1929*, p. 60; *BMOA 1930*, p. 177. It will be noticed that there is a suggestion that the system of *dasturi* went higher than jobbers, into the ranks of departmental masters. See also the Government Labor Officer's report on this, *ITJ*, XLVI, No. 7, April 1936, p. 230; and *BMOA 1920*, p. 243.

[31] *LG*, IX, No. 10, June 1930, pp. 1051–1052.

[32] *ITB 1934*, I, p. 49.

[33] *LG*, XIII, No. 2, October 1933, p. 111. See also F. E. Hawkins, "The Selection and Supervision of Workpeople," *ITJ*, XLIII, No. 3, December 1932, p. 99; and statement of the Bombay Textile Engineering Association, *ITB 1934*, II, p. 281. In 1933 the Sassoon Mills made a timid foray by appointing a mill labor officer. It was hoped that ultimately he would be able to break up the jobber monopoly of hiring. In an article, the labor officer indicated how deeply the system of jobber hiring affected work-force stability. He estimated that if he could eliminate the jobber from the hiring process he expected to be able to reduce the number of different substitutes employed at the Sassoon Mills from 30 to 40 per cent of the total work force to 10 per cent. *LG*, XIII, No. 2, October 1933, p. 112.

[34] Somewhat later the BMOA admitted that no significant change had occurred before 1934. *ITJ*, XLVII, No. 11, July 1937, p. 369.

[35] The BMOA appointed its labor officer in response to government pressure. *BMOA 1934*, pp. iv and viii; *LG*, XIV, No. 4, December 1934, p. 274.

Each *badli* received a registration card which assigned him to a specific mill. Each morning he was to appear at that department with first claim to any temporary employment. Only if no regular card-carrying *badli* was available could a department jobber go to the mill gate and recruit other labor. The new recruits were then also to be given registration cards which made them part of the regular labor pool. Each *badli's* card was to be marked every day he turned up, whether or not he received employment. When permanent jobs became available they were to be filled from among the substitutes who had been most diligent in attendance. Supported by the government, this proposal was quickly accepted by the Association and formally introduced into all mills in 1935.[36]

In 1936 the system was modified in an attempt to reduce the size of the *badli* labor pool. Each mill was instructed to report the absenteeism among its permanent employees in each department on the day after pay day (when absenteeism was highest). On the first of the next month registration cards were issued only to that number of *badlis*. The *badlis* were required to appear at the departments to which they were assigned every morning, whether they got work or not, and they could have their registrations revoked for irregular attendance. When a permanent vacancy occurred, the senior *badli* in the department was supposed to be appointed to fill it.[37]

The Association also recommended two other procedures to the mills. It urged that mills should provide retrenched hands with certificates of service so that they might be given preferential treatment for either temporary or permanent vacancies in other mills, "thus reducing, to some extent, the dependence of managers on their head jobbers or jobbers for the supply of labor." [38] The Association also proposed that mills keep service records for all jobbers. These service records would note the reasons why a jobber left or was dismissed so that those fired for taking bribes could be spotted.[39]

In 1938 the Millowners' Association further recommended that each of its member mills appoint labor officers. Among other functions, it was stressed that these officers could supervise recruitment of labor.[40]

By 1937 the BMOA was boasting that the coöperation of government

---

[36] *BMOA 1935*, pp. 29 and 150–151.

[37] The registration card contained in Marathi a description of how the *badli* control scheme worked and what was expected of the worker. For the text of these instructions, see *TLIC 1940*, p. 339.

[38] *BMOA 1936*, pp. 38–39. There is no evidence that this was ever implemented.

[39] *BMOA 1936*, p. 37; *ITJ*, XLVII, No. 10, July 1937, p. 369.

[40] *BMOA 1938*, p. 59.

and Association labor officers plus the working of the "*badli* control scheme" had removed the employing power and its possibilities of corruption from the hands of the jobber.[41] Although it is true that some improvement had occurred since 1934, the power of the jobber had not yet been broken.[42] The new system, applied with varying degrees of enthusiasm in the mills, was cumbersome and had many loopholes. In December 1938 one union official charged that *badlis* were still giving bribes in a quarter of the city's mills and that many mills ignored seniority claims to permanent posts.[43] In 1940 the Textile Labor Inquiry Committee concluded that these conditions still persisted. In fact they continued to bedevil the industry through World War II, although to a declining degree.[44]

The source of continuing weakness which prevented management's capture of effective control of the hiring process was the role of the mill labor officer. Although the BMOA had recommended that each mill create such a post in 1938, in 1940 only twenty-six of the sixty-eight working mills had complied, and as late as 1946 only thirty-four labor officers had been appointed.[45] Not only were the mills slow to appoint labor officers, but even in those which had created the post the power of the officer to affect recruiting decisions was seriously circumscribed by the refusal of management to concede effective authority to him. He was not permitted to infringe on the powers of departmental heads. Yet, if it were not to be subverted, the *badli* control scheme required a powerful labor officer with precisely this authority. On the whole, the appointment and survival of the labor officer in most mills was merely a grudging concession to external political pressures.[46]

Beyond the failures of application there was one additional weakness in the *badli* control scheme. The fact that substitutes were attached to individual departments in individual mills meant that there was a larger

[41] *ITJ*, XLVII, No. 10, July 1937, pp. 369–370; *BMOA 1938*, p. 59.

[42] For evidence of continuing and widespread *dasturi*, see the Government Labor Officer's monthly reports, *ITJ* & *LG*, issues for 1935–1939.

[43] R. S. Nimbkar, *TLIC 1940*, p. 340.

[44] *TLIC 1940*, pp. 337–347. M. M. Shah, "Labour Recruitment and Turnover in the Textile Industry of Bombay Presidency" (Unpublished Ph.D. dissertation, University of Bombay, 1941), *passim*, described from personal experience the chaotic state of mill record-keeping at the end of the 1930's. In the absence of careful records, the *badli* control scheme could easily be subverted. See also *ICEC 1948*, p. 61; Mehta, *ICTI*, p. 69; *BMOA 1948*, p. 201; and R. C. James, "The Casual Labor Problem in Indian Manufacturing," *The Quarterly Journal of Economics*, LXXIV, No. 1, February 1960, pp. 100–116.

[45] *TLIC 1940*, p. 341; *LIC, Enquiry 1946*, pp. 7–8.

[46] *TLIC 1940*, pp. 341–342; *ICEC 1948*, pp. 61–62.

pool of substitutes in the industry than would have been the case had the *badlis* been drawn from a central pool. Apart from the continuing possibilities of corruption that the arrangement permitted, it also meant a lower level of employment for each *badli*.[47]

The incomplete success of the mill labor officers and the *badli* control scheme forced the Bombay provincial government to return at the very end of my period to a proposal that had been advanced during the Indian Tariff Board hearings of 1926, the establishment of a central labor exchange. In May 1947 the government proposed the establishment of a central pool of all persons seeking employment in the industry. This labor exchange would issue *badli* registration cards in numbers sufficient to maintain an adequate supply of labor. No employer would be permitted to employ a substitute except through the exchange nor might permanent employment be granted to persons not on the official register.[48]

The Association objected strongly, arguing that this "decasualization scheme" was an attempt to use a technique applied to dock labor in other countries in an industry where conditions were entirely different.

To be frank, . . . the employer should have absolute freedom in this matter of employing any person who, in his opinion, will meet his requirements. In any event, the Officer-in-charge of recruitment in the mills under the *Badli* Control Scheme now in operation, may be expected to know better than the Exchange Manager under the proposed scheme, the type of person who will fit in with the mill's requirements.[49]

The Association succeeded in delaying the introduction of the new system until after the end of the period with which I am concerned. Finally, rising unemployment in the industry forced the government to take action and in mid-1949 the "decasualization scheme" was introduced over employer objections.[50] After nearly a century the recruiting power of the jobber had come to an end. However, the authority over employment, taken from the jobber, did not come into the hands of the employer. Instead, it was to be exercised by a State agency reinforced by legal authority.

---

[47] R. Mukerjee, *The Indian Working Class* (Bombay: Hind Kitabs, Ltd., 1951), p. 38; *BMOA 1947*, p. 202.

[48] *BMOA 1947*, pp. 200–203.

[49] *BMOA 1947*, pp. 204–206.

[50] For a detailed description of the scheme as it was introduced, *BMOA 1949*, p. 248. For an analysis of its operation and some of its consequences, James, "Labor and Technical Change," *passim*; and James, "The Casual Labor Problem in Indian Manufacturing."

(3)

In addition to his almost complete responsibility for hiring workers, the jobber had virtually uncontrolled power in the administration of labor discipline. Mill agents and managers established the general policies and shaped the framework of discipline through the standing orders, but these were very general. It was the jobber who, at least until the 1930's, gave meaning and content to the formal work regulations. In the absence of any strong system of superior supervision, the jobber had very wide-ranging responsibility for the performance and behavior of the work force.[51] In this section I propose to show how between 1856 and 1934 mill discipline, though formally a management function, was actually shaped by other less impressive hands.

It is not an easy phenomenon to describe. If one reads the standing orders one encounters the formal discipline as prescribed by agents and managers. If one reads the testimony and reports of the Bombay Millowners' Association one gets the impression of employers sure of their power and certain of the structure of discipline they had created within their enterprises. But the true character of mill labor discipline did not lie in the written regulations, and it cannot be found in the formal statements of the employers' association. It can be seen only in the subtle and elusive relations which existed among human beings in the mills. Evidence for the period before 1926 is not very extensive. The specific relationships between jobbers and work force, never formally described, were constantly changing in minor ways, but it is clear that the general pattern did become institutionalized very early. When the conventional façade was finally penetrated by the Tariff Board and Royal commission in the late 1920's there was exposed not merely a situation as it then existed but as it had been virtually from the beginning. Then it became clear that the disciplinary responsibilities held by the jobber contributed significantly to the kind of labor force which the industry had created.

From the earliest days the jobber seems to have borne the main responsibility for directing the operatives in his section or department, operatives who had been hired largely by him. Whatever training a new mill hand got, if any, was the jobber's responsibility. He saw to it that work progressed properly; he arranged work loads and rest intervals. He was responsible for mill hands turning up on holidays to clean their machines, and he had extensive power to fine or discharge workers for

---

[51] Obviously, the jobber was ultimately a subordinate employee and the extent of an individual jobber's control was sometimes challenged and limited. However, the general picture is one in which the employers until the 1930's had largely forfeited their authority to him.

breaches of discipline and bad work. In other words, it was he who determined whether the worker was efficient enough to remain on the job.[52] Moreover, when a hand wanted to quit, it was up to the jobber to accept or refuse the formal notice. If he refused — and he sometimes did — the worker would forfeit his accrued earnings when he left the mill.[53] Moreover, the jobber also largely controlled the granting of leaves. In the absence of formal provisions, a worker who wanted to take time off had to make individual arrangements, typically with his jobber. Weavers were customarily required to find their own substitutes, it being left to the jobber to accept or reject the replacement.[54] Other mill hands might also provide their own substitutes, but more frequently they seem to have been directly hired by the jobber from the mill gate.[55] It was up to the jobber to decide whether a worker who had taken leave, with or without approval, would get his job back when he returned.[56] Indeed, he was practically the only channel of communication between the operatives and management and it was his responsibility to see that trouble makers did not get hired or remain long employed in the mill.[57] He was, in effect, the key figure in the supervision of work and the maintenance of discipline.[58] And his authority was recognized and generally accepted by the employers.[59]

---

[52] *FC 1875*, pp. 90 and 144; *FC 1885*, pp. 104 and 142; *Bombay and Lancashire Cotton Spinning Inquiry, 1888*, p. 77; *BMOA 1905*, p. x; *IFLC 1908*, II, p. 106; *ITB 1927*, II, p. 106; *ITB 1927*, III, pp. 439–441 and 546–547; *LG*, VI, No. 12, August 1927, pp. 1111 and 1114; *RCL 1929*, I, Part 1, pp. 9, 46, 298, 501 and 503–504; *RCL 1929*, I, Part 2, pp. 172, 248, 257, 332, 386.

[53] *IFLC 1908*, II, p. 51.

[54] *ITB 1927*, III, pp. 439–441.

[55] Weaving required greater skill than any other occupation in the mills. Apparently, one way of guaranteeing that qualified substitutes would be available was to require the weaver to furnish his own substitute whose earnings were credited to the regular worker who then made his own arrangements for paying the replacement. *ITB 1927*, III, p. 61. It seems that the operatives often sought to place members of their own families as substitutes. *ITJ*, VI, No. 72, September 1896, p. 85.

[56] N. N. Wadia, *ITB 1927*, II, p. 223; *LG*, VI, No. 12, August 1927, p. 1111; *RCL 1929*, I, Part 1, pp. 351, 501, 503–504; *RCL 1929*, I, Part 2, pp. 248, 257, 386. ". . . few mills are willing to recognize a worker on his return from a holiday as an old employee. . . ." *RCL 1929*, "Report," p. 26.

[57] *BMOA 1905*, p. ii; *IFLC 1908*, II, pp. 78 and 110; *IDC 1921*, p. 17; Burnett-Hurst, *op. cit.*, p. 117; *RCL 1929*, I, Part 2, pp. 312, 319, 415. On the jobber's responsibility for keeping trouble makers out of the mills, *BMOA 1892*, pp. 10–11 and 27–28; *ITB 1927*, III, p. 440.

[58] *RCL 1892*, p. 124; *BMOA 1905*, p. x; *IFLC 1908*, II, pp. 66 and 72; *IIC 1916–18*, IV, pp. 39 and 41; *IIC 1916–18*, "Report," p. 156; *RCL 1929*, "Report," pp. 23–24.

[59] The draft standing orders prepared by the BMOA made formal acknowledgment of the jobber's authority. See regulation 16, appendix VI below. Although the draft

The jobber not only had power over workers, but he made that power pay directly, exacting *dasturi* from them in many ways while on the job.[60] Furthermore, his power on the job was matched by its ramifications into many other aspects of the operatives' lives and provided other sources of income. A large proportion of the work force seems to have depended on credit for survival.[61] The jobber frequently acted as a moneylender himself or served as an intermediary between the mill hands and outside moneylenders. The financial hold of the jobber on the mill hands was further strengthened by certain mill-sanctioned moneylending activities in which he engaged, the so-called *havala* system.[62] He also used his authority to induce workers to trade with favored merchants.[63]

Not only did the jobber supplement his income by these activities, but he was able to defend these perquisites and frustrate efforts to eliminate their disruptive consequences. For example, even government-supported attempts to provide a cheap food supply to mill workers during World War I inflation fell afoul of his power. In 1920 the Government of Bombay complained:

For the present there are many influences like those of jobbers, head jobbers, masters, and other such persons which come in the way of the poor workers and prevent them from making their purchases through the Consumer's Society's Shop where they have been started. These petty officers of the mill act as touts or Commission Agents of several Banias [merchants] and get regular commission for the purchases of grain and cloth made by the workers under them. These persons command a lot of influence over the actual workers, and

---

was not accepted by the industry, this regulation seems to have represented the codification of generally existing practice. At a later time, when the mills came under sharp attack for allowing the jobber to exercise the power he did, the BMOA, though denying the existence of that power currently, did admit its existence in the past, *RCL 1929*, I, Part 1, p. 386. See also the Bombay government statement, *ibid.*, p. 9.

[60] *ITJ*, I, No. 6, March 1891, p. 91; *ITJ*, X, No. 120, September 1900, pp. 356–357; Wacha, *op. cit.*, p. 74; *ITB 1927*, II, pp. 351–352; *ITB 1927*, III, pp. 439, 447, 453, 546–547, 567; *RCL 1929*, I, Parts 1 and 2, *passim*; Matheson, *op. cit.*, pp. 132–133; and the monthly reports of the Government Labor Officer, published in issues of *ITJ*, 1935–1937.

[61] The withholding of the first pay for as long as two months seems to have been a factor contributing to this need.

[62] *LG*, VII, No. 1, September 1927, pp. 57–59; *RCL 1929*, I, Part 1, pp. 479–481, 508–509; *RCL 1929*, I, Part 2, p. 329, 336–337, 341–342.

[63] *IFLC 1908*, II, pp. 52, 65, 124; *BMOA 1918*, p. xii; *BMOA 1920*, p. 243; N. M. Joshi, "Welfare Work in Bombay Cotton Mills," *Journal of Indian Industries and Labour*, I, No. 1, February 1921, p. 21; *RCL 1929*, I, Part 1, p. 509; *Bombay Provincial Banking Enquiry Committee, 1929–30*, III, p. 621; P. G. Kanekar, "Cooperation Among the Working Classes," *Cooperation in Bombay*, edited by H. L. Kaji, pp. 236–237, 241–242; *LG*, XIX, No. 1, September 1939, p. 25.

when they do not act according to their wishes, they are afraid of either losing their employment, or of not getting any facilities as regards the purchases on credit or loans in cash.[64]

The jobber's hold on his subordinates was reinforced by his social connections with them. The method of recruitment usually permitted him to hire workers, not infrequently his relations or caste brethren, who came from the same village or district. But the ultimate hold, making possible the jobber's resistance to considerable pressure from the employer, was that mill-hand loyalties necessarily tended to be identified with the jobber rather than with the employer. The jobber gave him his position and the jobber could take it away or at least make life miserable for him. Moreover, if the jobber was sacked a new jobber could well sweep a department clean of its old hands and replace them with his clients. Unprotected against arbitrary treatment, the mill hand had no alternative but to support the devil he knew against the devil he did not know. Here we have an explanation of cases of operatives striking in support of a discharged jobber or following him to another mill.[65]

The description of the system clearly indicates that the power of the jobber, his semiautonomous position as the disciplinary authority in the mill, derived not only from the arbitrary coercive rights he exercised in the name of the employer but also from the general insecurity of the work force for which he was responsible. The jobber was transformed, almost from the very beginning of the industry, from the insignificant subordinate which his position in the factory chain of command would have suggested, into a powerful figure whose interests were frequently at odds with any attempt to create a stable, efficient, and disciplined mill labor force.

I have already indicated that the jobber's exercise of this wide range of power was not only recognized but also accepted by the employers. Occasionally there were employer complaints that the jobber could not be easily controlled.[66] On a few occasions there were cases of clear con-

---

[64] *BMOA 1920*, p. 243. This statement also raises another issue, the extent to which the system of corruption involved higher management — departmental masters and the like. There is some evidence to suggest that this phenomenon did exist on a reasonably wide scale. However, it is only important to note that this merely served to bolster the power of the jobber who was the key to the whole system.

[65] *ITJ*, I, No. 6, March 1891, p. 91; *ITJ*, IV, No. 42, March 1894, pp. 149–150; *RCL 1892*, p. 124; *IIC 1916–18*, IV, p. 342; H.B.C., "Preliminary Thoughts on the Efficiency of Bombay Textile Labour," pp. 211–213; *ITB 1927*, III, 542, 565, 570; *RCL 1929*, I, Part 2, pp. 332, 337. From 1921 the *Labour Gazette* reported many cases of strikes caused by the discharge of jobbers.

[66] *FC 1885*, p. 79; *RCL 1892*, p. 124; *IFLC 1908*, I, pp. 14–17; *IFLC 1908*, II, pp. 49–50, 52, 56, 72, 84–85, 116; *IIC 1916–18*, "Report," p. 152.

flict between the employer and his jobbers. The classic instance, frequently cited, occurred when J. N. Tata took over a bankrupt mill at Kurla in 1886 and completely rationalized its equipment and reorganized its work practices. He seems, as a result, to have had trouble with his labor force for a year or two because of obstruction from jobbers who were holdovers from the previous administration. However, Tata successfully broke their power.[67] In the few other cases of serious conflict between jobbers and management which produced strikes, the discharge and replacement of jobbers and their supporters quickly resolved the problem.[68] My point is that when the power of the jobber did interfere with the objectives of a determined employer the jobber could be sacked and he and his hands, if they supported him, replaced with a minimum of difficulty.[69] But at no time before the 1930's were the employers at all interested in undermining the basic structure of jobber authority.[70]

Although there was no significant criticism of the role of the jobber from within the industry, this does not mean that the system was never under attack. Criticism began quite early, but it came almost entirely from interested outsiders. *The Indian Textile Journal*, from its founding in 1890, continually attacked the industry's uncontrolled concession of power to the jobber. Sorabji Rutnagur, its editor, blamed the lack of

[67] *ITJ*, I, No. 11, August 1891, p. 177; Wacha, *op. cit.*, p. 74; Mehta, *CMI*, p. 59; *RCL 1892*, p. 124. There is evidence that Tata's problem did not entirely stem from recalcitrant jobbers but from wage cuts and the withholding of pay. See the report by H. E. Winter, Thana District Magistrate, in East India (Factories Act), *Return to an Address of the House of Commons, 15 April 1889*, pp. 76–77.

[68] *ITJ*, I, No. 6, March 1891, p. 91; *ITJ*, IV, No. 42, March 1894, pp. 149–150; *ITJ*, X, No. 113, February 1900, p. 120; *ITJ*, XIX, No. 225, June 1909, p. 321; *ITJ*, XIX, No. 226, July 1909, p. 359.

[69] One manager described the pattern: "With [the introduction of] a strict supervisor, the chief feature is the frequency of strikes for a short period until things get fairly settled down." *ITJ*, X, No. 120, September 1900, p. 356.

[70] It is worth noting that many of the complaints against jobber power came from managers. This raises an interesting point. On occasion the jobber served as a spy for the managing agent, reporting to him on activities in the mill. Sometimes the jobber's influence with the agent was great enough to undercut completely the manager's authority. For one vivid example of this, *ITJ*, III, No. 35, August 1893, pp. 224–225. For general complaints of espionage and lack of managerial authority, *ITJ*, V, No. 54, March 1895, p. 134; *ITJ*, VIII, No. 88, January 1898, p. 102; *ITJ*, XIX, No. 228, September 1909, p. 405; *ITJ*, XX, No. 229, October 1909, pp. 2 and 4. The high rate of managerial turnover may also have accounted for some of the managers' weakness vis-à-vis the jobber. The *ITJ* fairly regularly reported the movement of managers from one mill to another. See, for example, *ITJ*, VI, No. 62, November 1895, p. 44. See also Mehta, *ICTI*, p. 75.

proper mill labor discipline on the owners' failure to do anything about the situation.[71] The official report on the working of the Indian Factories Act in Bombay for 1913 complained that the high labor turnover was encouraged by the jobbers and went so far as to suggest that trade unions were needed to solve the problem.[72]

Criticism grew sharper and more extensive during and after the World War when first inflation and then the industry's economic crisis, accompanied by rapidly increasing unemployment, produced a rising crescendo of labor unrest. The Tariff Board hearings in 1926 and the Royal Commission enquiry of 1929 brought to a focus all the long-standing criticisms of jobber power. But even in the face of all these criticisms the industry remained officially complacent and unyielding. It argued that given the character of the labor force the jobber system was the only possible method of administering the mill hands. Moreover, the mill-owners claimed that jobbers did not exercise actual disciplinary power in the mills and that final authority was in the hands of management.[73]

The employer description of the situation was vigorously challenged by a host of witnesses. To this the BMOA responded that to the extent that jobbers created problems in the administration of the work force, as much was being done as needed doing or could be done. It denied that bribery was at all widespread and stated that when cases of corruption were discovered, "the most severe disciplinary action is taken against the jobbers concerned." [74] But in 1929 the unofficial testimony was strongly bolstered by a memorandum submitted by the Government of Bombay which charged that despite millowner efforts to suppress corruption, it was widespread and the powers of the jobber were "still as great as formerly. . . ." [75] The government's analysis made it clear that the elimination of jobber authority was essential if a stable and coöperative labor force was to be created.[76]

Occasionally an employer showed some awareness that all was not well and that jobber power might be contributing to the labor difficulties which were paralyzing the industry. "The jobber class which is slightly superior in mentality to the laborers is getting impudent, playing upon the ignorance of the latter and is many times the main cause of strikes

[71] *IFLC 1908*, II, pp. 110–111.

[72] *ITJ*, XXV, No. 289, October 1914, p. 24. See also a similar statement by J. B. Petit, *BMOA 1913*, pp. vii–viii.

[73] For evidence by employers and contrary testimony from other sources see *ITB 1927*, II and III, *passim*, and *RCL 1929*, I, Parts 1 and 2, *passim*.

[74] *RCL 1929*, I, Part 1, p. 386.

[75] *RCL 1929*, I, Part 1, p. 9.

[76] *Ibid.*, pp. 8 ff.

by instigating and spreading dissatisfaction amongst the laborers behind the curtain for its own self-interests." [77]

But even in the few cases where managements recognized that the
jobber was at the root of the problem, they feared to move against him.
The authority that the jobber had been allowed to wield over the mill
hands now made him a formidable adversary. Having created a situation in which the jobber was virtually omnipotent, the employers found
themselves dependent on the continuation of his power.[78] The millowners feared that any attempt to eliminate him would cause more strikes.[79]

But though the jobber's "impudence" may have been part of the explanation of labor unrest, it was certainly not all of it. Some of the chaotic
situation arose out of the struggle of the mill hands against the uncontrolled exercise of power by jobbers. "The experience of the Union is that
among the workers there are often two camps — one pro-jobber and the
other anti-jobber — fighting against each other and occasionally going
to law courts and adding to the litigation." [80]

And this left the employers in some confusion. As the BMOA representative commented: "Things became topsy-turvey last year when the
workers wanted some jobbers to be dismissed." [81]

The subservience of the work force to the jobber was beginning to
break down and this added to the disorderly condition of the industry.
It was clear that the jobber as the key element in the administration of
the mill labor force had to be eliminated if some stability was to be re-
stored. The crux of the problem, however, was that the employers had
so long depended on the jobber to manage the work force that they apparently could not visualize any way to change basically their internal
disciplinary structure.

(4)

In 1926 various witnesses, primarily those from the unions, had suggested to the Indian Tariff Board a radical revamping of the entire
system of labor discipline. They pointed out that unrestricted jobber

[77] *ITB 1927*, IV, p. 204.

[78] *RCL 1929*, I, Part 1, p. 501.

[79] See the evidence of Mr. Stones, superintendent of the Sassoon group of mills,
RCL 1929, I, Part 2, p. 410. See also the description of the failure to break jobber
power at the Spring Mill. *RCL 1929*, I, Part 2, p. 332.

[80] *BTLU, RCL 1929*, I, Part 1, p. 298.

[81] *RCL 1929*, I, Part 2, p. 330. See also *BSEC 1928–29*, pp. 194–195, dispute 16.
Actually, strikes by workers for the dismissal of jobbers were not new phenomena.
See *ITJ*, XX, No. 239, August 1910, p. 387. However, in this particular case the
workers were demanding the dismissal of newly appointed jobbers. This may have
indicated a fear by mill hands that the new jobbers would replace them.

authority increased inefficiency, discontent, and instability of the work force. In order to minimize these characteristics, the powers of recruitment, discipline, and discharge had to be taken away from the jobbers. Formal and regular rules for discipline, leave, and discharge had to be established. Cases of corruption had to be punished with instant dismissal, and workers informing in such cases had to be protected against possible intimidation.[82] Although the Tariff Board made certain recommendations about the jobber system, it did not see to the heart of the problem.

The Royal Commission on Labor spent more time investigating the subject and clearly recognized that the largely uncontrolled powers of the jobber was responsible for much of the instability which characterized the labor force and accounted for the "general prevalence" of bribery. The commission recommended "the exclusion of the jobber from the engagement and dismissal of labor," these functions to be taken over by a specially trained labor officer who would be "subordinate to no one except the general manager of the factory. . . ." Among the benefits it saw flowing from such a change were suppression of bribery and the reduction of absenteeism and labor turnover.[83]

The combination of official pressure and an antagonistic public opinion forced employers to respond to the criticism somehow. They did not attempt to adopt the root-and-branch revision recommended by the Royal Commission. As the Millowners' Association saw it, the problem was really caused by the lack of effective communication between employers and worker:

In Bombay there is no equivalent to Mr. Gandhi [in Ahmedabad] nor is there the same close personal touch between the workers and the employers that one finds in Ahmedabad where the average millowner spends the greater part of his time in his mill. As has been pointed out the trade unions in the textile trade in Bombay are virtually nonexistent and recognizing this the millowners are endeavoring to get in touch with their men direct.[84]

In January 1930 the Association proposed to its members that all mills should take steps to "prevent the accumulation of grievances and remove them as they arise." [85] Its solution was that "a complaint box to which operatives should have free access should be put up in the compound of all mills." [86] In its public statement announcing this policy, the Association said:

---

[82] *ITB 1927*, III, pp. 439–454 and 565; *ITB 1927*, IV, pp. 178, 189, 192–193.
[83] *RCL 1929*, "Report," pp. 24–26.
[84] *BMOA 1930*, p. 177.
[85] *BMOA 1929*, p. 59.
[86] *Loc. cit.*

The management of the mills have been advised to make it clear to the work people that they are always ready and willing to consider sympathetically any complaints or suggestions that the workers may bring forward personally and the men have been told that whenever they feel they have cause for complaint they should speak about it to the head of their department at any time during the day and if the latter is unable to deal with a complaint the workmen should approach the manager personally when he comes into the department. . . .[87]

Even if good will had existed in the industry, such an approach would have been naïve. It did not come to grips with the basic problem, the disciplinary authority of the jobber. Moreover, the experiment did not work. Although most of the mills did set up complaint boxes and notified the workers of their presence, they were not widely used.[88]

During the period 1931 to 1934 it became clear that no decisive steps were being taken against jobber power. Employers persisted in their adherence to the traditional system of labor administration, "accepting the jobber line as an indispensable benefit or an equally indispensable evil. . . ." [89] An example of this can be seen in the case of a strike in the M. Dharamsi Mill in 1931. Having gone on strike, the mill hands elected a strike committee of one man from each of the factory's eleven departments. Some interested outsiders interviewed the management regarding its unwillingness to meet with the workers, "but the latter [the management] preferred to negotiate directly with the workers themselves. The management accordingly discussed the question with the jobbers and head jobbers of the mill. . . ." [90] At the beginning of 1934 only the Sassoon group of mills had attempted to comply with the Royal Commission recommendation by appointing a labor officer.[91] Barring this single exception, the traditional pattern of authority continued to exist.[92]

Having failed to get the industry voluntarily to introduce any major changes in mill disciplinary organization and practices, the government

---

[87] *BMOA 1930*, p. 177.

[88] *LG*, IX, No. 10, June 1930, p. 1050. The fact that complaint boxes were placed so that jobbers and officers could be witness to their use worked against the success of the device. F. E. Hawkins, "Medical Service in Bombay Cotton Mills," *ITJ*, XLV, No. 3, December 1934, p. 93. The fact that a majority of the employees were illiterate should also be allowed for.

[89] F. E. Hawkins, "The Selection and Supervision of Work people," *ITJ*, XLIII, No. 3, December 1932, p. 101.

[90] *LG*, X, No. 8, April 1931, pp. 853–854.

[91] *LG*, XIII, No. 2, October 1933, pp. 112–113. However, this labor officer was not intended to replace the jobbers immediately.

[92] F. E. Hawkins, "Need of a Labour Officer for Every Mill," *ITJ*, XLV, No. 4, January 1935, pp. 125–126. See also *ITB 1934*, II, p. 281.

turned in 1934 to legislation in an attempt to reduce the industrial tensions which it blamed on the ineffectual relations between employers and workers. As I have already pointed out, the passage of the Bombay Trade Disputes Act marked a great turning point. The official labor officer was given the responsibility to see to the enforcement of the standing orders, to represent the workers' grievances to the employers, and to secure their redress.[93] It was, in other words, the function of this government official to undertake some of those duties which a vigorous union would have discharged had one existed. These duties, conscientiously carried out, constituted a first step toward reduction of the arbitrary authority of the jobber.[94]

At the same time, the BMOA labor officer, appointed to act as an intermediary between the Government Labor Officer and the mills, also moved to directly strengthen controls over jobber corruption. In May 1935 he started building up a card file of information on jobbers in the industry and by mid-1937 he had records on about 2,600. The purpose of the file was to prevent a mill from giving employment out of ignorance to a jobber who had been discharged by another mill for bribe-taking.[95] In 1937 the Millowners' Association boasted that as a result of the coöperation between its own labor officer and the Government Labor Officer the power of the jobber had been sharply reduced:

. . . the power of engagement and dismissal of labor has been taken out of the hands of the jobber and has been placed in the hands of the heads of Departments and of the Managers. This alteration has, in itself, greatly reduced the capacity of jobbers . . . to extort payments to obtain or retain employment in the mills, and the operatives are now aware that it is their individual efficiency in their daily occupation which would govern the continuity of their employment and not the whim or greed of the jobber. . . .
The deterrent effect of a dismissal for bribery . . . has been further increased by the introduction of service cards for all . . . jobbers. . . . When a jobber is dismissed for bribery, the offense is noted on his record card by the Association and if he seeks to obtain a post in another mill, a copy of his previous record is available to the mill concerned.

---

[93] The authority of the Government Labor Officer was bolstered by a conciliation procedure established by the 1934 law. T. V. Baddeley, "Industrial Disputes and their Settlement," *ITJ Jubilee Souvenir*, p. 281.

[94] By insisting on proper enforcement of standing orders and by providing a channel of protest against arbitrary discharge, the Government Labor Officer began to restrict arbitrary exercise of power by the jobber.

[95] *LG*, XIV, No. 11, July 1935, p. 841; *BMOA 1935*, p. 29; *ITJ*, XLVII, No. 10, July 1937, p. 369; *ITJ*, XLVII, No. 11, August 1937, p. 424. The BMOA had advanced such a proposal as far back as 1918 but its members had refused to accept it. *BMOA 1918*, p. xiv; *ITB 1927*, II, p. 348.

In 1935, 25 persons . . . holding important posts in the mills were dismissed for bribery.[96]

But the willingness and coöperation of the Association were not enough. Attention to Association rulings was, in these matters, essentially a voluntary thing which could be disregarded by individual mills.[97] Although the Government Labor Officer and the Association officials could push their policies, only the individual mills could effectively break the jobber's power, and most mill managements were not easily or willingly brought to make the necessary changes. Reports of the Government Labor Officer for the years 1935 to 1939 are filled with evidence of the jobber's continuing power and of the overt and covert support he received from his superiors.[98] Higher officials refused to listen to mill-hand grievances; they intimidated workers who appealed to the Government Labor Officer; and they almost invariably supported the jobber against charges brought by the laborer. Furthermore, when it was proved that a jobber had demanded bribes, he was not always discharged. Even the combined pressure of the two labor officers was often resisted by managers and millowners.[99]

As late as 1940, despite some inroads into the grossest manifestations of jobber power, the situation was only slowly changing. Summarizing the evidence presented before it by many witnesses, an official committee reported:

Since the publication of the Report of the Royal Commission, the Millowners' Association, Bombay, claims to have restricted the influence of the jobber by transferring from him to the manager and departmental heads the powers of engaging and dismissing men and of inflicting fines and granting leave. But the action taken in this behalf does not seem to have been effective, and the jobber still continues to be the main instrument of labor management.[100]

Although this 1940 report suggests a tenacious survival of the jobber's power, his authority was in fact gradually being undermined by the intervention of the State. The application of the Payment of Wages Act in

---

[96] *ITJ*, XLVII, No. 10, July 1937, p. 369.

[97] Not only was the Association labor officer able to get service cards on only about two-thirds of the jobbers employed by the mills, but there was no requirement that the employer pay any attention to the past record of a jobber he intended to hire.

[98] The issues of *LG* and *ITJ* for the period contain these reports or extracts from them.

[99] For some specific cases see *LG*, XIV, No. 8, April 1935, p. 589; *ITJ*, XLVII, No. 10, July 1937, p. 376; *ITJ*, XLVIII, No. 7, April 1938, p. 118; *LG*, XIX, No. 1, September 1939, p. 25. In many cases it was clear that the jobbers continued to exercise the power of granting leaves, in clear violation of the standing orders ostensibly adopted by the industry in 1931. *BMOA 1937*, p. 37.

[100] *TLIC 1940*, pp. 337–338.

1937 and the passage of the Bombay Industrial Disputes Act in 1938 strengthened the process by which labor discipline was being made more regular and systematic. The measures, discussed in the previous chapter, regularized working rules, disciplinary measures, and discharge procedures. This did not mean that jobber power had been broken. Unwilling or incompetent managements could continue to thwart the spirit of the new legislation, but this became increasingly difficult in the face of the increased powers held by government officers to interfere in the internal affairs of the mills. The old system was truly on the defensive. At the same time the Bombay Industrial Disputes Act of 1938 strengthened the feeble trade unions which had reappeared after 1934. After 1938 the power of the trade unions became increasingly important and the arbitrary exercise of jobber power became subject to the check of another autonomous institution. By the end of the period with which I am concerned the role of the jobber had been significantly curtailed. The tradition of nearly a century by which the jobber exercised a virtually unrestricted and essentially arbitrary power had come to an end.[101]

---

[101] Mehta, *ICTI*, pp. 66–72.

CHAPTER IX

Wage Structure
and Labor Discipline

(1)

I have already dealt with wage trends as they related to the supply of labor. Let me now examine the wage structure and its administration as these affected the stability and discipline of the work force.

The wage structure in the mills — the rates for individual tasks and the relationship of rates among jobs — varied enormously among mills. Some hints of this can be found scattered in the various testimony presented to the factory commission of 1875 and 1885. And in 1892 the BMOA told a royal commission: "Rates of wages are very various, depending on the situation of the mills, the class of material operated upon and the general regulations under which the mills are worked." [1]

We can get a crude notion of the diversity which existed by comparing wages reported by the Petit Mill in 1893 and the maximum rates suggested for the industry by a BMOA committee in the same year. Not only was there diversity in the wage structure but the deviations were not systematic. Table XVI shows that for twelve comparable occupations the Petit Mill paid less in four and more in eight. At the extremes, full-time fly carriers received 22 per cent less than was recommended by the BMOA while full-time drawers could earn 32 per cent more. [2]

Nor did the situation change in subsequent years. For example, although the factory commission of 1908 claimed that wages tended to be standardized within Bombay, this was clearly incorrect even on the basis of the evidence presented to it. [3] The commission did not get much wage data, but there is scattered evidence that full-time earnings varied

[1] RCL 1892, p. 130. See Mr. Drewet, ibid., p. 132, and testimony by others for evidence of variations in rates of pay. See also ITJ, II, No. 20, May 1892, p. 155.

[2] The BMOA committee attempted to establish some compromise wage structure, acceptable to all or at least to a majority of the employers. But the fact that N. N. Wadia, an important figure at the Petit Mill, was largely responsible for the suggested wage scale makes it very likely that the variations between Petit Mill rates and the proposal rates understates the situation in the industry at large.

[3] For the 1908 claim that mill rates tended to be standardized, see IFLC 1908, I, p. 20.

TABLE XVI

Maximum Monthly Wages Recommended by BMOA Compared with Monthly Wages at M. Petit Mills, 1893[4]

(BMOA rates=100)

Occupation	BMOA	M. Petit Mill
Fly carrier	100	78.3
Winder	100	93.3
Card tender	100	98.5
Ring sider	100	99.7
Blow room machine hand	100	104.1
Grinder	100	105.0
Sweeper	100	107.7
Reeler	100	112.8
Slubbing frame tenter	100	123.1
Intermediate frame tenter	100	123.1
Roving frame tenter	100	123.1
Drawer	100	132.2

widely. In fact, even in mills under the same management the full-time earnings of an average weaver varied by 21 per cent.[5]

Not only did the wage structure vary between mills but the variations were not systematic over time, as can be seen in the Table XVII comparison of the average full-month earnings in the Petit Mill with those in the Bombay Dyeing and Manufacturing Company. This table indicates that in 1910 the Petit Mill was paying lower wages in all except the weaver classification. It continued to pay lower wages in the time-rated jobs in 1913 and 1918, but the differentials changed. And in 1918 the Petit Mill winders, previously paid considerably less, were now being paid more than the winders in the Bombay Dyeing Mill.[6]

These scattered bits of evidence suggest that there was a wide varia-

---

[4] *PW 1893* for Petit Mill rates; *BMOA 1893*, pp. 59–60, for BMOA rates. See Appendix III for discussion of the data.

[5] The Rachael Sassoon Mill paid an average full-time weaver Rs.21 per month whereas the Alexandria and E. D. Sassoon Mills reported that a weaver earned Rs. 25–Rs.26. *IFLC 1908*, II, testimony of Mr. Crabtree, p. 134, and Mr. Cooper, p. 149.

[6] It can be argued that the differences in earnings reported for piece rate jobs (winders and weavers) reflect different degrees of utilization of available labor. However, the implication in the sources is that all the figures represent earnings of full-time employees. If so, the shift in winder differentials for example, should represent a change in rates. See Appendix III.

TABLE XVII

Deviation of M. Petit Mill Average Full-Month Earnings in Five Occupations from Average Full-Month Earnings in Bombay Dyeing and Manufacturing Company, 1910, 1913, and 1918 [7]

	Years		
Occupation	1910	1913	1918
Blow-room hand (time rate)	—8.3	—21.4	—8.7
Card-room hand (time rate)	—5.6	—17.4	—7.8
Ring sider (time rate)	—5.8	—11.7	—10.9
Winder (piece rate)	—24.0	—20.0	+5.2
Weaver (piece rate)	+9.91	+36.4	+63.1

tion in rates for every classification in the industry during the nineteenth and early twentieth centuries, and the wage relationships between mills changed over time. This diversity of wage rates continued to exist during the interwar period. For example, in 1926 the Bombay Labor Office commented that there were "very wide variations . . . both in methods of payment and the manner in which rates are fixed . . . as between unit and unit." [8]

It is, in fact, possible that the variation in wages paid for the same job by different mills may have become greater rather than less after 1920. Though the evidence for the period before 1920 rarely shows a maximum range of more than 30 per cent between low and high mill for any job, during the interwar years the range of variation seems always to have been above that figure. For example, there is a survey of nineteen mills for July 1926 which gives us the range of difference in average daily earnings between lowest and highest paying mill. The lowest variation was for ring siders and amounted to 32.75 per cent. [9]

---

[7] Calculated from Petit Mill figures in *PW 1918* and Bombay Dyeing and Manufacturing Company figures in *ITB 1927*, I, p. 113, and *ibid.*, II, pp. 138 and 150. In each case the 1918 figure was adjusted to include the cost-of-living allowance of 15 per cent.

[8] *BLO 1926*, p. 29. In fact, the Labor Office went on to say that "Variations [in rates] were also found to exist for the same occupation in a unit." *Loc. cit.*

[9] For two-loom weavers the variation was 33.55 per cent; for warpers, 75.24 per cent; for gray winders, 86.87 per cent; and for reelers, 72.55 per cent. Calculated from *BLO 1926*, p. 35; and *BLO, Wages and Unemployment 1934*, p. 30. The figure for reelers relates to thirteen mills only.

It should be noted that these figures report differences in average daily earnings rather than in full-month earnings as was the case for the prewar data. The 1926 data were collected in such a way as to exclude most of the effects of absenteeism and underemployment. But it is still possible to argue that the figures for piece-rate

There is one additional conclusion that can be drawn from the 1926 survey. There is absolutely no consistency in the structure of average daily earnings among the nineteen mills. A mill with low average earnings in one category might well be close to the top in another occupational class.[10] In other words, the structure of wage rates in each mill bore no clearly apparent relationship to the structure of wages paid in any other mill.[11]

TABLE XVIII

Per Cent Difference in Average Daily Earnings
Between Low Mill and High Mill, July 1926
and December 1933[12]

Occupation	July 1926	December 1933
Ring sider (one side)	32.75	46.04
Weaver (two loom)	33.55	89.74
Gray winder	86.87	63.11
Reeler	72.55	175.00

Nor did the situation become more coherent as years passed. A survey conducted in December 1933 gives us data for thirteen of the nineteen mills surveyed in 1926, and we can see that the situation become more rather than less extreme in the interval.

In all categories except gray winders there was a notable increase in

workers (weavers, warpers, winders, and reelers) may be qualified by differences in effort. However, ring spinners were paid on time rates so that the 32.75 per cent difference in average daily earnings between lowest and highest paying mill should reflect differences in basic wage scales.

It is likely that the prewar data understated the wage range for a job because they involve comparisons only between two mills at any one date. The data for the interwar period make possible comparison among a large number of mills. As later discussion makes clear, the larger the number of mills in a sample the wider the range of variation tended to be. This being the case, it is probably safe to say that the wide diversities between low and high mill one finds during the interwar years can be taken as characteristic of the period before World War I as well. In fact, speaking in 1919, the Chairman of the BMOA referred to wage differentials of "no less than 30 per cent." *BMOA 1918*, p. xiv.

[10] *BLO 1926*, p. 35.

[11] The Indian Tariff Board confirmed this judgment from its own examination of the situation. Not only did wages for a job vary greatly between mills, but frequently they varied among mills controlled by the same managing agent. *ITB 1927*, I, p. 140.

[12] BLO, *Wages and Unemployment 1934*, p. 30. Six mills surveyed in 1926 had apparently closed down by the time the 1933 survey was made. These six mills in 1926 paid wages which fell between the extremes, and their exclusion therefore did not affect the range between low and high mill for that year. In none of the four classifications were the low or high mills in 1926 in the same position in 1933. *Ibid.*, p. 206.

the range of difference in average daily earnings between low and high mill. Weavers, winders, and reelers were pieceworkers and the changed differentials may reflect changes other than in basic rates. However, time-rated ring siders also show a substantial widening of the wage differential between low and high mill.[13]

It is possible that these figures do not indicate what I suggest that they do. It might be argued that the influence of differential effort and absenteeism on piece-rate earnings and of absenteeism on time-rate workers could have influenced the results.[14] But it is possible to exclude these influences. The 1933 survey provides information on full-month workers in three time-rated occupations in forty-nine mills. Earnings in these occupations would not be affected by worker effort. The effect of absenteeism is excluded by reporting only the earnings of mill hands who worked steadily through the month. The range of variation in December 1933 between low and high mill for full-time time-rated employees was as follows:[15]

Ring sider (one side) .... 37.16 per cent
Tarwallas .... 47.25 per cent
Doffers .... 39.64 per cent

Ring siders, the only category comparable to 1926, still show a substantial widening of the range between low and high mill when compared with 1926. Again we have proof of the wide disparity in basic wage rates in the Bombay mills. Despite the frenzied wage cuts of 1933, there had been no move towards some city-wide equilibrium rate. If anything the disparities had widened.[16] These differentials seem to have persisted until 1947 when an Industrial Court award established standardized rates for all occupations in all cotton mills.[17]

---

[13] If the percentage range of average daily earnings for ring siders in the nineteen mills of the July 1926 survey is compared with the range for all forty-nine mills actually surveyed in December 1933, the differential between low and high mill becomes even greater. In July 1926 it was 32.75 per cent; in December 1933 it was 51.08 per cent. Computed from *ibid.*, pp. 140–145.

[14] The data are ambiguous on this point.

[15] *Ibid.*, pp. 135 and 140–145. In order to guarantee comparability. I made use only of data from the thirty-eight mills which worked twenty-seven days during the month.

[16] The 1933 data when compared with the 1926 figures suggest that the general wage structures of individual mills were also undergoing severe changes, not all associated with the "rationalization" movement then underway. *Ibid.*, *passim.*

[17] It is possible that between 1937 and 1947 the range within each job classification narrowed somewhat. The wage increase of 1937 and the wartime cost-of-living allowances both gave higher percentage increases to lower paid workers in each classification. Mehta, *ICTI*, p. 36.

This apparent lack of systematic pattern in the wage structure over time raises problems about the nature of the Bombay labor market. One would expect that the rates for an occupation would tend to move toward a common level. Employers would have to pay the going rate or not get labor. Though we would not expect a perfect fit because of dynamic elements in the situation, we also would not expect the pattern of wide diversity which we have found in Bombay at various moments of time nor the persistence of such extreme differentials through time.

It is possible that the Bombay mills did not operate in a single labor market but in what, for transport or other reasons, constituted a series of quasi-independent labor markets. If true, one would expect that as we come closer to 1947 the differentials would narrow because urban transport and knowledge of the market certainly improved as time passed. But paradoxically, the data for pre- and post-World War I suggest, if anything, the reverse of this. The evidence I have presented suggests differentials of up to 30 per cent before 1920 and considerably more than 30 per cent after that date.[18]

However, for purposes of argument let me assume that even after World War I the improvements in transport and knowledge were still not sufficient to make a unified labor market on the island. The BMOA suggested as much when it told the Royal Commission on Labor in 1929 that individual mills set wage rates in accord with "the wages paid in neighboring localities or neighboring mills." [19] In an effort to test this proposition the Bombay Labor Office grouped forty-two mills by district, making the assumption that

In most industrial countries it is generally found that wages for the same kind of work in different units of the same industry, situated in the same locality, are ordinarily very nearly the same. We have examined variations in the earnings of operatives in the different wards of the city in the light of this principle.[20]

The Labor Office proceeded to report for each of three districts the range of average daily earnings between low and high mill for each of four occupations.

---

[18] I have pointed out that the pre- and post-1920 data are not of the same degree of reliability and that the variation of wages for any job was probably higher before World War I than the evidence actually shows. But at most this would only mean that the differentials were as great before 1920 as they were after. There is absolutely no evidence that would suggest a narrowing of wage differentials between mills over time.

[19] *RCL 1929*, I, Part 1, p. 398. A survey made in 1925 reported that the overwhelming majority of mill hands walked to work. *LG*, IV, No. 7, March 1925, pp. 745–747.

[20] BLO, *Wages and Unemployment 1934*, pp. 34–35.

TABLE XIX

*Per Cent Range of Average Daily Earnings Between Low Mill
and High Mill in Four Selected Occupations in Bombay Cotton
Mills Distributed by Location, December 1933* [21]

	Per cent range of average daily earnings		
Occupation	E Ward (10 mills)	F Ward (13 mills)	G Ward (19 mills)
Ring sider (one side)	21.56	36.36	49.64
Weaver (two loom)	56.43	104.66	113.85
Winder (gray and color)	107.38	85.37	249.12
Reeler	172.04	122.08	158.21

The table shows enormous ranges of variation for each occupation, even among mills clustered in the same ward. The differentials for weavers, winders, and reelers may possibly be dismissed as reflecting differential efforts of pieceworkers. The range for time-rated ring siders is much smaller and does offer some vague support to the notion of fragmented labor markets in the city. Though the all-city range between low and high mill was 51.08 per cent, the differential within each of the three wards was narrower than this. But does this support the BMOA proposition that the millowners set wages "with due regard to the wages paid in . . . neighboring mills"? Certainly the differential even in "E" Ward is much greater than one would expect in a perfect labor market. Moreover, the table suggests that the larger the number of mills in a ward the greater the differential between low and high mill, which is hardly what we would expect in a competitive situation.[22]

Looking at the history of the industry, we can say that all available evidence shows that wage differentials among mills were always very wide for every job classification. Over time there were changes in the wage structure in each mill and these changes affected the wage relationship for any single job in the industry. A mill which paid relatively high wages for a job at one time might be found to be paying relatively low wages for the same job a few years later.

It is difficult to explain why these great differentials existed. It is possible that they can be attributed to deviations from a competitive norm as individual enterprises attempted to obtain the labor they required. This notion is supported by the fact that although the wide differentials

---

[21] Computed from *ibid.*, p. 35.

[22] The assumption made by the Labor Office is that mills in the same ward were competing for the same labor force. A distribution of mills by geographical concentration independent of the city's political divisions would have been more satisfactory. It is impossible to reconstruct the data in this way.

persisted, mills typically seem not to have retained their same relative positions over time as low- or high-paying mills in any job category. We can expect no answer to the question until we get some studies of individual mills. However, the solution of this problem is not crucial to the issues with which I am concerned. All that we need to recognize is that these considerable differentials existed and that over time the relative ranking of the wage for a job in one mill as compared with other mills might sharply change. We would expect that such a situation would have important effects on the behavior of the labor force, stimulating labor turnover and encouraging unrest.

(2)

It is quite clear that as new mills opened in Bombay, they attempted to reduce the costs of training labor by luring experienced hands from other firms with the promise of higher wages. As one mill manager said in 1885: "There is a larger demand for trained hands, and these being scarce are leaving us as new mills spring up . . . New mills offer inducements in the ways of higher pay." [23] All observers agreed that this wage competition for trained workers existed although the entering wage for inexperienced workers remained relatively stable. Factory Inspector Jones described the situation as it existed during the booming years of the early 1880's: "There is undoubtedly a rush for employment [at going rates] by unskilled hands when a new mill is opened, but inducements have to be offered to trained hands in the shape of increased pay or by satisfying them of the advantages of working on newer machinery to induce them to leave their former employment." [24]

It should come as no surprise that a new and very rapidly expanding industry in a competitive environment would use the wage rate as the major device for reallocating needed skills. However, it is important to recognize the consequences. The industry developed during this early period a pattern characterized by a constant movement of labor from one mill to another as workers sought to take advantage of higher basic rates and more efficient equipment and the possibilities of greater output and income. [25]

---

[23] *FC 1885*, p. 18.

[24] *Ibid.*, p. 27. See also *ibid.*, pp. 85 and 126; and *Bombay and Lancashire Cotton Spinning Inquiry, 1888*, pp. 34–35; 61–62, 176, 188–191, 336, and 339.

[25] The process of wage setting was not an easy one. Mills experimented with the wage structure, and they ran into trouble if worker earnings were too low, as occurred during the early years at the Anglo-Indian and Empress mills. "The workpeople grumbled at not being able to earn as much as the hands employed in other mills. . . ." *FC 1885*, p. 55.

The wage sytem was unstable in other ways as well. For example, although piece-rate workers were ostensibly paid on the basis of output, one mill hand representative claimed that in some mills rates were reduced during the shorter days of the winter season.

The only complaint I know of was where the pieceworkers were paid less during the shorter days although they did as much work as they had done during the longer days. The hands can do as much work as they can in the longer days, consequently they naturally object to having their pay cut. I have seen hands on the roving, slubbing and intermediate frames do as much work in a short day as in a long day. I know about six mills where they cut the pay of the hands while they take from them the same amount of work.[26]

Employers did not hesitate to cut rates when productivity gains occurred. For example, in July 1892 the Sassoon Mills cut their basic weaving piece rates.

The reduction in the rate of pay was made in July last as was only on some sorts ¼ and others ½ to ¾ pie per lb. We took this step as owing to our having at some expense expedited the running of the looms the production was increased and certainly the benefit of such a step should by right go to the mill and not to the weavers.[27]

Moreover, individual mills cut rates and worked short days during periods of slack market demand.[28] Very frequently the reductions were surreptitiously made, the mill hands discovering the fact only when they received their pay. As a factory inspector pointed out in 1892, "the principle of giving notice beforehand is never practiced by the millowners even in the case of temporary reduction of wages. . . ."[29] This unsystematic and not infrequently furtive manipulation of wage rates and earnings by employers was a constant source of discontent and a cause of frequent, if usually abortive, strikes among mill hands.[30]

---

[26] N. M. Lokhunday, *ibid.*, pp. 119–120. Although this particular grievance was not explicitly confirmed by other sources, there is testimony that in a number of mills earnings did fall during the shorter days of the winter months. The fact that earnings of piece-rate workers did not fall in all mills suggests that there may have been some truth to the charge. See *ibid., passim.* Rate cuts in the winter months may have been related to the large influx of labor into Bombay during this season.

[27] *BMOA 1892*, p. 28.

[28] "In the whole history of our cotton industry it may be noticed that almost invariably our mill agents have thought the reduction in wages the first remedy against hard times." *ITJ*, X, No. 113, Feb. 1900, p. 129. See also *ITJ*, I, No. 12, Sept. 1891, p. 190; and *RCL 1892*, pp. 128 and 137.

[29] *RCL 1892*, p. 136, and also p. 169.

[30] East Indian (Factories Act), *Return to an Address of the House of Commons, 15 April 1889*, p. 72; *RCL 1892*, pp. 123, 132, 135–136, 137, 169; *BMOA 1892*, pp. 10–11 and 28; and various issues of *ITJ*, October 1892 to June 1895.

The plague outbreak in the fall of 1896 seriously disrupted the industry's labor supply as thousands of people fled the island. In January 1897 it was estimated that only about a third of the work force remained at their machines. Although a few mills closed down, most made every effort to continue working. The chairman of the BMOA urged this as a matter of *noblesse oblige* as well as a necessity to prevent the total disintegration of the labor force that had been mobilized over the previous forty years.[31] A more immediately practical motive was suggested by outside observers to explain the eagerness of the managing agents to keep their mills working. The Chief Inspector of Factories pointed out that the unanimous advice of English managers and technicians had been to close down to avoid rapid depreciation of equipment caused by restriction of output and difficulties of maintenance. However, he said, the managing agents were more interested in keeping production as high as possible, whatever the effect on equipment or quality of output, in order to maximize their commissions.[32]

Whatever the reasons, the general attempt to keep the mills working set in motion a ferocious competition for labor. Some mills made an initial attempt to hold their workers by lengthening the period between pay days. This very quickly failed because food prices were rising very sharply and, at the same time, the sources of regular credit on which the mill hands depended vanished as most moneylenders fled the plague-wracked city.[33] Mills then frantically sought to lure workers from their competitors and brought in untrained persons off the streets with promises of daily wage payments, free grain or grain bonuses, and generally higher wage rates. The records of the BMOA for 1896 and 1897 report

---

The complexity of methods of wage computation and the lack of information available to the operative constantly caused trouble. One manager referred to the "petty disputes and bickerings which invariably take place on the monthly pay day . . . between the operatives and the timekeeper or foreman of the department. . . ." *ITJ*, XI, No. 122, Nov. 1900, p. 35. Another mill officer, commenting on "the surreptitious manner in which the rates or wages of the work people are cut down without notice of any kind," also pointed out that it "is characteristic of the Indian mill hand not to take the trouble to check his pay so long as he gets about the same from month's end to month's end. If the wages of the roving tenters or weavers happen to be higher than usual on account of some favorable change in the production, he is not given a proportionate advance based on his usual rates. Nor is the laborer in a position to know how much has been taken away from him. A person earning Rs.10 on an average is satisfied if he receives an extra rupee although there may be two or more due to him." *ITJ*, XI, No. 123, December 1900, p. 67.

[31] *BMOA 1896*, pp. 136–137.

[32] *FA 1897*, p. 7. See also *ITJ*, VIII, No. 95, August 1898, p. 289; *ITJ*, IX, No. 99, December 1898, p. 66; *ITJ*, IX No. 104, May 1899, p. 235.

[33] *ITJ*, IX, No. 99, December 1898, p. 66; *BMOA 1896*, p. 136; and *FA 1897*, p. 8.

Wage Structure and Labor Discipline

the almost total disruption of the traditional wage structure.[34] This disruption was limited by the relatively short duration of the worst manifestations of the plague and the worsening of economic conditions in the countryside which willy-nilly drove the workers back to the city. Gradually, during the second half of 1897 and in 1898, as the labor supply began to return to a more normal level, daily payments, bonus payments, and higher rates were eliminated.[35] There was resistance to the cutbacks in earnings, but the restoration of wages to preplague levels was aided not only by continued economic distress in the countryside but also by the declining demand for textile products in 1898 and 1899 and by the closing of a number of mills in subsequent months.[36]

During 1900 the industry was in great distress. Although an attempt was made by the Association to get all mills to agree to close a fixed number of days per month, each mill seems to have acted as best suited its individual needs. Some mills closed altogether; some mills worked four days a week; some worked full time. Most of the working mills did not operate all of their equipment. Apparently there was a spate of wage reductions at the same time. The reduced earnings and the irregularity of mill response to the economic crisis produced a great many strikes.[37]

Beginning in 1904 a favorable market situation accompanied by the rapid introduction of electric lighting made it possible to push hours considerably beyond their traditional limits. This development, which lasted until 1907, produced a host of new wage stresses and accentuated instability in the labor force. Piece-rate workers quickly received increased earnings for their overtime work and greater output, but time-rate workers did not. This sharp increase in disparities promptly produced trouble in the mills.[38] Moreover, mills worked different hours and this

---

[34] For a vivid description of the chaotic situation, *FA 1897*, pp 7–8.

[35] For general information, see *BMOA 1896* and *BMOA 1897*. The Factory Inspector reported that the disruption of production resulted in greater demand for labor in some departments than in others. Weavers, for example, did not share in the crisis-period rise in wages unless they shifted to the carding rooms. However, as production returned to normal the weavers found themselves in a position to force raises for themselves whereas other wages were beginning to come down. *FA 1897*, pp. 8–9.

[36] *ITJ*, issues for December 1899 *et seq*. One cause of continued trouble in the immediate postplague period was the refusal of many mills to pay returning workers their earnings from late 1896 and early 1897 which they had not collected when they fled the city. *FA 1897*, p. 9.

[37] See *ITJ*, issues for 1900. Apparently, individual mills used wage cuts among their competitors as the occasion to lure away particularly skilled workers. *ITJ*, X, No. 113, Feb. 1900, pp. 129–130.

[38] *BMOA 1906*, speech of M. Ramji, p. viii; *IFLC 1908*, II, evidence at pp. 85, 109, and 152.

produced different levels of earnings and provoked additional tension. In fact, in mid-1905 the Commissioner of Police wrote the BMOA that the situation in the factories had become such that he could not guarantee public order.[39] Between 1905 and 1907, an epidemic of strikes struck the industry, strikes by time-rate workers for overtime pay and by piece-rate workers for changed basic rates.[40] The directing committee of the BMOA worried that the lack of employer discipline "is likely to disorganize the labor market and lead to further strikes and riots. . . ."[41]

The evidence given to the Indian Factory Labor Commission in 1908 yielded a picture of considerable disorder within the labor force, much of it directly originating as a reaction to the unstable wage structure. Not only were there strikes, but workers, seeing differential earning possibilities, shifted from mill to mill in quest of the combination of hours and earnings which suited them best. Virtually all mill representatives recognized the importance of wage-rate variations and earning possibilities as a cause of the high degree of labor turnover. As one employer said, "The present cause of the migration of labor was because one mill was pitted against another."[42]

(3)

In 1908 the Indian Factory Labor Commission concluded that the wage structure had little if any effect on labor force stability, attributing the mobility of labor, rather, to "natural inclinations."

The Indian operative is fond of change; he prefers to wander from mill to mill rather than remain settled; and the slightest causes are apparently sufficient to determine him to leave one employer in favor of another. . . . The inducements to change are occasionally pecuniary, of course; but as a general

---

[39] *BMOA 1905*, p. 8; L. Fraser, *India Under Curzon and After* (London: W. Heinemann, 1911), pp. 34–35.

[40] *BMOA 1906*, speech of N. N. Wadia, p. xv; *BMOA 1907*, speeches of B. D. Petit and J. B. Petit, pp. xiv and xv–xvi; *IFLC 1908*, II, evidence of H. Hawthorne, p. 152; *ITJ*, XVI, No. 184, Jan. 1906, p. 99.

[41] *BMOA 1906*, p. 18.

[42] *IFLC 1908*, II, testimony of N. N. Wadia, p. 113. There are innumerable references in the sources to the continuing unrest and turnover caused by the manipulation of wage rates by individual mills. See, for example, *FA 1909*, p. 2; *BMOA 1908*, pp. xiii–xv; *BMOA 1912*, pp. iii and ix; *FA 1914*, p. 5; and *ITJ*, No. 240, September 1910, p. 339.

A survey in 1913 of one hundred mill hands with long service records reported that sixty-three had worked in more than one mill. Forty-one had changed mills because of improved earning possibilities. G. K. Devadhar, "A Note on Cooperation Among the Mill Hands," Report of the Ninth Indian Industrial Conference (Amraoti, 1914), *op.cit.*, p. 159.

rule the same rate of pay obtains throughout each center, and in such cases the motive must be looked for elsewhere.[43]

But if the Commission thought that differential rates and earnings were not an important factor in labor force instability, the Bombay millowners thought otherwise. One of the constant preoccupations of many of the leading figures in the BMOA, at least after 1890, was the problem of establishing standardized wage rates and a rationalized wage structure to reduce labor mobility.

So long as the industry was small and very prosperous, this instability of the work force apparently caused no concern. However, in 1890 the sixty-five working mills were confronted by a major slump which forced most of them to close for two days a week. This situation brought to some employers a belief that the wide wage variations which existed were undesirable. If nothing else, the absence of standardization among the mills made wage reductions difficult to achieve without serious trouble.[44] Spurred by representatives of certain large and established mills, the BMOA convened a general meeting in February 1891 "for the purpose of considering the question of a general reduction of wages of mill employees [and] the fixing of a maximum rate of wages to be paid in each department." [45] A committee was appointed to get pay sheets from all the member mills and work out an appropriate schedule. Very few mills responded to the request. The Association pessimistically concluded:

---

[43] *IFLC 1908*, I, p. 20.

[44] At this point I ought to mention the sketchy evidence that suggests the existence of a Labroussian-type relationship which linked demand for textile products and the cost of living. Although this phenomenon has not been studied and waits on a detailed investigation of the relation of the Bombay industry to its domestic markets, there is some evidence that bad harvests and high food prices were linked with poor demand for the output of Bombay mills. Given bad harvests, demand for mill products would fall and food prices would rise. Mills would begin to work short-time, and wage rates and incomes would begin to be pressed downward. Workers would then be confronted with the combined threat of falling income and a rising cost of living. Under these circumstances strikes became much more frequent and employers had very serious difficulties when they attempted to reduce wages. This Labroussian situation may have existed in 1900 and certainly occurred in 1909 and explains why, in spite of the shutdown of many mills, employers could not reduce wages. See *ITJ*, No. 223, April 1909, p. 234; *ITJ*, No. 224, May 1909, p. 267; *ITJ*, No. 228, September 1909, p. 463; and *ITJ*, No. 240, September 1910, pp. 339 and 400.

The indexes of consumer goods prices that we have seem to support this conclusion. See K. L. Datta, *Report on the Enquiry into the Rise of Prices in India* (Calcutta: Superintendent of Government Printing, 1914), II, pp. 16, 280–281, and 288; and *ibid.*, III, pp. 194–195.

[45] *BMOA 1891*, p. 15.

"The conditions of labor at different mills are so extremely various that . . . ultimately it will probably be found that the question will have to adjust itself as hitherto by the usual operations of supply and demand." [46]

Depressed conditions continued through 1892 and 1893. The general meeting of the BMOA in July 1893 was largely concerned with how to lower the industry's costs. And at this time another attempt to standardize (and lower) wages was undertaken. An appeal was made to the example of Lancashire's standardized lists.[47] N. N. Wadia, a leading mill-owner, was directed to prepare a schedule of standardized wage rates. The recommendation was circulated among the member mills, but only thirty-nine of the sixty-nine mills indicated that they were willing to go along with the proposal, and the scheme collapsed.[48]

No new formal effort to standardize wages was made until after World War I, but the problem continued to exercise at least some employers. The issue periodically was raised at Association meetings. Advocates of standardization argued its necessity for reducing labor turnover, for limiting raiding of trained workers, and for preventing workers from using higher rates in another mill as an excuse for pressing their own employer for an increase. But no coöperation could be gotten from the employers as a collectivity.[49]

During World War I the rapidly rising cost of living caused a great deal of labor unrest in the industry. Finally, in August 1917 the employers granted a Dear Food Allowance of 10 per cent in an effort to stem the tide of discontent. The Association proceeded to authorize additional cost of living increments in subsequent years. These increases seem to have been paid by all mills and to this extent represent the industry's first successful coöperative venture in wage matters. However,

---

[46] *Loc. cit.*

[47] *BMOA 1893*, pp. 135–136. For an explanation of these Manchester lists, see S. J. Chapman, *The Lancashire Cotton Industry* (Manchester: The University Press, 1904), pp. 262–276.

[48] *BMOA 1893*, pp. 11–12 and 59–60; and *BMOA 1894*, p. 11. The BMOA records do not explain why millowners were unwilling to go along with the proposal. One reason seems to have been the reluctance of many employers to forego the use of higher wages as a device for pirating trained labor when it was needed. Another factor seems to have been linked with the great variations in labor deployment patterns between mill and mill. Standardization of rates would have required many mills to undertake drastic reorganization of their methods of labor utilization and operation. This of course, they were unwilling to do.

[49] See *BMOA 1904*, p. 162; *BMOA 1907*, p. xv; *BMOA 1908*, pp. xiii-xv; *BMOA 1911*, pp. ix and xiii; *BMOA 1912*, pp. iii and ix; and *BMOA 1918*, p. xiv.

these actions had nothing to do with the standardization of wage rates, which mills were still free to vary at will. [50]

In 1921 an official body investigated the still mounting industrial unrest, and concluded that the "uncorrelated raising of wages in one factory is almost invariably seized upon as a grievance in other factories of the same class, and instances of strikes caused in this way are within the memory of all." [51] Two mill representatives agreed that there was need for some system of wage standardization to eliminate one major cause of industrial conflict. But neither was sanguine about the possibility. One commented on the difficulty of standardizing wages "while the capacity of the machinery and quality of material used in different mills are so different." The other added that "a system with innumerable variations like the Manchester list is impossible here, as the workmen would not understand it." [52] Referring to these gloomy views in its report, the committee concluded:

It appears to us that the continual insistence of our witnesses on the differences of machinery and conditions of labor in the various factories, however justified, is liable to obscure the importance of a common practice in the scale of wages which if it is not reached by agreement from amongst the employers will eventually be arrived at by pressure from amongst the men at a greater sacrifice of industrial peace.[53]

Despite this prescient comment by the Industrial Disputes Committee, no standardization scheme emerged in the years that followed. The

[50] *BMOA 1917*, p. x. These cost-of-living increases were applied to basic wages. "The term 'basic' in the case of the Bombay mills may be generally considered to apply to the pre-war year although in the case of some individual mills it might apply to any year between 1913 and 1918 when the first increase of 15 per cent as a dearness allowance was granted." *BLO 1926*, p. 13. Most discussions of post-World War I wage trends have erred because they focus on the uniform movements of the Dear Food Allowance and imply a uniformity of rates and trends which did not in fact exist. Not only was the Dear Food Allowance applied to the individualistic structure of the early war period, but no attention has been given to the fact that the basic rates in individual mills were frequently varied even after the Dear Food Allowance was introduced.

[51] *IDC 1922*, p. 2.

[52] *IDC 1921*, pp. 5 and 8. See also *BMOA 1918*, p. xiv. The comment about the complexity of the Manchester Lists was gratuitous. All evidence suggests that the calculation of earnings in Bombay was at least as complicated and suffered from the fluctuations in rates associated with the variations in types of output. An inspection of the various Labor Office surveys will give some indication of the situation. See particularly *BLO 1934*, pp. 43–45.

[53] *IDC 1922*, p. 2. At the same time as the Committee was holding hearings the BMOA decided to coöperate with the Bombay Labor Office in a survey of wages in an effort to get a statistical basis for any standardization scheme that might be proposed in the future. *BMOA 1921*, p. 87; and *BLO 1921*, p. 1.

traditional pattern of individual mill-rate adjustments continued as before. After 1922 the impact of these adjustments was made more harsh by the economic crisis in which the industry found itself. Worker spokesmen charged that there was a systematic, if individualistic manipulation of rates in a downward direction.[54] They alleged that there were seven devices by which real rates and earnings were in effect being reduced by employers:

1. Introduction of new varieties of cloth which did not bring the level of wages to what was earned on the production of older varieties;
2. Reduction of piece rates to meet unanticipated high production by individual operatives;
3. Adjustments in rates by a mill to bring these in line with rates prevailing in other mills;
4. Failure to increase rates in cases where mills shifted to finer count production;
5. Introduction of artificial silk (rayon) and inferior raw materials;
6. Introduction of the method of calculating wages on the weight of cloth after it had undergone a subsequent process instead of on basis of the actual weight produced on the looms.
7. Gradual withdrawal of various bonuses which had previously existed.[55]

Though the millowners denied these allegations, arguing that the wage changes were merely normal adjustments stemming from variations in products produced, an official investigation concluded that some, at least, of the charges were true.[56]

The stepped-up momentum of wage modifications produced increasing industrial tension and a rising tempo of strikes during the years after 1922. In 1926 the BTLU, testifying before the Indian Tariff Board, urged the establishment of a system of wage standardization as one contribution to the relaxation of tension.[57] The Tariff Board raised questions about the possibilities of enforcing such a standardization scheme in the absence of strong unions capable of "delivering the goods." [58] But ulti-

---

[54] Evidence of Bombay Textile Labor Union, *ITB 1927*, III, pp. 446–447. Henceforth, the union will be identified as BTLU.

[55] *BSEC 1928–29*, p. 6. Few mills posted piece rates for various types of product, nor were workers informed when rates were changed. Evidence of BTLU, *RCL 1929*, I, Part 1, pp. 345–347. Employers agreed that this caused trouble and labor turnover. *Ibid.*, I, Part 2, p. 299; and *BMOA 1935*, p. 28.

[56] *BSEC 1928–29*, p. 65. The Committee preferred to avoid a thorough investigation of these charges. *RCL 1929*, "Memorandum," p. 117.

[57] *ITB 1927*, III, pp. 452–453.

[58] *Ibid.*, III, p. 539.

mately, though recognizing the problems associated with the "illiteracy and imperfect organization of labor," the Tariff Board did urge the adoption of such a scheme "in consultation with representatives of labor." [59]

By the time the Tariff Board's recommendations had been made, downward wage adjustments were becoming more common and some mills were also attempting to carry out a rationization of work process that promised to reduce labor costs sharply. The combination of reduced earnings and increasing unemployment produced a sharp rise in the number of strikes, particularly after mid-1927. This serious industrial situation became increasingly tense and finally culminated in the industry-wide strike which lasted from April 16 to October 6, 1928. The strike was ultimately terminated when the government agreed to appoint a committee to deal with the issues of wage standardization.

Out of the work of this committee and the concurrent negotiations of the BMOA with the Joint Strike Committee came a "Standardization Scheme" based on the principles of the Lancashire Lists.[60] The proposal embodied three basic features. First, there was to be industry-wide standardization of wage rates for workers doing the same kind of work, variations in earnings depending on the skill of workers. Second, earnings were not to suffer because of defects in equipment or poor quality of material. Finally, changes in rates were not to be made unilaterally but were to be subject to negotiations between the parties.[61]

The BMOA proposed that the Standardization Scheme, the first serious effort to come to grips with the industry's individualistic wage structure, should come into operation October 1, 1929. However, in April 1929 another general strike broke out. When it collapsed five months later the unions collapsed with it. The Association then claimed that it could not introduce such a radical innovation without the coöperation

---

[59] *Ibid.*, I, p. 140.

[60] For a detailed description of the scheme and its history, see *BSEC 1928–29*, pp. 86 ff. The BMOA had been dilatory in its response to the Indian Tariff Board's wage standardization recommendation. It was not until a year after the Board had published its report that the Association started to work on a proposal and then only because industrial discontent continued to spread. Apparently the opposition of many member mills frustrated any move by the directing committee. Finally the Association leadership was able to push through approval of its scheme in June 1928, when the mills were shut down by the general strike. The proposal, which formed the basis of negotiations with the Joint Strike Committee, was reluctantly accepted by the industry only because of the enormous public and official pressures which had been building up.

[61] *Ibid.*, p. 89.

of labor, and there remained no organized group of workers with which it could coöperate.[62]

There was more to the problem than is immediately evident. The proposal involved not only a standardization of rates but also a standardization of muster rolls. In the minds of the employers the standardization of wage rates was integrally linked with a rationalization of work. The two segments of the plan stood or fell together. This is clearly evident in the history of the proposal.[63] But it was precisely this fear of additional unemployment which provoked the implacable hostility of the employees, which led to the abortive general strike of 1929, and which kept the work force in turmoil even after the collapse of the unions.[64]

In 1926 the Bombay Textile Labor Union had told the Tariff Board that though settlement of other issues might require the coöperation of strong unions, "Standardization really requires [only] an organization among the millowners themselves." [65] The Tariff Board subsequently agreed that "the introduction of measures designed to increase the efficiency of labor and plans to standardize wages between one mill and another are really separate and distinct. . . ." [66] Unfortunately for labor force stability, the employers felt forced to face both problems at the same time. The economic crisis made it impossible to obtain any agreement among themselves on the issues of wage standardization except under circumstances that provided for agreement on a standardized muster. And no trade union in 1929 had the will or the power to enforce acceptance of such combined proposals on the workers, especially when this threatened additional unemployment.

The fate of the wage standardization proposal was also profoundly affected by the fact that between 1929 and March 1934 the number of mills working in Bombay dropped from seventy-seven to fifty-five.[67] The worsening economic crisis reduced employer enthusiasm for wage

---

[62] *BMOA 1930*, p. 5; and *ITB 1934*, I, p. 50.

[63] *BSEC 1928–29*, pp. 87 ff; and *ITB 1934*, I, p. 46. The scheme for wage rationalization and muster standardization was not the same as the "efficiency scheme" which was being tried out by a few mills at the same time. On the "efficiency scheme," see *BSEC 1928–29*, Chapter VII.

[64] *BLO, Wages and Unemployment 1934*, pp. 6–7 and 12.

[65] *ITB 1927*, III, p. 539.

[66] *ITB 1932*, p. 60.

[67] *BLO, Wages and Unemployment 1934*, pp. 8–9. Bombay was the only textile center in the Presidency so affected. The mills outside Bombay were enjoying a "reasonable measure of prosperity." Much of the problem in Bombay was caused by "the involved financial position of the mills," and by inefficiency in purchasing, manufacturing, and marketing. *Ibid.*, pp. 43–44.

standardization. Mills were much more interested in wage cuts. In 1933 and the first half of 1934 there was a frenzy of wage reductions spreading from one mill to another but without any apparent pattern whatsoever.[68]

These uncontrolled reductions caused a great deal of unrest among the by now desperate mill hands, culminating in another industry-wide strike which lasted from April 23 to June 20, 1934. Government intervention finally forced a halt to wage slashing, and in July 1934 the BMOA came forward with a new proposal to achieve some stability in the industry's wage structure. The object of the new scheme was to establish minima below which the earnings of various classes of fully employed time-rate workers could not fall. Unable to standardize piece rates, the Association recommended the establishment of a minimum cost-of-living allowance for piece-rate workers. Mills paying at rates and levels below these minima were to raise them, effective July 1, 1934.[69] It is not clear that this action was effective in itself, but at least the worst of the spasm of wage cuts ended about this time.

Government pressure on the industry continued and, stemming from this, in the next two years the Association recommended additional wage measures intended to reduce labor force unrest. In May 1935 it urged all mills to post piece-rate and Dear Food Allowance schedules in all departments.[70] In 1936 it recommended that mills end the practice, at least in certain classifications, of paying *badlis* (temporary workers) lower rates than regular employees.[71]

To deal with the continuing problem of downward pressure on basic rates, the Association also recommended in October 1936 that no changes in rates should be made by mills without previously notifying it and the workers concerned. It also suggested methods for setting piece-rates for new products.[72]

---

[68] The BMOA claimed to have authorized these individual wage cuts. *TLIC 1940*, p. 84. However, it is clear that the Association was able to exercise no authority over its membership in this matter. For a description of the reductions, *BLO, Wages and Unemployment 1934*, pp. 25 ff. My wage index, Appendix III, shows a wage decline of 16.3 per cent between 1926 and 1934. This is less than what contemporary observers assumed occurred. The Bombay Labor Office at one point concluded that owing to reduction in rates and allowances, earnings had fallen by no less than 21 per cent in this period. But there are also estimates of a smaller decline. See *ibid.*, pp. 25–39.

[69] *BLO 1934*, pp. 255–257; and *BMOA 1934*, pp. 36–38.

[70] *BMOA 1935*, p. 28. The proposal also suggested that these schedules be prepared in the vernacular.

[71] *BMOA 1937*, p. 40. *Badlis* were not always casual employees. Taken on as substitutes, they often ended up working regularly but at the lower rates at which they were initially employed.

[72] *BMOA 1936*, pp. 39–40.

The Association boasted in 1937 that as a result of these activities there had been a significant improvement in the average level of earnings.[73] However, the *Indian Textile Journal* challenged this conclusion:

Instead of dealing with the situation [the 1934 general strike] in a generous manner by conceding at least a part of the men's demands they [the Association] exploited the situation further by coming out with the so-called minimum schedule of wages which made the situation worse by offering an inducement to the better paying mills to make further wage cuts. . . . When the minimum schedule was laid down it was affirmed that it was devised to meet the needs of the weakest mills and that the better paying mills would continue to pay at the higher rates. This affirmation soon melted into thin air.[74]

The evidence suggests that the *Journal* was correct and the Association wrong. Between 1934 and July 1937 average monthly earnings had fallen at least slightly.[75]

It is, of course, possible that all this was consistent with a tendency toward wage standardization. Certainly the Association claimed to be moving in this direction.[76] There is no clear evidence on the subject. The BMOA schedule of 1934 merely attempted to establish a minimum rate below which time-rated jobs did not fall. It did not prevent mills from varying rates above that level. Nor did it prevent diversity in piece-rate occupations. And as late as 1940 an official committee concluded: "The introduction of the schedule cannot be said to have met the need for standardization of wages, the purpose of which is to place the wage rates in all units in the industry on a uniform level." [77]

The failure of the mills to rationalize and standardize the wage structure led to official intervention to achieve this end. Although wage standardization was not the initial objective of government action, the net effect of the steps it took was to move the industry inexorably in this direction. The Government Labor Officer, whose position was created by the Bombay Trade Disputes Act of 1934, played a decisive role in forcing mills with particularly low wages to raise their rates.[78] In 1936 the State

---

[73] "Labour and Welfare Work in Bombay Mills," *ITJ*, XLVII, No. 11, August 1937, pp. 424–425.

[74] *ITJ*, XLVII, No. 12, September 1937, p. 438.

[75] See Appendix III; *TLIC 1937–38*, pp. 22–25; and *TLIC 1940*, p. 57.

[76] *ITJ*, XLVII, No. 11, August 1937, pp. 424–425.

[77] *TLIC 1940*, p. 100. In addition to the lack of standardization among member mills, there were some companies which were not affiliated to the Association and not subject to its recommendations. A. W. Pryde, "The Work of the Labour Officer," in *Some Social Services of the Government of Bombay*, edited by Clifford Manshardt (Bombay: D. B. Taraporevala Sons & Co., 1937), pp. 87–89; and *TLIC 1940*, p. 85.

[78] *Ibid.*, pp. 83–85; Pryde, *op.cit.*, pp. 87–89; and reports of the Government La-

intervened more directly. The passage of the Payments of Wages Act required employers to post all wage rates in prominent places in the mills, thus giving legal force to the Association's recommendation made the year before.[79] This minimized the likelihood of employer manipulation of rates without the knowledge of the worker. Another step was taken in 1938 when the enactment of the Bombay Industrial Disputes Act made it illegal for an employer to make any changes in these posted rates before certain legal steps had been taken.[80]

In 1937 the official Textile Labor Inquiry Committee recommended an average wage increase of 11.9 per cent for workers in the industry. The award provided for a series of graded increases the net effect of which seems to have been the narrowing of margins of difference in wage rates for the same occupation and the reduction of the spread between lowest and highest paid occupations.[81] Having dealt with the urgent issue of a general wage increase, this committee in the next two years turned its attention to the problem of wage standardization, explaining its objective as an attempt to achieve greater stability in the labor force and the elimination of a most provocative source of industrial conflict.[82]

The BMOA submitted a standardization scheme to this committee which, on the whole, was much like the proposal developed in 1928–29.[83] Although there was general acceptance by all parties of the notion of standardization, two issues seem to have prevented agreement between the employers and spokesmen for the mill hands. The first was the level at which the lowest wage classification was to be set; the second involved the relationship between the standardization scheme in Bombay and wage rates in other textile centers in the Presidency. Agreement could probably have been reached on the first issue had the Bombay mill-owners not been so preoccupied with their competitive position vis-à-vis other textile centers. Failing to get a satisfactory solution via agreement, the Textile Labor Inquiry Committee submitted its own recommendations to the Government of Bombay at the end of December 1939.[84] But by then World War II had broken out, and the current government

---

bor Officer which appeared in *ITJ* and *LG*, 1935–1938. The evidence is quite clear that in the absence of official pressure Association efforts would have failed, as they had in the past.

[79] S. N. Bose, *Indian Labour Code (Central)* (2d ed., Calcutta: Eastern Law House, Ltd., 1950), p. 593; *LG*, XVI, No. 10, June 1937, p. 760.

[80] *LG*, XVIII, No. 3, Nov. 1938, pp. 183–191, particularly Clause 28 and Schedule III.

[81] *TLIC 1938*, pp. 89–94, particularly p. 90.

[82] *TLIC 1940*, p. 98.

[83] *Ibid.*, p. 109.

[84] For details, see *ibid.*, pp. 98–145.

thought it inadvisable to introduce such a radical reform at that time.[86] The wage structure remained more or less unchanged through the war.[86]

In 1946 the two major unions reopened through official channels the question of establishing a standardized wage structure.

As regards standardization, it is urged that there are no uniform wages and rates for the same kind of work in the different units in the Bombay mill industry and the manner in which they were fixed was entirely arbitrary with the consequence that there is considerable dissatisfaction among the workers. A uniform system of wages for time and piece work is, therefore, urgently needed. They [the unions], therefore, demand that the rates of wages payable to all classes of workers and all classes of work should be revised and standardized to secure a living wage standard and ensure a proper remuneration, in suitable recognition of the strain and skill required in different processes in the industry.[87]

The issue was submitted to the Industrial Court for settlement. The BMOA did not oppose the demand for standardization but it did object to the proposal being linked to an effort to raise wages. After long deliberation the Court handed down a wage-standardization decree which had the force of law. The wage structure established was based on the one submitted by the BMOA to the Textile Labor Inquiry Committee in 1938 and modified and recommended by that committee in December 1939. The Industrial Court's task was made easier because the industry was making very high profits, and it was possible to impose upon the employers a scheme that provided generalized wage increases at the same time. The award, made effective January 1, 1947, is most simply described in an Association report.

The award laid down a standardized uniform list of basic wages and rates for employees of the textile industry in the city of Bombay. Schedule I of the award prescribed a standard wage for each time-work operation listed therein for a calendar month of 26 working days, and Schedule II dealt with pieceworkers. In the case of certain piecework occupations . . . , a standard basic average earning for a month of 26 working days has been laid down, and mills were required to convert these basic average earnings into a piecework rate. To enable mills to carry out correctly the intentions of the award, members were instructed to convert the basic monthly earnings indicated by the

---

[85] *The Industrial Court Reporter, 1946–47* (Baroda: Office of the Deputy Commissioner of Labour (Information), Government of Bombay, 1951), p. 395.

[86] There is no evidence on the behavior of rates although it is typically assumed that these remained constant until 1947. However, to basic wages was added a Dear Food Allowance which rose with the cost of living. Being a flat absolute amount awarded to all employees, its net effect was to reduce somewhat the disparities between lower and higher paid workers.

[87] *The Industrial Court Reporter, 1946–47*, p. 394.

Court into a piecework rate on the basis of normal expected production in the department.[88]

Standards for weavers were settled on the basis of a rate established for weaving ten yards of cloth of set specifications on a loom of set dimensions. Variations from these specifications were provided for by establishing a complex set of allowances and deductions.[89]

The Government resisted all temptations to make the scheme a minimum wage guarantee. In answer to a question of interpretation, the Industrial Court ruled that "Standardized wages and rates did not mean minimum or maximum wages, but uniform wages according to one standard. . . . [All] mills were . . . bound to pay the same wages and rates for particular occupations mentioned in the award." [90]

Although the scheme was generally accepted by the work force, certain difficulties did appear. Two small groups of workers, warpers and drawers-in, being dissatisfied with the increases given them, started a slow-down and ultimately struck work. But vigorous action by the Government broke the strike. Various modifications were introduced after 1947 to provide for new situations or to remedy revealed inequities. Otherwise, the standardization scheme held intact.[91] The scheme, of course, did not eliminate industrial conflict, but one major source of tension and labor force instability had been removed.

(4)

From a look at the history of wage structure changes, it seems quite clear that the cotton mills of Bombay were behaving as competitors in the purchase of labor services. At one time or another all employers objected to the consequences, the creation of a labor force with a high degree of interfirm mobility. Moreover, this wage structure, which was so responsive to the pressures of the supply of and demand for labor, also generated a great deal of industrial tension and conflict. In fact, it can be suggested that the strike was a major institutional mechanism in the functioning of this competitive labor market. It was the device through which adjustments in the wage structure were validated or invalidated.

---

[88] *BMOA 1947*, p. 44.

[89] *The Industrial Court Reporter, 1946–47*, pp. 414–422.

[90] R. G. Gokhale, *Annual Review of the Labour Situation in the Bombay Cotton Mill Industry*, 1949, pp. 21–22.

[91] For details on the development of the standardization scheme, see *LG*, issues for 1946–1948; *BMOA 1946–BMOA 1949; The Industrial Court Reporter, 1946–47*, pp. 79–84, 265–267, and 386–422; Gokhale, *op. cit.*, 1947; and Gokhale, *op. cit.*, 1949.

Most employers, of course, objected to this on principal. But more important, as we shall see in the next chapter, the strike produced its own institutional results which ultimately threatened to yield some unpalatable political consequences of concern to the State.

Since 1897 the industry had attempted periodically to establish some degree of wage standardization. At no point was it able to muster the discipline or mobilize the authority to carry such a proposal into effect on its own. Nor were trade unions at any time sufficiently well developed to impose such a scheme on the industry. It was only after 1934, by the intervention of the State, that the possibility of eliminating unstabilizing wage differentials began to manifest itself. But even with governmental intervention, it was not until the very end of the period, and then only by the force of legal fiat, that such a proposal became effective.[92]

---

[92] It would be interesting to speculate on the effects of such a wage-standardization scheme, had one been established in the very earliest days. Given the rapid growth in the number of mills, such a device would have made it very difficult to shift trained workers from established enterprises into new mills. It might, therefore, have increased the costs of establishing a mill by raising the cost of training. Whether this would have been sufficient to slow up the rate of development is difficult to say. Certainly, the increased costs, to the extent that they would have occurred, would have constituted an infinitesimal proportion of total costs in an industry where profit rates seem to have been quite high. Moreover, it is likely that the costs of training would have been offset by the economies of reduced labor turnover and tension.

If a successful standardization proposal had been accepted in 1891, when the first scheme was broached, it is likely that it would have worked to the advantage of the industry. By that time virtually all the mills had been established and the basic labor force trained. The failure to standardize wages for more than a half-century after 1891 probably raised costs to the industry by giving it a much more unstable labor force — with effects on over-all efficiency and conflict —than would otherwise have existed.

But the issue is more complex than this. The institutional imperatives of a move toward the exercise of monopsony power in the labor market would certainly have affected the industry's behavior in other spheres, with consequent effects on its technology and organization. Moreover, such a step might well have provoked an earlier massive reaction from the labor force.

CHAPTER X

Trade Unions,

the State, and Labor Discipline

(1)

More than three decades ago the Royal Commission on Labor wrote: "Prior to the winter of 1918–19, a strike was a rare occurrence in Indian industry." [1] This statement certainly did not apply to the Bombay cotton textile industry.[2] As early as 1874 there had been strikes in individual mills and departments, and they were not uncommon in the 1880's.[3] By the early 1890's strikes had become "of frequent occurrence in every one of the mills in this city." [4] Nor was the possibility of multimill strike action unheard of. The District Collector hinted that though rare, such strikes had occurred.[5] The Factory Inspector feared that there would be a general strike if the employers succeeded in agreeing to the proposed wage reduction (and standardization) scheme. "If such a reduction [of wages] takes place, something like a general strike is not unlikely; as though the workers have no organized Trades Union, still they are mostly of the same caste and from the same district, and have a strong tendency to hang together; moreover, the old rates of wages are in their eyes sanctioned by the custom of more than a generation." [6]

During the bad years 1900 and 1901 there was another rash of strikes. In one case twenty mills in the Parel district combined to cut wages by

---

[1] *RCL 1929*, "Report," p. 333.

[2] A detailed history of the working class movement in Bombay has yet to be written. This chapter is not intended to remedy the deficiency. It will deal only with those aspects of organized mill-hand activity which bear on the problem of creating a disciplined industrial labor force.

[3] Presidency of Bombay, *Annual Report, 1874–75*, p. 137; and *FC 1875*, pp. 24, 42, and 82. The manager of the M. Gokuldas Mill pointed out that a major purpose of keeping pay in arrears was to prevent strikes. *Ibid.*, p. 42. For strikes in the 1880's, see *RCL 1892, passim*.

[4] *RCL 1892*, evidence of N. M. Lokhunday, p. 169. For confirmation, see the evidence of the District Collector, *ibid.*, p. 174; *BMOA 1892*, pp. 11 and 28–29; and *ITJ*, issues for 1892 and 1893. The frequency of strikes led the *Indian Textile Journal* to refer to "a strike mania." *ITJ*, III, No. 27, December 1892, p. 64.

[5] *RCL 1892*, p. 174.

[6] *FA 1892*, p. 14. See also *RCL 1892*, p. 128.

12.5 per cent and in response 20,000 mill hands struck, shutting down these mills for ten days. Unlike most strikes of which we have record, this one must be considered a work-force victory.[7]

I have already described the strikes and unrest accompanying the extension of working hours after 1904. Referring to these, the Factory Commission of 1908 stated that "while the operatives fully understand the machinery of local strikes, . . . they are as yet unable to combine over any large area with the object of securing a common end by concerted action."[8] The commission was probably generally correct, as the strikes of the period before World War I indicate. No formal trade unions appeared. Leadership was lacking.[9] But the work force was beginning to develop the capacities for large-scale collective action. In fact, as early as 1892 one government official suggested that though trade unions did not exist, the same effect was achieved "by an unnamed and unwritten bond of union among the workers. . . ."[10] Expanding on this point, another official stated: "I understand the chief influence of the unnamed and unwritten bond of union . . . to be by the threat of boycotting to prevent individual workmen in any branch of factory labor consenting to accept wages lower than what that form of labor has hitherto commanded. This secret influence, though little more than 'in the air,' is powerful."[11]

World War I was a period of great tension in Bombay. The work force became increasingly restless as the cost of living rose rapidly. Strikes became even more frequent and threatened to take on city-wide proportions. The millowners boasted that by their quick action in granting a cost-of-living allowance they were able to forestall a general strike in the middle of 1917, but in January 1919 an industry-wide strike involving 150,000 workers broke out and lasted twelve days. Exactly a year later a month-long general strike once again paralyzed the mills. These

---

[7] *ITJ*, XI, No. 129, June 1901, p. 235. For reports on many of the strikes during this period, see *ITJ*, issues for 1900 and 1901.

[8] *IFLC 1908*, p. 20.

[9] Even before 1880 there developed worker welfare associations organized by charitably inclined individuals. Among these was the Bombay Mill Hands Association which in 1884 held mass meetings of more than 5,000 workers to press for improved factory legislation. In 1890 the same association called a meeting of 10,000 workers to press for a six-day week. Other notable welfare groups included the Servants of India Society (founded in 1905), the Kamgar Hitwardhak Sabha (founded in 1909), and the Social Service League (founded in 1910). Although these organizations were mainly welfare agencies, they not infrequently intervened as spokesmen for the workers after strikes broke out.

[10] Mr. Drewet, *RCL 1892*, p. 132.

[11] Mr. Campbell, *ibid.*, p. 128.

general strikes in 1919 and 1920 were caused by the rapidly rising cost of living.[12] To this unrest was added the growing nationalist agitation.

It is difficult to describe with precision the way in which the Bombay mill workers developed their sense of unified action, but there is no question that it was during this period that an effective collectivity appeared. Perhaps it was the role of the middle-class intellectual appearing in his first full-blown opposition to British rule.

Another distinction is that for several years to come, we cannot disassociate the industrial questions from the political movements of the country. The political agitator knows that a powerful army of town laborers would be an asset of no mean value to his cause. Labor here has plenty of grievances, but it is yet too early to expect its own ranks to supply a sufficient number of men who are able to take the lead in the inevitable struggle with capitalistic management. The existing leaders are recruited from the educated middle classes which have no dearth of people with little personal experience of the life of the laborer, little association as a rule with the conduct of industry in any form, but possessing a good deal of intellectual sympathy with the cause of oppressed labor.[13]

Certainly the growing unrest over the rising cost of living produced the economic basis for action. Whatever the causes, they affected the entire work force. But the general strikes were not organized incidents; they represented the disorganized boiling over of resentments too hot to be contained. This can be seen from a brief description of the general strike of January 1920.[14]

The mill hands of the Jacob Sassoon Mill approached the assistant manager on January 1 and asked for a bonus payment to offset the high cost of living. The official apparently refused to listen to the employees and took a very high-handed attitude. The next morning 4,000 workers gathered in front of the mill and had an inconclusive discussion with the mill manager.[15] Dissatisfied, the men refused to return to work. Instead, they marched to the near-by Gokuldas Mill and by shouting and throwing stones induced the operatives there to go on strike. With their numbers thus augmented the strikers paraded to other mills in the district, and by noon twelve mills were closed and 20,000 workmen were out. By evening twenty-five mills were affected and the number of strikers had

---

[12] *BMOA 1917*, p. x; *BMOA 1918*, p. xi; *BMOA 1919*, pp. ix–x.

[13] G. L. Nanda, "Labour Unrest in India," *Indian Journal of Economics*, III, Part 4, January 1921, pp. 462–463. See also P. P. Laksman, *Congress and Labour Movement in India* (Allahabad: Economic and Political Research Department, All-India Congress Committee, 1947), pp. 16–18.

[14] Based on C. S. Deole, "The Bombay Strikes," *Journal, Indian Economic Society*, II, 4, December 1919, pp. 193–202; and *BMOA 1919*, pp. ix–xi.

[15] It is not clear who spoke for the workers.

risen to 40,000.[16] At this point the evidence is unclear. Some reports suggest that the processions of noisy, stone-throwing workers caused the general shutdown. Others stated that the BMOA ordered a lockout in the remaining mills. In any event the strike became city-wide by January 4. On January 5 there was distributed a Marathi leaflet containing four demands, signed by two or three men as "Joint Secretaries" of the Mill Hands Association. We don't know who these leaders were or what the Mill Hands Association was.[17]

The strike continued for several days without change. Its momentum was fed by the outbreak of strikes among other groups of Bombay workers. During this interval some of the labor welfare organizations rounded up representatives of different groups of workers and created the Labor Settlement League. In a series of meetings held from January 9 to 11, 1920, a list of formal demands was worked out. This was presented to the Millowners' Association by Sir Narayan Chandavarkar, head of the Labor Settlement League. The millowners refused to consider the demands unless the men returned to work and presented their grievances to the individual mill managements. This was rejected, and the strike continued until January 23 when the Governor of Bombay intervened and forced the BMOA to announce a series of concessions.[18] It was assumed by the Labor Settlement League spokesmen that these terms would be acceptable to the strikers. However, the workers refused to return to the mills. On January 24–25 the League issued a leaflet over the signature of Sir Narayan urging a return to work, but only a few workers accepted this advice. On the 26th the situation grew ugly as strikers attacked workers in the six working mills and forced these enterprises to close. It is not clear why the strike continued, but on February 2, for reasons equally obscure, opposition ended and the operatives quietly resumed work.

The workers as a whole had no articulate demands at the time the strike broke out, nor was there any clearly defined leadership. It required the intervention of outsiders to formulate the demands, and these outsiders negotiated with the employers.[19] The Labor Settlement League

---

[16] The way in which the strike spread is very similar to the pattern manifested during the early period of European working class activity. See E. J. Hobsbawm, "The Machine Breakers," *Past & Present*, No. 1, February 1952, pp. 57–70.

[17] Apparently it did not have any relation to the long defunct organization of the same name which had been led by N. M. Lokhunday.

[18] Among the worker claims were demands for a shorter workday, substantial rises in pay, prompt payment of wages, and prompt payment of a resigned employee's accrued earnings. A number were conceded by the employers. Deole, *op. cit.*, pp. 195–198.

[19] A conference of mill hands had been held in December 1919 under the auspices

had only tenuous contacts with the strikers. When a compromise was reached the spokesman could exercise no control over the mill hands; the workers returned to their work places only after indicating their rejection of their putative spokesmen. This strike illustrated qualities characteristic of virtually all strikes until 1928. There was unrest without discipline, strike without organization.[20] When the mill hands returned to work all that remained was the memory of common action on a city-wide basis.

During the next few years no trade unions developed in the cotton mills. Efforts by individuals involved in the growing nationalist agitation to establish unions among the textile workers inevitably failed. There were no general strikes although there were innumerable small disputes. A strike would break out, some individual or group would appear to organize the workers, a strike committee would be formed, and dues collected. When the strike ended the organization vanished.[21]

The general strikes of 1924 and 1925 had the same characteristics as the 1919 and 1920 affairs. Sympathizers from social welfare organizations had no control over the outbreak of the strikes. During the course of the struggles they intervened, provided financial support, and undertook to act as spokesmen for the employees, but when terms of agreement were reached between the employers and the spokesmen the workers returned to work only slowly.[22]

At the end of the 1925 general strike a number of representatives of labor welfare groups gathered with a handful of workers to plan a

---

of one of the welfare organizations, the Kamgar Hitwardhak Sabha. It was claimed that seventy-five mills were represented. At that time twenty-four resolutions dealing with improved working conditions were passed. It is possible that this conference may have crystallized worker thinking. However, the demands set forth during the strike were much more limited in scope and much more directly economic in character. Deole, *op.cit.*, p. 195; "A New Labor Movement in India," *Monthly Labor Review*, XI, No. 2, August 1920, pp. 175–176; and P. D. Kulkarni, "Textile Trade Unionism in Bombay," *The Indian Journal of Social Work*, VII, December 1946, p. 228.

[20] *IDC 1922*, p. 2.

[21] *LG* each month reported strikes in the city and gave a brief description of their apparent causes. For one example, see *LG*, I, No. 10, June 1922, p. 10. On employer hostility to trade union development, see annual reports of the BMOA for 1919–1921.

[22] For information on the 1924 general strike, caused by the millowners' decision not to pay an annual bonus, see *LG*, III, Nos. 6, 7, and 8, February to April 1924; *BMOA 1923*, pp. ix–xi; and *BMOA 1924*, pp. xiii and 166–168. For information on the 1925 general strike, caused by a threatened general 11.5 per cent wage reduction, see *LG*, V, Nos. 1–5, September 1925 to January 1926; and *BMOA 1925*, pp. vii–viii and 122–127.

genuine city-wide cotton textile union. The resulting Bombay Textile
Labor Union (BTLU) is customarily viewed as the first effective trade
union in the industry. Unlike the welfare organizations which attempted
only to speak for the workers, the BTLU tried to create an organization
in which the workers themselves would participate. Building on the
enthusiasm engendered by the successful 1925 strike, the union was
able by March 1927 to claim a membership of 9,800, slightly more than
6 per cent of mill employment.[23] Although it attempted to create a
Western-style trade union, oriented to wage-welfare objectives, the
BTLU never generated an independent momentum. No attempt was
made to create union administrative units within the individual mills
nor was a subsidiary leadership developed. The organization was a
creature of its prime movers, N. M. Joshi and R. R. Bakhale. When they
were busy elsewhere — as they often were — the organization stagnated.
Since the union was unable to cope with falling employment, sagging
wage rates, and the threat of rationalization, its membership began to
decline from its March 1927 peak.[24]

At this time the Communists made their first appearance in Bombay
and sought a mass base for their political activities. The mill workers,
making up more than half the total factory work force in the city, were
the obvious source of such support, and the disturbed conditions provided the ideal opportunity. In January 1928 the Communists began to
agitate for a general strike against the "efficiency scheme," the rationalization program being introduced by the Sassoon group of mills. At
first they were forestalled by the moderate leadership of the BTLU, but
the Communists were able to take advantage of millowner determination to push the new rationalized work system. Mill-hand discontent increased and a general strike broke out in April 1928. The Communists
created the Girni Kamgar Union (GKU) to direct the strike. Although
the BTLU leadership had been opposed to a strike, it was forced to go
along with the manifest sentiments of the great mass of the workers or
forfeit all of its support to the more radical organization. It joined the
so-called Joint Strike Committee. The strike lasted nearly six months and

---

[23] All trade union membership data, except when otherwise indicated, are from
"Principle Trade Unions in the Presidency of Bombay . . . ," a quarterly report appearing in the *Labour Gazette*. All membership figures are grossly overstated, and
this should be borne in mind whenever such figures are cited. Perhaps the most
reliable are those for the BTLU.

[24] The BTLU never had effective control over its membership. It gained support
when it satisfactorily settled strikes which the workers started on their own. It lost
members when it failed. The BTLU showed no capacity for success and no ability
to maintain loyalty in defeat.

ended only when the millowners agreed to the appointment of a government committee to investigate the issues.[25]

While the Bombay Strike Enquiry (Fawcett) Committee was sitting, trouble continued in the mills. Not only were the conditions which provoked the general strike still present, but the very fact of the strike had exacerbated the situation. There were continuing charges of discrimination against workers who had been active in the strike. While the BTLU leadership occupied itself entirely with negotiations before the Fawcett Committee, the GKU was also organizing in the mills. Between September and the end of December 1928 the BTLU membership fell to 6,749 whereas the GKU membership rose to 54,000.

In every mill the GKU set up a grievance committee to deal directly with the management. These committees, apparently encouraged by their union leaders, increasingly interfered in matters which the employers considered purely management affairs. Although the BMOA was negotiating with the Joint Strike Committee through the Fawcett Committee, this did not mean that the individual employers had admitted any limitations on their traditional arbitrary authority. The conflict produced a spate of new disputes during the negotiations and in one of them a weaving master was murdered.

In March 1929 the Fawcett Committee issued its report. The evidence suggests that the BMOA was willing to attempt the radical reorganization of labor discipline in the mills which was recommended. However, in meetings held in April 1929 between the BMOA and the Joint Strike Committee to consider implementing the Fawcett Committee proposals, the Communist leadership refused to go along until the employers settled all the outstanding disputes and rehired workers who had been replaced by strikebreakers. During this entire period the disputes were creating a feeling among the mill hands that individual millowners were systematically victimizing militant unionists. Mass meetings of workers whipped this fear, no doubt with a strong foundation of truth, into a willingness to join another general strike which was called at the end of April 1929. The strike was bitterly opposed by the leaders of the moderate BTLU, and in the seventeen or eighteen mills where its influence was greatest many of the workers did not strike. The employers took an unyielding position. The strike collapsed in September 1929 almost

---

[25] For materials on the general strikes of 1928 and 1929, see *LG* issues for the period; annual reports of the Millowners' Association for 1928–1930; *BSEC, 1928–29*; Government of Bombay, *Report of the Court of Enquiry, 1929* (Bombay: Government Central Press, 1929); *ITJ* issues for the period; and *The Police Report on the Bombay Riots of February 1929* (Bombay: Government Central Press, 1929).

immediately after an official Court of Enquiry sharply denounced the activities of the Communist leadership of the GKU. With this defeat the membership of the GKU dwindled to a few hundred members by the end of the year. Ironically, the membership of the BTLU also fell to insignificance.

The collapse of the unions did not mean the end of tensions, nor did it clear the way for the introduction of the revamped system of labor administration recommended by the Fawcett Committee. Instead, the deepening economic crisis resulted in mill closings and a frenzy of wage cuts. Frequent strikes continued to occur in individual mills between 1930 and 1934, but the leaders of the now virtually defunct unions, carrying on their efforts at organization, met with little success until mid-1933 when the chaotic race of employers to reduce wages provoked a renewed militancy among the now desperate mill hands. A general strike broke out at the end of April 1934. The strike movement had initially been in the hands of the moderate leadership of the old Bombay Textile Labor Union. As in 1928 and 1929, however, it quickly fell into the hands of the Communists. The strike lasted until mid-June when it finally collapsed because of the unyielding attitude of the employers.[26]

(2)

The violent and catastrophic behavior of the workers between 1928 and 1934 was to be expected in light of the industry's history. At the same time, the events after 1922 revealed the incapacity of employers individually or through their association to establish a more effective and responsive labor force. During the period of expanding markets and high profits before 1922 the efficiency with which labor was utilized and the discipline under which it worked were matters of little consequence to the employers. The lax organization of production and work I have described was sufficient to meet the requirements of the market. But by 1922 the industry's golden era was over. Japanese mills and mills in other parts of India — newer and on the whole more efficient — offered sharp competition in a slackening market. Millowners first sought to ease the burden of declining profits by lowering the wage bill directly. These efforts led to the general strikes in 1924 and 1925 which cost nearly twenty million man-days. The next step, beginning in 1926, was an attempt to rationalize the use of the work force. By the time the employers found themselves forced to attempt a rationalization of labor utilization,

---

[26] On this strike, see *LG*, XIII, Nos. 9–11, May–July 1934; and *ITJ*, XLIV, Nos. 4, 8 and 9, January, May and June 1934 pp. 137, 276–278 and 311.

they discovered that their traditionally lax methods of labor administration had become institutionalized.[27] Attempts to reduce labor costs along lines proposed by the Indian Tariff Board in 1927 produced the great strikes of 1928 and 1929. It became obvious that radical reform in the industry could be carried out only over the violent protests of an increasingly self-conscious work force or with its coöperation. The period during which the employers had been free to manipulate the work force without regard to mill hand sensibilities had come to an end. In this sense, the unilateral attempts of the millowners to impose a new system of labor discipline appropriate to their changed needs had come too late.[28]

In another sense, the long-run crisis in the industry came too early. It appeared just at the time when the mill hands showed a new-found militancy but before strong trade unionism could give that militancy any sense of direction and discipline.[29] The moderate and Communist union leaderships struggled, each in its own fashion, for the loyalty of the operatives, a loyalty denied to the employers. In the tumultuous, fear-ridden, and violent atmosphere of the mills, the demands of the Communists especially played on the workers' hostility to the employers. All efforts at compromise failed, and the infant unions vanished from the industry. The events of the period not only revealed the failure of voluntary groups to transform mill discipline but also showed the ease with which the operatives could fall under Communist influence and be turned into a revolutionary political force threatening the very fabric of the established social order. In these circumstances the State intervened.

---

[27] As Wilbert Moore has said, "past employment practices . . . may raise barriers to effective labor utilization. . . . [They] may have been frozen into employment policies that make subsequent development harder rather than easier." "Problems of Timing, Balance, and Priorities in Development Measures," *Economic Development and Cultural Change*, II, No. 4, January 1954, p. 240.

[28] There is some evidence that employer attempts to rationalize production not infrequently imposed higher production targets on mill hands without providing the improved raw materials, slower machine speeds and other features on which the "efficiency schemes" ultimately depended. See, for example, *TLIC 1940*, pp. 198–207.

[29] Some employers and the BMOA belatedly recognized the importance of strong unions as a disciplinary force in the industry. *RCL 1929*, I, Part 1, p. 482. In fact, the BMOA went so far as to say in 1932 that no great progress could be made in the absence of "a single effective [trade union] body with which it can negotiate. . . ." *ITB 1934*, I, p. 87. Though this was true to a great extent, there were many reforms in mill operation which did not depend on the coöperation of labor, but the millowners were far too unruly a group to carry these proposals through to completion.

The provincial government was determined that no group with the potential political and economic strength of the Bombay mill hands should come under Communist control. It took steps to provide limited and nonrevolutionary channels through which workers' grievances could be aired by passing the Trade Disputes Conciliation Act immediately after the end of the 1934 strike.[30] Earlier chapters have emphasized the important role of the State in contributing to the establishment of orderly working relations in the mills. The consequences of the Bombay Trade Disputes Conciliation Act were equally important in shaping the long-run development of trade unions. This act marked the beginning of governmental intervention in the sphere which in western countries had historically been reserved to voluntary association of workers.

The act created an official labor officer who was to function much as a union business agent in the United States would. He negotiated with employers about workers' grievances, and if his intervention was unsuccessful he could refer the issue to conciliation. The mill hands could select the labor officer or one of their own group to represent them in the conciliation proceedings, but precautions were taken that they did not select a Communist.[31]

The Millowners Association greeted the act with considerable enthusiasm, but spokesmen even of the moderate labor position had serious doubts, fearing that government intervention might prevent the growth of independent unions.

The Labor Officer himself would represent the workers if no qualified delegate could be secured to represent them, thus eliminating the whole of the labor view. . . . Government's conciliation is bound to imperil the militant vigor of the Girni Kamgar Union though it may not permanently establish moderation in the labor camp. . . . Labor . . . must stand independent and build up its own organizations by itself with a definite policy of independent negotiations with the owners direct.[32]

---

[30] The government was quite explicit about its objectives. The minister responsible for carrying the bill through the Legislative Assembly stated: "I wish to make it clear that . . . it [the legislation] is an open effort on the part of Government to prevent Communists and extremists (labor) from interfering in the textile affairs of Bombay City." *ITJ*, XLIV, No. 11, August 1934, p. 380. For the text of this legislation, see *LG*, XIII, No. 12, August 1934, pp. 865 and 904–912. Although this and subsequent legislation were extended at various times to other industries, the prime concern at the time of their passage was with the Bombay textile industry.

[31] Beyond conciliation and publication of the facts, nothing was to be done. It was assumed that such official pressure would be sufficient to achieve a redress of most grievances.

[32] *ITB*, XLIV, No. 11, August 1934, p. 376. For the BMOA position, see *BMOA 1934*, p. iv.

The government responded that "there was no desire that the labor officer should supplant the representatives of a properly organized trade-union." [33] Despite these protestations, the 1934 statute seems not to have helped the development of independent organizations. Generally speaking, the Government Labor Officer did usurp the functions of the small trade unions which had been resurrected during the 1934 general strike. In retaliation, they fought him at every turn, seeking to obtain for themselves the loyalty of the workers. Their efforts seem to have been largely fruitless.[34] At the same time the labor officer, by the settlements he sought in the years after 1934, gradually began to establish some notion of standardization of labor administration among the mills. His influence was strengthened with the passage of the Payment of Wages Act in 1936, which placed the structure of discipline at least partly under the authority of the State.

In 1937 the Indian Congress Party came to power in Bombay Province. On its accession to office in July the new government issued its statement of labor policy.

With regard to trade disputes, Government are determined to pursue an active policy with a view to maintaining industrial peace . . . , endeavoring all the time to see that the workers obtain a fair deal. It is the intention of Government to promote legislation aiming at the prevention of strikes and lockouts as far as possible. The basis of this legislation would be the requirement that no reduction in wages or other change in conditions of employment to the disadvantage of the workers should take effect till they have had sufficient time and opportunity for having the facts and merits of the proposed change examined and all avenues of peaceful settlement of the dispute explored either through the channel of voluntary negotiation, conciliation or arbitration or by the machinery of the law. A corresponding obligation would rest on the workers in respect of demands on their behalf. . . . While Government proposes to do all that is practical for the amelioration of the conditions of the working class, they are convinced that no legislative program can be a substitute for the organized strength of the working class and till organization of workers, run on genuine trade union lines, grow up in various fields of employment, no lasting good can accrue. Government are therefore anxious to assist in removing real hindrances in the way of the growth of the organization and to promote collective bargaining between the employers and the employees. Means will be devised to discourage victimization of workers for connection with a labor organization and participation in legitimate trade union activity.[35]

---

[33] *ITB*, XLIV, No. 11, August 1934, p. 376.

[34] Between 1934 and 1938 the five Bombay textile unions had fluctuating memberships, which in December 1937 totaled about eighty-seven hundred.

[35] *LG*, XVI, No. 12, August 1937, pp. 923–924.

The establishment of a Congress government, followed by the publication of its labor policy statement and the release from imprisonment of certain left-wing labor leaders, plus rising profits in the industry set loose a great number of strikes. To lessen discontent the government appointed an official committee (the Textile Labor Inquiry Committee) to investigate the whole question of wages and work organization. At government request the committee issued an interim report providing for an 11.9 per cent increase in wages.[36] At the same time the government began to draft legislation giving effect to its statement of policy. From its point of view the Bombay Trade Disputes Act of 1934 was inadequate because it did not make conciliation compulsory.[37] The Bombay Industrial Disputes Act, passed in November 1938, attempted to remedy this defect and at the same time establish the basis for more effective industrial relations by strengthening the hand of trade unions.[38]

The act required employers to register with the government the formal terms — the standing orders — under which workers were employed. Any intent by employer or workers to change wages or working conditions required notice to the affected party, and the two parties had to negotiate the change directly. In the event that direct negotiations failed the issue was referred to a government conciliator. If conciliation failed, the government could, by agreement of the parties, refer any important issue to an industrial court established under the law. Only after this procedure had been followed could a strike or lockout legally be called.[39]

Thus a more determinate system of labor regulation was established within each mill by the state, and the right to settle issues by direct trials of strength between employers and workers was limited by the enforced conciliation procedure. In 1941 the governor of Bombay, seeking to prevent strikes that might hamper the war effort, amended the 1938 act to provide that any important dispute not resolved by conciliation could be ordered into an industrial court for arbitration. Decisions of this court were to be binding on the parties.[40]

---

[36] *TLIC 1938*, pp. 89–94.

[37] *LG*, XVIII, No. 3, November 1938, p. 183.

[38] For a description of this act, see *ibid.*, pp. 183–191. On the special efforts of the government to strengthen trade unions as representative agencies, see *loc. cit.*, and *LG*, XX, No. 1, September 1940, p. 23.

[39] A strike declared before all legal steps had been taken could result in fines against the workers involved and the loss of all rights to re-employment and other claims against the employer. An employer who locked out his workers or made an illegal change in working rules could be fined.

[40] *LG*, XX, No. 9, May 1941, p. 653.

How was the functioning of trade unions affected by the 1934 and 1938 legislation? The 1934 Trade Disputes Act did not encourage the development of independent unions, nor was that its basic intent. The official labor officer usurped the functions claimed by the unions, which had been revived during the 1934 strike. Despite their vigorous efforts, the unions could claim no more than 8,700 members in December 1937. The Industrial Disputes Act of 1938 did seek to strengthen unions by making victimization of workers for union activity illegal. It also provided that when a union's membership reached 25 per cent of the industry's work force, it could officially represent workers in collective bargaining and official proceedings. But at no time during the life of the act (1938 to 1947) was a union able to achieve representative status. As a result, unions remained largely excluded from official participation in the industrial relations process. Worker representation continued to be provided by the labor officer or by workers chosen in elections conducted by him.[41] Further, the law tended to frustrate direct collective bargaining. Whenever a dispute arose, the participants forced the issue into official channels as quickly as possible. The Industrial Court, representing the State, ultimately became the key institution.

In October 1939 the Congress ministry resigned in protest against India's involvement in the war against Germany. On its return to power in 1946 it issued a new statement on labor policy:

. . . it is intended . . . to develop to a further stage the scheme of industrial relations embodied in the Bombay Industrial Disputes Act [of 1938]. Government could not now remain content with just removing hindrances in the way of labour's effort to organize itself. It proposes to supply a very real impetus for the growth of sound organizations of industrial and other workers. . . . The workers may feel assured that the Government of Bombay will explore further ways of checking arbitrary dealings on the part of employers and removing delays in the redress of grievances. Government is equally anxious to ensure that the course of efficient production is not hampered by thoughtless and needless stoppages of work . . . Government is concerned at the excessive frequency of illegal strikes in the City of Bombay. While offering to lend every aid in the speedy redress of legitimate grievances, Government wishes to make it plain that the workers who have recourse to illegal strikes should look for no sympathy or help from it and organizations which directly

---

[41] There is evidence that after 1938 unions in fact began to play a slightly more important role. The Labor Officer tended informally to consider the views of the unions in presenting his cases before the conciliator. And in a growing number of cases the workers, instead of choosing the Labor Officer to speak for them, selected representatives from their own ranks. Frequently these worker representatives were union activists.

or indirectly encourage such strikes will receive no countenance at its hands. . . . But in the case the workers apply for arbitration which is refused by the employer, any strike in consequence, as long as it is conducted peacefully, would be entitled to full sympathy and support from the community.[42]

The enactment of the Bombay Industrial Relations Act of 1946 was intended to give substance to the new statement of policy.[43] It created an elaborate system of labor courts to supplement the conciliation and arbitration functions established under the 1938 Act. The law endeavored to encourage actively the growth of "sound organizations," those which would support the official policy. A category of "approved unions" was created by the law — those whose constitutions accepted the principle of compulsory conciliation and arbitration and permitted no strike until all legally available methods had been exhausted and only after a majority of the members had voted by secret ballot in favor of the strike. An "approved union" received certain important privileges, including the right to post notices and collect dues in the mills; its officers could visit the members at their work; it could make use of the official conciliation-arbitration machinery; and it could receive legal aid from the government in presenting cases before the industrial courts. Any number of "approved unions" could exist, but when one union represented 15 per cent or more of the total industry work force (and had more members than any other union), it was designated the "representative union." An organization so designated was granted sole authority to speak for all workers in the industry in bargaining matters and it alone, under these circumstances, possessed the added rights of an "approved union." The law was purposely designed to encourage the development of a single union for the industry. Other unions could exist but the "representative union" alone received the special advantages. In a situation where dues collection was difficult and where most workers' grievances were settled before government agencies, restricting the right to collect dues inside a mill and to represent workers before official tribunals to a single union and at the same time providing it with government-financed legal assistance gave it an enormous advantage. Once a "representative union" was established, it would be very difficult to replace.

---

[42] *LG*, XXV, No. 9, May 1946, pp. 670–671.

[43] For a detailed description of the legal provisions, see Government of Bombay Political and Service Department, *The Bombay Industrial Relations Act, 1946 (Bom. XI of 1947) with the Bombay Industrial Relations Rules, 1947; the Industrial Court Regulations, 1947; and the Labour Courts (Practice and Procedure) Rules; and the Bombay Wage Board Rules, 1948* (Bombay: Government Central Press, 1950.)

(3)

When the first Congress ministry came to power in 1937 there were five small unions in the industry. Most important was the Communist-led Bombay Girni Kamgar (Red Flag) Union, with 5,500 members.[44] Although its membership had fluctuated erratically between 1934 and 1938, under the more tolerant Congress policy it tended to grow. By June 1940 its membership had risen to a claimed 32,000 whereas the combined membership of all other unions totaled less than 7,000. This rapid growth of the Red Flag Union was associated with its vigorous and sometimes violent support of strikes in various mills and its conduct of two general strikes. The first, in November 1938, was a token one-day protest against the passage of the Bombay Industrial Disputes Act of 1938, a strike which resulted in considerable violence and attracted new members.[45] The second general strike in March and April 1940 arose out of a demand for a cost-of-living allowance to offset the price increases which had occurred since August 1939. The Red Flag Union provoked considerable agitation on this issue. The government was forced in January 1940 to appoint a conciliation board to consider the matter. The Red Flag Union, unsatisfied with the award, called a general strike in March. During the strike, which was entirely dominated by the Communists, the Congress Party tried to take control but failed. The strike finally collapsed in April.[46]

By the time World War II broke out, two important groups were struggling for the loyalty of the mill workers, one identified with the Congress Party and the other associated with the Communists. Each rivaled the other in attempts to exploit the economic grievances of the operatives. Both sought to cultivate this large and restless labor force, seeking to capture its potential strength for use in shaping the economic and political character of the independent India that was visibly emerging.[47]

During the war the Indian National Congress was bitterly involved in

---

[44] This was a resurrection of the union which had been so active during 1928 and 1929.

[45] *Report of the Bombay Disturbances Enquiry Committee* (Bombay: Government Central Press, 1939.) This strike was conducted by the Communists and their allies as an attack on Congress ministry policy. See particularly *ibid.*, pp. 14–18.

[46] For details of this dispute, see *LG*, XIX, Nos. 6–9, February–May 1940, pp. 487–491, 661–663, and 756–758; and The Employers' Federation of India, *The General Strike in the Bombay Cotton Mill Industry* (Bombay, 1940.)

[47] The Congress Party was inhibited in its struggle for worker loyalty by many political factors, including its unwillingness to engage in direct organization of trade unions for fear of weakening the Independence movement. Laksman, *op. cit.*, pp. 27–28.

the struggle for independence and virtually all of the Congress Party
trade union leaders were in jail. The Communist union tended, therefore, to remain the dominant mill-hand organization. The Communist
Party's prowar stand after June 1941, its union's emphasis on full production, and the efforts to keep strikes to a minimum brought it informal
support from the government and millowners. Nevertheless, its numeri-
cal strength declined from its December 1940 peak of 36,500 to 26,000
at the end of 1945. The Red Flag Union represented the vast majority
of workers organized into cotton textile unions, but its hold on the
operatives was by no means firm. Although there was no effective Congress Party union during the war, on many occasions, in spite of Communist opposition, the Congress was able to bring the workers into the
streets in political demonstrations for independence.[48]

At the end of the war, with independence in sight, the Congress
turned its attention once again to capturing control of the Bombay operatives. In late 1945 it created the Rashtriya Mill Mazdoor Sangh
(RMMS) to organize directly among the mill hands. Its prestige en-
hanced by the vast enthusiasm for the Congress Party during the period
when independence came, this union quickly began to compete with
the Red Flag organization. By 1947 it claimed 32,000 members to the
Red Flag Union's 39,537.[49] On every possible occasion the new postwar
Congress government threw its support behind the RMMS which benefited from the popularity of the Industrial Court's wage and standardization award of May 1947. The situation was complicated at the time by
the appearance of the Socialist-dominated Mill Mazdoor Sabha. After
this the three political parties struggled to capture the support of the
operatives through the trade unions they sponsored and to some unknown extent financed.[50]

Both the Communists and Socialists recognized the direction in which
Congress government policy was moving. They called a one-day strike
of protest in December 1947 which brought out 209,000 workers and
closed all but one of the city's mills. In spite of this, the government a
few months later designated the Congress-dominated RMMS the "representative union" for the industry. No election was held to determine
which of the three major contending unions represented the largest

---

[48] P. D. Kulkarni, *op.cit.*, pp. 232–233.

[49] R. G. Gokhale, *Annual Review of the Labour Situation in the Bombay Cotton
Mill Industry*, 1947, p. 9. Actually, a predecessor to the RMMS had been organized
in 1938 and recorded a small membership in September 1940. See Kulkarni, *op.cit.*,
pp. 232–233; and *LG*, XX, No. 3, November 1940, pp. 216–217.

[50] It is necessary to take trade union developments slightly beyond the end of my
period in order to sketch out the important implications of the 1946 law.

number of workers. The Registrar of Trade Unions merely checked the membership lists of the RMMS.[51]

The fact that the RMMS was designated the "representative union" did not lessen Communist and Socialist competition for mill-hand loyalty, and the history of the period between 1949 and 1951 indicates that the representative character of the Congress union was merely a legal fiction at that time.[52] In 1949 the RMMS supported a government ruling that a part of the 1948 annual bonus was to be paid by the mills in the form of national savings bonds. This was sound anti-inflationary policy but it was bitterly resented by the workers who, encouraged by Socialist-Communist agitation, deserted the RMMS in droves. Its membership declined so much that on application of the Socialist union the registrar of trade unions canceled the representative status of the RMMS, but the decision was reversed by the Industrial Court.[53]

The next year the RMMS claim to represent the workers was challenged again, this time in devastating fashion. The 1950 annual bonus award by the Industrial Court was smaller than the workers had anticipated, and workers in four mills were excluded because their mills had no profits in 1949. Although the RMMS possessed the legal and organizational advantages as "representative union," the Socialist and Communist unions were able to call a great general strike.[54] Despite the exhortations of the Congress union and the vigorous legal and police action of the government, the strike continued for sixty-three days before it finally collapsed.[55] The breaking of the strike had important consequences. It led to the virtual collapse of the Communist union and

---

[51] It is impossible to determine the memberships of the various unions at this time. However, we do have one clue. Just before the designation of the RMMS as the "representative union," twenty-one workers were chosen from the Bombay mills in elections conducted by the Labor Officer to represent the operatives in a bonus dispute before the Industrial Court. Of the twenty-one, nine were followers of the Socialist union, four were followers of the Communist group, and only eight were adherents of the Congress-sponsored RMMS. Gokhale, *op. cit.*, 1949, p. 31.

[52] Even if its membership was actually larger than that of either of the other two unions, there is evidence which suggests that its plurality was concentrated in a limited number of mills. The other organizations had their centers of power in other mills. The Congress union, even if effective, was able to maintain authority only over the workers in its restricted number of mills.

[53] Gokhale, *op. cit.*, 1949, p. 7.

[54] The Congress union membership at this time was claimed as 46,546. On the basis of membership dues collected, my own estimate is that the membership was probably not more than 21,000. If some of the rumors circulating in Bombay in 1951 were correct, the effective membership was closer to 10,000. However, all union membership figures were grossly exaggerated if measured by dues collected.

[55] *LG*, XXX, Nos. 2–4, October to December 1950, pp. 126, 212–214, 258–259 and 358.

the serious weakening of the Socialist Mill Mazdoor Sabha. The Congress-supported union, although itself reduced in membership, emerged with no effective opposition against it.[56] After 1951 the union was able to increase its ability to force workers to operate through the formal channels of protest over which it had a government-supported monopoly.

(4)

There are two special characteristics which characterized textile unionism in Bombay. First, no trade union was able to lay effective claim to the loyalty of the mill hands, even of purported members. Membership figures rose during periods of tension before and during strikes but tended to decline afterward. Second, in periods of tension workers responded to the agitation of any well-organized and dynamic group. Even after trade unions had made their formal appearance, there was no guarantee that the leadership could carry the members with it. The mill hands were not bound by any of the discipline which their erstwhile leaders attempted to impose on them. In spite of the growth of a militant sense of self-consciousness among the workers and apparent government encouragement, trade unionism of the Western variety did not thrive.

The fact that the first manifestations of formal trade union organization did not appear until after World War I is relatively easy to understand. This was inevitable in an industry where the labor force was growing rapidly. New workers poured in from rural areas. They came from different regions, frequently with differing languages, cultures, and religions. There was, in addition, a constant turnover of workers among the mills, a phenomenon tending to disrupt organizational ties.

None of this actually worked against the building of a collective consciousness, even though effective unity was relatively slight during the pre-World War I period. Within the limits of discipline and efficiency set by the employer, some informal tradition emerged which was based on a web of custom and coöperation. The strikes which occurred in the industry's very earliest days are objective evidence of how quickly the process took place. Commentators have often implied that strikes in India were the evidence of the workers' lack of commitment to the industrial situation. On the contrary, strikes were an expression of their attachment to the industrial environment rather than an effort to destroy it. Strikes suggest the acceptance of customary work relationships and were an effort to preserve them. If the mill hands had been truly un-

---

[56] RMMS claimed membership fell to less than 40,000 in October 1951.

committed and had retained their fundamental loyalty to rural life, there would have been no strikes but only a flight to the countryside.

Though it is easy to explain the lack of formal trade unionism before World War I, it is more difficult to understand why, once started, it was not successful. The sense of unity and the willingness to strike were present. The general strikes showed a capacity for tenacity and sacrifice almost beyond belief. Yet from this no strong organization came.[57] This is not the place to consider the problem in detail, but it is appropriate to offer a few comments about a matter which has generally been ignored when this situation is considered.

For reasons never explored, Indian unions tend almost always to be industrial rather than craft in structure. This was certainly the case in the Bombay cotton textile industry. So far as I know, there has never been any attempt to organize workers along lines of skill.[58] An important factor would seem to be associated with the occupational structure in the industry. The Bombay industry developed with a technology that required minimum amounts of great skill and maximum amounts of semi- and unskilled labor, exactly the kind of work force that can be effectively organized only along industrial lines.[59] But whatever the correct reasons for the attachment to industrial-type unionism, the very acceptance of this form as the appropriate way to organize the cotton textile workers made it more difficult to establish strong unions.

The first strong permanent unions in Britain and the United States were craft organizations. Having solved the problems of organizing relatively well-paid skilled workers, industrial unions were ultimately erected on a base of administrative experience and cadres of organizers developed in the craft unions. It is important to note that despite frequent efforts to organize semi- and unskilled workers, successful

---

[57] As late as 1958 an observer wrote: "The nature and role of the RMMS is shaped by its legal status under the Bombay Industrial Relations Act (1946). The view is frequently put forth by government, labor, and management officials in Bombay that the RMMS would even collapse without this legislation." R. C. James, "Trade Union Democracy: Indian Textiles," *The Western Political Quarterly*, XI, No. 3, September 1958, p. 570.

[58] Strikes were often departmental and thus more or less occupationally organized, but industry-wide strikes never seem to have taken this form. On the other hand, in Ahmedabad the Textile Labor Association was organized on the basis of several craft unions. C. A. Myers, *Labor Problems in the Industrialization of India* (Cambridge: Harvard University Press, 1958), p. 72. But the Ahmedabad case was exceptional. A study that attempts to explain the differences between Bombay and Ahmedabad is certainly called for.

[59] The industry very early shifted from mule spinning to ring spinning, thus reducing the skill component in this particular occupation. Weaving, the other major occupational category, also seemed to use a technology that required relatively little skill.

industrial unions did not appear in Britain until the 1890's and in the United States until the 1930's. In other words, it was not until about a century after the appearance of the factory system in each country that the very complex administrative problems associated with the creation of strong responsible industrial unions were solved. Thus, the weakness of Indian unions — explicable in terms of poverty, illiteracy, and the rest — is perhaps best explained by the fact that the workers lacked any tradition of craft union experiences and did not possess any of the administrative talents therein developed. Industrial unions in the Bombay textile industry, in order to achieve that membership loyalty and discipline upon which their strength depended, required a bureaucratic structure too complex to be created by the talent available to them.

Governmental intervention increased the difficulties of building a bureaucratic apparatus suitable to the needs of the membership. The creation of an elaborate system of industrial jurisprudence based on the legislation of 1934 and after not only imposed more burdensome administrative requirements in industrial union structure; it may well have established a new linguistic barrier. The whole system of industrial courts functioned in English. This meant that all efforts to resolve conflicts between employers and workers through the mediation of the State were carried on in a language the workers could not understand. In effect, they were not direct participants in the manipulations which went on about them and which purported to settle their fates. They were disassociated from their employers and from the juridical apparatus by the barrier of language. This was a cleavage which to some extent divided the mill hands even from their leadership, at least during the crucial periods when that leadership was negotiating with others. This may explain in part the lack of loyalty to any trade union, the unwillingness with which mill hands responded to any call for aggressive action, and the tenacity with which they were so often willing to stand out against constituted authority.[60]

---

[60] Max Weber wrote: "One advantage for the entrepreneurs is that the caste division of the workers has thus far made any trade union organization and any real 'strike' impossible." *From Max Weber: Essays in Sociology*, edited by H. H. Gerth and C. W. Mills (New York: Oxford University Press, 1946), p. 414. Despite Weber's authority, it will be noted that I have made no reference to caste as a factor inhibiting the development of trade unions. Although the institution may have played some role, the evidence is notoriously silent on that possibility. Mehta, *CMI*, p. 121, has referred to untouchable strikebreakers in the 1929 general strike, but other evidence suggests that this was exceptional. The size and scope of many strikes from the end of the nineteenth century required the coöperation of all occupational groups in a mill or the industry, including untouchables. Moreover, there is no substantial evidence that caste has served as an overt bar to trade union development in the Bombay textile mills. However, this is another aspect of the relationship of caste to industrialization on which research is badly needed.

CHAPTER XI

Summary and Conclusions

(1)

Modern factory industry requires methods of organizing productive activity that are significantly different from those employed in preindustrial societies. If the shift from traditional modes of production to industrial technology is to be successful, it is necessary to mobilize a labor force which will serve the necessities of this novel situation. Labor must somehow be drawn out of the old and transferred into the new environment. It must be given new tasks and sufficient training to perform them; it must be taught to work to a different pattern of rules and relationships.

Scholars have tended to stress the radical character of this transformation and the difficulties of its achievement. For example, it has been the claim of students of the subject that during the past century Indian industrialization was inhibited in many ways by the tenacious persistence of commitments to the traditional social order in the countryside. Apart from its other purported consequences, it is argued that the institutions of the older social order seriously inhibited the creation of an industrial labor force. Claims of kinship, caste, and village supposedly served as bonds keeping people on the land or operated as powerful forces to bring them back. Thus any movement to the city was a temporary one. In this view, the expansion of the Bombay cotton textile industry, particularly before 1920, was inhibited by the limited supply of raw labor available to it and by the consequent effects of this shortage on work-force stability and discipline. Moreover, this shortage of labor, so it is said, forced employers to depend on the foreman-jobber for hiring and disciplining the workers, a dependence which added to the difficulties of properly organizing the labor force. And even after World War I, when all observers agree that labor was not in short supply, it is claimed that the persistence with which mill hands retained their rural connections made for a labor force only "partially committed" to factory employment, one characterized by indiscipline and rates of absenteeism "much higher than in more advanced industrial countries."[1]

---

[1] C. A. Myers, *Labor Problems in the Industrialization of India* (Cambridge: Harvard University Press, 1958), pp. 43–54.

Actually, however, very little systematic historical evidence has been adduced in defense of these notions. When the career of the Bombay industry is analyzed, quite a different interpretation emerges.

Not only did the industry steadily expand the size of its labor force, but the evidence suggests that during the critical period, the half century before 1920, mills were able to obtain new recruits without any significant upward pressure on the wage rates at which novice mill hands were employed. If labor shortages had persisted for long periods of time — i.e., if market conditions had favored a more rapid expansion of output than actually occurred — we would expect to find evidence of a steady upward trend of hiring-in wage rates, particularly when labor costs were a relatively small proportion of total costs and profit expectations were quite high. Moreover, we would have expected evidence of a shift in the industry's technology increasingly in the direction of more capital-intensive methods of production. Neither of these two tendencies can be found in the period before 1920.

Nor can it be argued that wage rates, for cultural reasons specific to India, were unresponsive to a labor shortage when it appeared. The general behavior of wages during the plague-induced labor shortage of 1897 as well as the changing occupational wage rate structure over time prove that we are dealing with a situation responsive to market forces. The relative stability of hiring-in rates is clear evidence that the industry never was faced by a problem of labor shortage. It generally could recruit all the new raw labor it required to meet its needs for expansion.

The overwhelming proportion of mill hands came from districts in the Bombay Presidency, but within the recruitment pattern there were certain specific features. The main body of workers did not come from the hinterland immediately surrounding Bombay but from more distant sources, from places at least 101 to 200 miles from the city. Initially, mill hands seem to have come from a limited number of districts, but as the years passed the operatives tended to be drawn from a greater number of localities and from increasingly distant regions. I have not been able to explain why these specific tendencies existed and were modified over time. To find an answer will require studies of the changing economic situations in the rural areas and changing employment opportunities in Bombay City itself. However, my data should at least put an end to the notion that the structure of Indian society and the character of the traditional ideology impeded the movement of people over long distances to places where economic opportunity existed.

The place-of-origin data I have been able to compile suggest an additional feature about the labor force, one running counter to the widely accepted view that the industry depended almost entirely on workers who migrated only temporarily from the countryside and returned to the countryside at the end of their period of service. My evidence, limited though it is, suggests that over time an increasing proportion of the work force was recruited from people born or permanently resident in Bombay. The fact is significant because it casts very serious doubt on the propositions which attributed labor force instability to the persistence of a rural nexus.

The instability theme itself seems to have been exaggerated, although it is difficult to be precise about the degree to which this has been so. My evidence suggests that a not insignificant and growing proportion of the work force exhibited considerable attachment to the industry, if not to an individual mill. The fragmentary length-of-service information suggests a steady rise in the proportion of the workers with records of long service in the industry. As would be expected, length of service in a single mill was shorter although even here there was a significant tendency toward increasing stability. There is no way, quantitatively, to determine the extent to which labor turnover in the individual mills was associated with transfers to other mills rather than with a return to the countryside. It is clear, however, that a great deal of the labor turnover in the mills was in fact a response to changing employment and income possibilities in the industry and in Bombay generally rather than to the lure of the countryside.

Just as the analysis supports the view that a growing proportion of the labor force was permanently tied to the industry for its livelihood, a reassessment of the materials on absenteeism suggests that these rates have been grossly overstated. It is likely that willful absenteeism by mill hands was typically less than 10 per cent, and much of this could be attributed to illness. Moreover, statistical evidence does not support the claim of an enormous seasonal swing in absenteeism associated with agricultural requirements of the rural sector.

Just as other traditional institutions did not seem seriously to inhibit either the movement of people to Bombay or their recruitment into the mills, so traditional village caste (*jati*) divisions apparently did not have overwhelming effect on the mobilization of a factory labor force. I have cautioned that the information on caste is particularly treacherous to deal with, and one must proceed with caution. Nevertheless, it seems safe to say that though there certainly were caste clusterings in Bombay mills, they were not exclusive and did not prevent members of different *jatis* from working side by side with one another.

The traditional subcaste distinctions of the countryside did not affect the employer's ability to recruit as much labor as he needed of the type that he wanted. This does not mean that certain caste attitudes did not persist in the mills, but they do not seem to have affected the employer's ability to utilize labor or to operate his enterprise profitably. At no place in the vast mass of material bearing on the industry's history have I been able to find a complaint by an employer that caste divisions made the working of a mill financially less rewarding. Moreover, whatever distinctions did persist survived only because they were irrelevant to mill operations. Whenever and wherever industrial functioning required the disruption of traditional distinctions, they were apparently swept away with ease.

There was only one significant exception to the general proposition that caste was unimportant in the industry. Hindu untouchable caste members seem to have been systematically excluded from weaving departments. This has been explained as a refusal of nonuntouchable weavers, Muslim as well as Hindu, to work with them because of the fear of a specific type of ritual defilement. Though the logic is ideologically impeccable, there is no strong evidence one way or another on this point. There is some indication that the fear of pollution was only one, and perhaps a minor, aspect of the situation. The weaving department was historically the highest paid section in the industry. Untouchable groups seem to have come into the mills relatively late and moved into the lower-paid jobs. The exclusion of untouchables from weaving jobs may well have operated as a device to preserve the monopoly of particularly well-paying jobs for all Muslims and clean-caste Hindus against all untouchables more than it constituted a carryover of traditional ritual barriers into the factories. This interpretation is supported by rather scanty evidence that untouchables were also excluded from other well-paid occupations in the industry, jobs in which the specific threat of ritual pollution did not exist.

The slow appearance of untouchables and their limited employment in cotton mills throws doubt on much that has been written about the sources of labor for modern Indian industry. The labor force did not, as Weber suggested, come mainly from the "declassed and parish castes" of the countryside.[2] Why this was so is not clear. It is possible that the traditional values held by the employers of labor may have had something to do with this. But once untouchables began to be employed in large numbers, they tended to seep into most occupations. Their exclusion from weaving may have been an apparent qualification to the tendency of industrial employment to act as a subverter of traditional social norms. But even this situation had no adverse effect on the adequacy of labor supply.

---

[2] Max Weber, *The Religion of India* (Glencoe, Illinois: The Free Press, 1958), p. 105.

One final point should be made about the persistence of traditional
attitudes in the mills. If comments of virtually all observers can be accepted, the group divisions which were created in the mills were of a
substantially different type in fact than those which existed in the countryside. Where employers found it necessary to grapple with work-force
distinctions, language, region, and religion were the operationally relevant ones. To the extent that caste appeared as a category, it was not
the *jati* concept so familiar in the villages. In the transition from village
to factory the institution seems to have undergone a major transformation which lumped all clean-caste Hindus together and pitted them
against all untouchable-caste groups. Nor did even these divisions persist with the sharpness that one might have expected. As strikes became
increasingly frequent and as union organization began to emerge, these
activities exhibited very few of the divisive features of the traditional
rural inheritance.

Since there was no difficulty in obtaining recruits for the expanding
industry and those who did enter were more firmly attached to it than
most observers assumed, it seems safe to conclude that the labor problems with which the industry had to contend did not flow primarily from
the psychology of the work force or from the rigid traditions and structure of the rural social order. Such instability and indiscipline as did
exist stemmed from the character of employer policies which were determined by the economic and technical characteristics of the enterprises and the competitive nature of the markets in which they operated.
In these terms it is probably safe to say that at least until the 1920's the
industry got precisely the kind of labor force and the kind of labor
discipline that it wanted and needed. And after 1920, when circumstances dictated the development of a different system of labor utilization and administration, the difficulty of modifying disciplinary patterns
arose out of the industry's own past organization and institutional arrangements.

(2)

The early mills laid down very stringent work rules, and these set the
model for all subsequent enterprises. Though penalties for infringement
were harsh, unlike the situation in many of the early British cotton factories, the work discipline actually demanded was quite lax. Perhaps
the most notable features of labor utilization in the Bombay mills were
the large amounts of labor employed and the looseness of the regulations imposed at the work place. All observers were struck by the fact
that, compared with the situation in Lancashire, there was always a very
large number of millhands away from the machines.

Given the supply of labor available to them, there is no question that early employers were free to choose virtually any pattern of work organization they desired. Moreover, they were in a position to model their labor deployment schedules on British experience. But the industry very quickly adjusted its forms of operation and its labor routines to the specific conditions it confronted — to the relative costs of capital and labor in Bombay and to the markets in which it had the greatest comparative advantage. Mills were established with the knowledge that capital costs were relatively high, unskilled labor was relatively cheap, and the industry's competitive advantage lay in the production of coarse yarns and cloth from cheap, short-staple local cottons.

The adjustment of the industry to its specific relative factor costs and market requirements clearly determined the forms of labor utilization. The object was to run the expensive equipment as continuously each day and every day as circumstances permitted and at the highest achievable speeds. These practices made it possible to use very large amounts of absolutely minimally trained labor, precisely the sort that was easy and cheap to obtain in Bombay. But the work schedule also made it necessary to employ enough labor to permit workers to take breaks while the machines were running, to develop what in effect amounted to an informal shift system.

Not only did the output on which the Bombay mills concentrated not require a highly trained labor force in any of the numerically significant occupations, but production did not depend on an elaborate system of expensive supervision. A manager and a few skilled masters, supported by a small cadre of fairly well-trained artisans, sufficed to determine operational requirements and guarantee the continued working of the machines. There was no need to lay down a rigorous set of regulations which defined with precision the relation of each worker to his task. Recruitment and supervision could be left to the jobbers because the quality of output and the stability of individual mill hands were not critical to the success of an enterprise.

There is no question that employers could have initiated a tighter and more precise system of labor utilization and discipline had they so wished. But such an approach would have required more expensive supervision than could be obtained from the jobbers without producing any obvious immediate benefits to the enterprises. Given the particular competitive advantages which the Bombay mills possessed, it is unlikely that a more elaborate and exact system of labor recruitment and supervision would have contributed to the enhancement of profits. The added costs may in fact only have reduced them. In other words, thoroughly rational economic calculation encouraged what seemed to so many outsiders to be a thoroughly ramshackle system of labor use and discipline. But this casual organization of the mill labor force, early introduced and long preserved, created a tradition of work that was to be difficult to change.

In this respect, a good deal has been said on the effects of *dasturi*, the payments jobbers exacted from workers as the price of getting and holding jobs. Most of what has been written on this subject has been concerned only with the immorality of the exploitation of helpless workers. Doubtless the phenomenon encouraged a much higher labor turnover rate than might otherwise have existed. But apart from the minimal effects of labor instability on mill profitability, a fact which explains the employers' lack of concern with the situation, it seems unlikely that *dasturi* could have been eliminated by a reduction in the power of the jobber. The pervasiveness and persistence of *dasturi* was an expression of the desperate eagerness with which people sought employment. Lacking any device to stem the flow of job seekers, no system of labor recruitment and administration could have remained uncorrupted by the opportunities for making money out of the pressing demand for jobs at going wage rates.

In addition to factors within individual mills which made for labor instability, there were intermill forces also at work. The industry was very competitive, not only in the product market but in the labor market as well. During the first six decades, when new mills were being opened rapidly, experienced workers were lured from factory to factory by the promise of higher wages. It was this phenomenon about which already established mills complained most bitterly and which led them, unsuccessfully, to propose wage-standardization schemes at a fairly early date.

Furthermore, the product mix in each mill tended to vary with changing market demand, and wage rates seem to have fluctuated accordingly. Workers tended to move from mill to mill in search of the most advantageous rates. The absence of clear lines of promotion within an individual mill also encouraged workers to seek improvement by moving to another factory.

There is no question that the lack of any necessity for stable work relations within the individual mill and the specific forces which encouraged mobility among mills created what to all intents was a casual labor force in the industry. There were no rewards for constancy and many encouragements to instability. Skills were easily learned, and there were no incentives which encouraged workers to stick with their jobs. When to all this were added the effects of arbitrary discharges and not infrequent cutbacks of work by individual mills to meet market fluctuations, it is easy to understand why those workers who could refused to sacrifice their connections with the countryside. The village link, frail bulwark though it was, offered the only protection against the uncertainties of employment in the cotton mills.

(3)

This situation existed without substantial challenge until the 1920's. But with the collapse of the post-World War I boom the industry found itself confronted by a major crisis caused by increasingly vigorous competition from up-country and Japanese mills. The first attempt to deal with the problem, an all-industry assault on the wage level, produced a dramatic reaction in the general strikes of 1924 and 1925. An alternative solution, supported by the Indian Tariff Board's 1927 report, involved a shift toward finer count output combined with a rationalization of production which would lower labor costs. This development, involving more costly raw materials and a higher value of product, necessitated the transformation of traditional methods of labor utilization and discipline. But attempts to carry through these reforms provoked the great strikes of 1928 and 1929.

The four general strikes in six years made it clear that the older methods of administering the work force could not easily be modified. All efforts at change provoked the hostility of an aroused and suspicious labor force, particularly in the context of declining employment opportunities. Radical changes of work and discipline in the mills could be obtained either over the violent protests of mill hands who had become self-consciously militant or with their coöperation. The employers were no longer free to manipulate the situation without regard to mill-hand sensibilities. In this sense, the unilateral attempts by millowners to transform the methods of labor utilization, to intensify discipline, had come too late.

In another sense the great crisis in the industry came too early. It occurred just as the mill hands were generating a strong sense of militancy but before trade unions were strong enough to channel that combative spirit toward the achievement of orderly objectives. The unilateral efforts of the millowners to solve their problems had generated a tumultuous and suspicion-ridden atmosphere in the mills. The moderate and the Communist union leaderships struggled for the operatives' loyalty, a loyalty denied to the employers who were now beginning to pay the price for the loosely organized system of labor administration which had existed for three quarters of a century. The bitter conflicts and all-round mistrust made efforts at compromise unavailing. The 1929 strike collapsed and the infant unions vanished from the industry.

The great strikes from 1924 to 1929 suggest a point which had been ignored or misinterpreted. Strikes were evidence of work force attachment to the industry, of acceptance of a web of working rules and customs. Had workers been only casually attached to factory employment, they would not have struck when confronted with unsatisfactory conditions. They would have voted with their feet, quietly returning to their villages. The willingness to strike and to resist — often for unbelievably long periods — any undesirable changes in work circumstances suggests a profound involvement in the industrial situation.

Nor does it seem reasonable to argue that the occurrence of industry-wide strikes only after World War I indicates some change in work-force attitudes after that date. Certainly there was no dramatic change in rural social structure which would account for the difference. Moreover, we have to recognize the existence of serious, if less extensive, strikes before World War I. The explanation of increased militancy lies rather in the conjunction of three factors at work in Bombay itself.

First, the changes which a number of mills began to undertake after 1924 were far more profound than any which had previously occurred. Earlier adjustments to changed competitive circumstances had typically been achieved within a general environment of expansion and usually involved the addition of new mill functions and new workers. The rationalization which began in the 1920's, on the other hand, required a thorough-going revision of tasks and a reduction of employment. Second, the end of labor force growth meant that the existing labor force was no longer diluted by masses of raw recruits from the countryside who did not possess the experience of the industry's long-standing traditions of work. And finally, the sharp increase of Nationalist activity and the appearance of the Communist Party produced elite groups anxious to provide leadership for existing discontent. These are the elements which explain the generalized character of the outbursts after World War I.

The collapse of the unions in 1929 did not end the tendencies toward modification of work organization. The worsening economic crisis, causing mill after mill to close, forced the survivors to push ahead. For example, between 1930 and 1933 the Bombay mills reduced their labor requirements in the weaving sheds from ninety-four to sixty-one men per one hundred looms.[3] This process of reorganization was not carried out in an orderly fashion or with coöperation of the unions which the Fawcett Committee had envisaged in its 1929 report. The changes, typically accompanied by drastic wage reductions and pushed through over enfeebled protests from the exhausted work force, were achieved

---

[3] Mehta, *CMI*, p. 179.

by the mills on an individualistic and piecemeal basis. Pressed by urgent financial difficulties, not comprehending the scope and complexities of the total task, reluctant to undertake changes along lines unfamiliar to them, virtually all employers attempted to make only the obviously necessary modifications while preserving most of the old order of things. They intensified the work load without redefining specific work responsibilities and without accompanying adjustments in the quality of materials and in the supervisory setup.

In immediate terms, the cotton mills of Bombay which survived seem to have worked their way out of the worst of the crisis by 1937, but, as the general strike of 1934 indicated, the long-run consequences, both economic and political, were ominous. The frantic individualistic and typically inchoate efforts of the employers to grapple with the desperate financial situation, though capable of yielding some of the productive adjustments needed, accomplished these only by exacerbating work-force fears and hostilities. And no technical transformation could be economically viable in the long run if the industry was to be wracked by continuing industrial tension and disrupted by periodic general strikes.

The unrest of the work-force was being caused not only by ruthless wage reductions but also by the fact that the work rules remained ambiguous and extremely cavalier in application. Whatever else it had achieved, the industry had failed to produce any orderly system of labor administration which would provide stable expectations for the operatives. The millhands were not themselves capable of imposing a more rational system upon their employers. In this state, their sullen frustration could only express itself in seething discontent and a susceptibility to strike at the slightest provocation. Whenever articulate leadership appeared to kindle the spark, protest could burst out in an industry-wide conflagration. The 1934 general strike merely confirmed what had been discovered in 1928 and 1929, not only that voluntary groups within the industry were incapable of grappling coöperatively with the task of reforming labor discipline but also that the demoralized work force could, in this condition, easily come under the control of the Communists.

The cotton mill operatives, large in numbers and concentrated at one of the key urban centers of the country, constituted a potential revolutionary force of disturbing dimensions. In a situation where the employers were unable to solve the problem autonomously, where moderate unions powerful enough to force solutions upon the industry had failed to appear, the State, fearful of a contingency that threatened to undermine the established social order, was forced to intervene.

The initial objective of the State in the Trade Disputes Conciliation Act of 1934 was a very limited one, to induce employers systematically to apply their own work rules. However, the initial intervention revealed how difficult it was to obtain an orderly response when the work regulations within individual mills were themselves so vague. In an effort to achieve greater precision of administration than employers were willing to develop voluntarily, the State was forced step by step to undertake after 1934 its own definition of the terms of employment, discipline, and wage payment. In the process, much of the authority of the individual mills to determine the framework of their own labor discipline was eliminated. Not only did the State establish new and more systematic forms of labor administration consistent with the new requirements, but its intervention gradually established, by the end of my period, a high degree of industry-wide conformity to the solutions. Moreover, at the very end of the period, when trade unions once again began to make their appearance in a substantial way, the State, through these same statutory devices, had created the legal apparatus by which the role of unions could be subjected to the sharp constraints of public policy. The effects of these developments on the subsequent career of the industry's labor force were to manifest themselves in the period after 1947, years that are beyond the scope of this study. But by 1947, the year of Independence, the main lines of the new direction had been laid down.[4]

(4)

The history of the Bombay cotton mills suggests that it was not difficult to create an industrial labor force in India. The acceptability of my analysis as a general interpretation, however, waits on comparative evidence from other industrial situations. As I pointed out in Chapter I, there have been very few intensive studies of this problem in any society and there is none that explores the experience of other Indian industries in detail. However, there is a very brief discussion of the development of an industrial labor force at the Tata Iron and Steel Company (TISCO) plant at Jamshedpur in Bihar which does support my analysis of Bombay developments.[5]

---

[4] For some discussion of the post-1947 consequences, see R. C. James, "Labor and Technical Change" (Unpublished Ph.D. dissertation, Cornell Washington, 1957); and M. D. Morris, "Labor Discipline, Trade Unions, and the State in India," *Journal of Political Economy,* LXIII, No. 4, August 1955, pp. 293–308.

[5] What follows is based on M. D. Morris, "The Labor Market in India," in *Labor Commitment and Social Change in Developing Areas,* edited by W. Moore and A. Feldman, pp. 173–200. For some tentative international comparisons, see M. D.

The Jamshedpur enterprise, established in a very lightly populated district in 1908, built up a labor force which by 1957 amounted to 40,000 workers. The entirely new city which grew up around the steel plant claimed a population of nearly a quarter of a million in 1951. As in the Bombay situation, the evidence suggests that at no time during the first half-century did TISCO suffer from an inadequate supply of raw labor which it could train to its needs.

As I have suggested, it has not been possible to eliminate ambiguities in the Bombay evidence regarding stability and instability of the labor force. Given the very large number of cotton mills as well as the alternative employment opportunities in the city, it has been impossible to prove conclusively that a very large part if not most of the labor turnover involved a movement of workers between mills rather than from mill to countryside. However, in Jamshedpur, where there was only one important employer, the situation is much clearer. Within a decade of the production of the first iron ingots there is evidence of substantial stability in the labor force. In fact, by the 1950's the firm found itself actually embarrassed by the lack of labor turnover.

The relative work-force stability in Jamshedpur as compared with Bombay certainly did not arise from any fundamental differences in the cultural characteristics of the workers recruited. What are involved are dissimilarities in the technical necessities of the two industries and the consequent variations in policies demanded of the employers.

For the bulk of its career the Bombay textile industry required workers who needed only very casual training and the most limited sort of supervision. The stability of individual workers was of no fundamental concern to employers; recruitment and administration of labor therefore could be turned over to jobbers. By contrast, the steel operation required a much broader range of skills and more elaborate investment in training. On the whole, TISCO could not tolerate a free-floating, near-casual work force if efficient and profitable operation was to be maintained. As a consequence, recruitment and administration of the labor force was always a matter of strong concern to the Company. Although the labor recruited was certainly as cosmopolitan and the cultural and linguistic distinctions as complex as in Bombay, the management never found itself forced to give to its low-level jobber equivalents the basic responsibilities for the administration of its work force. The ramshackle discipline appropriate in Bombay mills until the 1920's was never feasible in Jamshedpur, and it never appeared.

Morris, "The Recruitment of an Industrial Labor Force in India, with British and American Comparisons," *Comparative Studies in Society and History*, II, No. 3, April 1960, pp. 305–328.

The evidence from Bombay and Jamshedpur suggests that the creation of a disciplined industrial labor force in a newly developing society is not particularly difficult. A comparison of the cotton textile and the steel industries makes it clear that the difference in worker stability cannot be accounted for by any substantial difference in the psychology of the raw labor recruited. Nor can it be attributed to dissimilarities in the traditional environment from which the workers came. If there were differences in work-force behavior, these flowed from employer policy. The necessities imposed by industrial technology and markets required employers to select different systems of discipline, and these determined the way labor would work.

Appendices

APPENDIX I

Average Number of Mill Hands Employed Daily on All Shifts, Bombay Cotton Textile Mills, 1865-1947

Year [a]	Number of mills	Average daily employment [b]	Year [a]	Number of mills	Average daily employment [b]
1865	10	6,557	1895	69	75,740
1866	10	6,733	1896	71	78,455
1867	10	7,630	1897	75	69,530
1868	10	7,715	1898	82	70,728
1869	10	7,857	1899	82	77,169
1870	10	8,103	1900	82	72,914
1871	10	8,553	1901	81	82,162
1872	11	8,816	1902	80	86,122
1873	14	10,714	1903	80	86,913
1874	15	11,398	1904	79	89,915
1875	27	13,551	1905	81	92,924
1876	29	14,718	1906	84	100,798
1877	31	20,347	1907	85	98,101
1878	32	26,942	1908	86	101,536
1879	32	28,860	1909	89	105,751
1880	32	29,417	1910	89	104,550
1881	32	31,351	1911	87	104,500
1882	36	31,801	1912	86	109,691
1883	38	34,736	1913	90	110,033
1884	43	36,071	1914	85	109,860
1885	49	41,545	1915	86	111,924
1886	50	44,111	1916	86	118,303
1887	55	43,270	1917	87	125,713
1888	61	47,789	1918	87	124,199
1889	69	52,490	1919	85	126,368
1890	70	59,139	1920	83	140,208
1891	67	61,981	1921	83	147,740
1892	68	65,087	1922	82	149,224
1893	69	67,870	1923	81	148,771
1894	69	70,553	1924	82	148,414

[a] For the period 1865 to 1913, reporting year ends 30 June; For the period 1914 to 1947, reporting year ends 31 August.

[b] For the years 1865 to 1930, day-shift employment only; For the years 1931 to 1947, second and third shifts included.

Continued

Year	Number of mills	Average daily employment	Year	Number of mills	Average daily employment
1925	82	153,009	1935	74	136,052
1926	83	149,069	1936	74	137,326
1927	83	154,398	1937	69	139,215
1928	82	129,275	1938	69	168,130
1929	81	106,710	1939	68	156,046
1930	81	136,774	1940	65	140,093
1931	81	136,404	1941	64	175,656
1932	81	143,120	1942	66	192,430
1933	78	129,213	1943	66	210,735
1934	75	105,271	1944	65	212,471
			1945	65	213,085
			1946	65	207,956
			1947	65	207,245

SOURCES:

All years 1865 to 1930, except 1876, from BMOA annual reports. 1876 figure taken from Presidency of Bombay, *Annual Report, 1875–76.* For the years 1931 to 1947, day-shift figures from BMOA annual reports were combined with September–August annual average night-shift employment calculated from figures reported monthly in *LG.*

NATURE OF THE SOURCES:

The basic source for Bombay cotton mill employment figures is the statistical appendix entitled "Cotton Spinning and Weaving Mills Working and in the Course of Erection in India," found at the end of each annual report published by the BMOA. Although the Association was not established until 1875, the employment series goes back to 1865.[1] BMOA data represents only day-shift working. Before 1930 this did not result in significant distortion; night shifts were rarely worked. Beginning in 1930, night shifts became a more or less regular practice in an increasing number of mills. Consequently, BMOA for 1931 to 1947 systematically and increasingly understated average daily employment. To correct this deficiency in the BMOA data, I have added an annual average of night-shift employment, calculated from figures published monthly in *LG*, to the BMOA figure. Beginning in 1931, my figures are therefore higher than the BMOA published series.[2]

---

[1] It is not possible to tell how the BMOA got its 1865 to 1874 data. However, the Presidency of Bombay *Annual Reports* for the period contain cotton mill employment figures which are not inconsistent with the ones given by BMOA. For 1876, when BMOA did not report an employment figure, I felt safe in using the official source.

[2] I calculated an annual average night-shift figure based on a September to August year to make it consistent with the BMOA day-shift figure. There were short periods just after World War I when a few mills worked nights. There may also have been

The BMOA figures comprise the longest and best employment series we have, and they have been universally accepted. However, they have been used so uncritically that it is worth-while pointing out some of their major limitations. I have already mentioned the exclusion of night-shift employment. Perhaps the most important difficulty is that we do not know who is included in the employment figure. At no point did the BMOA define the work force covered. We do not know whether the figures provided to the BMOA by individual mills represent production workers only or other groups of industry employees as well. So far as I have been able to determine, each mill reported what it wished. It is likely that the series represents production workers.[3]

Apart from the problem of work-force coverage, the "average daily employment" concept is itself ambiguous. Beginning about 1930 the BMOA statistical appendix contained a footnote to the effect that for each mill the "average number of hands employed daily is arrived at by adding together the number of hands *actually* working on each day the Mills were open [during the year] . . . and dividing the result by the number of days actually worked."[4] In fact, this was not always true even after this notation began to appear. Occasionally, previous year's employment figures were used. But more important, the addition of the footnote in itself suggests the possibility that during the previous seventy-five years the mills were not reporting on any standardized basis. There are two suspicious features which persisted for varying periods of time and tend to support this notion. There was, first, the fact that employment figures for many individual mills quite frequently ended in zero or five. Second, employment for many mills often remained unchanged from one year to the next.[5]

In the absence of any precise instructions from the BMOA and given the specific peculiarities I have noted, I doubt that mills were actually reporting a calculated arithmetic mean of employment. Some may have, but in many cases it seems clear that mills were reporting "muster roll" employment, the number of workers required to work the machines under specific full-operation conditions. Actually employment could certainly be lower than this if all machines were not working or were not working full time; employment might possibly be higher under specific conditions of very brisk market demand.

Apart from these obvious difficulties, there is the fact that an arithmetic mean, even if properly constructed, doesn't tell us very much. The annual average blurs the extent of employment fluctuation during the year. This is a matter of considerable importance.[6]

---

similar occasions before World War I. But in all cases the length of time and number of workers involved were small. Failure to find satisfactory data for these instances do not seriously affect the results.

[3] The BMOA series refers to "hands," which suggests that only production workers were being reported. However, it is entirely possible that in some mill reports, at least, clerical staff was also included.

[4] Italics in the original.

[5] Both phenomena occurred more frequently than chance would dictate.

[6] It might be possible, by very careful year-by-year analysis of the brief comments which appear in the statistical appendix, to get some notion of fluctuations in the demand for labor. For example, *BMOA 1911* reported employment as 104,500. However, of the eighty-seven mills listed, seventeen enterprises, with a minimum of

10,841 employees, were closed for all or a substantial part of the year. In other words, at least 10.4 per cent of the work force shown as employed had, according to the appended notes, no employment or only very curtailed employment.

The only other important source of employment data is the annual report on the working of the Indian Factories Act for Bombay Presidency. This source is not as useful as BMOA. It begins much later, in 1892. There are some subsequent gaps, years when mill employment data were not provided. The data also suffers from the same ambiguities as do the BMOA figures. Since the factory act series, on the whole, moves in much the same way as BMOA, it did not seem worth-while to present a separate series from this source.[7]

---

[7] Comparison with my series is possible by reference to the "total employment" column in Appendix II. The differences between FA and BMOA data seem partly associated with the fact that different reporting years were used.

APPENDIX II

Average Daily Employment of Men, Women, and Children,

Bombay Cotton Textile Mills, 1884-1947 [a]

(All shifts)

| Year | Total employment | Adults | | Children |
		Men	Women	
1884[b]	39,716	30,383	8,816	517
1892	64,830	45,252	15,969	3,609
1893	68,483	47,404	17,716	3,363
1894	71,276	50,225	17,637	3,414
1895	73,865	52,454	18,275	3,136
1896	75,010	53,340	19,035	2,635
1897	67,391	49,135	15,703	2,553
1898	72,670	53,639	16,255	2,776
1899	80,498	59,195	18,952	2,351
1908[c]	103,082	76,304	22,915	3,863
1909[c]	101,135	75,970	21,599	3,566
1910[c]	102,775	77,446	21,581	3,748
1911[c]	104,195	79,280	21,198	3,717
1912	109,806	83,029	22,722	4,055
1913	108,686	82,017	22,402	4,267
1914	105,057	79,262	21,404	4,391
1915	113,495	86,099	22,296	5,100
1916	116,877	88,860	24,065	3,952
1918	121,210	94,601	24,108	2,501
1919	130,593	101,169	26,545	2,879
1920	140,898	109,505	28,717	2,676
1921	146,300	114,062	29,970	2,268
1922	151,241	120,232	29,770	1,239

[a] Except where otherwise noted, information is taken from *FA* for the appropriate year. Very little need be said about these data. They apparently suffer from the same limitations as the BMOA figures used in Appendix I.

[b] *FC 1885*, p. 236. The low figure for children as compared with 1892 is probably the result of a different legal definition of a child. See *FA 1892*, pp. 15–16. Under the Factories Act of 1881 a child was defined as a person between the ages of seven through eleven. Under the law of 1891, the legal age of employable children was nine through thirteen years.

[c] D. E. Wacha, "Bombay Mill Labour: A Statistical Analysis," *ITJ*, XXIV, No. 285, June 1914, pp. 317–18.

Continued

Year	Total employment	Adults		Children
		Men	Women	
1923	144,676	114,423	29,600	653
1924	144,556	112,904	31,065	587
1925	146,244	113,580	32,396	268
1926	148,254	114,658	33,541	55
1927	145,005	112,925	32,048	32
1928	118,617	92,796	25,817	4
1929	118,368	92,994	25,356	18
1930	127,578	98,377	29,163	38
1931	124,963	97,482	27,441	40
1934[d]	128,420	104,099	24,319	2
1937	148,137	124,556	23,581	—
1939[e]	145,691	123,934	21,757	—
1944[f]	220,681	193,897	26,784	—
1947[g]	205,491	182,529	22,962	—

[d] *BLO 1934*, p. 13. Does not include the two Kurla mills.

[e] *LIC, Enquiry 1946*, p. 6. Information for August 1939 only.

[f] *Loc. cit.* Information for November 1944 only.

[g] R. G. Gokhale, *Annual Review of the Labour Situation in the Bombay Cotton Mill Industry, 1947*, p. 77. Information for July 1947 only.

APPENDIX III

Index of Monthly Full-Time Wages in the Bombay
Cotton Mill Industry, 1875-1947

Many complexities arise in the attempt to construct an index of wages for the cotton textile industry. Some are typical of all such efforts whereas others are specific to the Bombay situation. I will consider only those which bear significantly on the interpretation of Table XX, below.

So far as the evidence is concerned, the period must be divided into two parts, pre-1921 and post-1921. A different type of information is available for each and should be discussed separately. Let me examine first the material available for the years before 1921.

There is no usable wage information for any year before 1875. There is one cluster of figures for 1875 and then nothing until 1882. The basic wage source for the period 1882 to 1921 is the annual official publication, *Prices and Wages in India* (*PW*). Initially, wages were reported for thirty-five job classifications at the M. Petit Mill; by the end of the period these had been reduced to twenty-nine. In the early years *PW* stated that it was reporting the "Average wages (piece work and monthly wage) paid at the Manockjee Petit Mills, Bombay, in January. . . ."[1] However, even a cursory examination makes it clear that in many cases we were not being given an average but a range of wages. Subsequently, a footnote was added to clarify the situation to the effect that "The rates for piece work are the highest and lowest wages earned by a laborer during the month working full days and those for fixed wages are the amount of salary fixed for that class of work plus the bonus paid for that month."[2] Ambiguity persisted because a range of rates was also given for some of the time-rated jobs. Another note was added to the effect that the "difference in the wages (though fixed) of a 'side minder' in the Ring Throstle Room is owing to the wages being fixed according to different counts of yarn."[3]

It seems very doubtful that *PW* rates represented the actual situation at the Petit Mill. Two obvious causes for skepticism stand out immediately. First, there is the very striking stability of individual job rates for long periods, something quite at odds with what we generally know about mill wage-rate behavior.[4] Second, we know that at least in one year, 1897, labor was in very

---

[1] *PW 1890*, p. 186.

[2] *PW 1922*, p. 217. The bonus mentioned may possibly have been paid for good attendance.

[3] *Ibid.*, p. 218.

[4] Apart from the lack of year-to-year fluctuations, which one would normally anticipate of an "average" or even of a range of earnings, there also was a peculiar stability during periods when the press commented that because of bad business conditions wages were being cut in virtually all mills. For example, *PW* shows not one

short supply and wage rates rose precipitously. But *PW* data from the Petit Mill does not show this at all.[5] It can, of course, be argued that in this case *PW* reported rates as of January 1897, before the BMOA authorized the increases. But we know that labor shortages and wage rises began to be very noticeable as early as November 1896. It is inconceivable that the Petit Mill escaped this experience.[6] These and other bits of evidence all point to the probability that *PW* figures were not actual full-month earnings but some sort of muster rates from which actual full-time wages diverged in unknown ways.[7]

Apart from my doubts about the meaningfulness of the Petit Mill series, there is also the question of representativeness. Even if we are bold enough to accept the Petit data as a correct statement of the situation in that enterprise, the evidence should not be interpreted as necessarily representative of the industry's wage structure. As shown in Chapter IX, the range of rates for individual occupations was so great and the relationship of rates for occupations was so diverse among mills that it is impossible to accept data from a single factory as representative of the industry. We must therefore be extremely cautious about treating any year-to-year movement of individual job rates or of the general index derived from the Petit figures as a true indicator of the city-wide situation.

Whatever the weaknesses, these are the data with which I was forced to work. I started with the wage rates for seventeen classifications from *PW* and obtained an unweighted average wage for each year, 1882 to 1921.[8] Using 1882 as my base year, I then calculated an index for the period. This appears as the unbracketed figures in Table XX.

For the jobs where only a single rate was given, I had no problem of choice.

---

wage reduction between 1899 and 1901 whereas *FA 1900*, pp. 1 and 3, reported that in 1900 twenty-nine mills were either partly or totally closed and that most working mills had cut wages by 12.5 per cent.

[5] In fact there were only three changes in minimum rates between 1896 and 1897 and all were in a *downward* direction.

[6] *BMOA 1896*, p. 2. Statements made during the early plague period by N. N. Wadia, an important figure at the Petit Mill, clearly suggest that his enterprise was affected. *Ibid.*, pp. 137–139 and 145–146.

[7] The "standard muster" was a register maintained by each mill, showing the number of operatives allowed for each department and machine. It also showed the monthly rate allowed for operatives on time wages and the rate per unit allowed on piece rate. *ITB 1927*, I, p. 109. To me the evidence seems convincing that actual full-month rates typically fell below these standard muster rates. At best, the "muster rate" would have gone to a fully experienced hand and would have been above the hiring-in rate.

[8] As can be seen in the notes to Table XX, I selected all the main, clearly distinguishable classifications. In the period 1921 to 1937 these seventeen categories provided employment for at least 50 to 60 per cent of the total labor force. Calculated from *BLO 1921*, *BLO 1923*, *BLO 1926*, *BLO 1934*, and *TLIC 1940*. This understates the pre-1921 situation because the BLO surveys used much more narrowly defined categories than *PW*.

But where a range was given, I took the minimum figure. A host of problems are associated with this decision, but there would have been even greater problems had I decided to use some sort of average. By using the minimum figure it seemed more likely that I would be getting closer to the "hiring-in" rate for the occupation and therefore closer to the supply price which is my objective.[9]

In addition to *PW* data, one can find other bits of wage information for various years. On examination of all the rates I was able to locate, it became clear that most of them very obviously had been derived from *PW* and added nothing to our knowledge. The remaining observations constitute a mixed bag, at least as treacherous to use as the *PW* series. Typically, they purport to represent "average monthly earnings" for various occupations. We are never told how they were compiled, the number of mills represented, or the specific period of the year to which they relate.[10] However, in some cases these data seemed more realistic than the basic *PW* figures.[11] For the years in which I was able to substitute observations from other sources, I recomputed the average wage for the seventeen occupations and then obtained a revised index number for each of those years, using 1882 as a base. These figures appear in brackets in Table XX. In Chart II I have used the adjusted (bracketed) figures instead of *PW*. [12]

The *PW* series was terminated after 1921 because of a widespread discontent with its inaccuracy. Beginning in 1921 information comes mainly from a series of wage surveys conducted by the Bombay Labor Office (BLO). Although I am uncertain about the precise meaning of my data to 1921, I treat the figures I have used as more or less representative of the hiring-in rate. The BLO surveys did not produce such a figure. In each survey, I was forced to use the "average daily earning" figure multiplied by twenty-six days to get the

---

[9] By using the minimum figure, I hoped to avoid the upward wage drift caused by increasing skill. However, if I am right in assuming that even the minimum rate was scheduled for a fully trained operative, then I cannot be certain that productivity effects have been excluded. For a brief summary of some productivity changes, see D. H. Buchanan, *The Development of Capitalistic Enterprise in India* (New York: The Macmillan Company, 1934), p. 373.

[10] It must be mentioned that employers did not keep the kind of records that made it easy to determine precise occupational rates or earnings. See, for example, the continual difficulties encountered by the Bombay Labor Office when it conducted its surveys. These problems are described in *BLO 1921*, *BLO 1923*, and *BLO 1926*. See, also, discussions in *ITB 1927*, I–IV, *passim*. The difficulties faced by the Labor Office, even when it sent its own investigators to examine the mill wage sheets, makes me all the more certain that the Petit Mill series in *PW* is based on muster rates rather than on actual rates paid.

[11] They seemed reasonable in terms of other evidence that was available.

[12] The five years in which the *PW* data were modified are 1892, 1893, 1895, 1897, and 1905. Except for 1897, I used an alternate figure only when it was lower than the *PW* minimum figure for the job. I did this in order to indicate the possibility of lower hiring-in rates. For 1897 I used a set of figures that was higher than *PW* because they show the effect of the plague-induced labor shortage.

full-month rate. Theoretically, the BLO figures, representing *average* full-month earnings, should be significantly higher than the *PW* series which is intended to represent the minimum full-month rate.

The only year when *PW* and *BLO* overlap is 1921. It is true that in fourteen of the sixteen categories for which comparisons are available, the *BLO 1921* figures are higher than *PW*, but the differences are not as great as one might expect. And Table XX, below, indicates that *BLO 1921* average wage (the bracketed figure) is only 9.4 per cent higher than *PW*.[13]

It is important to recognize that I am splicing two different kinds of data at 1921. Between 1875 and 1921 the index attempts to represent the trend of the average hiring-in rate in the industry. From 1921 the index reveals the movement of average full-month earnings. But there are other problems as well. One is the issue of changing job classifications. The seventeen categories appear throughout the *PW* series. It would seem that since the *PW* data came from a single mill there would be no question of comparability between one year and the next. However, equipment and job content changed over time. For example, we get no information on the changing number of spindles minded by a ring sider. We are not told whether the weaver rates are for one loom or two looms. Moreover, the classifications (as in the case of sweepers) ignore the quite different rates for men and women.

In moving from *PW* to the subsequent data, we face another problem of compatability. How do we relate the *PW* categories to the BLO classifications which typically tend to be narrower and more precise? Moreover, BLO surveys broke down the classifications by male and female and time-rated and piece-rated employees, which *PW* did not. Faced with these complexities in the BLO surveys, I was ultimately forced to fall back on reasonable judgments. Where BLO surveys made these distinctions, I used female rates for winders, reelers, and sweepers. Where operatives were paid on both time rates and piece rates, I selected the category which included the larger number of employees. When, as between BLO surveys, there was ambiguity in the occupational classifications, I used the most obvious comparable category.

One further general point: the index is unweighted. There are no employment figures before 1921 which make it possible to weight the individual classifications, nor are there distinctions of rates for men, women, and children. Forced to use an unweighted index before 1921, I decided not to weight it for the 1921 to 1947 period. The unweighted index has its obvious dangers, but they are unavoidable.[14]

---

[13] In fourteen classifications, *BLO 1921* exceeded *PW* by amounts ranging from 0.3 to 35.2 per cent. The two categories for which *BLO 1921* was lower than *PW* were weavers and sweepers. This suggests an interesting point. Weavers constituted about half of the labor force in my seventeen categories. An average wage weighted by employment would probably produce a result in which *BLO 1921* was little, if any, higher than *PW*. This indicates the possibility that the *PW* Petit Mill series substantially overstated the average level of wages in the industry.

[14] There is another reason for not using a weighted index for 1921 and after. Employment data by job classification are available for 1921 to 1937 but not for 1944

The frailty and ambiguity of the evidence makes it impossible to construct a time series with any clear degree of reliability or any predictable range of error. I have put the available data together for what they are worth, conscious at every point of their weakness and uncertainty. The reader is warned that there can be no more than a pretence of accuracy in the levels recorded for any single year; nor can the movement between any two years be considered completely reliable. But the index yields a more accurate estimate of general wage trends in the industry for a longer period than any other I have encountered.[15]

Let me add one final note of caution. This index cannot be used directly in conjunction with any cost-of-living index that might be constructed to produce a real income series. My index ignores statutory changes in the hours of work; it excludes the effects of absenteeism, unemployment, and underemployment; it makes no adjustments for changing job content, for shifting weights of employment by occupation, or for changing proportions of men, women, and children in various categories. Therefore, no welfare judgements can be derived from this index.

TABLE XX

Index (Unweighted) of Monthly Full-time Wages in Seventeen Selected Occupations, Bombay Cotton Mills, 1875–1947.

(1882=100)

Year	Wage	Year	Wage	Year	Wage
1875 .. —	(91.4)	1898 .. 100.0		1916 .. 131.8	
		1899 .. 100.0		1917 .. 133.6	
1882 .. 100.0		1900 .. 100.0		1918 .. 164.7	
1883 .. 101.6		1901 .. 100.0		1919 .. 194.0	
1884 .. 102.7		1902 .. 100.0		1920 .. 254.1	
1885 .. 104.3		1903 .. 100.0		1921 .. 266.3	(291.2)
1886 .. 104.8		1904 .. 100.0			
1887 .. 105.4		1905 .. 100.0	(98.9)	1923 .. —	(293.9)
1888 .. 105.9		1906 .. 100.0			
1889 .. 105.9		1907 .. 118.0		1926 .. —	(298.2)
1890 .. 107.5		1908 .. 124.0			
1891 .. 105.4		1909 .. 125.6		1934 .. —	(249.5)
1892 .. 105.5	(93.4)	1910 .. 125.6			
1893 .. 104.2	(100.3)	1911 .. 121.9		1937 .. —	(246.0)
1894 .. 102.9		1912 .. 121.4			
1895 .. 102.9	(98.9)	1913 .. 124.6		1944 .. —	(562.0)
1896 .. 102.1		1914 .. 131.1			
1897 .. 100.0	(171.6)	1915 .. 131.8		1947 .. —	(710.5)

or 1947. I did compute a weighted average for the 1921 to 1937 period and discovered that the trend was not substantially altered.

[15] K. Mukerji, "Trend in Real Wages in Cotton Textile Mills in Bombay City and Island, From 1900 to 1951," *Artha Vijnana*, I, No. 1, March 1959, has attempted a weighted index of wages. His analysis begins only at 1900. For the period we both cover, our trends are roughly similar.

SOURCES:

The index was constructed from unweighted wage rates for the following job classifications: (1) scutcher, (2) card tenter, (3) grinder, (4) fly carrier, (5) drawing tenter, (6) slubbing frame tenter, (7) intermediate frame tenter, (8) roving frame tenter, (9) ring sider (double side), (10) spinning doffer, (11) gray winder (female), (12) reeler (female), (13) warper, (14) front sizer, (15) back sizer, (16) weaver (two loom), and (17) sweeper (female).

All unbracketed figures were computed from *PW*. Bracketed figures made use, wholly or in part, of observations taken from other sources which are identified below).

1875. No *PW* information. All observations came from *ITJ*, XVI, No. 191, August 1906, p. 331. The same figures can also be found in S. M. Rutnagur, *Bombay Industries: The Cotton Mills* (Bombay: *The Indian Textile Journal*, 1927), p. 352. Based on fourteen jobs only. No rates available for jobs numbered 2, 16, or 17.

1892. Jobs numbered 1, 2, 5, 6, 7, 8, 9, 10, 12, and 14 from *RCL 1892*, pp. 133 and 122, 139, and 170; and *ITJ*, II, No. 20, May, 1892, p. 155.

1893. Jobs numbered 1, 3, 5, 6, 7, 8, 12, and 17 from *BMOA 1893*, pp. 59–60, and *FA 1893*, p. 12.

1895. Jobs numbered 3, 5, 6, and 9 from *ITJ*, V, Nos. 55 and 56, April and May 1895, pp. 156 and 187.

1897. No *PW* data used. Rates calculated from *BMOA 1896*, pp. 26–27, and FA 1897, p. 8. I used the authorized daily rates plus the daily bonus and multiplied this total by twenty-six days. These were the official rates set during the period of peak labor shortage.

1905. Jobs 3 and 7 from *ITJ*, XVI, No. 191, August 1906, p. 331; or Rutnagur, *op.cit.*, p. 352.

1918. PW observations adjusted upward 15 per cent to include Dear Food Allowance (DFA).

1919. PW observations adjusted upward 35 per cent to include DFA.

1920. PW observations for time-rate categories adjusted upward 55 per cent and for piece-rate categories adjusted upward by 75 per cent to include DFA.

1921. PW observations for time-rate categories adjusted upward 70 per cent and for piece-rate categories adjusted upward 80 per cent to include DFA.

Bracketed figure calculated entirely from *BLO 1921*, pp. 23–36. Based on survey of 91 per cent of labor force. Sixteen job classifications only; no data for job numbered 5.

1923. Calculated entirely from *BLO 1923*, pp. 27–40. Based on survey of all workers in all mills.

1926. Calculated entirely from *BLO 1926*, pp. 90–98. Based on sample of nineteen mills employing nearly 35 per cent of all operatives in the industry.

1934. Calculated entirely from *BLO 1934*, pp. 149–154. Based on an industry-wide survey.

1937. Calculated entirely from *TLIC 1940*, pp. 11–57. Based on an industry-wide survey.

1944. Based on wages of 1937, to which was added the increase authorized by the Textile Labor Inquiry Committee in 1938 plus the sum of Rs.31-5-0, which was the average monthly DFA paid in 1944. For justification of this method, see *LIC, Enquiry 1946*, pp. 10–12. I did not use figures from this source but calculated my own for each category and arrived at slightly different results in a number of cases.

1947. Taken from the Industrial Court's standardized uniform list of basic wages and rates for employees of the textile industry of Bombay City. See *LG,* XXVI, No. 10, June 1947, pp. 770–807. To these wages has been added the sum of Rs.41-0-0, which was the average monthly DFA paid in 1947. See R. G. Gokhale, *Annual Review of the Labor Situation in the Bombay Cotton Mill Industry,* 1947, p. 27.

The Industrial Court did not set specific twenty-six day wages for reelers and weavers. I was forced to use the most likely figures. For reelers I used the rate of Rs.30-0-0, the basic minimum full-month wage. For two-loom weavers I used Rs.53-15-0, the average monthly earning in 1949. See Gokhale, *op. cit.,* 1949, p. 23. To both figures I added the DFA of Rs.41-0-0.

APPENDIX IV

Places of Origin of Cotton-Mill Work Force

SOURCES:

1911. Total mill-hand population of 118,512 comes from *Census 1911*, VII, Table XV, "Occupation or Means of Livelihood," pp. 302–447. I have used Class B, Sub-class III, Order 6, Suborder (22), "Cotton spinning, sizing, and weaving."
District of origin data are computed from *Census 1911*, VIII, Table VI, Part II, pp. 48–61, "Special Statistics Regarding Birthplaces Combined with Age, Caste, and Occupation for Bombay City."
1921. Total mill-hand population of 153,569 is taken from *Census 1921*, IX, Part II, City Table IX, p. clxxx. The figure includes skilled workmen, unskilled workmen, and unskilled workers less than fourteen years old. Directors, supervisors, and technical and clerical staff have been excluded.
District of origin data are compiled from *ibid.*, City Table VI, Part II, pp. xxxi-xlv, "Special Statistics Regarding Birth Place Combined with Age, Caste, and Occupation." Only the "mill hand" classification was used; "other ranks" was excluded. In determining the number of migrants whose district of origin was not given, I excluded those born in Europe as being people not likely to be employed as mill hands. The effect of this is minor.
1931. Total textile employment of 116,534 comes from *Census 1931,* IX, p. 50. Cotton textile employment represented more than 97 per cent of this total figure. *Ibid.*, p. 195. I used the textile employment figure rather than the more precise cotton textile classification because the district of origin data was for all textile workers rather than for cotton mill workers only. District of origin data was compiled from *ibid.*, City Table VI, Part II, pp. 184–193, "Special Statistics Regarding Birth Place Combined with Age, Caste, and Occupation."

General Limitations of Materials and Method of Their Use

There are serious weaknesses in Indian birthplace data, especially for the analysis of an urban population. In many parts of India it is typical for a woman, even if permanently resident in a town, to return to her parents' residence to give birth to her child. In such cases a technically accurate statement of place of birth will understate the reality of urban origins and overstate the extent of migration into an urban area. Moreover, there is a tendency for Indians to report their "native place" (the ancestral village or district) as their birthplace even though they may have been born in the city. For these reasons birthplace data for the population of a city like Bombay probably tend to overstate the immigrant characteristics by a substantial margin.[1] However, there is no way to resolve this problem; we must use the data as they are given to us.
The censuses of 1911, 1921, and 1931 contain information on the district of origin of all persons in Bombay who identified themselves as mill hands. To

---

[1] K. Davis, *The Population of India and Pakistan* (Princeton: Princeton University Press, 1951), pp. 107 and 134.

determine the distance these people migrated, I ranked the districts of origin by distance from Bombay. I arbitrarily assumed that all persons coming from a district came from that district's capital city and have calculated the shortest rail distance between that town and Bombay from *Newman's Indian Bradshaw* for February 1957.[2] In a few cases (e.g., Ratnagari), voyages were typically made by sea, and in these cases I calculated the sea distance instead.[3]

The census data as they stand suffer from many weaknesses other than those already mentioned. One difficulty is that many mill hands were lumped into the "laborers otherwise unspecified" classification because they merely reported themselves as *mazdoor* (laborer). There is no way of determining what percentage of this "labor unspecified" classification from each district should be allocated to the textile industry. I have, therefore based my calculations entirely on figures in the "mill hand" column for each census.[4]

An aspect of this particular problem is that the totals of mill hands reported in the censuses bear no discernible relations to the mill-hand figures for the census years that we find in Appendix I.

Year	Census	Appendix I
1911	118,512	104,500
1921	153,569	147,740
1931	116,534	136,404

Appendix I figures are annual averages of daily employment reported by the industry; the censuses reported anyone who classified himself as a mill hand. Given labor turnover, absenteeism, and casual employment in the industry, one would expect census figures always to be substantially higher than Appendix I data. But census figures are always lower than they might otherwise be by the unknown number of workers appearing in the "labor unspecified" classification.

Another problem is associated with the fact that the censuses did not always list all the districts or regions from which immigrants came to Bombay.[5] Even when the census seems to list all regions from which immigration came, it may not give an occupational breakdown for each district.[6] In addition, there were always some migrants into Bombay for which no place of origin was reported. But most distressing for my purposes is the fact that none of the three censuses

---

[2] *Newman's Indian Bradshaw* (Calcutta: W. Newman & Co., Ltd., 1957), No. 1,093, February 1957.

[3] There are a number of problems associated with the assumption that all persons came from a district's capital city. But in the absence of any greater precision on place of origin, this seemed to be the most reasonable decision to make. All other studies I have seen that discuss migration identify place of origin by geographical region — e.g., Konkan, Deccan, etc. Such a classification may be useful for some purposes, but it throws no light whatsoever on distance of migration.

[4] The census authorities, in discussing this problem, always argued explicitly that a very large segment of the "labor unspecified" classification were properly mill workers. In fact, *Census 1921*, IX, Part I, pp. 36 ff., made an attempt to allocate these unclassified workers to their proper occupational classifications. However, the effort is of no use for my purposes.

[5] This is true in *Census 1911*.

[6] This is the case in *Census 1931*.

gave an occupational breakdown for people born in Bombay. A consequence of all of these features in the censuses is that in each case the total number of mill hands reported is significantly larger than the number of mill hands identified by district of origin. For example, in 1911 19.08 per cent of all mill hands were not identified by district of origin. In 1921 the figure was 21.54 per cent and in 1931 it was 34.52 per cent. From where did these mill hands come?

There are three possibilities. Some mill hands, those whose place of birth was for some reason not recorded, may have been born in districts which were listed in the census breakdown. Others may have been born in districts which were not specifically listed by the census. The others must have been born in Bombay City. The problem is to decide how to allocate the unidentified group in each census between migrants and Bombay-born mill hands.

When one examines the general birthplace data in the 1911, 1921, and 1931 census, it turns out that only for a very tiny fraction of the population of Bombay do we have no place of birth reported.[7] This consideration can therefore be disregarded. The crux of the matter is to determine how significant was mill-hand immigration from districts not listed in the census breakdown. The census authorities were particularly interested in mill-hand migration, and it is unlikely that they would have excluded from their lists any district from which a number of mill workers came. Under these circumstances there is reason to argue that all (or at least the vast majority) of the undistributed mill-hands were in fact born in Bombay.[8]

I certainly do not feel completely secure in allocating all the undistributed mill hands to the Bombay-born group. The best alternative is to assume that the undistributed mill hands were Bombay-born or migrant in the same proportion as the total Bombay-born population in the city was to all immigrants from the unlisted districts.

Let me give an example using the 1911 census. The census reported a total mill-hand population of 118,512, of which 95,898 came from the nineteen districts for which an occupational breakdown was provided. This left a balance of 22,614 mill hands for which no place or origin was indicated. What proportion were migrants and what proportion were Bombay-born?

The total population in Bombay in 1911 was 979,445. The total immigration from the nineteen districts for which we have an occupational breakdown was 644,672. The total Bombay-born population was 191,581. This leaves a total of 143,192 immigrants coming from districts for which no occupational breakdown was provided. I have allocated the undistributed mill hands between Bombay-born and migrant classifications in the same ratio as total Bombay-born population stands to total unclassified immigrant population.

Bombay-born population .... 191,581 ...... 57.23%
Unclassified migrants .... 143,192 ...... 42.77%

Total   334,773 ...... 100.00%

In other words, of the 22,614 undistributed mill hands, 57.23 per cent (12,-

---

[7] Place of birth cannot be established for 4.14 per cent of total Bombay population in 1911, for 3.10 per cent in 1921, and for 0.2 per cent in 1931.

[8] Had I treated all the undistributed mill hands as Bombay-born in Table VI, this group would be reported there as 19.08 per cent in 1911, 21.54 per cent in 1921, and 34.52 per cent in 1931.

942) were allocated to the Bombay-born classification and 42.77 per cent
(9,672) were added to the migrant mill-hand group. The same method was
applied to the 1921 and 1931 data. I would argue that the Bombay-born
figure obtained in this way represents a minimum estimate.[9]

Some Contradictory Evidence

No other census data are available. The only other large scale studies were
conducted by the Bombay Millowners' Association in 1940 and 1955.[10] Only
the 1940 survey gives results that can be broken down in approximately the
same detail as the census materials.

TABLE A

Place of origin (Miles from Bombay)	1940 (per cent)	1955 (per cent)
Bombay and suburban	3.47	
1–100	9.29	
101–200	59.84	77.6
201–300	2.89	
301–400	5.12	
401–500	0.10	
501–750	—	22.4
751 and over	19.29	
Total	100.00	100.0

The districts which provided the largest proportion of millhands in 1940 were
as follows:

TABLE B

District	Distance from Bombay (miles)	Proportion of all millhands in survey (per cent)
Ratnagiri (Konkan)	101–200	38.4
United Provinces	Over 750	13.6
Satara (Deccan)	101–200	13.2
Kolaba (Konkan)	1 –100	8.5
Poona (Deccan)	101–200	6.5
Kolhapur (Deccan)	301–400	4.3
Sholapur (Deccan)	201–300	1.2
Total of above districts		85.7

[9] This is a statement that can be made more assuredly for 1921 and 1931 when the
census breakdown of mill hands by place of origin included virtually every district
or region in India.

[10] R. G. Gokhale, *The Bombay Cotton Mill Worker* (Bombay: Millowners' Association, 1957), pp. 87–89 for the 1955 survey data and pp. 117–118 for the 1940
survey data. The 1940 survey material first appeared in slightly greater detail in The
Millowners' Association, Bombay, *Confidential Summary of Workmen's Service
Records* (Bombay: The Millowners' Association, 1941). The 1940 birthplace survey
was based on 37,577 mill hands from nineteen mills; the 1955 survey was based on
74,580 workers in twenty mills.

The 1940 survey, summarized above, shows certain superficial similarities to the pattern suggested in the three census tabulations. The bulk of the work force came from the 101 to 200 mile circle, predominantly from Ratnagiri; the vast majority of all immigrants came from the Deccan and Konkan regions; the work force from the United Provinces continued to rise as a proportion of the total. However, the 1940 survey shows a narrowing of range of districts from which the work force was drawn. In fact, the proportion drawn from these seven most important districts produced 85.7 per cent of the total labor force, a much higher proportion than the census data showed at any time, even in 1911. The most striking deviation from the census data and the most critical problem are the incredibly low figure given for Bombay-born in 1940, 3.47 per cent.

There are at least two main reasons why these statistical differences could, in fact, be true. The first arises out of the difference in method between census and survey. The census data was based on what people said their occupation was whereas the BMOA survey was based on data for those actually employed. The census data (assuming that the "unspecified labor" category did not seriously distort the results) would imply that a very large proportion of the casual labor force in the industry came from other areas. A second reason might be that there was a fundamental shift in the composition of the work force between 1931 and 1940. The great difference in census and survey figures on Bombay-born can be explained in the same fashion. A final possibility that cannot be ignored, of course, is that my method of calculation of Bombay-born in the census data is quite wrong.

There are, however, reasons for assuming that the BMOA survey was seriously defective, both with regard to the extreme concentration of labor from a few districts and the very low proportion of Bombay-born labor. There is very serious question about the representativeness of the mills used in the two surveys.[11] To the extent that labor tended to cluster in mills by place of origin because of hiring practices, there is a good possibility that a fundamental distortion of the industry situation occurred.[12]

Moreover, there is serious question in my mind about the source of the information from which the BMOA survey was derived. The 1940 survey consisted of a tabulation of employee service record cards which at that time had only recently been compiled by the mills. My discussions in 1956 with various authorities on the subject, particularly clerks who had helped compile the records in a number of mills, suggested that a great deal of the personal information placed on a worker's service record was likely to be erroneous. It was not considered very important, and clerks tended to fill it in on the basis of what they thought they knew about the individual workers. One major distortion, particularly affecting the Bombay-born figure, was that there was a very clear bias toward entering "native place" rather than place of birth.[13]

---

[11] In the 1940 survey, ten of the nineteen mills belonged to one managing agency group. Gokhale, *op. cit.*, pp. 5–6.

[12] R. C. James, "Labor and Technical Change" (Unpublished Ph.D. dissertation, Cornell University, 1957), lays great stress on the clustering phenomenon.

[13] For confirming evidence about the poor quality of the employee record cards, see M. M. Shah, "Labour Rercruitment and Turnover in the Textile Industry of Bombay Presidency" (Unpublished Ph.D. dissertation, University of Bombay, 1941), pp. 10–12.

A final factor affecting my judgment of the value of the 1940 BMOA survey is that most qualitative evidence favored the view that particularly after 1920 the labor force was becoming more, rather than less, cosmopolitan and that a substantial proportion of workers were Bombay-born.[14] Qualitative judgments about textile workers are notoriously suspect, but in this case the logic of general population trends would seem to support them. If we accept the 1940 BMOA survey data about Bombay-born, we would then have to explain why so few Bombay-born residents found employment in the industry.[15]

There is one additional source of support for the 1940 estimate of Bombay-born. *Census 1921*, IX, City Tables XI and XII, pp. clxxxiv-cxcii, give information on birthplace of skilled and unskilled workmen. These tables do not give a detailed birthplace breakdown, but they do furnish what purports to be a tabulation of Bombay-born operatives and the results — 2.58 per cent of total mill hands — are significantly lower than my estimate.

I reject this source, not only because the tables show very few Bombay-born even among skilled workers, a situation which seems quite unreasonable.[16] Apart from intuitive disbelief, there are two substantive reasons which can be advanced. First is the fact that the data for City Tables XI and XII, unlike the material in City Table VI, were not actually collected by the census enumerators from the population but were provided by the employers.[17] Whatever the weaknesses of the birthplace information obtained by census enumerators from each person, it certainly is likely to be superior to the information provided by the employer from scanty or (at that time) virtually nonexistent records.

Second, and even more important, I consider my estimate of Bombay-born mill hands for 1921 the most reliable of the three census years. So far as I can tell, every district or region in India was listed and the occupational breakdown for each of these districts was given. In other words, in this year the overwhelming bulk of mill hands with place of origin not identified must have come from Bombay itself. It is because of this that I reject with considerable confidence the very low figure for Bombay-born reported by the same census in City Tables XI and XII.

Of the other evidence that bears on this topic, the data from the 1890 factory commission is more or less consistent with later census data. The commission took evidence from a seemingly random sample of thirty-six textile

---

[14] For example, in 1929 a millowner representative estimated that about 30 per cent of the work force was Bombay-born. *RCL 1929*, I, Part 1, p. 385. See, also, Mehta, *CMI*, p. 120.

[15] The 1940 survey reported 3.47 per cent of the work force as Bombay-born whereas the 1941 census showed 27.4 of the city's population born in Bombay.

[16] *Census 1921*, IX, City Table XI indicates that less than 3 per cent of weavers and fewer than 6 per cent of all jobbers were Bombay-born. Yet it has been widely accepted by all observers that of all classifications, weavers and jobbers were drawn in large numbers from the Bombay-born group. *FA 1897*, p. 9; S. M. Rutnagur, *Bombay Industries: The Cotton Mills* (Bombay: *The Indian Textile Journal*, 1927), pp. 317–18; S. M. Edwardes, *The Gazetteer of Bombay City and Island* (3 vols., Bombay, The Times Press, 1909), II, p. 210; *IDC 1922*, p. 1, and Shah, *op. cit.*, p. 180.

[17] *Census 1921*, VIII, Part I, pp. 209–10.

workers. Of the thirty-two cases for which place of origin can be identified, five (more than 15 per cent) were Bombay-born.[18] However, the numbers are so small that they can hardly be convincing.

The only other source is the length-of-service survey of 1,348 workers conducted by the Bombay Labor Office in 1927 and 1928.[19] Though no details were given, the report on the survey refers to the "remarkable fact that not a single worker gave his place of origin as Bombay City itself." [20] Unfortunately, the investigation suffers from serious methodological flaws. There is, first of all, the total ambiguity in the Indian context of a question about "place of origin." There is also a very substantial possibility of bias flowing from the worker residences picked to provide the sample. There is also a strong potential bias inherent in the types of workers deliberately excluded from the sample. On the whole, these factors lead me to dismiss this survey as a source of birthplace information.

Although I have rejected the 1921 census data from City Tables XI and XII, the results of the Bombay Labor Office survey of 1927 and 1928 and the BMOA survey data of 1940 for what seem to be good reasons, one must still accept my conclusions for 1911 to 1931 only as a cautious approximation to a correct description of the situation.

---

[18] Tabulated from evidence in *FC 1890*, pp. 22–50.

[19] *LG*, IX, No. 5, January 1930, pp. 457–461.

[20] *Ibid.*, p. 458.

APPENDIX V

Bombay Cotton Mill-Hand Caste Information

SOURCES:

1872. *Census 1872*, Table 71, pp. 133–147. For total and untouchable ("Hindu outcaste") cotton textile workers, I used occupations under Class VI, orders D-1, D-2 and K-3. These classifications are certainly broader than cotton mill employment alone. There is no way to narrow the categories. However, the effects on total and untouchable employment should be similar.

1881. *Census 1881*, Table 125, pp. 179–187. For both total and untouchable ("Hindu Low Caste") mill labor, I used occupations numbered 181 and 186. In neither *Census 1872* nor *Census 1881* is it possible to tell what groups were included as untouchables.

1911. *Census 1911*, VIII, Table VI, Part 2, pp. 48–61. I used the "mill hands" column for both total workers and untouchable workers. I selected the following caste categories as untouchable: Bhangi, Chambhar or Mochi, Dhed or Mahar. The figures for both total mill hands and untouchable mill hands are for immigrants only. See my discussion below.

1921. *Census 1921*, IX, City Table VI, Part II, pp. xxxi–xlv. Same comments as for 1911.

1931. *Census 1931*, City Table VI, Part II, pp. 184–193. Same comments as for 1911.

1941. *Census 1941* did not give any occupation-*cum*-caste information. As an alternative source I used the results of a 1940 survey conducted by the BMOA which appears in R. G. Gokhale, *The Bombay Cotton Mill Worker* (Bombay: Millowners' Association, 1957), p. 116. The caste data in the survey related to 37,639 workers in nineteen mills, representing 26.86 per cent of the average daily cotton mill employment for 1940. The information in this survey came from the employee record cards. I have been unable to determine how the caste information was obtained for these records. There is some suggestion that at the time the information on these record cards was not very reliable. See M. M. Shah, "Labour Recruitment and Turnover in the Textile Industry of Bombay Presidency" (Unpublished Ph.D. dissertation, University of Bombay, 1941), pp. 10–12. As will be indicated below, it is quite possible that, as compared with the census data for 1911, 1921, and 1931, the proportion of untouchable mill hands shown in 1941 has an upward bias.

Whatever weaknesses exist in the 1872 and 1881 figures, both the untouchable mill hand and total mill-hand figures can claim to represent industry totals. This is not true for 1911, 1921, or 1931. The censuses for these years did not provide a breakdown by caste for all mill hands. The occupation-*cum*-caste information relates only to immigrants from selected districts, although between 1911 and 1931 the number of districts and proportion of immigrant population included rises.[1] Moreover, the migration data were not given

---

[1] See Appendix IV for a discussion of these occupation-*cum*-caste tables.

for every caste from each district listed but only for those castes which contributed a fair number of people to the total migration from that district.[2]
In a number of cases untouchable castes were not reported.

In order to get the figures for 1911, 1921, and 1931 in Table XI, column
(3), I selected only those districts which did report migration figures for at
least one untouchable caste. Column (3) therefore represents the ratio of
immigrant untouchable mill hands to all immigrant mill hands from those
districts which reported figures on any untouchable castes. In other words, if
a district reported any untouchables, it was included in my calculations even
if none of these untouchables was reported as working in the cotton mills. This
method minimizes the effects of those districts which reported mill hands but
did not report any untouchable caste migration.

My method probably has a tendency to overstate somewhat the proportion of immigrant untouchable mill hands in the total immigrant mill-hand
situation. Untouchable immigrants were reported only from certain districts.
I have used the total of mill hands from these districts as my base. I excluded
the remaining reporting districts which apparently ignored untouchable castes
because they did not constitute numerically significant elements. But these
excluded districts did contribute mill hands to Bombay in varying numbers.[3]
As an extreme possibility such a district could contribute a sizable number of
mill hands of whom none was an untouchable. By excluding mill hands from
these districts from my base, I understate the number of immigrant mill hands
and thus inflate the proportion of immigrant untouchable mill hands. In other
words, if I tabulate the figures of all immigrant mill hands from all districts
reported by the censuses and use this as the base against which to calculate
the untouchable proportion (which remains unchanged), the untouchable
mill hand share in the industry's immigrant labor force will be somewhat
lower, as can be seen in Table XXI.

TABLE XXI

Immigrant Untouchable Mill Hands as a Proportion
of Total Immigrant Mill Hands, 1911–1931 [4]

(Per cent)

Year	Immigrant untouchable mill hands as proportion of all immigrant mill hands from districts reporting untouchable caste migration	Immigrant untouchable mill hands as proportion of all immigrant mill hands from all districts
(1)	(2)	(3)
1911	9.05	8.63
1921	11.91	11.02
1931	11.28	10.30

[2] For example, in 1911 caste identification was provided for only about two thirds
of the people who reported Ahmednagar district as their place of birth. Calculated
from *Census 1911*, VIII, pp. 48–61.

[3] The census always tabulated mill hands from a district, if there were any to
report.

[4] Calculated from censuses for 1911, 1921, and 1931. See Appendix IV for sources.

Column (2) represents the method used to get the figures in Table XI. As compared with the alternate method used for column (3), the upward bias is not overwhelming.[5]

There is a slight possibility that my maximum figure (column 2) is an understatement of the proportion of untouchable mill hands to total immigrant mill labor. First of all, the districts reporting untouchable caste migration may not have reported all the untouchable groups that did migrate. Though likely, it was probably not a significant factor. Second, the districts in the census tables which did not report untouchable migration and those districts excluded from the tables entirely probably contributed some untouchables to the city's total. However, these districts produced a small proportion of total migration to Bombay, a very minor share of mill labor and probably, as a result, very few untouchable mill hands.[6]

There are two other possible sources of bias in the 1911 to 1931 figures. The first arises from the fact that, representing the situation only among immigrant mill hands, the figures ignore the caste composition of Bombay-born mill hands. Unfortunately, there is no way of telling whether the Bombay-born mill hands would contribute a higher or a lower proportion of untouchables, to the work force. We must therefore use our immigrant figures as representative of the total industry situation.

The second source of possible bias arises out of a specific weakness in census enumeration. A very great many people properly classifiable as mill hands were reported in the census as "general labor."[7] This would not be a serious issue if the percentage of untouchables among "general labor" was roughly the same as among mill hands. But this is not the case. In each of the three censuses the proportion of untouchables classified as "general labor" is strikingly high. For example, if I make the arbitrary assumption that all "general labor" was in fact occasional or full-time mill labor, the proportion of untouchable mill hands plus untouchable general labor would be 15.90 per cent of all mill hands plus all general labor in 1911, 15.23 per cent in 1921 and 15.94 in 1931.[8] This would raise the proportion of putative untouchable mill hands, but the picture would not be altered substantially. This group would still have been a relatively small part of total mill-hand population.

Summarizing, I think it is safe to suggest that untouchables as a proportion of the immigrant mill labor force will fall within the ranges I have derived from the data. Their share of employment was no lower and certainly no higher than the following: [9]

---

[5] Column (3) in Table XXI represents a lower limit. It includes all districts which produced mill hands. Where no untouchables were reported, the assumption of the calculations for column (3) is that there were none.

[6] I suspect that the proportion of untouchables to total mill hands from these districts is less than from the reporting districts and therefore the danger of understatement does not arise. However, the possibility of understatement does exist and is a further justification for using the Table XXI, Column (2) rather than Column (3) figures in the text.

[7] On this point, see, for example, *Census 1921*, IX, Part I, pp. 36–37.

[8] Calculated from tables in censuses for 1911, 1921 and 1931, cited in Appendix IV. These figures represent maximum possibilities, based on the assumption that all "general labor" should be classed as mill labor.

[9] It should be stressed that the upper limit is probably higher than is reasonable,

Year	Per cent
1911.................	8.63 to 15.90 per cent
1921.................	11.02 to 15.23 per cent
1931.................	10.30 to 15.94 per cent

The 1941 figure in Table XI, derived from the BMOA survey, is not inconsistent with the upper range of my 1911 to 1931 data, although it is higher than any other figure in Table XI. It can, of course, be argued that the 13.81 per cent figure for 1941 merely represents the continuation of an upward trend. But there is one important reason why I think that the BMOA 1941 figure has an upward bias built into it as compared with the figures for earlier years in Table XI. The census data for 1911 to 1931 which I used represented only those persons who reported themselves as mill hands. Many workers listed themselves as *mazdoor* (laborer) and were not incorporated. The BMOA survey figure could not suffer from such a weakness. Everyone who had a record card in the nineteen mills was counted. In this sense, it is not that the BMOA figure was biased upward but rather that the census data I used for 1911 to 1931 was possibly on the low side.[10]

But whether the 1911 to 1931 census data in Table XI are low or the 1941 figure is high, it is possible to conclude that for the period 1911 to 1941 there was probably no significant change in the proportion of untouchables employed in the mills. This conclusion raises another rather interesting point. If we assume that the BMOA figure for 1941 is approximately correct and that the figures for 1911 to 1931 are of roughly the same order, this pushes the appearance of the untouchables in large numbers in the industry back to an earlier period and makes the increase more dramatic between 1881 and 1911. Untouchables would have increased in that thirty-year period from about 2 per cent of total employment to about 13 per cent and then held at that level.

---

based as it is on the assumption that all "general labor" should properly be classified as mill hands. This assumption is certainly excessive but to what degree it is impossible to say. I would expect that the maximum figure in each case should be reduced by at least one or two percentage points.

[10] There is a possible bias in the BMOA survey associated with the nature of the sample. Of the nineteen mills, ten belonged to the E. D. Sassoon group. I have already pointed out that there are possibilities that different employers had different patterns of worker group concentration. To draw a sample so heavily weighted with the mills controlled by a single managing agency may well have distorted the survey results. Let me give an example of the distortion that is possible. Kanji Dwarkadas, *Forty-Five Years with Labour* (Bombay: Asia Publishing House, 1962), p. 117, did a survey of 1,282 women employees in five mills for which he was the labor officer. Of the women employed in his mills in 1944, only 9.28 per cent were Harijans but the BMOA survey reported 25.2 per cent. For non-Hindus as a group, the Dwarkadas mills employed 8.74 per cent and the BMOA sample reported 2.7 per cent. Actually, the five mills on which Dwarkadas reported were members of the Sassoon group of mills. This suggests that the Sassoon enterprises biased the proportion of Harijans in the BMOA sample downward. But since we do not know how representative of the entire industry the sample was, I cannot make any adjustments to allow for this.

There is no evidence that such an invasion, if it occurred, caused any particular tension in the industry. Such a movement into the industry between 1881 and 1911 would fit with my explanation of the relative shift of "clean caste" Hindus from the spinning side into the more rapidly expanding weaving sector. It would also lessen the significance of the post-1921 strikes as the vehicle of entry for untouchables into the mills. But at the present state of knowledge, all of this is speculation.

APPENDIX VI

Uniform Code of Work Regulations Proposed by the Bombay Millowners' Association, 1892 [1]

Attendance

1. Every person employed in the factory shall punctually attend to and commence and cease his respective work at the respective hours which may from time to time be fixed for those purposes by the Bombay Millowners' Association.

2. The opening and the closing of the factory will be signaled by means of a whistle, bell, or gong. Persons employed in the factory shall enter by such gate or gates only as may be directed or notified by the Manager.

3. No person shall under any circumstances absent himself from the factory during the working hours without leave of the Manager, and (subject to rule 9) any person who shall absent himself for four consecutive days without such leave, shall be considered to have left his employment without notice and shall forfeit all wages due to him.

Wages

4. No person will be employed by the month but, unless employed on piece work, shall be employed on fixed daily wages. All persons, whether employed on daily wages or on piece work, will be paid their respective wages once in every month. Those who receive fixed daily wages shall be entitled to receive payment only for the number of days they may have worked in such month. Out of the wages payable to every person employed at the factory, eighteen days' wages may be deducted and kept in arrear as security or guarantee for the proper and faithful discharge of his duties, and for his obedience to all lawful orders, rules, and regulations from time to time in force in that behalf, and the amount of any fine or forfeiture which any such

---

[1] *BMOA 1891*, pp. 172–73. A preliminary draft of these rules was prepared by an eleven-man committee appointed by the Association. *Ibid.*, p. 15. This initial draft was submitted to the Association's legal adviser who then rewrote it as it appears here. The first draft apparently assumed that workers would make themselves familiar with the regulations; the lawyer seems to have added Rule 16. The first draft apparently provided much more arbitrary authority to fine workers and forfeit all accumulated wages than emerged in the final regulations. And it would seem that the provision in Rule 9, that where a factory was to be stopped for more than thirty days workers would be able to leave a mill's employment without notice, was added by the legal adviser. For all this, see the legal adviser's letter to the Association. *Ibid.*, p. 171.

person shall have incurred by reason of any breach or infringement of such orders, rules, or regulations may be deducted out of the wages payable to him.

5. Any dispute or complaint regarding wages shall be brought to the notice of the Manager immediately after the receipt by or tender to complainant of the wages appearing to be payable to him, and it shall be the duty of the Manager, or the person appointed in that behalf, to attend to such complaint and adjudicate thereon forthwith.

6. Persons desirous of leaving their employment shall give one month's previous notice to the Manager of their intention to leave; such notice must be given on the 1st or 15th of the month, subject to rule 9; every person who shall leave his employment without having given such notice shall forfeit all arrears of wages then due to him.

7. The Manager, on behalf of the Company, shall also give one month's previous notice, either on the 1st or the 15th of the month, to any person whose services he may think fit to dispense with, or in default of such notice shall pay to such persons one month's wages in lieu of notice. Provided always, that in case any person shall misconduct himself, or disobey orders, or in any manner act negligently, incompetently, disorderly, intemperately, or fraudulently, the Manager may dismiss him summarily, and the person so dismissed shall thereupon forfeit all wages due to him.

8. Wages to substitutes shall under no circumstances be payable day by day, but shall be payable only on one of the regular pay days.

9. Except in cases where the factory requires to be stopped for more than 30 consecutive days the stoppage of the factory, from whatever cause, shall not entitle any person employed to be absent without leave. If the factory requires to be stopped for more than 30 consecutive days, the Manager, on behalf of the Company, shall forthwith give notice to that effect, in which case it shall not be necessary for persons absenting themselves to obtain the leave required by rule 3, and, moreover, they shall be entitled to leave the Company's service without notice, and to receive their wages up to the time of the stoppage of the Factory.

10. In any suit or action for wages brought against the Company by any person, the Company shall be entitled to set off against the claim in such action or suit the amount of any fines or forfeitures which the Plaintiff in such action or suit may have incurred under these rules.

Fines, Forfeitures, and Dismissals

11. Persons committing theft or robbery in regard to any article or property belonging to the Company, or aiding or abetting in any such act, and all persons committing any fraud on the Company shall forfeit all wages which may have accrued due to them, or as an alternative shall submit to such fine as the Manager shall think proper, and shall also be liable to be prosecuted.

12. Persons soliciting, enticing, intimidating, or conspiring with other persons employed in the factory to leave the service of the Company, may be summarily dismissed, and shall be liable to forfeit all wages then accrued due to them, and also to be prosecuted.

13. Persons striking work, or intimidating or conspiring with other persons employed in the factory to strike work, may be summarily dismissed, and shall be liable to forfeit all wages then accrued due to them, and also to be prosecuted.

14. Persons found taking bribes from, or giving bribes, to other persons employed in the factory, or from or to any other individual having dealings with the Company, as a motive or reward for doing, or omitting to do, any act the performance or omission whereof would be prejudicial to the interests of the Company, will be liable to summary dismissal, and to the forfeiture of all wages.

15. Smoking is strictly prohibited, except at the places set apart for that purpose, and every person found smoking within any part of the mill premises, except at the places set apart for that purpose, shall be liable to fine or dismissal, or both, at the discretion of the Manager; separate places in the mill compound will be provided for those in the habit of smoking.

General

16. The Mill Manager shall see that all the compulsory provisions of the Factories Act, 1881 (as amended by Act XI of 1891), and all rules from time to time passed by the Governor-General in Council, or by the Local Government in regard thereto, are strictly and faithfully carried out so far as the Company and its mill operatives are concerned; and that the superior officers and heads of departments in the factory are made thoroughly acquainted with what is required of them. Under the said Act and rules the jobbers should in their turn also be directed to carry out and, so far as may be, to enforce obedience to such parts of the said Act and rules as relate to matters coming under their immediate notice or supervision.

APPENDIX VII

Standing Orders for Mill Hands in the Bombay
Cotton Textile Industry, 1937 [1]

1. These Orders shall come into force as and from 1st March 1937.
2. In these Orders, unless there is anything repugnant in the subject or context:

   (a) "Operatives" means all work people male or female employed in the Mill and includes Jobbers and Overseers;

   (b) "The Company" means .... Mills Co. Ltd; and

   (c) "The Manager" means the Company's Manager, or Acting Manager for the time being;

   (d) The masculine includes the feminine.

3. Operatives will be classed as (1) Permanent Operatives; (2) Probationers; and (3) Badlis.

   A "permanent" operative is one whose name has been entered in the Muster Roll and has been given a permanent ticket and has completed a probationary period of two months in the same or another occupation in the Mill.

   A "probationer" is one who is provisionally employed to fill a permanent vacancy, and has not completed two months' service on that post. If a permanent operative is employed as a probationer in a new post, he may, at any time during the probationary period of two months, be reverted to his old permanent post.

   A "badli" is one who is employed on the post of a permanent operative or probationer, who is temporarily absent.

4. The decision of the Manager upon any question arising out of, in connection with, or incidental to these Orders, shall be final subject, however, to appeal to the Managing Agents and without prejudice to any right of an operative aggrieved by his or their decision to resort to legal proceedings in a Court of Law.

5. The Mill will work each day for such number of hours as the Manager may from time to time fix in accordance with the Indian Factories Act, and the periods of work for all classes of operatives will be posted up on the Notice Board at the Time Keeper's Office as required by the Indian Factories Act, 1934. If a shift system is being worked in the Mills, operatives may be transferred from one shift to another.

6. Every permanent and probationary operative without exception will be provided with a departmental ticket showing his number, and on attendance each day, shall deliver up the ticket at the place provided.

---

[1]BLO 1934, pp. 260–263.

Every "Badli" will be provided with a "Badli" Card, which shall be surrendered if he obtains permanent or probationary employment.

7. Operatives attending late are liable to be shut out and treated as absent.

Any operative who after presenting his ticket is found absent from his proper place or places of work during working hours without permission or other sufficient reason, is liable to be treated as absent for the period of his absence.

8. Any operative who desires to obtain leave of absence, except for a temporary purpose within the mill premises, must apply previously to the Head of his Department or any officer appointed by the Manager for the purpose who, if he thinks fit, may grant him leave for a period not exceeding two months. If the leave granted exceeds two days, the officer granting it shall keep a record of its grant and give the operative a written and signed certificate as to the period of leave granted to him. In special cases, the Manager may grant leave for period exceeding two months. In the event of an operative remaining absent in excess of the period granted, he shall lose the lien on his appointment, unless he has previously secured written permission to extend the leave originally granted and returns to work on the first working day following the period covered by any such extension. If, however, on his return to work he gives a satisfactory explanation to the Head of the Department, or such other person as may have been appointed for the purpose, for his omission to apply for such an extension, his case for reinstatement when a suitable vacancy occurs shall be considered.

Requests or applications for nonurgent leave of more than seven days' duration will be received on two fixed days per week, and sanctioned leave in respect of such applications will ordinarily commence on the third day following the day fixed for receiving applications.

9. No operative shall enter or leave the mill premises except by the gate appointed for the purpose.

10. All male operatives are liable on leaving the mill premises to be searched by the gateman, and all female operatives are liable to be detained by the gateman for search by the female searcher, if acting without malice he suspects that any operative so detained or searched has wrongful possession of property belonging to the Company.

Provided that no search shall be made except in the presence of two other persons of the same sex as the suspected employee.

11. Notices specifying (a) the days on which the Mill will be closed, and (b) the days on which wages will be paid will be posted as required by the Indian Factories Act and the Payment of Wages Act respectively.

12. Notices specifying the rates of wages payable to all classes of workers and for all classes of work will be displayed in a conspicuous position in the Departments in which the operatives concerned are actually working. No alterations in the rates of wages will be made without giving 14 days' notice by means of a general Notice specifying the nature of the changes proposed.

13. The Company may, at any time or times, in the event of a fire, catastrophe, breakdown of machinery or stoppage of the power supply, epidemic,

civil commotion or other cause, whether of a like nature or not, beyond the control of the company, stop any machine or machines or department or departments, wholly or partially for any period or periods, without notice and without compensation in lieu of notice.

In the event of a stoppage of any machine or department under this Order during working hours, the operatives affected shall be informed, as soon as practicable, when work will be resumed and whether they are to remain or leave the Mill. The period of detention in the Mill shall not ordinarily exceed one hour after the commencement of the stoppage. If the period of detention does not exceed one hour, operatives so detained shall not be paid for the period of detention. If the period of detention in the Mill exceeds one hour, operatives so detained shall be entitled to receive wages for the whole of the time during which they are detained in the Mill as a result of the stoppage. In the case of pieceworkers, the average daily earnings for the previous month shall be taken to be the daily wages.

14. The Company may, at any time or times, in the event of shortage of orders or for any other trade reason, stop any machine or machines, or department or departments wholly or partially, for a period not exceeding three consecutive days in any one week and not exceeding twelve days in the aggregate (excluding statutory holidays) in any one calendar month without notice and without compensation in lieu of notice. If an employee is played off under this rule for a period of twelve days in the aggregate in any one calendar month, he may leave the company's service on intimation of his intention to do so without any further notice.

15. Any employee played off under Order 13 or Order 14 will not be considered as dismissed from service, but as temporarily unemployed, and will not be entitled to wages during such unemployment except to the extent mentioned in Order 13. All operatives played off will be given prior rights to reinstatement on the resumption of normal work, provided they present themselves for work when normal working is resumed.

16. The Company may, in the event of a strike affecting either wholly, or partially, any one or more department or departments of the Mill, close down, either wholly or partially, such department or departments, and any other department or departments affected by such closing down, and for any period or periods, and without notice or payment of compensation in lieu of notice to the operatives employed in such department or departments.

17. (a) The employment of any permanent operative may be terminated without assigning any reason by fourteen days' notice or by payment of 13 days' wages in lieu of notice. If he draws wages on a piece-rate basis, the 13 days' wages shall be computed on the average daily earnings of such operative for the days actually worked during the previous wage period.

(b) Probationary operatives other than those transferred from permanent posts in the Mill and "Badlis" may leave, or be discharged from service without notice by an officer not below the rank of the Head of a Department.

(c) Where the employment of any person is terminated by or on behalf of the Mill, the wages earned by him shall be paid before the expiry of the second working day from the day on which his employment was terminated.

18. Any permanent operative desirous of leaving the Company's service shall give 14 days' notice to the Head of the Department concerned. The wages due to such an operative must, if possible, be paid on the day the notice expires and in any case within two days after the expiry of the notice.

If any permanent operative leaves service without notice, he shall be liable to be sued for damages.

If ten or more employed persons, acting in concert, absent themselves from work without due notice as required in this Order, and without reasonable cause, they will, at the discretion of the Manager and in accordance with the Payment of Wages Act, be liable to a deduction from their earned wages of an amount not exceeding eight days' earnings in each case.

19. Any wages due to an operative but not paid on the usual pay day on account of their being unclaimed will be paid by the Company on the unclaimed wages pay day succeeding the date on which a substantiated claim was presented by the operative or on his behalf by his legal representative, provided that such claim is submitted within three years.

20. Any operative who is adjudged by the Manager on examination of the man, if present, and of the facts to be guilty of misconduct is liable to be dismissed without notice or, alternatively, to be suspended for a period not exceeding four days.

The following acts or omissions will be treated as misconduct:

(a) Willful insubordination or disobedience whether alone or in combination with another or others to any lawful and reasonable order of a superior.

(b) Striking work either singly or with other operatives without giving 14 days' previous notice.

(c) Inciting whilst on the premises any operative to strike work without giving 14 days' previous notice.

(d) Theft, fraud, or dishonesty in connection with the Company's business or property.

(e) Taking or giving bribes or any illegal gratification whatsoever.

(f) Habitual absence without leave or absence without leave for more than six consecutive days without sufficient cause.

(g) Habitual late attendance.

(h) Habitual breach of any Standing Orders.

(i) Collection of any moneys within the mill premises for purposes not sanctioned by the Manager.

(j) Drunkenness or riotous or disorderly behavior during working hours or any act subversive of discipline or efficiency.

(k) Habitual negligence or neglect of work.

(l) Habitual breach of any rules, or instructions for the maintenance and running of any Department or maintaining its cleanliness, and any other serious act of misconduct.

An operative suspended under this Order will not be permitted to work in the Mills for the period of suspension and no remuneration will be paid or be due to him for this period.

21. Operatives may be fined for any of the underquoted offences, but the offense if repeated, or in any gross case, may be treated as misconduct under Order 20. Fines will be imposed in accordance with the provisions of the Payment of Wages Act for the following offences, or at the discretion of the Manager for acts of misconduct specified in Order 20 as an alternative to dismissal or suspension:

(a) Absence without leave without sufficient cause.

(b) Negligence in work or neglect of work.

(c) Smoking on the Mill premises except in places where smoking is permitted.

(d) Entering or leaving, or attempting to enter or leave the Mill premises except by the gate provided for the purpose.

(e) Absence without leave or without sufficient cause from appointed work in the Mill.

(f) Breach of any rules or instructions for the maintenance and running of any department and maintaining its cleanliness.

(g) Damage to work in process or to any other property of the Company.

(h) Interference with any safety devices installed in the Mills.

(i) Distributing or exhibiting inside the Mill premises handbills, pamphlets or posters without the previous sanction of the Manager.

No fine shall be imposed except by the Officers authorized under the Payment of Wages Rules and until the operative concerned has been given an opportunity of being heard.

22. All fines imposed on operatives and realized will be credited to a special fines fund which will be utilized for such purposes as may be approved in this behalf by the Local Government in accordance with the provisions of the Payment of Wages Act.

23. When any probationary or permanent operative is summarily dismissed, suspended, or discharged, or leaves the service of the Company, or is granted leave of absence, he will, except in cases of general retrenchment, closing down of departments, strike or lock-out, be given a written order in the form prescribed by the Millowners' Association from time to time.

24. Each Overseer, Jobber, or Mucadam will be personally held responsible for the proper and faithful observance of the Standing Orders and of the special rules made under the Factories Act and posted in the Mill, particularly regarding the employment and working of women and children under him.

25. A copy of these Orders in English and Marathi will be posted near the Time Keeper's Office and in all departments and in such other places on the Mill premises as the management may decide, and shall be kept in a legible condition.

An abstract of these Standing Orders will be supplied to every permanent operative and every probationer engaged after the 1st March 1937.

26. Except to the extent of making by-laws or rules not inconsistent with these Standing Orders for the maintenance or running of any departments, maintaining cleanliness or other similar matters of internal administration, the Company will not rescind, add to or otherwise alter these Standing Orders without the previous written consent of the Millowners' Association, Bombay.

27. Notwithstanding anything to the contrary contained in these Standing Orders, it shall be lawful for the Company by a resolution of its Board of Directors that circumstances require or justify that such action shall be taken and with the previous written consent of the Millowners' Association, Bombay, and after giving not less than fourteen days' notice to its operatives of its intention to do so, to substitute for the then existing system of employment of its labor a system of day to day employment. Upon the introduction of a system of day to day employment, such of these Standing Orders as are inconsistent with a system of day to day employment shall cease to apply, and the employment of an operative shall be terminable by either the Company or the operative at twenty-four hours' notice.

When considering applications from mills under this Order, the Millowners' Association shall not give permission to work on a day to day system for a period of more than three months in respect of any one application.

Bibliography

A. B. F. *Statistical Tables Relating to Indian Cotton.* Bombay: Times of India Steam Press, 1889.

Acharya, Hemlata. "Creative Response in Indian Economy: A Comment," *The Economic Weekly* (Bombay), IX, No. 17 (April 27, 1957), 547–549.

Anand, Mulk Raj. *Untouchable.* Bombay: Jaico Publishing House, 1956.

Anonymous. *A Description of the Port and Island of Bombay.* London. 1724.

Anstey, Vera. *The Economic Development of India.* 3d ed. London: Longmans, Green and Co., 1949.

Aubrey, Henry G. "Industrial Investment Decisions: A Comparative Analysis," *The Journal of Economic History,* XV, No. 4 (December 1955), 335–351.

Babbage, Charles. *On the Economy of Machinery and Manufactures.* Philadelphia: Carey & Lea, 1832.

Ballhatchet, Kenneth. *Social Policy and Social Change in Western India, 1817–1830.* London: Oxford University Press, 1957.

Bombay and Lancashire Cotton Spinning Inquiry: Minutes of Evidence and Reports. Manchester: Manchester Chamber of Commerce, 1888.

Bombay Bank Commission. *Minutes of Evidence.* 3 vols. London: Her Majesty's Stationary Office, 1869.

Bombay Chamber of Commerce. *Report of the Bombay Chamber of Commerce for the Year 1852–53.* Bombay: Bombay Steam Gazette Press, 1853.

Bombay Millowners' Association. *Confidential Summary of Workmen's Service Records.* Bombay: The Millowners' Association, 1941.

———. *Report of the Bombay Millowners' Association.* For 1875, 1875–76 and 1878 through 1951. Bombay: The Millowners' Association, 1876–1952.

Bombay Provincial Banking Enquiry Committee, 1929–30. *Evidence.* Vol. III. Calcutta: Government of India Central Publications Branch, 1930.

The Bombay Quarterly Review. Vols. I–VII, January 1855–September 1858.

"The Bombay Railway," *The Bombay Quarterly Magazine and Review,* I, No. 2 (January 1851), 132–148.

The Bombay Saturday Review of Politics, Literature and Commerce. Vols. VI–VII, January 2, 1864 to June 10, 1865.

Bose, S. N. *Indian Labour Code (Central).* 2d ed. Calcutta: Eastern Law House, Ltd., 1950.

Broughton, G. M. *Labour in Indian Industries.* London: Oxford University Press, 1924.

Buchanan, Daniel Houston. *The Development of Capitalistic Enterprise in India.* New York: The Macmillan Company, 1934.

Burnett-Hurst, A. R. *Labour and Housing In Bombay.* London: P. S. King & Son, Ltd., 1925.

Cassels, Walter R. *Cotton: An Account of Its Culture in the Bombay Presidency.* Bombay: Bombay Education Society's Press, 1862.

Census of the Island of Bombay, Taken 2nd February, 1864. Bombay: Bombay Education Society's Press, 1864.

Census of the City of Bombay Taken 21st February, 1872. Bombay: Bombay Education Society's Press, 1873.

Census of the City and Island of Bombay Taken on the 17th of February 1881 by T. S. Weir, Surgeon-Major, Health Officer, Acting Municipal Commissioner. Bombay: Times of India Steam Press, 1883.

Census of India, 1891. Vol. VIII. *Bombay and its Feudatories.* Part II. *Imperial Tables.* Bombay: Government Press, 1892.

Census of India, 1901. Vol. XI. *Bombay (Town and Island).* Part V: *Report.* Bombay: Times of India Press, 1901.

Census of India, 1901. Vol. XI–A. *Bombay (Town and Island).* Part VI. *Tables.* Bombay: Times of India Press, 1901.

Census of the Town and Island of Bombay Taken on the 9th of February, 1906, with the sanction of the Government and of the Municipal Corporation for the City of Bombay accorded under Section 454 of the Bombay Municipal Act III of 1888, by the Municipal Commissioner. Bombay: Bombay Education Society Press, 1906.

Census of India, 1911. Vol. VII. *Bombay (Presidency).* Part I. *Report.* Bombay: Government Central Press, 1912.

Census of India, 1911. Vol. VIII. *Bombay (Town and Island).* Parts I and II. *Reports and Tables.* Bombay: Government Central Press, 1912.

Census of India, 1921. Vol. VIII. Parts I and II. *General Report and Tables (Imperial and Provincial).* Bombay: Government Central Press, 1922.

Census of India, 1921. Vol. IX. *Cities of the Bombay Presidency.* Part I. *Report.* Poona: Superintendent, Government Printing 1922.

Census of India, 1921, Vol. IX. *Cities of the Bombay Presidency.* Part II. *Tables.* Bombay: Government Central Press, 1922.

Census of India, 1931. Vol. IX. *The Cities of the Bombay Presidency.* Bombay: Government Central Press, 1933.

Census of India, 1941. Vol. III. *Bombay.* Delhi: Manager of Publications, 1942.

Chaloner, W. A., "John Galloway (1804–1894), Engineer of Manchester and His 'Reminiscences'," *Transactions of the Lancashire and Cheshire Antiquarian Society,* LXIV, 1954, pp. 93–116.

Chapman, Sydney J. *The Lancashire Cotton Industry: A Study in Economic Development.* Manchester: The University Press, 1904.

Cola, P. R. *How to Develope* [sic] *Productive Industry in India and the East.* London: Virtue and Co., 1867.

Condon, J. K. *The Bombay Plague, Being a History of the Progress of Plague in the Bombay Presidency from September 1896 to June 1899.* Bombay: Education Society's Steam Press, 1900.

Conybeare, H. "Report on the Sanitary State and Requirements of Bombay," *Selections From the Records of the Bombay Government.* New Series, XI. Bombay: Bombay Education Society's Press, 1855.

Cumming, J. G. *Review of the Industrial Position and Prospects of Bengal in 1908.* Calcutta: Superintendent of Government Printing, 1908.

Datta, K. L. *Report on the Enquiry into the Rise of Prices in India.* 5 volumes. Calcutta: Superintendent of Government Printing, 1914.

Davis, Kingsley. *The Population of India and Pakistan.* Princeton: Princeton University Press, 1951.

Deolalkar, P. V. "Textile Industries in India." Unpublished Ph.D. dissertation, University of Bombay, 1927.

Deole, C. S. "The Bombay Strikes," *Journal of the Indian Economic Society*, II, No. 4, December 1919, pp. 193–202.

Department of Economic Affairs, Ministry of Finance, Government of India. *Final Report of the National Income Committee, February 1954.* Delhi: Manager of Publications, 1954.

Department of Statistics, India. *Prices and Wages in India.* Thirty-six issues. 1882–1921. Calcutta: Superintendent of Government Printing, 1883–1922.

Deshpande, C. D. *Western India: A Regional Geography.* Dharwar: Students' Own Book Depot, 1948.

Devadhar, G. K. "A Note on Cooperation among the Millhands," in *Report of the Ninth Indian Industrial Conference Held at Karachi on the 25th December 1913.* Amraoti: General Secretary, The Indian Industrial Conference, 1914.

Director of Land Records and Agriculture. *Report on the Economic Condition of the Masses of the Bombay Presidency.* Bombay: 1888.

Dutt, Romesh. *The Economic History of India in the Victorian Age.* 7th ed. London: Routledge & Kegan Paul, Ltd., 1950.

Dwarkadas, Kanji. *Forty-Five Years with Labour.* Bombay: Asia Publishing House, 1962.

East India (Factories Act). *Return to an Address of the Hon. House of Commons, dated 15 April 1889 for a Copy of Reports on the Working of the Indian Factories Act made to the Government of India in Reply to Inquiries recently directed by the Secretary of State for India.* Ordered Printed by the House of Commons, 16 April 1889.

Edwardes, S. M. *The Gazetteer of Bombay City and Island.* 3 vols. Bombay: The Times Press, 1909.

Edwardes, S. M. *The Rise of Bombay: A Retrospect.* Bombay: The Times of India Press, 1902.

The Employers' Federation of India. *The General Strike in the Bombay Cotton Mill Industry: Its Lessons for Indian Industries.* Bombay, 1940.

Final Report of the Industrial Conditions Enquiry Committee Together with Suggestions for a Labour Code, Bombay State. Bombay: Government Central Press, 1950.

Fisher, F. J. "The Development of the London Food Market, 1540–1640," *The Economic History Review*, V. No. 2, April 1935, pp. 46–64.

Forbes, James, *Oriental Memoirs*, 2nd ed. 2 vols. London: Richard Bentley, 1834.

Fraser, Lovat. *India Under Curzon and After.* London: W. Heinemann, 1911.

Fremantle, S. H. "The Problem of Indian Labour Supply," *Journal of the Royal Society of Arts*, LVII, May 14, 1909, pp. 510–519.

From Max Weber: Essays in Sociology. Edited by H. H. Gerth and C. W. Mills. New York: Oxford University Press, 1946.

Gadgil, D. R. *The Industrial Evolution of India in Recent Times.* 4th ed. London: Oxford University Press, 1942.

The General Gazetteer; or Compendious Geographical Dictionary . . . Originally Written by R. Brookes, M. D. 8th ed. London: B. Law and Son, 1794.

Gokhale, R. G. *Annual Review of the Labour Situation in the Bombay Cotton Mill Industry for the Year 1947.* Bombay: Millowners' Association, n.d.

Gokhale, R. G. *Annual Review of the Labour Situation in the Bombay Cotton Mill Industry, 1949.* Bombay: Millowners' Association, n.d.

Gokhale, R. G. *The Bombay Cotton Mill Worker.* Bombay: Millowners' Association, 1957.

Government of Bombay. *Greater Bombay District Census Hand Book (Based on the 1951 Census).* Bombay: Government of Bombay, 1952.

Government of Bombay. *Report of the Bombay Strike Enquiry Committee, 1928–29.* Vol. I. *Report.* Bombay: Government Central Press, 1929.

Government of Bombay. *Report of the Court of Inquiry, 1929.* Bombay: Government Central Press, 1929.

Government of Bombay, Political and Services Department. *The Bombay Industrial Relations Act, 1946 (Bom. XI of 1947), with the Bombay Industrial Relations Rules, 1947, the Industrial Court Regulations, 1947, and the Labour Courts (Practice and Procedure) Rules and the Bombay Wage Board Rules, 1948.* Bombay: Government Central Press, 1950.

Government of India, Ministry of Commerce and Industry. *Report of the Working Party for the Cotton Textile Industry.* Delhi: Manager of Publications, 1953.

Graham, D. C. "Statistical Report on the Principality of Kolhapur," in *Selections from the Records of the Bombay Government,* Number VIII — New Series. Bombay: Bombay Education Society's Press, 1854.

Grant, C. W. *Bombay Cotton and Indian Railways.* London, 1850.

Great Britain. Royal Commission on Labour. *Foreign Reports.* Volume II. *The Colonies and the Indian Empire. With an Appendix on the Migration of Labour.* Presented to both Houses of Parliament by Command of Her Majesty, 1893. Command 6795–XI. London: H. M. Stationary Office, 1893.

A Guide to Bombay from the Bombay Times Calendar of 1855. Bombay: The Times' Press, 1855.

Habakkuk, H. J. "Free Trade and Commercial Expansion, 1853–1870," in *Cambridge History of the British Empire,* II, pp. 751–805. Cambridge: Cambridge University Press, 1940.

Habib, Irfan. *The Agrarian System of Mughal India.* London: Asia Publishing House, 1963.

Hall, Basil. *Fragments of Voyages and Travels.* Second Series. Vol. III. 2nd ed. Edinburgh: R. Cadell, 1852.

H. B. C. "Preliminary Thoughts on the Efficiency of the Bombay Textile Labour," *Journal of the Indian Economic Society,* II, No. 4, December 1919, pp. 203–212.

Hearn, W. M. "Statistical Report of the Colaba Agency," in *Selections from the Records of the Bombay Government,* Number VII — New Series. Bombay: Education Society's Press, 1854.

Hobsbawm, E. J. "The Machine Breakers," *Past and Present,* No. 1, February 1952, pp. 57–70.

Hopkins, E. Washburn. *India Old and New.* New York: C. Scribner's Sons, 1901.

Howard, Louise E. *Sir Albert Howard in India.* London: Faber and Faber Ltd., 1953.

Humphrey, D. F. "Forces of Disequilibrium and World Disorder," *American Economic Review,* XLIV, No. 2, May 1954, pp. 552–564.

Hutton, J. H. *Caste in India.* 3rd edition. London: Oxford University Press, 1961.

India. Factory Labour Commission, 1908. *Report of the Indian Factory Labour Commission, 1908.* 2 vols. Simla: Government of India, Central Press Branch, 1908.

India. Fiscal Commission. *Minutes of the Evidence Recorded by the Indian Fiscal Commission.* Vol. III. Calcutta: Government of India, Central Publications Branch, 1923.

India. Indian Industrial Commission. *Report of the Indian Industrial Commission, 1916–18. With Minutes of Evidence.* 5 volumes. Calcutta: Superintendent of Government Printing, India, 1918.

India. Tariff Board. *Report of the Indian Tariff Board (Cotton Textile Industry Enquiry), 1927.* 4 vols. Bombay: Government Central Press, 1927.

India. Textile Factories Labour Committee. *Report of the Textile Factories Labour Committee Appointed by the Government of India on the 17th of December 1906 to enquire into the conditions of FACTORY LABOUR IN INDIA — with Appendices.* Bombay: Government Central Press, 1907.

Indian Tariff Board. *Report of the Indian Tariff Board Regarding the Grant of Protection to the Cotton Textile Industry.* Calcutta: Government of India Central Publication Branch, 1932.

Indian Tariff Board. *Cotton Textile Industry, 1934.* 4 volumes. Delhi: Manager of Publications, 1934.

Indian Textile Journal. Vols. I–LXI. October 1890–September 1951. Bombay: The Indian Textile Journal Limited, 1890–1951.

The Indian Textile Journal: Jubilee Souvenir 1890–1940. Bombay: The Indian Textile Journal Limited, 1941.

The Industrial Court Reporter, 1946–47. Baroda: Office of the Deputy Commissioner of Labour (Information), Government of Bombay, 1951.

Industrial Disputes Committee. *Minutes of Evidence.* Bombay: Government Central Press, 1921.

Industrial Disputes Committee. *Report of the Industrial Disputes Committee.* Bombay: Government Central Press, 1922.

Interim Report by the Industrial Conditions Enquiry Committee on the Cotton Textile Industry in Bombay City and Bombay Suburban District. Bombay: Government Central Press, 1948.

James, Ralph C. "The Casual Labor Problem in Indian Manufacturing," *The Quarterly Journal of Economics,* LXXIV, No. 1, February 1960, pp. 100–116.

James, Ralph C. "Labor and Technical Change: The Bombay Cotton Textile Industry." Unpublished Ph.D. Dissertation. Cornell University, 1957.

James, Ralph C. "Labor Mobility, Unemployment, and Economic Change: An Indian Case," *Journal of Political Economy,* LXVII, No. 6, December 1959, pp. 545–559.

James, Ralph C. "Trade-Union Democracy: Indian Textiles," *The Western Political Quarterly,* XI, No. 3, September 1958, pp. 566–572.

Jathar, G. B. and S. G. Beri. *Indian Economics.* Vol. II. 7th ed. London: Oxford University Press, 1945.

Joshi, N. M. "Welfare Work in Bombay Cotton Mills," *Journal of Indian Industries and Labour,* I, No. 1, February 1921, pp. 17–24.

Kanekar, P. G. "Cooperation among the Working Classes," in *Cooperation in*

Bombay. Edited by Hiralal Lallubjai Kaji. Bombay: D. B. Taraporevala Sons & Co., 1930.

Karve, Irawati. "What is Caste?", *The Economic Weekly* (Bombay), X. Annual Number, January 1958, pp. 125–138.

Kelman, Janet Harvey. *Labour in India.* George Allen & Unwin Ltd., 1923.

Kerr, Clark, and F. H. Harbison, J. T. Dunlop and C. A. Myers. "Industrialism and Industrial Man," *International Labor Review,* LXXXII, No. 3, September 1960, pp. 236–250.

Kerr, Clark, and Abraham Siegal. "The Structuring of the Labor Force in Industrial Society," *Industrial and Labor Relations Review,* VIII, No. 2. January 1955, pp. 151–168.

Kulkarni, P. D. "Textile Trade Unionism in Bombay," *The Indian Journal of Social Work,* VII, December 1946, pp. 224–238.

Kumar, Dharma. "Caste and Landlessness in South India," *Contemporary Studies in Society and History,* IV, No. 3, April 1962, pp. 337–363.

Kumar, Dharma. "The Growth of Agricultural Labour in Madras Presidency in the Nineteenth Century." Unpublished Ph.D. dissertation. Cambridge University, 1962.

LaBouchardiere, M. P. "Some Aspects of the Bombay Industrial Disputes Act and the Present Work of the Labour Officer, Bombay," *The Indian Journal of Social Work,* II, No. 1, June 1941, pp. 58–67.

Labour Gazette. Vols. I–XXXI. September 1921–August 1952. Bombay: Labour Office, Government of Bombay, 1921–1952.

Labour Investigation Committee, Government of India, *Main Report.* Delhi: Manager of Publications, 1946.

Labour Investigation Committee, Government of India. *Report on An Enquiry into Conditions of Labour in the Cotton Mill Industry in India.* By S. R. Deshpande. Delhi: Manager of Publications, 1946.

Labour Office, Government of Bombay. *General Wage Census.* Part I: Perennial Factories. Third Report. *Report on Wages, Hours of Work and Conditions of Employment in the Textile Industries (Cotton, Silk, Wool and Hosiery) in the Bombay Presidency (excluding Sind). May 1934.* Bombay: Government Central Press, 1937.

Labour Office, Government of Bombay. *Report on an Enquiry into the Wages and Hours of Labour in the Cotton Mill Industry* (1921). Bombay: Government Central Press, 1923.

Labour Office, Government of Bombay. *Report on an Enquiry into Wages and Hours of Labour in the Cotton Mill Industry* (1923). Bombay: Government Central Press, 1925.

Labour Office, Government of Bombay. *Report on an Enquiry into the Wages and Hours of Labour in the Cotton Mill Industry, 1926.* Bombay: Government Central Press, 1930.

Labour Office, Government of Bombay. *Report of an Enquiry into Deductions from Wages or Payments in Respect of Fines.* Bombay: Government Central Press, 1928.

Labour Office, Government of Bombay. *Wages and Unemployment in the Bombay Cotton Textile Industry.* Bombay: Government Central Press, 1934.

Laing, Samuel. "Correspondence," *The Economist,* XX, No. 998, October 11, 1862, pp. 1126–1128.

Laksman, P. P. *Congress and Labour Movement in India*. Congress Economic and Political Studies No. 3. Allahabad: Economic and Political Research Department, All-India Congress Committee, 1947.

Lamb, R. K. "The Entrepreneur and the Community," in *Men in Business*. Edited by W. Miller, Cambridge, Massachusetts: Harvard University Press, 1952.

The Late Government Bank of Bombay: Its History. London, n.d.

Lokanathan, P. S. *Industrial Organization in India*. London: G. Allen & Unwin, Ltd., 1935.

Maclean, James Mackenzie, *A Guide to Bombay*. 3rd ed. Bombay: Bombay Gazette Steam Press, 1877.

Maclean, James Mackenzie. *A Guide to Bombay*. 5th ed. Bombay: Bombay Gazette Steam Press, 1880.

Madhava, B., and K. V. Krishna Sastry. "A Further Study of Statistics of 'Absenteeism' in Indian Labour," *Sankhya*, No. 2, 1941, pp. 215–222.

Mann, James A. *The Cotton Trade of Great Britain: its rise, progress & present extent*. London: Simpkin, Marshall & Co., 1860.

Martin, Montgomery. *The Progress and Present State of British India*. London: Sampson Low, Son & Co., 1862.

Materials Towards a Statistical Account of the Town and Island of Bombay. Being Vol. XXVI, Parts 1–3, of the Gazetteer of the Bombay Presidency. Bombay: Government Central Press, 1893.

Matheson, M. Cecile. *Indian Industry, Yesterday, Today and Tomorrow*. London: Oxford University Press, 1930.

Meade King, W. O. "The Indian Factories Act, 1881, with the Alterations therein Proposed." Memorandum to the Secretary to Government, 24 June 1882.

Mehta, S. D. *The Cotton Mills of India, 1854–1954*. Bombay: The Textile Association (India), 1954.

Mehta, S. D. *The Indian Cotton Textile Industry: An Economic Analysis*. Bombay: The Textile Association (India), 1953.

Mehta, S. D. "Professor Morris on Textile Labour Supply," *Indian Economic Journal*, I, No. 3, January 1954, pp. 333–340.

The Millowners' Association, Bombay, *Glossary of Textile Terms (Used by Bombay Cotton Mill Workers)*. Bombay: Millowners' Association, 1943.

Minutes by His Excellency Sir Richard Temple, Bart., G. C. S. I., Governor of Bombay, 1878. Bombay: Government Central Press, 1879.

The Monthly Miscellany of Western India. (Bombay), I, 1850.

Moore, Wilbert E. "Problems of Timing, Balance and Priorities in Development Measures," *Economic Development and Cultural Change*, II, No. 4, January 1954, pp. 239–248.

Moore, Wilbert E. and Arnold S. Feldman (eds.). *Labor Commitment and Social Change in Developing Areas*. New York: Social Science Research Council, 1960.

Morris, Morris David. "Caste and the Evolution of the Industrial Workforce in India," *Proceedings of the American Philosophical Society*, CIV, No. 2, April 1950, pp. 124–133.

————. "The Labor Market in India," in *Labor Commitment and Social Change in Developing Areas*. Edited by W. E. Moore and A. S. Feldman. New York: Social Science Research Council, 1960, pp. 173–200.

————. "The Myth of 'Paradise Lost': Unesco's Study of Bombay Labour," *The Economic Weekly* (Bombay), IX, Nos. 26–28, July 6, 1957, pp. 857–862.

————. "The Recruitment of an Industrial Labor Force in India, with British and American Comparisons," *Comparative Studies in Society and History*, II, No. 3, April 1960, pp. 305–328.

————. "Some Comments on the Supply of Labour to the Bombay Cotton Textile Industry, 1854–1951." *Indian Economic Journal*, I, No. 2, October 1953, pp. 138–152.

————. "Towards a Reinterpretation of Nineteenth-Century Indian Economic History," *The Journal of Economic History*, XXIII, No. 4, December 1963, pp. 606–618.

Morris, Morris David and Burton Stein. "The Economic History of India: A Bibliographic Essay," *The Journal of Economic History*, XXI, No. 2, June 1961, pp. 179–207.

Mukerjee, Radhakamal. *The Indian Working Class*. 3rd edition. Bombay: Hind Kitabs, Ltd., 1951.

Mukerji, Kshitimohan. "Trend in Real Wages in Cotton Textile Mills in Bombay City and Island, from 1900 to 1951," *Artha Vijnana* (Poona, India), No. 1, March 1959, pp. 82–95.

Mukhtar, Ahmed. *Factory Labour in India*. Madras: The Annamalai University, 1930.

Myers, Charles A. *Labor Problems in the Industrialization of India*. Cambridge, Massachusetts: Harvard University Press, 1958.

Newman's Indian Bradshaw. No. 1,093, February 1957. Calcutta: W. Newman & Co., Ltd., 1957.

Nanda, Gulzari Lal. "Labour Unrest in India," *Indian Journal of Economics*, III, Part 4, January 1921, pp. 460–480.

"A New Labor Movement in India," *Monthly Labor Review*, XI, No. 2, August 1920, pp. 175–176.

Nurkse, Ragnar. "The Problem of International Investment Today in the Light of Nineteenth Century Experience," *Economic Journal*, LXIV, No. 256, December 1954, pp. 744–758.

Ornati, Oscar A. *Jobs and Workers in India*. Ithaca: The Institute of International Industrial Relations, Cornell University, 1955.

Palekar, Shreekant A. *Problems of Wage Policy for Economic Development*. New York: Asia Publishing House, 1962.

Pandit, D. P. "Creative Response in Indian Economy: A Regional Analysis," *The Economic Weekly* (Bombay), IX, Nos. 8–9, February 23 and March 2, 1957, pp. 283–286 and 315–317.

Papers Regarding the Management of the Bank of Bombay During the Late Commercial Crises. 2 vols. Calcutta: Superintendent of Government Printing, 1868.

"Papers Relating to the Introduction of the Original Survey Settlement into 144 Villages of the Sangameshvar Taluka of the Ratnagiri Collectorate," *Selections from the Records of the Bombay Government*, No. CLXXI — New Series. Bombay: Central Government Press, 1885.

Parliamentary Papers, 1831–32. House of Commons, Volume X, Paper 735–II.

Parliamentary Papers, 1840. House of Commons, Volume VIII, Paper 527.

Parliamentary Papers, 1888, XXVI, Command 5328. "Report of the Chief Inspector of Factories and Workshops for the Year Ending 31 October 1887."

"Parsi Prakash." Unpublished records (in Gujarati) on file at the Parsi Panachayat, Bombay.

Patel, S. J. *Agricultural Labourers in Modern India and Pakistan.* Bombay: Current Book House, 1952.

Pearse, Arno S. *Indian Cotton.* Manchester: International Federation of Master Cotton Spinners' and Manufacturers' Associations, 1915.

The Police Report on the Bombay Riots of February 1929. Bombay: Government Central Press, 1929.

Prabhu, Pindhari Nath. "A Study on the Social Effects of Urbanization on Industrial Workers Migrating from Rural Areas to the City of Bombay," in *The Social Implications of Industrialization and Urbanization: Five Studies in Asia.* Calcutta: UNESCO Research Centre on the Social Implications of Industrialization in Southern Asia, 1956.

Pradhan, G. R. "Untouchable Workers of Bombay City." Unpublished Ph.D. dissertation, University of Bombay, 1936.

Presidency of Bombay, *Annual Factory Report.* 1892–1947. Bombay: Government Central Press, 1893–1948. (Early issues were listed as Presidency of Bombay, Collector of Land Revenue, Customs and Opium. *Provincial Report on the Working of the Indian Factories Act.*

Presidency of Bombay, *Annual Report of the Administration of Bombay Presidency* for the years 1861–62 through 1880–81. Bombay, various dates. (The issues for the years 1864–65 and after carry the title, *General Report on the Administration of Bombay Presidency.*)

Presidency of Bombay. *Report on the Famine in the Bombay Presidency, 1899–1902.* Volume I: *Report.* Bombay: Government Central Press, 1903.

Pryde, A. W. "The Work of the Labour Officer," in *Some Social Services of the Government of Bombay.* Edited by Clifford Manshardt. Bombay: D. B. Taraporevala Sons & Co., 1937.

Report and Proceedings of the Commission Appointed to Consider the Working of the Factories in the Bombay Presidency. Bombay: Government Central Press, 1885.

Report of the Bombay Disturbances Enquiry Committee. Bombay: Government Central Press, 1939.

Report of the Commissioners Appointed by the Governor of Bombay in Council to inquire into the condition of the operatives in the Bombay Factories, and the necessity or otherwise for the passing of a Factories Act. Bombay: Government Central Press, 1875.

Report of the Indian Factory Commission, Appointed in September 1890, under the orders of His Excellency, the Governor General in Council, with Proceedings and Appendices. Calcutta: Office of the Superintendent of Government Printing, 1890.

Report of the Textile Labour Inquiry Committee, 1937–38. Vol. I. *Interim Report.* Bombay: Government Central Press, 1938.

Report of the Textile Labour Inquiry Committee. Vol. II. *Final Report.* Bombay: Government Central Press, 1940.

Rosenberg, Nathan. "Capital Goods, Technology and Economic Growth," *Oxford Economic Papers.* XV, No. 3, November 1963, pp. 217–227.

Royal Commission on Indian Labour. *Memorandum of Written Evidence of*

Government Witnesses, Bombay Presidency. (For Official Use Only.) Bombay: Government Central Press, 1929.

Royal Commission on Labour in India. *Evidence.* Vol. I, Part 1. *Bombay Presidency (including Sind.) Written Evidence.* London: His Majesty's Stationary Office, 1931.

Royal Commission on Labour in India. *Evidence.* Vol. I, Part 2. *Bombay Presidency (including Sind.) Oral Evidence.* London: His Majesty's Stationary Office, 1931.

Royal Commission on Labour in India. *Report of the Royal Commission on Labour in India.* Calcutta: Government of India Central Publication Branch, 1931.

Rutnagur, S. M. *Bombay Industries: The Cotton Mills.* Bombay: The Indian Textile Journal Limited, 1927.

Saklatvala, S. D. *History of the Millowners' Association,* Bombay: Bombay Millowners' Association, 1931.

Shah, Maneklal Maganlal. "Labour Recruitment and Turnover in the Textile Industry of Bombay Presidency." Unpublished Ph.D. dissertation, University of Bombay, 1941.

Shiva Rao, B. *The Industrial Worker in India.* London: George Allen and Unwin, 1939.

Siegfried, Andre. "Cotonniers aux Indes," *Revue de Paris,* LVII, December 1950, pp. 12–28.

Smith, Samuel. *The Cotton Trade of India.* London: E. Wilson, 1863.

Sovani, N. V. "British Impact on India Before 1850–57," *Cahiers d'Histoire Mondaile,* I, No. 4, April 1954, pp. 857–882.

Srinivas, M. N. "Social Anthropology and the Study of Rural and Urban Societies," *The Economic Weekly* (Bombay), XI, Special Number, January 1959, pp. 133–140.

Srinivas, M. N., and A. M. Shah. "The Myth of the Self-Sufficiency of the Indian Village," *The Economic Weekly* (Bombay), XII, No. 27, September 10, 1960, pp. 1375–1377.

Statistical Department, Government of India. *Financial and Commercial Statistics of British India.* 12th Issue. Calcutta: Superintendent of Government Printing, 1906.

Statistical Department, Government of India. *Monthly Statistics of Cotton Spinning and Weaving in Indian Mills.* Issues for 1901–1933.

Sulivan, R. J. F. *One Hundred Years of Bombay: History of the Bombay Chamber of Commerce, 1836–1936.* Bombay: Times of India Press, 1937.

Thorner, Daniel and Alice. *Land and Labour in India.* London: Asia Publishing House, 1962.

Thornton, Edward. *Statistical Papers Relating to India.* London, 1853.

Utley, Freda. *Lancashire and the Far East.* London: George Allen & Unwin Ltd., 1931.

Wacha, D. E. *A Financial Chapter in the History of Bombay City.* 2d ed. Bombay: A. J. Combridge & Co., 1910.

————. *The Life and Life Work of J. N. Tata.* 2d ed. Madras: Ganesh & Co., 1915.

————. *The Rise and Growth of Bombay Municipal Government.* Madras: G. A. Natesan and Co., 1913.

————. *Shells from the Sands of Bombay: Being My Recollections and Reminiscences, 1860–1875.* Bombay: K. T. Anklesaria, 1920.

Wadia, R. A. *The Bombay Dockyard and the Wadia Master Builders.* Bombay: Privately Published, 1955.

Walker, W. *Facts for Factories: Being Letters on Practical Subjects, Suggested by Experiences in Bombay.* Bombay, 1857.

Weber, Max. *The Religion of India.* Glencoe, Illinois: The Free Press, 1958.

Young, H. A. *The East India Company's Arsenals and Manufactories.* Oxford: Clarendon Press, 1937.

Index